Glen Coe

Rock and Ice Climbs

including

Glen Etive and Ardgour

K V Crocket
R Anderson
D Cuthbertson

edited by
R D Everett

'In here and now no step is up or down,
on in pain and hope and joy I go
until I love but do not linger on
each footstep in the snow.'

From: *Men on Ice* by Andrew Greig
(Canongate, Edinburgh, 1977)

SCOTTISH MOUNTAINEERING CLUB
CLIMBERS' GUIDE

Published in Great Britain by the Scottish Mountaineering Trust, 1992
Copyright © the Scottish Mountaineering Trust

British Library Cataloguing in Publication Data
Crocket, Ken
    Glen Coe Rock and Ice Climbs: Including Glen Etive and
    Ardgour
    I. Title
    796.5
    ISBN 0-907521-32-0

Maps drawn by Jim Renny
Diagrams drawn by Kevin Howett
Production by Peter Hodgkiss and Donald Bennet
Typeset by Westec, North Connel
Colour separations and graphic work by Par Graphics, Kirkcaldy
Printed by Martins of Berwick
Bound by Hunter and Foulis, Edinburgh

Distributed by Cordee, 3a DeMontfort Street, Leicester, LE1 7HD

Acknowledgments

So many climbers have helped in the production of this guide that at times it has felt like a private club ! Firstly, however, we acknowledge our debt to the authors of the previous editions, without whose work the writing of the present edition would have been made doubly difficult.

Guiding lights were held steadily by Donald Bennet and Roger Everett, Publications Manager and Editor of Climbers' Guidebooks respectively. Kevin Howett and Davy Gardner produced outstanding diagrams complementing the clear maps by Jim Renny.

Photographers whose slides made it past the scrutineers are acknowledged elsewhere; it was a difficult and sad task not to be able to use other excellent slides, and their owners, and other climbers who helped by reading drafts, providing information and egging us on with encouragement are listed here alphabetically. We apologise for any inadvertently missed out:

> Chris Anderson, Susan Cuthbertson, Brian Dullea, Allen Fyffe, Billy Hood, Ken Johnstone, Gary Latter, Donald McIntyre, Mark McGowan, Colin Moody, Stuart Murdoch, Alex Small, Donald Smith, Kenny Spence, Colin Stead, Ian Taylor, Professor D.S.Thomson, Andy Tibbs and Tim Whitaker.

Thanks are also due to Canongate Publishers, Edinburgh, for permission to quote from Andrew Greig's *Men on Ice*.

Ken Crocket
Rab Anderson
Dave Cuthbertson

January 1992

Contents

List of Illustrations

List of Diagrams and Maps

The Climber And The Mountain Environment

With increasing numbers of walkers and climbers going to the Scottish hills, it is important that all of us who do so should recognise our responsibilities to those who live and work among the hills and glens, to our fellow climbers and to the mountain environment in which we find our pleasure and recreation.

The Scottish Mountaineering Club and Trust, who jointly produce this and other guidebooks, wish to impress on all who avail themselves of the information in these books that it is essential at all times to consider the sporting and proprietory rights of landowners and farmers. The description of a climbing, walking or skiing route in any of these books does not imply that a right of way exists, and it is the responsibility of all climbers to ascertain the position before setting out. In cases of doubt it is always best to enquire locally.

During the stalking and shooting seasons in particular, much harm can be done in deer forests and on grouse moors by people walking through them. Normally the deer stalking season is from 1st July to 20th October, when stag shooting ends. Hinds may continue to be culled until 15th February. The grouse shooting season is from 12th August until 10th December. These are not merely sporting activities, but are essential for the economy of many Highland estates. During these seasons, therefore, especial care should be taken to consult the local landowner, factor or keeper before taking to the hills.

Climbers and hillwalkers are recommended to consult the book *Heading For The Scottish Hills,* published by the Scottish Mountaineering Trust on behalf of the Mountaineering Council of Scotland and the Scottish Landowners Federation, which gives the names and addresses of factors and keepers who may be contacted for information regarding access to the hills.

It is also important to avoid disturbance to sheep, particularly during the lambing season between March and May. Dogs should not be taken onto the hills at this time, and at all times should be kept under close control.

Always try to follow a path or track through cultivated land and forests, and avoid causing damage to fences, dykes and gates by climbing over them carelessly. Do not leave litter anywhere, but take it down from the hill in your rucksack.

The increasing number of walkers and climbers on the hills is leading to increased, and in some cases very unsightly erosion of footpaths and hillsides. Some of the revenue from the sale of this and other SMC guidebooks is used by the Trust to assist financially the work being carried out to repair and maintain hill paths in Scotland. However, it is important for all of us to recognise our responsibility to minimise the erosive effect of our passage over the hills so that the enjoyment of future climbers shall not be spoiled by landscape damage caused by ourselves.

As a general rule, where a path exists walkers should follow it and even where it is wet and muddy should avoid walking along its edges, the effect of which is to extend erosion sideways. Do not take short-cuts at the corners of zigzag paths. Remember that the worst effects of erosion are likely to be caused during or soon after prolonged wet weather when the ground is soft and waterlogged. A route on a stony or rocky hillside is likely to cause less erosion than on a grassy one at such times.

Although the use of bicycles can often be very helpful for reaching remote hills and crags, the erosion damage that can be caused by them when used 'off road' on soft footpaths and open hillsides is such that their use on such terrain must cause concern. It is the editorial policy of the Scottish Mountaineering Club that the use of bicycles in hill country may be recommended on hard roads such as forest roads or private roads following rights of way, but is not recommended on footpaths and open hillsides where the environmental damage that they cause may be considerable. Readers are asked to bear these points in mind, particularly in conditions when the ground is wet and soft after rain.

The proliferation of cairns on the hills detracts from the feeling of wildness, and may be confusing rather than helpful as regards route-finding. The indiscriminate building of cairns on the hills is therefore to be discouraged.

Climbers are reminded that they should not drive along private estate roads without permission, and when parking their cars should avoid blocking access to private roads and land, and should avoid causing any hazard to other road users.

Finally, the Scottish Mountaineering Club and the Scottish Mountaineering Trust can accept no liability for damage to property nor for personal injury resulting from the use of any route described in their publications.

Introduction

This is the fourth Glen Coe climbers' guide to be published by the Scottish Mountaineering Club. The pace of climbing in the area has probably increased somewhat, but more dramatically so has the number of climbers. These increases have placed more demands on the supply and style of climbing information, demands which we have tried to meet here. The guide is fully comprehensive, and includes all the routes which the three authors have been able to find. Technical gradings are used, where known. Colour photographs give a clue as to the climbing found here, mostly on sunny, clear blue days! But there should be a two-way flow of information. To help update the record, we rely on climbers to write in with their discoveries, new or old. The Scottish Mountaineering Club Journal, published annually in July records new climbs and notes in addition to more general mountaineering information. The Journal also gives the name and address of the New Routes Editor, to whom such information can be forwarded. Only then can the accuracy of our guidebooks be maintained.

But to the area itself. Glen Coe has long been in the forefront of high standard mountain routes, two hours' travelling time for the majority of those living in Scotland, and with unrestricted access granted through the purchase of much of the area for the National Trust for Scotland. Its rough lavas provide some of the most enjoyable rock climbing in the country at any grade, while many of Scotland's classic winter climbs are found here. Standards continue to be pushed up in this area, both in summer and winter as, amazingly enough, there is still untouched rock to be found, unclimbed icicles or turfy grooves to be picked at, and the new challenge of climbing hard summer lines under snow or ice to be attempted. In researching and writing this edition we have attempted to provide more than just the skeleton of a guidebook. The area deserves more. Comprehensive sections on the geology and climbing history, the amenities and other aspects should help to provide the unfamiliar visitor with not only a good working guide for any trip, but a guide which can be read as a book in its own right.

The three authors of this guide have all been steeped long in the climbing described here. They might even be described, in their own ways, as 'experts'. But even experts make mistakes, or miss some detail through being too close to the canvas. We apologise in advance for any errors in description, which will be inadvertent. Help us to correct any such errors by writing to us; and enjoy the climbing in this priceless mountain area, as we have.

The Geology of Glen Coe

In attempting to explain the present-day rocks and scenery of Glen Coe, four major chapters in geological history will have to be condensed and simplified. In essence, these are:

1. The formation of the Caledonian Mountain System, a period of immense pressures and temperatures, when vast areas of the planet's crust were in violent movement and change.

2. The Devonian period, marked both by the erosion of a mountainous hinterland of rocks to the north, and the fizzle and froth of volcanic activity in the area itself.

3. The comparatively recent Tertiary volcanic phase, when swarms of dykes associated with the great Hebridean volcanoes on Skye, Rum, Mull and Ardnamurchan pushed through existing rocks, promoting the formation of gullies with subsequent erosion.

4. The pruning, polishing and buffing of the ice-ages, virtually yesterday in geologic terms.

Before expanding on these four chapters however, it would do no harm to delve even deeper into the very mists of time, before life itself appeared on this planet and even (though this may be difficult to accept) before the formation of the SMC. So we go back to the late Precambrian, when a Proto-Atlantic Ocean began to form. It will come as no surprise to those of a nationalistic bent to learn that in all probability this early ocean, given the name Iapetus, divided what was to become the future Britain, with Scotland and the north of Ireland on the northern side, and England, Wales and the rest of Ireland on the southern side.

Iapetus was narrow at first, during the late Precambrian, gradually widening through the Cambrian. It then began its final closure as the great continental plates, driven and dragged inexorably by deep currents of molten rock, drifted together. This narrowing began in Ordovician times, and accelerated during the Silurian. By the close of the Silurian, the British region of the ocean had slammed shut, welding together the two halves of Britain. The join was probably somewhere in the region of the Solway Firth. The ancient geological borders thus eerily presage the present.

Some 1000 to 800 million years ago then, we have to try and picture high mountains to the north-west, made of Lewisian rocks. The erosion of these formed gorge-like areas with a very irregular relief, leading seawards to a deltaic coastline and, offshore, a developing trough. Into this trough or oceanic basin were deposited the first shelf-edge sediments of the early Iapetus, sediments which under later pressure would form the Moine rocks underlying much of Scotland's mountainous regions. These Moinian rocks are themselves overlain by the Dalradian rocks, which reach a thickness of over 8km, and were probably deposited in areas to the east and south-east of the Moine region. The Dalradian rocks, as measured by the chirrup of the radiometer, are some 500-440 million years old.

The approximate boundary of the Precambrian and Cambrian epochs was marked by a long-lasting, and probably world-wide glaciation, lasting some 100 million years. Interesting theories have been suggested for the cause of this, such as interstellar dust clouds casting a dismal gloom like some cosmic poll tax, but basically the boffins remain ignorant, (which last point may at least satisfy some).

The Caledonian Earth Movements lasted several million years - the length of time represented by the closing of Iapetus. In early Ordovician times, the Moine and Dalradian rocks were intensely folded and metamorphosed to make the first Caledonian Highlands. Silurian times saw the final rapid closing of Iapetus. In all their glory, these first Highlands were at least as high as the modern Alps of Europe.

So where in the Glen Coe area is the evidence of these old metamorphic rocks? The oldest of these schistose rocks is the Glen Coe Quartzite. This is a metamorphosed sandstone which forms both the Pap of Glencoe and Sgorr nam Fiannaidh; its light coloration contrasts with the darker andesite lava of the rest of the Aonach Eagach, while different layers or strata of the quartzite can be seen running along the flanks of the Pap and Sgorr nam Fiannaidh, inclined steeply. A younger rock is the Leven Schist, which forms Meall Mor and Aonach Dubh a'Ghlinne, across the glen from the Clachaig Inn. A short stretch of this schist, which is a metamorphosed siltstone, is crossed on the start of the Coire nam Beith path, its typically contorted grey layers forming a few rocky outcrops.

To see the youngest of these metamorphic Caledonides, hang over the old, lichen-encrusted wall of the Bridge of Coe, and while admiring the deep, green pools with their flashing trout admire also the Ballachulish Limestone, a lower Dalradian impure calcareous rock. To appreciate the great upheavals of the Caledonian Mountain Chain it can be demonstrated that the quartzite of the Pap runs under the limestone of the Bridge of Coe, indicating a large fold, while on the south side of the Glen the Leven Schist on Meall Mor and Aonach

Dubh a'Ghlinne lies on top of the limestone, though the schist is the older of the two, indicating a complete inversion of the original order of these rocks.

None of these three metamorphic rocks, however, are of any real climbing importance in the area, and we have to take the ferry at the Corran Narrows to the beautifully folded and striped Moine rocks on Garbh Bheinn of Ardgour to climb on the gneiss found there. While crossing over on the ferry, bear in mind that you are passing over the water-filled shatter belt formed by the huge Great Glen Fault, which extends from south of Mull in the south-west to the Moray Firth in the north-east. This ancient fault, (probably Precambrian in age), was responsible for a horizontal displacement of about 100km, with the land to the west moving south-west. The splendidly rough gneiss of Garbh Bheinn is better than most Moine rocks, which tend to consist mainly of smoother, holdless quartzites. Different layers of the original sediments are easily spotted as banding in the metamorphic gneiss. As with any rock containing a high occurrence of quartz, be careful of small flakes, which have a tendency to snap under stress.

As a last treat on Ardgour, observe the sneaky way up to the South Wall, via the steep and heathery Coire a'Chothruim, 3km west of the normal approach up Coire an Iubhair. The ancient Gaels named Coire a'Chothruim with great accuracy, as its name translates as the *corrie of the balance*. The burn coming down the corrie enters the main glen close to the watershed, so that it has on occasions flowed in either direction, east and west. The term *corrom* is now used to name such a delta-watershed. We are looking ahead of ourselves however, and must return to the rocks of the area that most concern climbers - the great volcanic layers of Glen Coe.

The closing of Ocean Iapetus was followed by a period known as the Old Red Sandstone, occurring from 400-350 million years ago. The sides of the Proto-Atlantic were not only firmly welded together, but the sediments of the basin and its margins were folded up into mountainous areas, visible away to the north-west, and rivalling the modern Himalaya. In basins between parallel mountain ranges, erosion laid down sediments: breccias, conglomerates and sandstones. The erosion continued for a long time, periods of relative calm giving finer sediments, raging torrents spreading out coarse breccias and conglomerates through the mouths of river gorges, the whole effect being to grind down the huge mountain chains visible on the far-off horizon. Oceanic crusts had long since descended from view, forced below the surface as the continental plates sailed majestically on, but on melting at great depths they were recirculated and pushed up or intruded through covering rock layers to form the Newer Intrusives. About 410-380 million years old, these intrusive rocks, mainly granites, include the Glen Coe ring complex.

One of the best sites from which to view the Glen Coe lavas is from near Loch Achtriochtan, at the Clachaig road-end, looking up towards Coire nam Beith. The west face of Aonach Dubh, on the left, is seen to consist of easier-angled, grassy buttresses, leading up to a steeper line of cleaner rock. Both of these rest on schists already mentioned, crossed on the first part of the track up into Coire nam Beith. The grassy buttresses are of augite-andesite, weathering readily and giving no climbing, while the steeper line of cliffs resting on the andesite is of rhyolite, which in Glen Coe provides most of the excellent, rough rock that is particularly suited for climbing. The hornblende-andesite lavas also provide good rock, as found on the higher cliffs of Stob Coire nan Lochan and Bidean. The sequence of volcanic rocks visible, from bottom to top, is 1. Augite-andesite and basalt lavas (450m). 2. Rhyolite lavas (135m). 3. Agglomerate (75m). 4. Hornblende-andesite lavas (270m). Don't worry about the strange names - augite and hornblende are minerals found in these rocks.

In all, there are 17 separate flows or bands of the augite-andesite, and three flows of the rhyolite, each of about 45m thickness, which might explain the current lengths of climbing ropes. The boundary between the augite-andesite and the rhyolite is most evident on the north faces of Gearr Aonach and Aonach Dubh. On Gearr Aonach, a narrow ledge runs across the face, with the steeper, cleaner rhyolite shooting up above the ledge. This ledge, in fact, continues on the east flank of the hill, forming the first, and main ledge taken by the Zig-Zags. On Aonach Dubh's north face, the boundary between the two lava types is indicated by the approach route known as Sloping Shelf. This boundary continues round onto the west face. Boundaries between individual lava flows, particularly those of the andesites, can often be discerned, again by ledges. The waterfalls coming down from Coire nam Beith, just right of the start of Dinner-time Buttress, probably mark different flows; slight variations in hardness would be quickly emphasised by water erosion.

Petrologically, rhyolite is an acid igneous rock of fine grain, with individual crystals in the groundmass being invisible to the unaided eye. Geologists further divide the rhyolites by their feldspar content, but while interesting to a specialist, further discussion on this point might cause acute narcolepsy in the average reader. The most striking point about rhyolite, and the cause of its name, is the flow banding often exhibited by these rocks, with parallel stripes of differently-coloured groundmass swirling through the rock. The thin, contorted bands give a vivid feeling for the condition of the rock when it was a newly-erupted molten magma, flowing viscously over the landscape. Enclosed crystals or phenocrysts include albite, orthoclase, biotite and quartz.

Fairly typical Glen Coe rhyolite is a pinkish-brown rock, with flesh-coloured banding being commonly found. It fractures to give sharp, well-defined edges, so that good holds in Glen Coe are just that, good. Obviously the amount, type and thickness of lava varies from site to site through the area, so that, for example, on the Buachaille there is no great layer of andesites underlying the rhyolite, there being instead two layers of rhyolite alternating with two layers of agglomerates and sediments. Agglomerate, it should be mentioned, is a pyroclastic rock, formed from fragmentary material associated with explosive activity by a volcano, as compared with the less violent flowing of the andesite and rhyolite lavas. A good exposure of agglomerate can be seen on the Buachaille, low down on the hill when approaching via the Jack-sonville path. Several slabby exposures of rock cut across the path, and when examined more closely the various shapes and sizes of contained rock fragments will be well seen, embedded in a finer matrix. Agglomerate is often seen at or near the base of a lava flow, sugges-ting that the ancient volcano first blew its top, then continued to grumble on for a while, lava flowing more quietly.

Periods of relative calm saw erosion of the new volcanic rocks, with deposition of sedimentary rocks occurring between volcanic episodes. A few thin layers of these deposited rocks have been found, with one, on the Buachaille, providing a clue as to the age of the Glen Coe lavas. In a thin, shaly layer near the Waterslide, fossil remains of an alga called *Pachytheca fasciculata* have been identified. This was a small, spherical alga, found perhaps typically in shallow water and growing up to about 1.5mm in diameter. While not spectacular as fossils go, it marks the lavas as belonging to the Lower Old Red Sandstone age.

Now we examine the emplacement of the Glen Coe lavas. Both the Glen Coe and Ben Nevis volcanic activities were accompanied by caldera subsidence, associated with outpourings of andesite and rhyolite. They are known as ring complexes, unconnected with those besotted with the music of Wagner and more to do with its ring-like shape. The Glen Coe caldera, which is a classic of its type, was formed by the two-stage subsidence, on encircling ring faults, of a cylindrical block of lavas and underlying schists. Each stage of the cauldron subsidence led to the upwelling of granite magma along the fractures. The analogy used in the previous edition of this guide, likening the upwelling to whisky spilling out of an overfull decanter when the stopper settles down, happily remains a valid one.

The huge reservoir of molten rock - the magma chamber underlying the cauldron - must have been formed by magma ascending from great depths. Tensile fractures were formed in the roof of the magma chamber as the magma, under pressure, neared the surface. Molten rhyolite, derived from the acid layer at the top of the magma chamber, penetrated these fractures, and dissolved gases were violently released, transferring more material to the surface. The emptying of the magma chamber then allowed the central block to subside into the chamber. This sequence would have been repeated several times, explaining the different flows of lava. Most of the rhyolite lavas were derived from vents on the west and north-west margins.

The western position of the ring fault is very clearly seen on An t-Sron, where the fault has been eroded to form the Chasm of An t-Sron. Standing near Loch Achtriochtan and looking up at the Chasm, the rock on the left, or Coire nam Beith side, is augite-andesite overlying schists, while the rock on the right of the Chasm is granite, squeezed up through the fault when the central block was foundering. The granite close to the gully indicates that it was rapidly chilled on intrusion, as it came into contact with the relatively cool sinking block. The granite further away from the fault however was not chilled, indicating that it must have come into contact with hotter rock, in other words with rocks contemporary with the subsidence.

The ring fault crosses the Glen and runs up the slopes of the Aonach Eagach, close to the Clachaig Gully (whose rocks are of lava). It then bends east, close to the ridge, continuing over the small hill of Stob Mhic Mhartuin, just west of the Devil's Staircase. Its position there is marked by a small crag. Bending south-east, it enters Glen Etive close to the minor road down that glen, becomes indistinct due to granitic intrusions, runs south of the Buachaille then turns west along the south side of Bidean's summit, thus completing the ring.

The other major intrusions were of course those of the granite Etive complex. There are three types of granite in the area which cut or push through the lavas in Glen Coe, and are therefore younger. The earliest granite on the scene is also the major part and is the Moor of Rannoch Granite, essentially a granodiorite. This is cut by the Ben Cruachan Granite, an adamellite, which is itself cut by the Starav adamellite.

These granites were emplaced in the form of bosses, circular in cross-section (and perhaps often similar in shape to a thickly-stalked mushroom). Connected to deeply sited batholiths which are probably connected underground, they have provided the vast exposure of slabby climbing on Beinn Trilleachan and elsewhere down Glen Etive.

The Starav adamellite has the minerals plagioclase and feldspar in approximately equal amounts, and is disconcertingly less coarse-grained than, say, the Moor of Rannoch Granite. Lighter veins of minerals trace their way up the slabs, indicating that different fractions of minerals existed in the granitic magma, being injected into the parent mass later. One particularly prominent one is followed on Swastika; the quartz content being more resistant to weathering than the surrounding granite, it protrudes slightly above the surface of the slab, providing an exciting ride for two crucial pitches. Don't expect any runners from it however. Expansion and contraction from heating, cooling and the freezing of water has prised off sections of the slabs, providing overlaps to dangle from and heave over. If the glassy Trilleachan Slabs overstimulate nerve endings, try the granite on Creag Chaorach, steeper but rougher and with protection!

One last act remained to be played out on the igneous stage - the Etive swarm of intrusive dykes. This phase overlapped and followed the granitic and lava flow phases, and is responsible for many of the existing gullies found throughout the Glen Coe area. The swarm was caused by the rising of molten rock into a series of closely spaced, parallel fractures running from north-east to south-west. Ossian's Cave on Aonach Dubh is one of the more spectacular examples, the cave being formed when the dyke rock fell away from the surrounding rhyolite. The dykes are mainly of a porphyritic microdiorite, which is very closely related to andesite.

The dykes are recognised, apart from the differential erosion, by their darker colour; a good example may be seen on the East Face of Aonach Dubh, where one descends for a short distance as a gully from the top of the east face. The gully has been formed by the erosion of the softer dyke rock. The flanks of the Aonach Eagach are seen to be seamed by dykes, whose easy weathering along with that of the andesite adds to the huge scree slopes found close by the road, and yes, we continue to resist the quarrying of these highly visible and no doubt valuable deposits (on National Trust for Scotland land).

The Ice Age. Long, cold and miserable, this took place during the last million years, so it is obvious that vast periods of time have been skipped in this brief description. These 'missed' years saw much erosion, but luckily for the modern climber the cauldron subsidence, by plunging some lavas deep underground, preserved the same rocks, which gradually saw the light of day again as the covering layers were slowly worn away. Before the ice-age gives the rocks their final buffing, we have one interesting facet to relate, that of the original Glen Coe river which once flowed to the North Sea.

In early Tertiary times, about 40 million years ago, magnificent volcanoes dominated the western seaboard, with vents on Skye, Rum, Ardnamurchan, Mull and Arran pouring out lavas almost continuously. Access to the Atlantic was denied to much of the drainage, and a river, rising in Ardnamurchan, flowed east along the line of Loch Sunart, Glen Tarbert, Glen Coe, over the Rannoch Moor and hence to the North Sea. The softer granites of the Moor have allowed the valley shape to be obliterated, while the harder rocks further east still show some of the ancient valley outline. The Coe has obviously at some point reversed its flow. Firstly the shatter belts of the Great Glen Fault and Loch Leven allowed drainage in a south-westerly direction, cutting across the original river so that the Coe was beheaded, immediately losing much of its power. Tributary streams blocked the remaining river with deltaic cones (long since removed by glaciation), which reversed the drainage towards Loch Linnhe. This reversal acounts for the fact that Scotland's watershed, on the Rannoch Moor, is barely noticeable.

The new, shortened Coe flowed eagerly to the Atlantic, cutting through the rhyolites of upper Glen Coe. Then came the glaciers. At their maximum the ice-shed was on the Rannoch Moor, with ice flowing west across and through the glen, carving it into a typical U-shape. There are boulders of Rannoch Moor Granite on the Aonach Eagach, while the Pap of Glencoe summit has south-west-aligned scratches from the time when ice carried rocks over the ridge. The basin of Loch Achtriochtan was scoured by ice out of an area of softer, slaty rock, while of course the high corries, mostly facing north-east, were sculpted by the erosion of thawing and freezing cycles and moving ice. The fine little Coire nan Lochan, with its tiny lochans, is a good example of such a corrie. With the retreat of the ice came floods of stones and other debris, fanning out to provide a flat floor to the west end of the glen.

A raised beach at Invercoe attests to the varying sea-level during the ice-ages (at least three of recent times, the last being from about 70-10 thousand years ago). During periods of glaciation world-wide sea-level was at least 100m lower; in a heavily glaciated region the land was actually pushed down, only to rebound upwards once the ice had gone. A large landslip occurred on Gearr Aonach, the falling debris being sufficient to dam Coire Gabhail. The valley behind the landslip developed an alluvial flat, forming that haven of peace known to climbers as the Lost Valley.

Humankind appeared on the scene and began to grub an existence, first by hunting and fishing, then by agriculture, and finally by building bunkhouses for itinerant travellers and charging ridiculous prices for a teabag.

The forces of nature continue unabated, and in the last decade several noticeable rock-falls have taken place in Glen Coe, e.g. near the foot of Chancellor Gully. In 1990 a large chockstone radically altered the Converging Walls pitch of The Chasm. In the same year heavy rain caused flood damage on the approach to the Trilleachan Slabs. These changes will not be the last, a salutary warning when strenuously pulling up on even a familiar flake. But take normal care and the robust rhyolite of Glen Coe will be found to be as reliable as any rock.

Ken Crocket

A History of Climbing in Glen Coe

1. The Golden Age

It is remarkably easy to overlook how difficult it once was just to reach Glen Coe. When climbing took off as a distinct game in Scotland in the late 19th Century, that new-fangled device, the steam locomotive, ran into its buffers at Tyndrum, where the Oban Line terminated. The pioneer climber then had to hire something on wheels pulled by a horse. If the rough track to Glen Coe was not blocked by snow, the cart would bump its way over the high pass above Tyndrum, skirt Loch Tulla by its west shore, then grind up over the Black Mount, staying tucked into the hills on the west for illusory shelter, with an ever widening vista over the Moor of Rannoch to the east. Kingshouse Inn would be reached with relief. (This hotel is named after George III, during whose reign General Wade worked on the Scottish road and bridge infrastructure, and stopped at the Inn.) Some tourists would have reached the Kingshouse after a boat trip up Loch Etive, considerably easier than the track from Tyndrum, while many would have taken a boat from Fort William to Ballachulish and would then have been disappointed not to be taken any further than the foot of Glen Coe.

This sorry state of affairs lasted until 1931, with the opening of 'the wonderful new highway', as George Abraham called it. Before then, however, those with time, energy and money managed to mount several successful expeditions, some of which will be covered later. But let us begin with the first recorded ascent in Glen Coe, that of Ossian's Ladder on the North Face of Aonach Dubh, climbed in 1868 by a local shepherd, Neil Marquis. Very little information seems to exist on this, though one description of Marquis is not very flattering, painting him as being somewhat dim-witted. Modern climbers might agree, the route being one to avoid. William Brown described the climbing required to gain the cave in a Journal article of 1896: 'Hands, knees, toes and eyelids had to be awkwardly spread over a mixture of mud and vegetable, which affords a support as treacherous as it is dirty, and which no respectable mountaineer, having regard to his Norfolk, will care to depend on.'

The Cave was subsequently visited by many prominent climbers, who left their cards in a tin box supplied by Norman Collie. Many years later, this custom was ended by another prominent climber, one Dougal Haston from Edinburgh, who was prompted to throw the box out of the Cave. The reference to Norfolk above was to the climbing clothing of the day, the Norfolk Jacket, whose stiffly warm woollen weave protected many a daring ascent in bad conditions. Contemporary photographs indicate that the climbers of these early days, just as in the present, fell roughly into two camps. Those who had some regard for fashion, and carried their equipment in neat little sacs, and those who crammed their paper-wrapped hotel lunches into the spacious side pockets of their Norfolks, hairy ropes draped languidly round their open necks. There was no obvious correlation between fashion consciousness and climbing ability, though the convenience of being able to dredge up morsels of food from a deep pocket in between pitches may have helped on some ascents.

The SMC was founded in 1889, while the Fort William Line opened in 1894, but Norman Collie beat both to Glen Coe with his ascent of Great Gully on the Buachaille, 'some years prior to 1894'. Collie also climbed the North Face of Aonach Dubh, by a route whose line is sadly unknown. He was back again in 1894, briefly present at an SMC Meet which should be regarded as a historical milestone in Scottish climbing - the Easter Meet at Inveroran Inn. Some ten miles from Tyndrum Station, this small hostelry on Loch Tulla afforded one base for attempting the Glen Coe hills.

Collie and his two guests, Solly and Collier, stayed one night at the crowded inn before moving to the Kingshouse on the next day. On Friday, March 23rd they climbed the Buachaille by its first rock climb, Collie's Climb, a 300m Moderate taking in the mixed ground left of Central Buttress. On the same day, and unaware of the other party, or for that matter the earlier ascent, Naismith, Thomson and Brown climbed Great Gully, mostly on wet snow. Collie's party, staying on in Glen Coe for a few days (training for their first ascent of Tower Ridge, made the following week), pioneered ways up several routes, including Collie's Pinnacle on Bidean, and a re-ascent of the North Face of Aonach Dubh. Collie returned to Glen Coe with Hastings, following his Ben Nevis trip, and on a day in early April 1894 he did a 'rather difficult climb up the face of Aonach Dubh just to the left of Ossian's Cave'. This climb was looked for in 1932 by Jimmy Bell, who recorded the East Wall Climb, Very Difficult. In 1894, it is safe to state, a psychological barrier, the invincibility of the Glen Coe rocks, had been breached.

In the following year, 1895, Brown, Rose and Tough recorded North Buttress on the Buachaille in July. This rock climb, still a respectable route of about Difficult depending on conditions (during the first ascent it was chucking it down), may be looked on as the first climb in Glen Coe recognisable as a clean, distinct and lengthy rock climb, Collie's other ascents notwithstanding. Other notable routes from this first, Golden Age, include the Aonach Eagach Ridge (August 1895), and Curved Ridge (July 1896), the latter soloed by G.B. Gibbs who found the climb 'not difficult'. But the top guns were aimed at the magnificent steep ridge which fell almost directly from the summit, when viewed from the Kingshouse. It was named the Crowberry Ridge, after the tempting berries which Naismith and Douglas encountered *en route* in August 1896. By skilled route finding, this purple-tongued pair bypassed the steep crux of the Crowberry Direct on the right, climbing the ridge for the first time by Naismith's Route.

It required the attentions of Lake District rock technicians, the Abraham brothers, in company with Puttrell and Baker, to climb the Crowberry Ridge Direct. This was in May 1900. It is still a crux to fall off with great ease, a sloping foothold on a steep nose of rock with little in the way of a handhold above. In their report in the Journal, the Abrahams complained of a misleading diagram in an earlier Journal, perhaps the first recorded instance of outsiders being unable to comprehend the Scottish philosophy of generalisation in diagrams and route descriptions for the larger scale. This misunderstanding continues today, with some unable, or unwilling, to make the necessary mental adjustment required for route finding. The small-scale diagram is useless for following a route - it is only intended to help in finding the route.

Crowberry Direct obviously induced much irritation in certain Scottish nostrils. The Abrahams recognised it as the most difficult climb then in existence. Harold Raeburn, then the hardest climber in the SMC, called it one of the most difficult climbs in Scotland. He was qualified to make this remark, having made the second ascent in June 1903. He arranged to meet the good Edinburgh climber Dr Inglis Clark and his wife at the Kingshouse. Making the most of life, Raeburn had been yacht-racing off the east coast in the afternoon and caught the night train to Tyndrum, from whence he cycled to Glen Coe, arriving there at 5.45 am. After a few hours of sleep the trio set off. Arriving at the crucial belay ledge, Raeburn changed into *kletterschuen*, soft climbing boots, while Inglis Clark attempted a photograph. Mrs Inglis Clark pretended to belay Raeburn (no sexist remark this, the belay was useless.) Unfortunately the camera was so close to the action and the situation so awkward for Clark that a headless photograph resulted, showing that some things never change. As for the crux moves by Raeburn, 'An anxious and silent interval was only broken by the slow movement of the rope...'. Clark returned later and caught his successful photograph with another team. Elsewhere on the Buachaille, in October 1903 Newbigging's party climbed the Difficult D Gully Buttress, an ascent which went unrecognised for 87 years, being overlooked by several guidebook authors.

Not all efforts were aimed at the rocks during this period. The gullies suffered from the sustained attacks of the long-axed climbers, with 1898 being a particularly rich year - Easy Gully, D Gully and Crowberry Gully all fell in April of that year. The ascent of the latter, by Raeburn and Green, has met with an awkward appraisal by various guidebook authors, unable to grant it the status of either a summer or a winter ascent. Raeburn himself avoided claiming anything, but then with the first three ascents of the gully - 1898, 1909 and 1910 (the last in summer conditions) - he could leave it to others to decide. He did describe all three ascents in a Journal article, which would prompt at least this writer to grant him the first winter ascent, in 1898, if not 1909.

Bidean nam Bian also fell under relentless forays by the early climbers, with Church Door Buttress a particular favourite (see route description for an interesting account of their first ascent antics). Stob Coire nam Beith was poked at by George Abraham and wife on honeymoon, with Arch Gully, a 200m Difficult receiving an ascent. In April 1906 a winter ascent was made of North-West Gully by Glover and Worsdell. Probably a mini-epic this, involving five hours of step-cutting and an appearance back at the Meet's Hotel at 11 pm. (To miss dinner was to guarantee a somewhat strained atmosphere at the breakfast table the next morning...).

There were only a few more years left of this glorious outpouring of exploratory climbing. Central Buttress on Stob Coire nan Lochan was, and is, a classic winter route, first climbed by the Inglis Clarks, Dr and Mrs, and Raeburn, in April 1907. Shadbolt's Chimney on the North Face of Aonach Dubh is still a Severe, despite being first climbed in June 1908. Over the ferry in Ardgour, the rocks of Garbh Bheinn had also been gaining attention, with the ascent by J.H.Bell (no relation of the later J.H.B.Bell) and Willie Brown in April 1897 of the Great Ridge, at 300m one of the longest Difficults to date outwith Ben Nevis. Brown was to die of an illness at the tragically early age of 33, with a string of good, hard ascents already recorded.

After about 1910 the Golden Age in Glen Coe lapsed into a Golden Twilight. Climbers were exploring elsewhere, it is true, but activity was decreasing in general. There were very few young climbers coming up, and increasing standards had run into a technological barrier. It was possible, physically, to do longer and more serious runouts on rock, but with virtually no protection (and climbers during this period fully realised this point) to do so was next to suicidal. In winter the overlong and heavy ice axes were clumsy and exhausting in the confines of a gully. Finally the Great War, with its high demands on every aspect of life, slammed shut any chance of climbing right through to 1920.

II. Renaissance

There was no immediate rebirth of climbing during the 1920s. The country was exhausted: physically, financially and spiritually. In September 1920, visiting climbers Wilding and Pigott ran amok in Glen Coe, recording Shelf Route on Crowberry Ridge (Difficult and exposed), and Crypt Route on Church Door Buttress among other routes. This was an anomaly however, at least as far as climbing in Scotland was concerned. We have to go forward to 1928 before the next new route was recorded, that being another variation to Crowberry Ridge. Then in 1929 J.H.B.Bell and Sandy Harrison began a series of fruitful visits to the glen.

In 1929 Bell was 33, and Harrison 41 years of age. They were therefore a bridge between the pioneering Victorians and the new breed that was about to emerge in the 1930s. Bell and Harrison, either together, or with different partners, were responsible for about 25 routes in Glen Coe between 1929 and 1940. Highlights included North Face Route on Central Buttress (1929), Cuneiform Buttress (1930), Diamond Buttress Direct (1931). All of these broke new ground on steep buttresses.

The new generation of climbers consisted of the Establishment (albeit a somewhat laid-back one), and the Others, a state of affairs consistent with one of the natural rules of the Universe. The Establishment formed the JMCS in 1924, frustrated by the conservatively-minded SMC, while the Others formed half-a-dozen clubs, including the Grampian Club (1927), the Ptarmigan Club (1929), the Creag Dhu Club (1930), and the Lomond Club (1933). The universities would shortly follow suit.

The Others were very different hill people from their predecessors. Many were either unemployed or poorly paid, their visits to the country

a relief from the grind and grime of the cities. They were commensur-
ately tough, taking the art of sleeping under newspapers to a height
that would only be rediscovered with the depths of the divisive politics
of the 1980s. Climbing, walking or just plain howffing was to be a
revelatory experience for many, with the rule of thumb the key to the
highway and things higher.

The new generation rapidly increased the pace of exploratory
climbing, The Chasm receiving its complete ascent via the Cauldron
Direct by Robinson and Jack in August 1931, thus completing some
33 years of investigation. In March 1934 the expatriate Pat Baird made
the first winter ascent of SC Gully while on a Cambridge University
meet. Later that year, in June, the Rannoch Wall was opened up with
Route I by Williams, Todd, Macphee and Jack. The route had actually
been climbed in its entirety in May 1933, but as Williams had had a
rope from above to safeguard the difficult part this was not recorded.
A new spirit of competition was beginning to flicker, with rumours of
other parties and a new guide in the making (eventually written by Bill
Murray, another of the new generation). A 'new guide in the making'
turned out to be an unfortunate phrase for some decades with the
SMC, as it was not to be published for another 16 years. Competition
was certainly in force on the day Agag's Groove was climbed, in August
1936, as the party of the first ascent beat the second party to the foot
of the climb by mere minutes.

That the SMC was at this time conservatively-minded was shown
by their reaction to the ascent of Route I. When Macphee (himself a
member of the SMC) heard that it was still possible for routes to be
included in the guide book he made diplomatic approaches, only to
be told that several other routes he and his companions had made in
May 1934 were 'not worth recording' (though in fact they later were),
and that a footnote might be allocated to the Rannoch Wall route. This
was a mere hiccup in mountaineering politics however, as the Establishment slowly realised what changes were taking place. By the time
the guide was eventually published in 1949, all of these routes and
many more modern lines were included.

This period of pre-war renaissance saw not only social changes,
but crucial improvements in equipment and techniques. When Murray
began climbing in 1935, for example, he and his friends increased the
recommended length of rope from 80 feet for three climbers to at first
60, then 80 feet between individual climbers. By 1936 they were using
100 feet for the leader on rock, 120 feet in winter. Also during the
1930s, the rope used switched from full-weight hemp to a thinner line,

one-inch or one-and-a-quarter inch circumference. Nailed boots were commonly used, with thin-soled 'Woolworth's' plimsolls being useful for the harder rock.

By 1936 the JMCS was 200 strong. Murray, Mackenzie, MacAlpine and Dunn formed an efficient climbing machine. They had transport and they used it to good effect through a series of hard winters. Ice axes were finally coming down in length, just as hems were going up. Douglas Scott, in 1936, had a very short axe made for himself by a blacksmith. With this he made the third winter ascent of Crowberry Gully. Bill Mackenzie had made the second a week earlier, though using a longer axe. On hearing of Scott's short axe, Murray bought a 14-inch slater's hammer. With its side claw removed, this short ice hammer facilitated the cutting of steep ice. Head torches began to illuminate the Stygian gloom of many a long, dark day, though crampons were still a tool of the future. With such equipment, Murray and Mackenzie made the first winter ascent of the Shelf Route on Crowberry Ridge (March, 1937), a hard and exposed climb, years ahead of its time. They followed this with the winter ascent of Deep-Cut Chimney in April 1939, at its time reckoned to be one of the hardest winter climbs in Glen Coe.

Though the flourishing climbing scene was not to know it, the Second World War was about to apply the brake, albeit less crushingly than had the First. Raven's Gully on the Buachaille was climbed by a strong party of the Others, including Jock Nimlin, in June 1937, while in 1938 Clachaig Gully finally succumbed to Murray's party. Norman Collie had been the first to attempt its flowery delights as early as 1894, while George Abraham had failed in 1900. In September 1939, as the world slid into another war, Iain Ogilvy and Miss Esme Speakman recorded Satan's Slit and Red Slab on the Rannoch Wall, the latter belatedly upgraded to Very Severe with the publication of the 1980 edition of this guide. With that, and Raven's Gully, a new standard had been set, one that would be continued and extended by the vigorous explorations of the young Scottish clubs - and one in particular - the Creag Dhu.

Ken Crocket

III. Post War to 1991 (Rock)
In an extract to the Editor of the SMC Journal in 1939, entitled 'Pitons on Crowberry', the use of a piton to protect the crux of the Direct Route caused quite a stir amongst the establishment. Perhaps the most

celebrated piton incident of the thirties occurred when a group of visiting German climbers used pitons on the first ascent of Munich Climb on Tryfan in North Wales. Leading activists were so outraged that they rushed up, repeated the route and removed the offending ironmongery! Evidently British climbers considered themselves far superior to their continental counterparts, remaining generally unaware of the great achievements taking place in the Eastern Alps! Is it then possible that a similar situation arose between Scotland and the development taking place in England and Wales? A propaganda war followed which ensured an almost total rejection of the piton and built into the mentality of British climbers an aversion (or stubbornness) that persists to the present day!

During the war it was simply a matter of opportunity. Of note, however, was the ascent of the Very Severe route Hangman's Crack (1941) on the Buachaille, climbed by Donaldson and McCarter. Frith Finlayson led this route in nails in the 1950s. In 1947 W.H.Murray's 'Mountaineering in Scotland' stimulated interest in the Highlands, as did Murray's preparation for the new Glen Coe Guide, due to be published in 1949. Leading the field were the Creag Dhu and leading the Creag Dhu, amongst other notables, were John Cunningham and Bill Smith.

Cunningham's Autumn Slab (HVS 1946) hinted of things to come whilst Crow's Nest Crack was interestingly graded Severe in rubbers (a good VS today). The quantum leap in standards appeared in 1947 when a young Cunningham added Gallows Route on the East Face of the North Buttress. This was a climb rivalled only by Preston's Suicide Wall (E2 1945) in North Wales and Haworth's Steeplejack Staircase (E2 1940) on Salisbury Crags in Edinburgh. Bill Murray continued to add many now classic routes while Cunningham completed a soul-searching lead on Slime Wall with Guerdon Grooves (HVS 1948). Climbing was no longer a middle-class sport.

By the mid-fifties, Jimmy Marshall led a strong Edinburgh school which included Robin Smith and Dougal Haston. In the west, Pat Walsh came to the forefront. Walsh was apparently so short-sighted that he often had no idea of the size of the holds he was pulling on! He and Hamish MacInnes climbed Bludger's Route (HVS 1952), an impressive line on the steep central section of Slime Wall. During the fifties few others were to make such an impact as Walsh. Amongst his most powerful leads were a blitz of routes made on Slime Wall in 1956. These were Doom Arete (E1), Bloody Crack (E1), and Nightmare Traverse (E2). It was clear that on a return trip to the Alps, Robin Smith expressed how they kept in touch with recent trends, 'with a pause in Wales in the Llanberis Pass at a daily rate of four a piece of climbs that Englishmen call XS. (X is a variable, from exceptionally or extremely through to very or hardly to merely or mildly severe)'. On the East Face of Aonach Dubh Cunningham introduced new heights with The Gut (VS 1956), whilst across the water on Garbh Bheinn Smith did likewise with Blockhead (E1 1957).

Exploration of the Etive Slabs began in 1954 when E.Langmuir and M.O'Hara discovered the superb Spartan Slab (VS). The next developments came three years later when M.Noon and Cunningham climbed the remaining corners, Hammer, Claw and Agony. Noon and E.Taylor then tackled the central slabs with the fine Swastika (E2). This fantastic period of exploration peaked when a nineteen year old Smith climbed Shibboleth (E2 1958), returning the following year with the talented Creag Dhu climber John McLean to add the True Finish (E2). Also impressive is Cunningham and Noons' ascent of Carnivore (E2 1958) on Creag a' Bhancair and Bluebell Grooves also by Cunningham. 'Padding' took on a whole new meaning when Smith and Cunningham combined in an ascent of The Long Wait (E2 1956) on Etive.

Marshall's eye for a line was unsurpassed when he unravelled the complexities of Trapeze (E1 1958) on the West Face of E Buttress on Aonach Dubh and the magnificent Apparition on Slime Wall (E2 1959) which he climbed with John McLean. Haston and Moriarty established Hee Haw (E1 1959), possibly the hardest of a fine E Buttress trilogy - the third, Big Top, added in 1961 by Smith. On the North Face, where seepage rarely dries, Smith and D.Hughes completed Yo-Yo (E1 1959), a line which had already rebuffed the mighty Whillans. (It was winter, and it was wet, when Whillans looked at the line). Smith again succeeded where Marshall failed on a new route called Marshall's Wall (E2 1960) on the East Face of Gearr Aonach.

Don Whillans, the man who resolved the entry pitch to Carnivore, returned with D.Walker to settle the score with a hard direct known as the Villain's Finish (E2 1962). And that man again, Walsh, climbed a line based on what was later to become the first pitch of Crocodile and the second pitch of the Girdle Traverse on the North-East Nose of Aonach Dubh. Tragically, Britain lost one of its most talented mountaineers when Robin Smith was killed in the Pamirs.

Haston went to Switzerland, Walsh south, Cunningham to Antarctica and climbing in general found a new direction in other parts of the Highlands and Islands. Nonetheless a period of consolidation followed. New climbs were added and the big routes saw repeats dispelling their aura of impregnability. These activities induced a new edition of the guide written in two volumes by L.S.Lovat; The Buachaille (1959) and Glencoe II (1965). Good routes from this period include the Girdle of the North Face of Aonach Dubh (E2 1963) by a big Edinburgh team, Via Dolorosa (HVS 1964) by Bugs McKeith and B.W.Robertson. Unicorn (E1 1967) was cleaned and climbed by Jimmy Marshall and Robin Campbell, and the fine King Pin on the West Face of Church Door Buttress by J.Hardy and W.Thomson (E2 + aid 1968).

Another feature during the sixties was the increasing popularity of aid climbing, a trend which possibly began in California's Yosemite Valley. Exemplary in the art were two talented climbers from Edinburgh, 'Bugs' McKeith and Dave Bathgate. A number of the Coe's major lines only succumbed after a mixed amount of free and artificial moves. Freak Out, Flip Out and the line now taken by The Clearances were all climbed in this style.

Where the Edinburgh Squirrels dominated the scene in the East the Dumbarton-based 'Rock Kids' did likewise in the West. This small group consisted of such talented notables as J. Jackson, Rab Carrington, Ian Fulton, Robin McFarlane and Big Ian Nicolson. Providing influence and inspiration to this group were various Creag Dhu members, including Con Higgins, Jimmy Gardiner, Davy Todd, and John McLean. Big Ian stepped in with the much prized second ascent of the Girdle of the North Face of Aonach Dubh, and a new route called Apocalypse (E3 1968) which he climbed with Higgins. Having climbed a number of new routes with Dave Knowles, Kenny Spence and others, Ian showed his mettle by soloing The Long Reach and Pause, albeit a few years later in the early 70s.

The ideas and exploits of the talented Edinburgh climber Kenny Spence were quite futuristic, one such being an ascent of the line now taken by Massacre. Two points of aid were used on what he considered to be a free route. The ascent was never recorded. Spence with John Porteous also climbed many major lines including Lecher's Direct (E2 1968), Tumbler (E1 1967) and a free ascent of Pendulum (E2). Jackson and Carrington added the hard Pinch (E3 1968) on the Etive Slabs, Belk and Jenkins The Cough (E2 1971) and Tut Braithwaite with Geoff Cohen found the improbable Scansor (E2 1972).

On the South-East Face of the Buachaille further exploration by Ken Crocket, Colin Stead and Dave Jenkins (amongst others) led to some excellent discoveries in the VS-HVS grades, most notably Whispering

Grooves and Flamingo on the Blackmount Wall and Waterslide Corner on Central Buttress. Throughout the 1970s and early 80s, Crocket and partners, including Stead and Ian Fulton, recorded a series of good routes over the water on Garbh Bheinn of Ardgour, mainly at VS.

In 1974 Pete Livesey was influential. Inspirational were the likes of Ron Fawcett, John Allen and Tom Proctor. Chalk, indoor climbing walls, magazines and the then bible of British climbing - *Hard Rock,* all played an important role. The most significant climb in the area was Nick Colton's death-defying lead of Le Monde (E4 1976) on Creag a' Bhancair. Pride of place however, goes to The Clearances (E3 1976) by Ed and Cynthia Grindley. Dave Cuthbertson reduced the aid on Freak Out and Ken Johnstone added Spacewalk with a sling for aid. By 1977 attitudes were such that if you couldn't climb it free then you didn't do it at all. Representative of this new wave were Dave Cuthbertson, Murray Hamilton, Willie Todd and Ken Johnstone, later joined by Kenny McClusky, Pete Greenwell, Rab Anderson, Alan Taylor, Derek (Spaz) Jamieson, Spider McKenzie, Dougie Mullin and Kenny Spence.

Cuthbertson led Bannockburn (E4 1977) based on a line known as Tight Rope, which had been climbed in the sixties by Cunningham and freed at a later date by Arthur Paul. Todd freed Bluebell Grooves (E4 1977). Hamilton freed Clearances, King Pin and added Grogblossom on Slime Wall (E4 1978) and Pinch Direct on the Etive Slabs (E3 1978). Pete Greenwell and Johnstone's Triceptor (E5 1978) was as hard and serious as any route in the Coe. Mullin relieved Freak Out of its aid and with Hamilton did likewise to Eldorado, Cuthbertson and Johnstone adding a new top pitch the following day (E5 1980). Massacre was restored to a state of respectability courtesy of Spider and Spence (E3 1980).

It was at this time that the SMC refused to accept that there were enough climbers operating in Scotland to justify the use of the extreme grade. However, the new edition of the guide by Ken Crocket did feature E grades (alongside the extreme grade) but despite the misgivings of the author was selective, and still combined summer and winter in one volume without technical grades.

1980 saw yet another incursion by an Englishman, The Risk Business (E5) by Pete Whillance. This was influential in that inspection was carried out most professionally. Up until now the majority of first ascents were climbed on sight but down south pre-inspection had become the norm. At long last the next major rise in standards came from a Scot. After a brief interlude on sight (resulting in a 70-foot fall)

Cuthbertson pre-inspected Revengeance (E6 1981). In contrast Prophet of Purism was climbed on sight (E6 1981), an attempt which lasted two to three days with much down-climbing and familiarisation. In 1982 Pete O'Donovan's clean ascent of Spacewalk (E5) was worthy of note, and Whillance took on a mammoth task when he climbed the Lost Ark (E4 1983), a line previously attempted by leading climbers of the sixties and early seventies. Garbh Bheinn received a modern approach with Hamilton's Chela (E3 1982), True Cut (E3 1982) and the most stunning route yet, The Kelpie (E6 1986). Cuthbertson's Romantic Reality (E7 1984) marked a considerable rise in standards and as a traditional climb it is still the hardest undertaking in the area.

The next developments of any great importance were controversial. Graeme Livingstone climbed Fated Path (E6 1986) and Cuthbertson added The Railway Children (E6 1986/7) to the Tunnel Wall of Creag a' Bhancair, two of the finest pitches to be found anywhere in the country, but featuring bolts for protection. The second ascent of Revengeance (pitch 1 only) fell to the talented late Colin Gilchrist and a long-standing ambition was fulfilled when Paul Laughlan repeated Romantic Reality and the main pitch of Gone With The Wind. Mark McGowan repeated Gone With The Wind as well as adding The Chant of Jimmy Blacksmith to Aonach Dubh and Creag Dhon't Woll on the Buachaille. Perhaps reflecting future trends and a very high level of fitness were the on-sight ascents of Admission, Fated Path and Uncertain Emotions by Dougie Hall and a flashed ascent of The Railway Children by Glen Sutcliff. Grant Farquhar and Gary Latter showed that it is still possible to climb hard new routes without bolt protection on the Tunnel Wall when they produced Up With The Sun (E6) in July 1991.

Glen Coe's future is bright. There are many challenging lines for everyone to climb and enjoy. I do believe, however, that there is a place for bolts in Scottish climbing, but only in the right hands and on the right crags. For the majority of us bolt protected climbing is all about pushing oneself to the limit in relative safety. In Glen Coe and the Highlands in general there are quite simply no accessible crags of the type necessary to produce satisfactory bolted climbs. Elitist? All I'm saying is spare a thought for others and make space for a little fun.

Dave Cuthbertson

IV. Winter Climbing 1940 to 1991

'That there are almost innumerable possibilities of winter climbs in Glencoe is self evident, but the intervention of the war temporarily halted our exploration.' This quote by W.M.Mackenzie from a 1947 SMC Journal illustrates the effect that the Second World War had on the development of winter climbing; it was to be some years before exploration fully resumed. The number of winter climbs recorded in the Coe during the 1940s further illustrates this fact - a mere six. Amongst these however was the very fine 1942 ascent of Flake Route (IV) on Church Door Buttress by G.R.Scott and F.W.Cope of the Grampian Club. On their ascent snow and ice-covered holds caused delay below the arch with Raeburn's chimney beyond proving almost insurmountable until combined tactics were used. When submitted to the SMC Journal, the Editor noted that although no ascents had been recorded he knew that the route had been done in the month of April, probably under easier snow conditions. It appears strange (or does it!) that such a significant first ascent was treated in this off-hand manner. It is also interesting to note that the route was subsequently claimed by the Smith/Holt partnership in 1959 (EUMC Journal), and then by MacInnes in 1960.

Another two routes worthy of mention from this period are the now classic Twisting Gully (III 1946), added to Stob Coire nan Lochan when Bill Murray teamed up with Douglas Scott and J.Cortland-Simpson, and Crowberry Gully Left Fork (IV 1949) by C.M.G.Smith, R.J.Taunton and I.C.Robertson. This latter route is still considered hard, although short and, nowadays, well protected.

The 1950s saw a significant increase in activity and also the emergence of a number of new names soon to become, dare it be said - legendary. The first of these was the 'Old Fox' himself, Hamish MacInnes, whose first foray into the Glen Coe winter scene would appear to be the undistinguished Right Chimney on Stob Coire nan Lochan (II 1950). It didn't take him long to learn and his second offering in 1952 was much 'meatier' - a recognised ascent of Clachaig Gully (IV/V) in the company of R.Hope. I say recognised, for an earlier ascent had been disallowed by the SMC, as ever acting in the role of judge (and probably jury). In the 1949 SMCJ it was noted 'The Editor of the Glencoe Guide has noticed that winter ascents are being claimed when the rocks are free from snow and ice. The fact that a climb has been made during the six winter months does not of itself qualify the climb as an ascent under winter conditions for guide book purposes. Such a claim merely misleads other climbers. The Editor has therefore disallowed the claim to a first winter ascent of Clachaig Gully published in the last issue of the Journal. The rocks were free of snow. Similar ascents have been disallowed for the Chasm, Church Door Buttress and Rannoch Wall.' It is interesting to note that then, as now, controversy has surrounded the ascents of those attempting to increase standards. This is not to say that the claims for these ascents are valid, merely to illustrate that all may not be what it seems! Quite often there is a very thin dividing line between a route being in winter condition or not. The modern definition, and also that of the pre-front pointing era, is that any route is fair game should it be of wintery appearance and be made easier by the use of crampons, gloves and axes.

In 1951 D.H.Munro and P.D.Smith climbed the now classic No.6 Gully. No.4 Gully (III/IV) was ascended in 1952, which in itself is nothing spectacular until one notes that its first ascentionists were Messrs Joe Brown and Don Whillans. It was not until 1953, however, that the next major and long overdue leap in winter standards took off. This was not for the lack of trying or knowing what routes to go for, as can be seen by the controversy surrounding some earlier ascents. (At this juncture it is worth bearing in mind that the difference between the summer grades of the winter routes that were being attempted was a lot less than it is now - in other words these climbers were really pushing it.) This time it was MacInnes and he was firmly at the controls. Within the space of a week he clocked up three exceptional ascents of well-tried and sought after routes. Firstly, Agag's Groove (V) went in the company of Chris Bonington along with Hamond and MacIntosh, then, on consecutive days, Raven's Gully (V) and Crowberry Ridge Direct (V), both with Bonington. MacInnes thought Crowberry the hardest, then Agag's and last Raven's - remember, this was the pre-front pointing era! This makes the 1938 ascent of Crowberry Ridge, which included the crux, stand out as a considerable achievement - to date these are the only known ascents. Agag's has had two other known ascents, and has been rated at least a grade harder than Raven's Gully. The similar Eagle Ridge (V) on Lochnagar, climbed a month previously, is now a classic, whilst Agag's and Crowberry are ignored.

Another name which springs up in the mid-50s is that of Len Lovat. Amongst a number of his first ascents were the excellent Hidden Gully (III/IV 1955) and Lady's Gully, Right Fork (IV 1958) both with W.J.R.Greaves. He also succeeded with N.G.Harthill on the often tried Crack Climb (III 1958). Undoubtedly though his finest route was the excellent Scabbard Chimney (IV 1956) of which he made the first summer ascent in 1954. One of Glen Coe's classics, this climb is still thought hard - not surprising when it is noted that along with A.H.Hendry, one Jimmy Marshall was in the party. Having cut his teeth on Scabbard, Marshall was to go on to make his mark as one of Scotland's finest exponents in the art of winter climbing.

Also of note from this period is the D. and R.Goldie ascent of Shadbolt's Chimney (IV 1955), a route of which little is known, though it is likely to be harder than the grade given to it. In 1957 John Cunningham bounced onto the winter scene when, along with Mick Noon, he climbed his own summer VS, Deep Gash Gully (IV) to produce an interesting sounding, and rarely climbed route. However, despite his summer knowledge of the Coe and his Creag Dhu roots, Cunningham was not to be involved in the new route scene there, eventually moving to Glenmore Lodge and developing his skills on ice in the Cairngorms. In December 1957 the two Cuneiform Buttress routes on the Buachaille were climbed on the same day by the two main exponents from Edinburgh; Robin Smith and Leaver did Long Chimney (IV) whilst Marshall, Mill and Ritchie did Ordinary Route (IV). Shortly after, in January 1958, while brother Jimmy was on The Italian Climb on the Ben, Ronnie Marshall, with J.Stenhouse, climbed North Face Route (V) on the Buachaille to produce an excellent, hard mixed route. Developments in the east included Savage Slit (V) and Sticil Face (V).

January 12th 1958 was a busy day on Stob Coire nam Beith, with Lovat and Harthill on Crack Climb; Jimmy Marshall and I.Douglas on The Pyramid (III) and then The Sphinx (III/IV), and J.Clarkson and J.Waddell on the now classic Central Gully (III/IV). The same day over in the Lochan, K.Bryan and J.Simpson added the fine Spectre (IV) up the ramp beneath Scabbard Chimney.

The following year (1959), John McLean and Mick Noon, talented rock climbers from that most famous of brotherhoods 'The Creag Dhu', went in search of a hard route on which to test their mettle, and finding this on Diamond Buttress they produced the very hard Direct Route (IV). Alternative venues were also being sought, and in 1959 Jimmy Marshall opened up the Lost Valley Minor Buttress with various partners including Dougal Haston, Graham Tiso, Elly Moriarty and J.Stenhouse. This was the year that Marshall and Cunningham repeated Raven's Gully, on the very same day that Smith and Holt did the Orion Face on Ben Nevis. Also to fall that year were Point 5 Gully on the Ben and Smith's Gully on Creag Meagaidh.

A new decade had arrived and, having been out of the new routes scene for a while, MacInnes was keen to make up for lost time. In 1960, among his crop of new routes were Old Man, Big Chock and Chancellor Gullies on Am Bodach, Rev Ted's Gully, Crypt Route by The Tunnel, and the excellent Avalanche Gully (IV) via the upper right fork. Other routes of note during this period were Pterodactyl (V 1964) with some aid and Gully A, Right Fork (IV 1964) both by MacInnes and D.Crabbe.

In the winter of 1965 attention was turned to a number of icefalls. Dougal Haston and Bugs McKeith accounted for Drain Pipe Corner (IV), The Screen (IV) went to Dave Bathgate and Jim Brumfitt, and Shiver (IV) was climbed by J.Knight and M.Harcus. In 1966 Ian Clough, G.Lowe and John Hardie climbed Amphitheatre Scoop (IV), Clough returning later to add the direct start and in so doing producing one of the best routes on the face. Over in the east Jim McArtney, soon to join the Coe scene, did Djibangi (V 1965); Pinnacle Face (V 1966) was also climbed.

The winter of 1969 was brilliant, good conditions arrived and, unusually for the Coe, lasted some time. A staggering total of just over fifty new routes were climbed, mainly by instructors and their parties from the Glencoe School of Winter Climbing (GSWC). Routes were ripe for plucking and the pace was frantic. Climbs of particular note were; The Graduate (IV) Dave Knowles and party, the superb West Chimney (IV) Allen Fyffe and MacInnes, the hard Frostbite Wall and Frostbite Groove (IV) MacInnes and parties, Adagio (IV) MacInnes and party, Tyrannosaur (IV) Ian Clough and party, Innuendo (IV) MacInnes and party and the excellent Great Gully (IV) on Garbh Bheinn by the motley crew of Chris Bonington, Tom Patey and Don Whillans.

Three routes in particular, however, stand out from this very exceptional winter. On February 16 two parties attacked the blatantly obvious and patently hard-looking icefalls high on the exposed East Face of Gearr Aonach. Taking the icefall to the left side of the icicle fringe, Fyffe and McArtney climbed Mome Rath Face Route (V), whilst the icefall down the right side of the fringe was climbed by MacInnes, Hardie and Clough, The Wabe (V) - both are superb. The other route was even bigger and since the ascent was never written up (ie sent to the SMC Journal) and it was only ever mentioned in hushed whispers amongst The Starav Club, it was some years before much, if anything, was known about it. This was Wilf Tauber and Davy Gardner's ascent of the very obvious Fingal's Chimney (V) on the North Face of Aonach Dubh, an impressive achievement. After the 1984 ascent by Chris Dale and J.Moffat (they thought they had made the first ascent) the route was rated highly, both in quality and difficulty.

So out went the 'swinging 60s' with a flourish and in came the 70s and the visit of Yvon Chouinard. This was to trigger a change that would revolutionise winter climbing. In February 1970 Chouinard made a brief visit to Scotland, primarily it would appear, to publicise his prototype curved ice-hammers. With him came Doug Tompkins, another superb ice technician, and together they illustrated the effectiveness of the curved picks - in Glen Coe they repeated Raven's Gully in fast time, adding the Direct Finish (V). The simple change from a straight to a curved pick enabled upwards progress to be made in a totally different manner and with a greater degree of security than ever before. Prior to then, although there had been some experimenting, the idea of hanging off a dropped pick without cutting as a means of climbing ice just hadn't been considered. The Americans, their tools and their techniques therefore arrived like a bombshell. Chouinard visited Glenmore Lodge where he met Cunningham, whom he had heard about because of the Scot's experiments with the precarious dagger technique, the high point of which was his ascent of The Chancer (V 1970) in the Cairngorms. The daggers were actually a red herring, the importance was the fact that Cunningham was front pointing on steeper ice. 'Bold as hell' on ice, Cunningham was immediately and understandably converted. Change was in the air, Chouinard and Tompkins visited the Clachaig. Cunningham and March came through from Glenmore Lodge, MacInnes was there, as was Spence and a host of others from the GSWC. Underlying the revelry there was serious conversation. For those present step cutting virtually died overnight, and what is commonly know as the front pointing era began.

The Glen Coe 'School' realised the limitations of the curved picks and their construction for mixed ground and thin ice, and within a remarkably short period MacInnes had produced his own prototype, the Pterodactyl. In its fully finished form the 'Terror', as it was commonly known, was an awesome tool; steeply inclined, straight, dropped pick; short shafts; shovel-head adze and large square, weighty hammer-head. Versatility and robustness were its hallmarks and it proved ideal for use on the varying types of terrain in Scotland. Unfortunately, (there is always a price to be paid) since the pick was close to the shaft the knuckles suffered tremendously under the continual battering. Soon Chouinard's curved tools and the Terrors were in full production and widespread use. Due to the immense psychological barrier of trusting oneself to the new techniques, and the Scots' usual resistance to change, it actually took upwards of two years before everyone was converted. Once these barriers had been broken it enabled those who would previously never have ventured onto steeper ground to approach such climbs with confidence. The original timings for ascents of routes on ice as an indicator of difficulty became meaningless as was pointedly illustrated by Ian Nicolson and Dave Knowles's solos of Zero Gully, with Nicolson continuing to solo Point 5 in a combined time of 3 hours. The emphasis had moved away from technically hard mixed ground and it was to be some years before it was to start turning back in its former direction.

There was remarkably little new route activity in the Coe for most of the 70s, perhaps due to a number of reasons; in search of fresh pastures the GSWC took courses to the North-West; leading climbers were involved in various projects abroad and the front pointing techniques were enabling good repeat ascents to be made as well as a allowing many hard new ice routes to be put up in other areas, especially the Ben. This could therefore be considered as a period of consolidation.

A few routes, however, were added in the early part of this decade. Kenny Spence and Dave Knowles had joined the Coe team. Spence, a talented rock climber from Edinburgh, had drive and initiative. Always seeking difficulty he was to be one of the main instigators in the eventual shift back to mixed climbing. Knowles from Preston was a determined winter climber, though not too good at recording his ascents, who produced some excellent routes before his untimely death whilst filming on the *Eiger Sanction*. Routes of note from this period were: the fine Midnight Special (V 1970) Spence, Clough and party; Evening Citizen (IV 1970/1) Spence, MacInnes and Alan Thomson; Ordinary Route (IV 1971) Spence and party; Route 1 (IV 1972) by MacInnes and the fine Moonshadow (IV 1972) by Ken Crocket and Colin Stead. Two routes stand out though, Midnight Cowboy (V 1972) Dave and Dud Knowles with Wull Thompson, and Direct Route (V 1972) Dave Knowles and J.Loxham. Both are of different natures; Midnight Cowboy being long and on ice is bold with some long runouts, whilst Direct Route is short and being on snowed-up rock is technically hard. For years it was incorrectly thought that Knowles had climbed the more obvious chimney of what was to become Chimney Route, but Spence, with whom Knowles had previously attempted the line, confirms that it was the summer line they were following in order to establish a difficult face route (the reason for Astronomy on the Ben: Spence, Fyffe and MacInnes, 1970).

Apart from Nicolson's fine icefall, Findlay's Rise (IV 1978), little else happened until 1979 when another good winter saw ice forming low down again and a fresh influx of young climbers who, being weaned on front pointing, were there to take up the challenges. Rab Anderson, Dave Brown, Zander McAllister and Mal Duff climbed the two parallel lines of White Snake (IV) and Venom (IV/V). Dave Cuthbertson, another gifted rock climber, like Cunningham before him turned his attentions to steep ice. First he climbed The Flute (IV), then he went on to climb one of the biggest problems in the Coe, the free standing, hanging icicle which forms the direct start to No.5 Gully. It had been eyed by many but the techniques with which to climb it were not available until the 70s and since it formed very rarely the challenge was never taken up. A local personality, Willie Elliot, whose house it hangs above, had proclaimed it impossible - hence the name Elliot's Downfall (V). Another fine ice route was Heart of Glass (V) Cuthbertson, Willie Todd and Ken Johnstone, however, full marks go to John 'Spider' McKenzie and Gerry Rooney for their gem on the Aonach Eagach, Blue Riband (V) - one of the longest routes in the country. MacInnes reappeared and with C.Williamson he climbed another long thought-about route, The Dalness Chasm, via the Right Fork (IV). On the Buachaille, Arthur Paul and Davy 'Paraffin' Sanderson, on the same day, climbed Misty High (IV) and Cuneiform Corner (IV).

Undeterred by all the ice antics going on around them, Kenny Spence teamed up with Murray Hamilton, another talented rock climber who had the same will to succeed on hard routes as himself. Putting well-discussed tactics into operation, they decided to utilise their rock climbing abilities to a better extent by attempting routes that would be likely to give them similar technical and physical difficulty to that which they sought in summer. Their first success was Direct Route (V) on Great Gully Buttress. Not being able to miss out on rare opportunities they, in the company of Alan Taylor, also climbed the first and much thought about winter line on the Etive Slabs by following ice near the summer route Ba's (IV). Over in the east things never really changed during this period, they simply carried on winter climbing; Bower Buttress, The Carpet and Hourglass Buttress (V's 1970) and Labyrinth Direct (V 1972) were fine routes. In 1977 Cumming Crofton (V) and Vertigo Wall (V) showed potential, however in 1979, simultaneously with, but independent of, developments in the west, the pace started to change with Central Route (V), and The Link (V/VI). On The Ben harder ice was done, Shield Direct and Shadow (both VI). Prospects for the next decade looked rosy.

Having experimented with what was possible, Spence and Hamilton along with Alan Taylor returned in 1980 to push standards further. Clough's summer line Tilt, provided them with an excellent hard route (VI). In 1980 this team also climbed Postern (VI), Mousetrap (V/VI) and Citadel (VI) in the east. With these routes a significant step forward had been made. It should be noted that prior to this it had not been clear just what was possible and to what extent of difficulty one could climb in the prevailing weather conditions. What was clear, however, was that catching these steeper routes, especially in the west, with sufficient snow on them would be difficult indeed. Terms such as torquing and hooking were not yet around; these techniques were found by experimenting and using one's tools as extensions of the hands. Here then was where the development of Scottish Winter climbing lay, back on course again after the intervention of the 'ice-age'. The 80s were to become a period of diversification where snowed-up rock, ice and mixed climbing standards were all pushed up even further with the addition of many excellent routes.

On the Mome Rath Face, the first routes to be added since the winter of '69 were Outgrabe Route (V 1980) by Rab Anderson and Rob Milne, followed closely by Dave Cuthbertson and Mal Duff on the hard but excellent Rainmaker (V), which the previous pair had attempted. The Wabe saw numerous ascents and was soloed by Spider McKenzie. In December 1980, Spence and Anderson climbed Consolation (V), short but hard and Spence began an affair with Central Grooves. This was the next obvious line to go for after Tilt, but being steeper and graded VS it was sure to be harder and less often in condition. Numerous trips with various partners ensued; in 1981, having climbed the first pitch, Spence and Hamilton broke out of the cornerline to produce the very good Central Buttress (VI), but the main line remained.

Good routes continued to be added; the fine Darwin's Dihedral (V 1981), Cuthbertson and Martin Lawrence; Closer (IV 1982), Chris Dale, Adam Kassyk and D.Talbot; East Face Route (V 1982), Hamilton and Anderson and on consecutive days in 1982 the remaining branches of the Dalness Chasm - the Left Branch (V) to Andy Nisbet and Sandy Allen and the even more impressive Central Branch (V) to Cuthbertson and E.McArthur. A route to rival, if not beat, Elliot's Downfall was well spotted and climbed by the dynamic duo of Mick Fowler and Tony Saunders up on yet another raiding party, Mr Softee (V) is impressive. Spence and McKenzie like McLean before them sought a hard route on the complex Diamond Buttress and came up with Winter Route (V 1983). Success on Central Grooves (VI 1983) finally went to Spence and McKenzie (the third time up the first pitch for Spence) and one of the Coe's best routes had been produced, a fine achievement. On the same day Hamilton and Anderson arrived in the car park to find that the occupants of the other car which had arrived just in front of them were Spence and McKenzie. Rather than have a farcical race for the route, Hamilton and Anderson went elsewhere, returning to make the second ascent in 1985. With the addition of Centurion (VII 1986) on the Ben, this short-lived but fruitful partnership of Spence and McKenzie stopped winter climbing to concentrate on rock; Hamilton was to do likewise also.

January 21 1984 was the day of the big storm which cut Glen Coe off for days. Many parties were active when the storm hit and most were caught on the hill. Fortunately all managed to struggle back down at some time or other and the only work the rescue team had to do was dig out cars. Four new routes were climbed that day including Brian Sprunt and Sandy Allen's good effort on Ordinary Route/Raven's Edge (V), whilst across the gully Cuthbertson and Arthur Paul failed high on Guerdon Grooves, a route Al Rouse had tried a few days previously. A week later Cuthbertson and Paul finally succeeded on Guerdon Grooves to give the area its first VII, a very bold and serious undertaking. A few days later, on consecutive days, they also added two fine routes to the Mome Rath Face, Jabberwock (V) and Snow-stormer (V).

Another much thought about possibility was the soaring cornerline of Unicorn, and in January 1985 Andy Nisbet and Colin McLean found it in very rare hoar-frosted condition. The resultant route, the area's second VII, is extremely hard and utilises some aid; a free ascent, if possible, will undoubtedly be impressive, although a long wait will doubtless be required for the right conditions. Also of note from this period were: People's Friend (V/VI 1985) Nisbet and Duff; Silent Running (V 1986) and King Cobra (V/VI 1986) by Duff and Rick Nowack; Willie Todd's ascent of the fine, hard-looking icefall which forms beside Lady Jane (V 1986), and to show that there were still good easier lines, Anderson and Hamilton did Crest Route (IV 1985) and Crocket, Walker and Craig found Ephemeron Gully (IV 1985).

The exploration of some other areas started to take place: on Beinn Starav, Graham Little and Dave Saddler found the excellent Hidden Ridge (IV 1986); on Garbh Bheinn, Simon Richardson and Nick Kekus did Route I (III 1986); on the obscure Beinn Fhionnlaidh a huge cleft was sought out and climbed by Robin Clothier and Simon Richardson,

Rapunzel (IV 1987); on Sron na Creise, R.A.Napier and S.Downie found the classic Inglis Clark Ridge (III 1987). Back in the Coe a very obvious line on Bidean's West Top, although noticed by many, was left for F.Yeoman and J.Mathie to climb, hence Dubiety (IV 1987).

In 1987 the Lost Valley Buttress was brought into the 80s when at the second attempt Anderson and Grahame Nicoll succeeded on the superb Neanderthal (VI). Anderson returned over the next few seasons with various partners to add a string of very good routes, notable amongst which was the short but ferocious Savage (V 1988). This route illustrates an interesting trend in modern winter climbing, as others had already climbed the crux in summer (HVS 5a) during exploration for new winter lines, but the party concerned failed to find an amenable approach on their return in winter.

Over on Stob Coire nan Lochan, Nisbet and Cunningham returned with Newton (the three Andy's) to succeed on a line they had checked in summer, Para Andy (V 1988), while Anderson and Nicoll added the neighbouring Intruder (V 1988) which had seen a number af attempts by others. Three routes, however, stand out from this very good winter. Firstly, Red Slab (VI) on the Rannoch Wall went to the young hot rock team of Colin Gilchrist and Mark McGowan to give a technically hard and bold outing, an impressive achievement. Tragically, Gilchrist was killed a short time later in an avalanche. On the North Face of Aonach Dubh the superb chimney line of Fall-Out went to Anderson and Gavin Taylor at VI; reaching the top in the dark in a full blown storm they couldn't crawl into, they were forced to abseil back down the route whereupon the whole of Sloping Shelf avalanched nearly taking them with it - they arrived back at the road some 19 hours after leaving it. In fact, in just over a week Anderson and Taylor did three new routes in the Coe all involving climbing in the dark and very late arrivals back at the road. The winter game is not an easy one.

What was fairly clear was that the steeper routes needed snow and being in the west they had to be caught and climbed before the snow disappeared. If they were in condition there would more than likely be even more fresh snow at their bases - prime avalanche conditions. Catch 22. This was also illustrated when Sloping Shelf got Fowler, taking him and two of his companions for some 190m, mostly in mid-air. Being the lucky fellow that he is, Fowler, and companions, survived this harrowing ordeal with minor abrasions. Rumours of Fowler being up to something on the North Face of Aonach Dubh were obviously true but luckily for him the route stayed in condition and before anyone could go for a look the long trip up from London was made again and together with Chris Watts he climbed the aptly named Against All Odds (VI) up the big fault left of Fingal's Chimney. A hard route which uses some aid, it will be interesting to see if there will be any takers for a second ascent.

Little was produced in 1989. After a previous failure and subsequent summer inspection, The Long Crack went under heavy snow cover to Anderson, Chris Greaves and Alick Williams on a day when people were failing to wade into Coire nan Lochan. A technical 'cragging' style route with descent by abseil off a tree made this an entertaining excursion. An interesting point is that Williams, a mechanic on his first winter route, was the only one not to fall off - fiddling with spanners is obviously good for modern winter climbs! Double Entendre (IV), an obvious line left of Innuendo, went to Andy Nelson and George Szuca and Directosaur (V) on Lost Valley Buttress to Anderson, Graeme Ettle and Rob Milne.

1990 produced nothing and 1991 was little better although some routes were climbed. Rab and Chris Anderson with Rob Milne added two IVs to the Far Eastern Buttress, produced the technical Isis (V) and managed to climb the very good and very hard Inclination (VI) beside Tilt. In Glen Etive two good icefalls were climbed, The Whore's Apron (III) by Steve Kennedy and D.Ritchie, and The Fall Line (III) by Kennedy and Arthur Paul.

Despite the past three seasons being relatively unproductive, there is a healthy future for winter climbing in Glen Coe, with many new routes on all types of terrain and at all grades still to be climbed. There are also many routes awaiting second ascents. It is fair, therefore, to say that in the period of this review there has been over half a century of exceptional development and it is evident that there are still numerous possibilities for winter climbs in Glen Coe and its environs.

Rab Anderson

Notes on the Use of the Guide

CLASSIFICATION OF ROUTES

Summer
The normal British grading system of Easy, Moderate, Difficult, Very Difficult, Severe, Very Severe (VS), Hard Very Severe (HVS) and Extremely Severe has been used. The Extreme grade is sub-divided into E1, E2, E3, E4, E5, and so on.

Technical grades are given for routes of VS and above where known. Much effort has been made to elicit information from active climbers about routes, some of which will have all the relevant pitches graded, while others will have only the crux pitch so described. The normal range of technical grades expected on routes of the given overall grade are as follows: VS - 4b, 4c, 5a; HVS - 4c, 5a, 5b; E1 - 5a, 5b, 5c; E2 - 5b, 5c, 6a; E3 - 5c, 6a; E4 - 5c, 6a, 6b; E5 - 6a, 6b. Routes with a technical grade at the lower end of the range will be sustained or poorly protected, while those with grades at the upper end of the expected range will have a short and generally well-protected crux section.

Although the British system is thought to be second to none by those who use it, it is known to confuse visitors from abroad. For their benefit it can be assumed that 5a, 5b, 5c and 6a correspond approximately to the American grades of 5.9, 5.10a/b, 5.10c/d and 5.11a/b respectively. Eurocraggers should note that there is little or no fixed protection on most of the climbs here, and that if they are used to cruising bolted French 6c, they may suffer some distress while attempting the corresponding 6a pitches here, with their sometimes spaced and fiddly protection.

Grading information is in some cases scanty or even almost totally lacking, particularly in some of the older or more obscure routes. Climbers should therefore be even more circumspect in their approach to such routes, which have been indicated in the text by a dagger symbol. Information about these routes is always welcome.

Winter

Winter climbs have been graded from I to VII.

Grade I indicates simple snow climbs, with perhaps a corniced exit.

Grade II includes gullies with either individual or minor pitches, or high angled snow with difficult cornice exits, and the easier buttresses under winter conditions.

Grade III incorporates gullies which contain ice or mixed pitches. There will normally be at least one substantial pitch and possibly several lesser ones. Also sustained buttress climbs without great technical difficulty.

Grade IV gullies may include nearly vertical ice sections, while the buttresses will require a good repertoire of techniques.

Grade V climbs are difficult, sustained and/or serious. Some may be well protected but technically very hard.

Grade VI and VII routes have exceptional overall difficulties.

Split grades indicate uncertainties due to the route being known to be variable in condition, or a borderline case. Routes are graded for average to good conditions. It should be borne in mind that winter grades are often an approximation, because conditions (particularly in this area) can vary rapidly. The advent of extremely difficult buttress climbs, which differ so radically from the more traditional gullies and icefalls, has put the grading system under some strain. As an experiment, a two-tier grading system, which incorporates some of the principles of the summer technical grades, has been proposed. An explanation of this system is given at the back of the book, together with the proposed two-tier grades for the harder climbs in the area. If this system becomes accepted by the majority of active climbers, then it will be used in future guidebooks. If not, it will go the same way as all other failed experiments.

Terminology

Left and right refer to a climber facing the cliff or facing downhill in descent. In cases of potential ambiguity a compass direction is also given. An arete may also be described as an edge. A diedre can be described as a groove or a corner. Pegs, bolts and other fixed gear are for protection only, except where specifically stated that they are for direct aid. Do not assume that they will either be in place or in a safe state of repair.

Pitch Lengths
Pitch lengths are given in metres, to the nearest 5m (except for very short distances). 45m ropes should be adequate for the vast majority of routes, though 50m ropes are useful in winter.

Diagrams
The climbs on some of the cliffs have been numbered. This indicates that there is a diagram depicting the cliff, which will be found close to the relevent text. The numbers of the climbs in the text correspond to the numbers on the diagrams. If a numbered climb is not shown on the diagram it will be located in relation to the numerical order of those that are. For each separate area the numbering begins again at 1, so make sure you're looking at the correct diagram.

Recommended Routes
Some unfortunate routes have been singled out by using the three star system of recommendation. This has been arrived at through the personal experience of the authors and through information received from active climbers. In most cases the consensus of opinion has not varied by more than one star. Undoubtedly some deserving but obscure routes will have been missed, while starry-eyed personal bias, always a danger, may have intervened in a few cases.

First Ascensionists
The year of first ascent is given in the text. The full date and pioneers are listed in chronological order at the back of the guide. Further relevant details of the first ascent and subsequent ascents (where known) are also listed in this section.

Style
All thinking climbers should be concerned with the quality of their climbing; this includes style, which is about the way you climb, including protection. It is assumed that a good range of modern nuts and perhaps also some camming devices will be carried. For rock climbs in this guide pegs are not required, and climbs are so graded. A few ancient pegs may be found *in situ;* these should be left as they are, to avoid further rock damage. With time they will corrode gracefully and disappear. On some occasions pegs may be found necessary for winter belays; however, all efforts must first be made to seek a safe alternative.

The use of chalk will creep down the grades unless discipline is used. Chalk marks have been seen on Agag's Groove, which must mark a new low point for climbing competence. Chalk should really only be advantageous for climbs graded HVS and above, or some VS routes on a sweaty day.

The SMC deplores the use of bolts for aid, protection or as belays on any mountain crag, and regrets that bolts have been used and are in position on Creag a'Bhancair. Given that this crag has had bolts for many years, it is probably too late to realistically consider their removal, though it is hoped that future climbers with both greater skill and alternative means of protection will eventually render these bolts redundant. Bolts, likewise, have no place in winter mountaineering. Climbing in Scotland has a strong tradition of boldness and adventure at every grade of climb: this spirit should be preserved for future generations of climbers.

Mountain Rescue

In case of an accident requiring rescue or medical attention, contact the police, either by phone (999) or in person (Police Station at Glencoe Village). If a victim has to be left, be sure that the exact location is known before leaving the site of the accident, and that if possible the nature of any injuries can be reported. Try and leave someone with a victim, who should in any case be made comfortable and well sheltered if injuries allow. As participants in a potentially dangerous sport such as climbing, some knowledge of first-aid is a worthy thing. An awareness of the 'coma position' for example, may save a life. Booklets abound on both first aid and rescue techniques, including respect and proper use of rescue helicopters. Read them.

Maps

The following Ordnance Survey maps cover the area of this guide:-
1: 50 000 Sheet 40 (for Ardgour)
1: 50 000 Sheet 41 (for Glen Coe)
1: 50 000 Sheet 50 (for Glen Etive)
Also useful is the map of Glen Coe, at a scale of 1:20000, drawn by James Renny and published by the Scottish Mountaineering Trust. The meaning and pronunciations of local place names can be found in *Scottish Hill and Mountain Names* by Peter Drummond, published by the Scottish Mountaineering Trust (1991). The Scottish Mountaineering Club District Guides to the Central Highlands and the Northwest Highlands contain much useful general information concerning the mountains of Glen Coe, Glen Etive and Ardgour.

Avalanches

In Glen Coe avalanches occur most often following heavy snowfall or during thaw. All gullies and most slopes between 22 and 60 degrees should then be suspect. Some gullies are more prone than others and are so highlighted in the text. The greater the amount of fresh snow, the higher the risk. Fresh snow can include wind-blown deposits, so that stormy weather can maintain an avalanche risk for prolonged spells. Past and present weather conditions are very important. Climbers preparing for winter climbing should familiarise themselves with basic avalanche theory, using one or more of several useful books available on the subject. In the field, much can be learned by digging a hole and examining the snow profile, looking especially for different layers of snow with different degrees of bonding. Slab avalanches, for example, will be caused when a weakly cohesive layer of snow collapses underfoot. Such a weak layer is usually hidden under a firmer layer, hence its great potential as a killer. The top layer will often break into slabby fragments, the first warning. If descent of a dubious slope is unavoidable, each person should stay apart and trail a rope while descending. This will greatly ease the location of a buried climber.

If avalanched, try and either jump free, or anchor yourself for as long as possible, depending on circumstances. If swept down protect your access to oxygen by 'swimming' to stay on the surface, by keeping your mouth closed, and by preserving a space in front of your face if buried. Wet snow avalanches harden rapidly on settling, so try and break free if possible at this point. If trapped try to stay calm, which will reduce oxygen demand.

If you are a witness to an avalanche, it is vital to start a search immediately, given it is safe to do so. Victims will often be alive at first, but their chances of survival lessen rapidly if buried. Unless severely injured, some 80% may live if found immediately, but only 10% after three hour's delay. Mark the burial site if known, listen for any sound, look for any visual clues and search until help arrives if possible. Again, a working knowledge of first aid may save a life, as many victims may have stopped breathing. Glen Coe is one of the three mountain areas in Scotland which is currently being monitored on a regular basis throughout the winter for snow conditions and avalanche risk, so regularly updated information is available in the national press and with the Climbline telephone weather information service.

AMENITIES

Accommodation

Camping: There are numerous roadside campsites in Glen Coe, Glen Etive and Ardgour which have traditionally been used without any restriction, though it should be remembered that camping and lighting fires in the Scottish countryside without permission is an offence. This traditional freedom to camp should be treated as a privilege and respected by considerate behaviour for local inhabitants, other campers, tourists and the wildlife which inhabits the countryside. Most of all one should respect the environment. This is a beautiful and scenic place; please help keep it that way and leave no trace of your passing.

Unfortunately it is a small minority of campers who create problems for those who do behave with due care and consideration. The area covered by this guide has become extremely popular with a large number of outdoor enthusiasts, and as a result the environment can only suffer under the considerable strain. Rough camping although free has one major drawback, there are no sanitary facilities. For this reason it is strongly recommended that where possible an official campsite should be used. These are:-

Glen Coe Campsite (113 576): This extensive site, run by the Forestry Commission, is by far the best in the area. It lies just off the main road some 2km east of Glencoe village. Camping and Caravanning Club listed, there is always a friendly welcome and the facilities are excellent. Toilets, showers, drying room (all free to campers), launderette and mini-market shop. There is also a more secluded area on the fringes of the site for those who wish to keep away from the holidaymakers. Unfortunately, at the time of writing, the site is closed from 30 September until Easter. However, due to the problems that rough campers are creating elsewhere, pressure is being brought to bear on the Forestry Commission and it is hoped that soon the site will be open all year round. Highly recommended. (Tel: 08552 397)

Red Squirrel Campsite (120 573): Situated on a loop of the old road to Glencoe village, 1km west of the Clachaig Hotel. Although Camping and Caravanning Club certified, this pleasantly situated country site is fairly basic. Portaloo toilets and showers, but no shop or laundry facilities. Open all year. (Tel: 08552 256)

Invercoe Caravans (098 593): This camping and caravan site lies by the shore 500m north of Glencoe village, on the road to Kinlochleven. Facilities are excellent: toilets, showers, launderette and shop.

Caravans for hire. Closed from the end of October until Easter. Self-catering cottages available all year. (Tel: 08552 210)

Caolasnacon Caravan and Camping Park (139 612): Situated on the shore just over 5km along the Kinlochleven road from Glencoe village. Caravans for hire also. Closed November to March. (Tel: 05554 279)

For those wishing something more substantial over their heads there are a number of alternatives:-

Glen Coe Youth Hostel (118 576): About 1.4km west of the Clachaig Hotel, along the old single track road to Glencoe village. Grade 1 hostel with 62 bedspaces, laundry facilities, store, family rooms available and members own kitchen. Open all year, although booking is advised at peak times: July, August, New Year and weekends. (Tel: 08552 219)

Glen Coe Bunkhouse (117 577): About 50m west of the youth hostel, the bunkhouses are at Leacantuim Farm, sleeping up to 70. Toilets, showers, hot and cold water. There is also slightly cheaper 'Alpine' type accommodation. (Tel: 08552 256)

Glen Coe Outdoor Centre, Carnoch House, Glencoe. Bunkhouse, rooms sleep 2-8, more pricy. (Tel: 08552 350)

There are also seven climbers' huts in the area available for booking to members of clubs affiliated to the MCofS or the BMC. Addresses and phone numbers of current hut custodians should be obtainable through your club or by contacting the MCofS who issue an annually revised hut list covering all the huts in Scotland. These are:

Blackrock Cottage (267 531) LSCC Hut; just off the access road from the A82 to the White Corries ski area.

Lagangarbh (222 560) SMC Hut; just over the River Coupall opposite Altnafeadh on the A82 road.

Inbhirfhaolin (158 507) Grampian Club Hut; down Glen Etive.

The Smiddy (116 457) For Venture Hut; at the foot of Glen Etive.

Kyle MC Memorial Hut (128567); next to the Clachaig Inn.

Alex McIntyre Memorial Hut (046 612) BMC and MCofS Hut; on the A82 roadside adjacent to the Creag Mhor Hotel, Onich.

Manse Barn (033 613) Lomond MC Hut; on the A82 roadside at Onich.

There are a number of other frequently used climbers' huts in the area. These are not 'open dosses' and should be treated with respect. Unless invited, enter at your own peril. One club has been known to roast intruders alive over an open fire! Rumours apart, as long as the huts are not abused hospitality will be extended to those caught *in extremis* or found staggering off the hill, lost in a blizzard. For those of more prosperous means there are numerous bed and breakfast establishments, guest houses and self-catering cottages within the area. For details contact the local Tourist Information Office in Ballachulish. (Tel: 08552 296) There are three main hotels which as well as providing food and accommodation also provide useful watering holes for thirsty climbers and walkers, or as can often be the case places for watery climbers to shelter. These are:-

Kingshouse Hotel (259 543): Situated on a loop of the old road, this 22-roomed hotel is visible (weather permitting!) to the north of the main A82 road, about 2km west of the access road to the White Corries ski slopes. Commanding a fine view of the Buachaille and the entrance to Glen Coe, the hotel specialises in catering for climbing club dinners. Restaurant available to non-residents for dinner or breakfast, room permitting. Bar food midday to 7pm at weekends, also served midweek. The bunkhouse run by the hotel is scheduled to close permanently on 1/5/1992. Planning is underway for a new bunkhouse and other facilities. Rough camping is tolerated just over the bridge from the hotel, however, due to previous misuse the hotel's sanitary facilities are no longer available for campers. (Tel: 08556 259)

Clachaig Inn (128 567): Lying at the western end of Glen Coe, on another loop of the old road, this 19-roomed hotel sits beneath the Clachaig Gully and commands a fine view of the West Face of Aonach Dubh. Reasonably priced accommodation can be obtained in the lodge facility (9 rooms) which is available during the winter for groups of 3-5 (minimum let 4 days). Drying room facilities in the lodge and in the hotel. There are also three 6-bed self-catering chalets (minimum weekly let). Hotel dining room open to non-residents for dinner and breakfast. Bar food available all day whilst bar is open; winter bar meals (vegetarians catered for); selection of real ales; entertainments programme including live music most weeks and winter programme of lectures and slide shows; maps, guides, batteries and other sundry items available for sale. (Tel: 08552 252) Rough camping in the Clachaig environs is generally on National Trust for Scotland property and has been barely tolerated. This situation is likely to change due to the problems created by the large numbers of campers using (and abusing) this area. Hotel facilities are not available for campers. The National Trust Visitor Centre used to allow campers to use its toilet facilities, but due to previous misuse this is no longer the case.

Glen Coe Hotel (098 587): Beside the A82 road on the edge of Glencoe village. 15 rooms, bars, dining room open to non-residents, breakfast and dinner. Entertainments at weekends. (Tel: 08552 245)

Local Information

Climbing Shop (095 586): A few hundred metres west of Glencoe village at Tigh-phuirt, just off the main road, is 'Glencoe Guides and Gear', an excellent little shop run by Paul Moores who being a qualified guide knows a lot about the area and the gear he sells. (Tel: 08552 402)

Glencoe Village: Two petrol stations. Police station (Tel: 08552 222). Doctor (Tel: 08552 226). Two shops; 'McCubbins Stores' (grocer and general merchant) and 'General Stores' (post office and general merchant). Two Cafes; 'Clan Mackenzie Restaurant', 1km south of Glencoe village on the main road, open 9am - 8pm (climbers breakfasts etc but being a tourist area slightly pricy) and 'Crafts and Things', opens 9.30 am, Tigh-phuirt (next door to Glencoe Guides and Gear). Banking services available, enquire locally for times and places.

National Trust for Scotland Visitor Centre (129 564): Just off the A82 road on the opposite side of the River Coe from the Clachaig Hotel. Most of Glen Coe is under National Trust for Scotland care and the Centre provides much local information on sights (including a 10-minute audio-visual programme), events and accommodation. Picnic area, snack bar, bookshop and toilets. One can become a member to support the Trust in their work. Closed October to Easter, thereafter seasonal opening 9.30/10am to 5.30/6.30pm.

Ballachulish Village: Tourist Information Office, open 7 days, can arrange accommodation in the locality, free booklet available covering most of the accommodation in the area, (Tel: 08552 296). Petrol station and 'Chisholm's Garage', (Tel: 08552 217). Two shops; 'Spar' and 'Co-op'. Cafe, 'Highland Chef', at the west end of village just off main road. Isles Hotel, under construction, planned to open Easter 1992.

Onich: Small campsite open March to October (Tel: 08553 208), three locations for caravan hire, shops, hotels, petrol etc. Inchree Bunkhouse, toilets, showers and drying facilites, sleeps up to 30, chalets available. (Tel: 08553 287)

Ardgour: Most climbers visiting Ardgour do so for the day, crossing via the ferry. However, there are campsites at and to the west of Strontian, which also has shops and hotels, etc.

Weather Forecasts

Mountain Call: 0898 500 441 for the west (442 for the east) Climbline: 0891 654 669 for the west (668 for the east) Notice boards giving weather details and avalanche reports are placed at strategic locations.

Buachaille Etive Mor

Rising gracefully in the angle between Glen Coe and Glen Etive, the Buachaille Etive Mor (1022m) watches over the wild expanse of Rannoch Moor and the bounds of Blackmount. The mountain is a long ridge with four tops, a good walk in its own right, stretching south-west towards Loch Etive. The summit is the north-east top, Stob Dearg, popularly known as 'The Buachaille'. It provides, in summer and winter, climbing which is fabulous, infinitely varied and steeped in history. After Stob na Broige and Stob Coire Altruim, the routes on Stob Dearg are described from left to right under three main headings: the South-East Face, the North-East Face, and the North Face.

STOB NA BROIGE

956m   (Map Ref 191 526)

Dalness Chasm (Map Ref 196 520)
This is the huge triple-forked gully system located some seven kilometres down the Glen Etive road on the south-east flank of Stob na Broige, the most southerly of the Buachaille summits. In summer it is not recommended and seldom climbed (for obvious reasons). In winter, however, an ascent by any one of its three branches will give a magnificent and arduous expedition. Good conditions are very rare, as both heavy snow and a long hard frost are necessary. The best descent is down the broad south-west ridge to a small top at (180 519) from where a descent south-east leads down to Glen Etive.

There are a number of pitches below the first fork which vary in length and difficulty depending on the volume of water. Above this the gully narrows. Notable pitches are a slab left of the watercourse, then a rib (again on the left) followed by a traverse into the gully bed above a waterfall, then a short strenuous cave pitch up the line of the watercourse. After a long pitch the first bifurcation is reached at The Amphitheatre, which is easily accessible from the right bank. The main left and right forks branch off here; the central fork springs up right from the left fork not far above the bifurcation.

Left Fork   350m   VS
(1951)

The left branch is the main gully and the pitches are loose and somewhat vegetated. An overhanging cave is climbed to the right and the great barrier pitch to the left. Three further pitches follow to the top.

Winter: 460m   V **
(1982)

The lower gully gave a series of ice pitches, some on precarious icicles covering a substantial flow of water. From The Amphitheatre, the left branch starts with a 60m ice pitch of medium angle, then low-angled ice for another 60m to an icicle pitch. This was passed by a separate icefall on the right then a grass ramp led to the barrier pitch. This was avoided by leaving the gully at a point below a vertical wall well out on its left bank. The gully was re-entered as soon as possible (easy). Snow led to another icicle pitch and then a huge icefall, visible from the road, gave the last and hardest pitch, about 40m of very steep ice.

Central Branch   350m   VS   (1955)

Leave the Left Fork by a scramble right around a corner to the foot of a steep water-worn pitch. Straddle and gain the left wall, and so to the barrier pitch. Climb the left wall by an obvious cracked slab topped by an overhang (peg). Now climb a steep open corner and embark on its left wall at about 20m. Go up and right (vegetated) then go right to a small tree. Traverse a little wall, then move right to the pool above the pitch (crux, 30m). The next pitch is climbed on the left and right walls. A large number of pitches follow, notably a wide chimney on the left with a traverse on to its right-bounding rib, a red wall on the left with a traverse right below an overhang to the gully bed and another red left wall with a delicate left traverse. Some distance above, the gully widens with a false grassy continuation on the left and the watercourse coming down a rocky wall to the right. Climb a long chimney on the right (apparently an off-shoot). Higher up, beyond some easier pitches, the gully opens out on to the face of the large right wall. The water comes over a cave, well above. Climb broken rocks to an exposed line of good holds on distinctive grey rock leading up to a point left of and above the cave. The gully now eases and scrambling leads to the top.

Winter: 500m   V ***
(1982)

An easy pitch goes out right after the first 60m ice pitch of the left fork. The second of four difficult pitches, the summer crux, is the hardest section. Above, the gully opens out and a short steep ice column on the right leads to easier climbing in the gully bed, with a huge cul-de-sac above. Gain the true watercourse by an awkward right traverse and a steepening ice pitch which leads to the easier upper section.

Right Hand Branch   360m   E1   (1955)
This is the most difficult fork. At about half way the gully slants up left in a series of pitches to finish near a rock pinnacle.
Winter: 360m   IV ***   (1979)
From the junction follow the right branch by short steep pitches, bearing right at a further fork. Climb to and up the final narrowing section of gully.

STOB COIRE ALTRUIM
939m   (Map Ref 197 532)

The north-facing crag just below the summit of this top consists of a main rock buttress bounded by a snow gully on the left. A lower, more broken buttress lies to the left of the gully. The best approach is straight up very steep slopes from the Lairig Gartain.

Dream Topping   100m   III   (1989)
The buttress left of Central Couloir is cut by a narrow slanting gully in its lower half. Follow the crest of the buttress to a large cornice, which can be avoided by a long left traverse. This climb takes much the same ground as Huandoy Revisited (1991).

Central Couloir   100m   II   (1950)
The 100m main buttress forms the vertical right wall of the gully. At 60m the gully forks; take the left branch. Two short pitches lead to the cornice.

Dalmatian Couloir   100m   IV **   (1991)
An obvious deep chimney splits the centre of the main buttress. Climb the chimney in two pitches passing over several large chockstones. A little gem, somewhat reminiscent of a mini Raven's Gully.

STOB DEARG
1022m   (Map Ref 223 543)

Approaches
There are two paths. The Jacksonville path starts from a parking place (237 554) on the south side of the A82 road about 1km west of the Glen Etive turnoff. Cross the river to Jacksonville, a private hut owned by the Creag Dhu M.C. (entry by invitation only), then follow the path directly up to the left side of the prominent Waterslide slab. The Lagangarbh approach leaves the A82 at Altnafeadh (222 564). Follow the track down to the bridge across the River Coupall, then about a hundred metres beyond the white cottage of Lagangarbh take the left branch of the initially wet path. The other branch goes straight on into Coire na Tulaich and is the normal hillwalkers' way to the summit. The path gently rises, crosses the outflow of Great Gully and converges with the Jacksonville approach just below the Waterslide. From there the route zigzags up towards the foot of D Gully Buttress, and then makes a rising traverse with some easy scrambling to the right, staying close under the lowest rocks of Curved Ridge. The path emerges at the bottom of a gully system below Crowberry Ridge, fed by both Easy Gully above and Crowberry Gully further right. This is Crowberry Basin, the start of Curved Ridge. In winter it is usual to start from Altnafeadh, where the normal descent path finishes. It is important to note that the whole area leading up to and including Crowberry Basin is subject to avalanche in deep soft snow.

Descent
In summer, the usual routes of descent from the summit are Curved Ridge and North Buttress. To reach Curved Ridge from the summit, descend due east to Crowberry Tower Gap, skirt the Tower by an easy gully on the right, and go left (facing out) at its base to the cairn at the top of Curved Ridge. Scramble down the ridge to its foot at the Crowberry Basin and descend the ascent path described above. In winter, there is only one reasonable descent route. From the summit follow the fairly level ridge south-west for about 400 metres, then go due west for a further 400 metres down uncomplicated slopes to reach a flat cairned col at 870m. Navigation on this section can be difficult in a white-out. The most common mistake is to continue too far south-west and descend into Glen Etive, which is relatively safe but may be very inconvenient. However, great care should be taken not

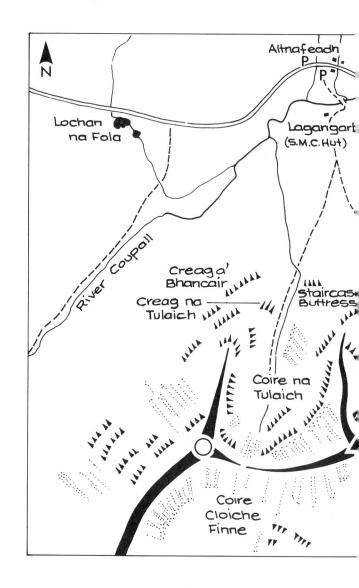

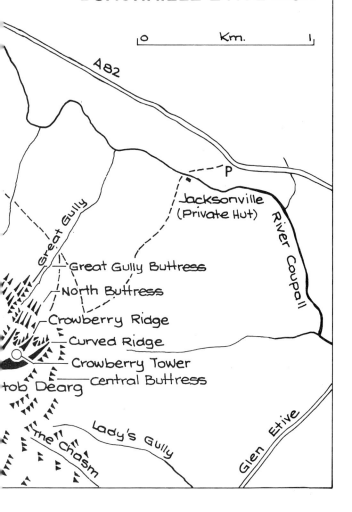

BUACHAILLE ETIVE MOR

Km.

A82

Great Gully

P

Jacksonville
(Private Hut)

River Coupall

Great Gully Buttress

North Buttress

Crowberry Ridge

Curved Ridge

Crowberry Tower

Central Buttress

tob Dearg

Lady's Gully

Glen Etive

The Chasm

to stray too far north or west or to turn west too early as there are large cliffs at the head of Coire na Tulaich. From the col turn north down the steep narrow gully leading into the corrie. This often icy slope has been the scene of many accidents. The lower part of the corrie leads easily down to Lagangarbh.

SOUTH-EAST FACE OF STOB DEARG

When viewed from Glen Etive just south of Coupall Bridge, this face presents a complex series of interconnecting buttresses and dividing gullies. The major features are, from left to right: The Chasm, The Chasm North Wall, the Blackmount Buttresses, Lady's Gully, Collie's Climb, Waterslide Gully, and Central Buttress. Rising diagonally right across the whole face is the prominent slanting line of The Chasm to Crowberry Traverse. Almost halfway up the traverse line is a prominent undercut cave. This is a useful landmark in locating the Blackmount Buttresses, which are situated above the lower end of the traverse. The routes are described from left to right.

South Gully   150m   Moderate   (1920)
This gully, which gives no more than a scramble, is situated some 200 metres south of The Chasm.

The Chasm   450m   VS ***
This deep gully, some 400 metres left of Central Buttress, is best approached from Coupall Bridge. There is a much easier and shorter gully about 200 metres to the left. The Chasm is one of the most enjoyable gully climbs in Scotland, and is highly recommended. With few exceptions the rock is clean and sound and the gully can be climbed in the wet, the limiting factor being the volume of water. Interest increases with height as does the scenery, culminating in the Devil's Cauldron (Pitch 15). Below this, sunlight may be plentiful, and escape routes obvious.

The standard is mainly Very Difficult below the Devil's Cauldron, from which there are three finishes. The easiest of these may be Severe in the unlikely event of dry rock; otherwise, expect VS climbing. It is traditional, and indeed more convenient, to climb in Vibrams.

The gully starts at an altitude of 360m, with several easy pitches. Pitch 4 is topped by a huge chockstone, best climbed by the groove and crack on its left. Pitch 5, the Red Slab, climbs the left wall (25m). Above, a huge boulder blocks the gully. Climb a crack on the left wall about 6m back from the boulder, then step back right into the gully. The left fork is a short tributary; the true gully is the right fork. Pitch 8 is the Hundred Foot Pitch, where the stream forms a fine waterfall. Pitch 9 is the Piano Pitch. Cross the watercourse to the left wall, and above a small but beckoning pool make a right traverse, ending by a delicate move onto a sloping chockstone. At pitch 10, The Converging Walls, a ramp on the right leads to a 20m cave pitch, with narrowing walls and a waterfall at the back. A few metres out on the left wall is a small ledge. Gain the ledge and then bridge up, facing in, until it is possible to reach good holds on the right wall. This pitch can be avoided by a ridge on the left. Several short pitches then lead to the Devil's Cauldron, a singularly confined and impressive cleft. There are three exits, two on the left wall, and the Direct Finish up the water-course.

The South Chimney   30m   VS 4c   (1920)
This is the hardest finish, usually damp and unattractive. On the left wall is a chimney. Climb it to a ledge on the right. Above the ledge some difficult moves lead to broken ground.

The South Wall   30m   VS 4b **   (1934)
This finish is usually damp, but otherwise technically Severe and the easiest finish out of the Devil's Cauldron. Start as for the South Chimney. Climb the chimney for 6m to a runner, then make a very awkward move onto a ledge on the wall on the right. Traverse round the edge onto a broad ledge and take the line of least resistance to the top.

The Direct Route   40m   VS 4b   (1931)
The grade is justified by the ever-present stream. Climb straight up the watercourse to a small cave (20m). Now chimney well out from the cave and make for an obvious foothold on the right wall, with a good jug within reach (crux). Beyond are two small chockstones, 3m apart. Back and foot work between them requires care on slabby rock. Above, the climbing gradually eases.
*Winter: V ***
In common with the other gullies on this aspect of the Buachaille, The Chasm is seldom in good condition, especially in the lower reaches. However, in exceptional conditions the whole route (including the Direct Finish, which is the crux) can be climbed to give an outstanding outing.

The Chasm to Crowberry Traverse   1000m   Moderate   (1898)
This scramble takes a line rising right across the south-east face of
the mountain, most easily seen from Glen Etive. It starts at the edge
of The Chasm below the first high wall of The Chasm North Wall, at
about 540m altitude. It is easy to follow and leads through some
interesting rock towards Crowberry Tower. The worst section is encountered at an undercut cave, where there is much loose scree, while
the most difficult section follows the crossing of Lady's Gully Left Fork,
where a wet corner up a pink slab is followed by a right traverse to
easier ground. The rocks of Curved Ridge and the top of the Rannoch
Wall should then be visible ahead.
Winter: II *
This takes more or less the line of the summer route, but it is possible
to make harder variations from the ascending rake towards the
summit. Otherwise the line can be continued to the top of Curved
Ridge.

The Chasm North Wall   360m   II   (1895)
This climbs the rock walls which bound The Chasm on the right, a
useful route when snow conditions are poor elsewhere. Climbing
begins about 100m above the start of The Chasm, and includes two
steep buttresses.

BLACKMOUNT BUTTRESSES

This fine group of buttresses lies between the upper part of The Chasm
North Wall and stretches rightwards above (and below) The Chasm
to Crowberry Traverse. As the area is complex and little-known, its
topography is detailed here, in the hope that climbers with imagination
may enjoy the excellent, remote-feeling climbing. There are three main
buttresses, with several smaller, associated crags. At their maximum
they are some 150m in height. Towards the lower end of the Traverse
a narrow Very Difficult chimney-gully springs up, broadening to a
grassy bay after 90m. Above this lies a splendid 60m pink wall. This
forms the left-hand or south buttress, the Blackmount Wall, with some
of the best climbing on this part of the Buachaille. From the grassy bay
an easy gully runs up left to the final rocks of The Chasm North Wall.

Some distance up and right from the start of the Very Difficult
chimney is a prominent undercut cave. The central Blackmount

Buttress is situated between these two features, and is broken at half-height by a terrace easily attainable from the grassy bay. The upper part of the central buttress projects beyond the faces of the two flanking buttresses, and its southern face bends round to a junction with a prominent chimney (the line of Limbo) at the right end of the Blackmount Wall.

Above and right of the undercut cave is a rocky bay (the back wall of which comprises steep ribs and chimneys). Higher up lies a steep face overlooking a chimney-gully curving up left, the Left Fork of Lady's Gully. This separates the central buttress from the north buttress, which has long been named the South Tower of Lady's Gully. (Strictly speaking, it should really be the north tower of the Left Fork, as the Right Fork finishes at a cave below the Traverse.) The south-east face of this buttress contains a prominent crack (Saturday Rock). It is possible to reach the Half-Way Terrace of the central buttress by scrambling up and left from the Left Fork just above The Chasm to Crowberry Traverse. Most climbs on the buttresses finish on scree slopes, so care is required to avoid dislodging rocks.

Approach and Descent
Scramble up The Chasm North Wall to The Chasm to Crowberry Traverse, go right then climb the Very Difficult chimney to the grassy bay below the wall. On approach the pink wall assumes a shy and retiring nature, and is easily missed. Descent from the Blackmount Buttress routes is on the north side of The Chasm, via The Chasm North Wall. Go left and scramble down tricky rock ribs until the ascending rake of the Chasm to Crowberry Traverse is crossed. Alternatively, cut back north sooner to gain the easy gully which leads easily back below Blackmount Wall. From there routes on the Wall or right of the South Tower are easily reached. It is also possible to continue further left above The Chasm and descend slopes towards Glen Etive, or traverse right to gain Curved Ridge, which is closer than you may think. The routes are described from left to right.

BLACKMOUNT WALL

Littlekin   45m   Hard Severe 4a   (1973)
Follows the obvious line of weakness to the left of the Mutchkin. Climb the groove to a ledge. Move left and then right to gain and follow a left-slanting crack.

The Mutchkin   60m   VS *   (1973)
The pink wall is bounded on the right by an impressive chimney, the
line of Limbo. Some 10m left of this is an obvious crack leading to a
small niche. (There used to be a small pinnacle, the Mutchkin, but it
fell, or was pushed..)
1. 15m Climb the crack to belay in the niche.
2. 20m 4c Climb the groove above, turning the overhang by the nose
on the right, then go left and belay at the foot of a corner.
3. 25m Climb the corner and the wall above.

Whispering Grooves   75m   VS ***   (1972)
Start 6m left of Limbo at a prominent groove.
1. 40m 4c Climb the groove for 12m, step right into a parallel groove
and continue to belay on ledge.
2. 35m 4b Move left then back right and continue to the top.

Flamingo   70m   VS **   (1972)
On the steep wall a few metres left of Limbo there is a thin crack.
1. 40m 4c Climb the crack and the wall above directly in the same line
to a small ledge and belay.
2. 30m 4b Continue directly to the top.

Limbo   55m   VS *   (1972)
1. 25m 4c Climb the chimney direct to belay in the cave.
2. 30m 4b Climb the wall on the left to the top.

The following two routes start from The Chasm to Crowberry Traverse,
just left of the prominent undercut cave, and climb the central of the
three Blackmount Buttresses.

Paleolith   150m   VS *   (1970)
Start approximately 15m left of the overhung cave at an obvious
undercut flake crack. Climb the crack and follow the line of least
resistance to the halfway terrace. The steep face above is recessed
in its centre. Climb for one pitch on the left of the central line, then
traverse awkwardly right to reach the recess, finishing by the line of
least resistance.

Neolith   150m   VS   (1972)
Start just left of the overhung cave, at the first prominent corner some
6m right of Paleolith.
1. 40m 4b Climb the corner and the continuing chimney to a ledge.
2. 20m Climb the wall above to the halfway terrace.
3. 40m Cross the terrace and continue at a mossy groove some 10m
right of Paleolith on the front of the face. Climb the mossy groove to
a ledge and follow the obvious steep rib to a ledge.
4. 40m Continue up the rib to a large ledge and follow the obvious
line leading right and up the steep rib above. Continue to the top.

THE SOUTH TOWER
The next four routes are on this, the rightmost of the Blackmount
Buttresses. The first three start from a crowberry ledge part way up,
and may be reached either from below or by traversing in via the
halfway terrace from below Blackmount Wall. The climbing is better
than first appearance might suggest.

Saturday Rock   90m   VS **   (1974)
This climb lies on the wall right of Lady's Gully, Left Fork, where it starts
to narrow, and is conveniently reached by scrambling up from The
Chasm to Crowberry Traverse. It takes the very obvious crack, starting
close to the two adjoining routes but soon bending up and left away
from them. Start at a block embedded in turf.
1. 45m 4c Climb the crack above and slightly left to a peg belay.
2. 45m 4c Continue up the crack to easier ground and finish by the
steep wall above.

The Snake   90m   Severe **   (1991)
The obvious, snaking crack immediately right of Saturday Rock.
1. 50m Climb the crack to a belay.
2. 40m Continue directly by a thin crack then a shallow corner to finish.

Paleface   90m   VS **   (1991)
Start opposite an embedded block, 3m right of Saturday Rock, at a
pale streak on wall.
1. 50m Climb the thin crack, moving slightly right at 40m, then up to
belay.
2. 40m Continue up a short corner, then a wall to a grassy ledge right
of the prominent skyline arete. Finish up a corner.

South Tower, Lady's Gully   75m   Very Difficult †   (1937)
Start from the Chasm to Crowberry Traverse, just right of the continuation of the Left Fork of Lady's Gully. Make a rising leftward traverse
to a notch behind a rock flake. About 45m higher a crowberry-covered
ledge is reached, where the route divides. Finish either by a crack and
crazy arete to a platform, which is level with the top of Lady's Gully, or
up a crack to the top of the tower.

Lady's Gully   240m   Very Difficult   (1900)
This is the first gully to the right of The Chasm, and bounds the left
flank of Collie's Route. It contains about 12 pitches and forks at 180m.
Start where the watercourse suddenly steepens in long deep chimneys. Climb the chimneys, mainly on their left walls, for about 60m
then walk over scree (escapes to right and left) to a 45m wall forming
a barrier. The watercourse comes down over the right end of the wall.
Start in the centre right of the watercourse and climb 20m by two steep
chimneys. Step left across the chimney and round the corner and
make a long rising traverse left across the watercourse wall to a tight
chimney which leads to easy rocks and the gully bed. Climb the corner
above (25m, crux). Easy pitches then lead to the gully fork.

Left Fork   Severe   (1954)
Below The Chasm to Crowberry Traverse the only difficulty is a cave
formed by a huge boulder. The geological, and logical continuation of
the gully then crosses the Traverse, splits the central and north
Blackmount Buttresses and steepens to a chimney. This 75m final
section finishes abruptly above the crux overhang.

Right Fork   Moderate   (1946)
This is the direct continuation which leads to a cave about level with
the top of Central Buttress, which is accessible to the right. The cave
is at the bottom left of a small crag containing conspicuous overhangs
- Eagle Buttress.
Winter: 240m   IV **   (1957)
This climb is usually in condition after a heavy snowfall low down.
There is normally a pleasant entry pitch followed by numerous short
steep pitches leading to a big pitch in the vicinity of the 45m wall (thin
ice on rock, otherwise avoided on the left). Exit by either fork then
continue right to Curved Ridge or left above The Chasm to descend
slopes towards Glen Etive.

EAGLE BUTTRESS

This is the small crag above the finish of the Right Fork of Lady's Gully.
The buttress is defined by a slab forming an inverted V topped by a
barrier of overhangs, and split by a crack from top to bottom. Access
is by easy scrambling via The Chasm to Crowberry Traverse and the
Right Fork of Lady's Gully.

Raptor   50m   HVS ***   (1991)
1. 25m Starting at the left end of the slab, ascend diagonally right,
skirting an overhang, then climb a corner to belay beneath overhangs.
2. 25m Climb through the overhang, moving left to gain and follow a
crack to the top.

Collie's Climb   300m   Moderate   (1894)
Apart from Collie's earlier scramble up Great Gully, this route is the
first recorded on the Buachaille. The following week, Professor Collie's
party made the first ascent, in winter conditions, of Tower Ridge on
Ben Nevis. The climb lies up the series of short but steep buttresses
between Lady's Gully and Central Buttress. Start at the lowest rocks
and go straight up for 75m to a grass saddle beneath a sheer 25m
face. This Severe face has been climbed but is not part of the route.
Descend right to a gully then rejoin the crest of the buttress and
continue straight up. Below the saddle the rocks are good and almost
continuous, above they are more indefinite and heathery. In winter this
area of the mountain can provide interesting route-finding and a
difficulty of about Grade II.

CENTRAL BUTTRESS

This two-tiered 200m crag lies low down on the south-east flank of the
mountain. On the left the buttress slopes up into the indeterminate
rocks of Collie's Climb, while on the right it is bounded by D Gully
Buttress. The two tiers are separated by the conspicuous Heather
Ledge which crosses the buttress some 120m up. The right flank of
the buttress juts out somewhat, producing a narrow but distinctive
north face which overlooks Jacksonville. The upper tier of this face
displays a prominent white scar. Between the north face and the left
flank of D Gully Buttress a grassy gully leads up then left to Heather
Ledge, while higher still the rocks close in to form a succession of
chimneys. Bounding the left flank of the buttress is the shallow
Waterslide Gully. The approach, by a left traverse below the rocks of

D Gully Buttress from a point approximately 60m above the Waterslide, takes no longer than 45 minutes from Jacksonville.

Descent
From the top of the buttress, which merges with the finish of D Gully
Buttress, an easy right traverse above the top of D Gully leads to
Curved Ridge, giving a useful connection to climbs on Rannoch Wall.
The safest way down from there is to descend Curved Ridge.
    The routes are described from right to left in three sections: the
North Face, the Upper Tier, and the South Face. Only the first route
climbs both tiers.

NORTH FACE

1   North Face Route   220m   Very Difficult **   (1929)
This route gives an entertaining variety of climbing at the upper limit
of its grade. Scramble up easy slabs to the bottom rocks of the
north-east edge of the buttress. Start at a prominent spike just left of
a rock niche. Climb a series of corners and walls. The left-hand crack
on the last steep wall is exposed but boasts a perfect handhold. Easy
scrambling then leads to Heather Ledge at the extreme right of the
south-east face. Hidden from the ledge, but visible while approaching,
is a prominent white scar (with a recess below it) on the north face
above. The route goes round the edge and gains the recess by an
obvious and well-marked traverse. Now descend rightwards to a ledge
and climb an awkward 3m wall to a ledge slanting right. Follow the
ledge to a 20m chimney. Climb the chimney, with a long step right at
10m, to a grass ledge. Traverse hard left on sloping holds to a short
steep crack near the buttress edge. Follow the edge to the top on
splendid rock.
Winter: V **   (1958)
A hard mixed climb which follows the summer line throughout.

2   North-East Crack Variation   30m   Hard Severe *   (1942)
This cuts out the right traverse from Heather Ledge by means of a
long crack on the left side of the corner pillar. It rejoins North Face
route above the white scar and just before the sloping left traverse.
Start 10m from the right edge of Heather Ledge, to the left of Hiccup.
Climb 5m up the wall, then traverse right on small holds to the crack,
avoiding its lower part. Follow the crack with a delicate exit until easy
but loose rock leads to a well-defined ledge on North Face Route.

THE NORTH FACE OF CENTRAL BUTTRESS

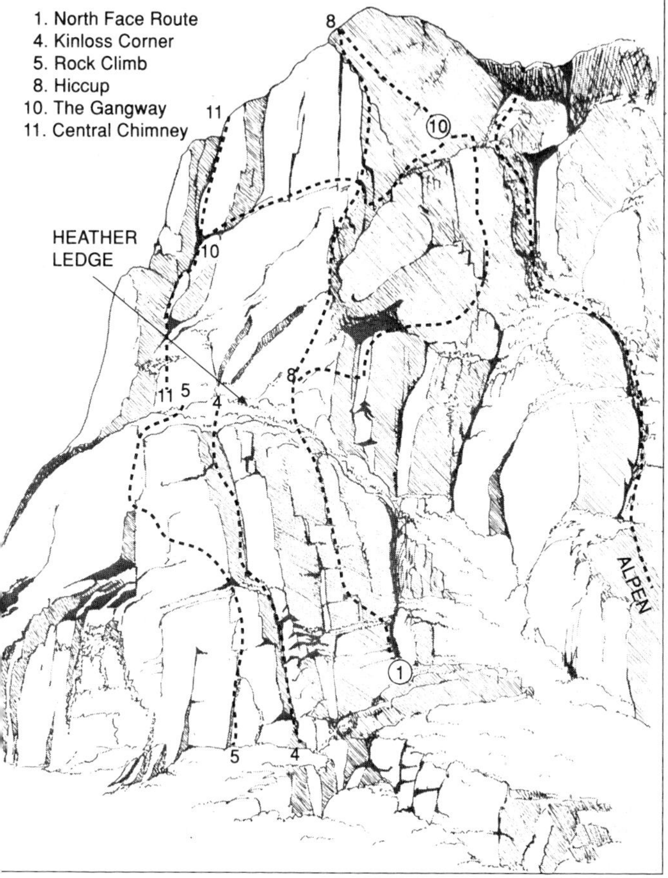

1. North Face Route
4. Kinloss Corner
5. Rock Climb
8. Hiccup
10. The Gangway
11. Central Chimney

HEATHER LEDGE

ALPEN

3 Appauling 90m VS †   (1966)
Start below and to the right of Heather Ledge at the left end of the
overhangs directly below the recess of North Face Route (arrow).
1. 25m Traverse up and right into a groove which leads to the recess.
2. 10m Climb on the right of the crack splitting the roof of the recess,
then move left past a jammed block to swing across the lip of the roof
to a ledge and block belay.
3. 20m Climb the corner forming the right edge of the prominent white
scar, first by a narrow shelf, then a vertical groove (2 pegs), then by
the exposed right edge of the corner to a ledge and block belay.
4. 35m Finish up North Face Route.

4 Kinloss Corner 120m Severe   (1954)
This route follows a line of square-cut open corners adjacent to the
left edge of the lower tier of the north face. Slow to dry. Start 15m left
of and below North Face Route, where a slab leads to a corner. Climb
the slab and corner. Above, a second easy slab leads to a short open
corner, which is the crux. The next corner, bounded by two steep ribs,
is vegetatious; climb the left rib which leads to Heather Ledge.
Winter: V **   (1984)
Although short, the difficulties are both sustained and technical.

5 Rock Climb 125m VS   (1965)
A wandering route through some interesting scenery. Traversing left
below the start of Kinloss Corner, the main part of the south-east face
will be seen to start at a higher level. Scramble up past a tree to a
grass ledge at the right of the face, where two cracks spring up. Start
below the heathery right crack.
1. 35m Climb the crack to a ledge, go up and left along the ledge to a
small stance at its left end below a crack.
2. 30m Climb the crack and wall above, continue up the arete until it
steepens, then traverse left to a stance.
3. 40m Traverse left above an obvious roof. Above is a mossy corner
with, on its right, a short groove. Climb the groove and traverse right
to a belay.
4. 20m Finish up a steep slab. Scrambling leads to Heather Ledge.

6 Rock Climb Direct Start Severe   (1966)
Start on a heather ledge midway between the start of Swansong and
Rock Climb. Go up a thin crack and traverse right to join Rock Climb
above the first belay.

7 Swansong 90m   Severe †   (1959)
Start approximately 30m left of Kinloss Corner.
1. 35m Follow the line of an obvious crack to a ledge and belay.
2. 35m Traverse left for 20m to an overhang; climb this then go right
up a thin crack to the top.

UPPER TIER

8 Hiccup 75m   VS **   (1962)
This fine little route climbs the steep wall just left of the edge of the
upper tier of Central Buttress. Start from Heather Ledge where the
traverse pitch of North Face Route begins, below a prominent crack.
1. 35m 4c Climb the crack, then the left-hand of two cracks above to
a peg belay on a small ledge.
2. 40m 4c Climb to a ledge below the right arete of the steep wall
above, then follow the arete to the top.

9 Has Been 70m   HVS †   (1984)
Between Hiccup and The Gangway is a large crack going straight up
the wall. Start at a large square slab with a small roof at 6m.
1. 40m Climb the right side of the slab to a thin crack. Step left and
climb the roof, then follow the thin crack to a larger crack. Climb to an
undercling, step right then up left to a large ledge on Gangway.
2. 30m At the left end of the ledge, climb the wall at overhangs to a
small ledge. Above is a right-slanting crack. Follow this briefly, then
break left by grooves and slabs to the belay.

10 The Gangway 90m   Severe *   (1946)
An amusing route. Start below the right-hand of two inset corners,
some 10m left of the buttress edge.
1. 35m Climb the corner and traverse left along grass to a good thread
belay on Central Chimney.
2. 20m This pitch demands a steady nerve and a windless day. Climb
the short corner above the belay. The large, sloping rock shelf above,
leading right, is The Gangway. Climb the wall, as high as possible,
then traverse right and descend to the shelf (few holds and even fewer
runners). Tiptoe right along the shelf to a big loose spike and belay.
3. 5m From the spike descend slightly and go round the edge to a
ledge and belay.
4. 30m Climb right, then up on good rock to finish up the final slabs
of North Face Route.

11   Central Chimney   75m   Very Difficult   (1931)
The right half of the upper tier is set back from the left, so that a central
rib is formed, just right of a steepening of Heather Ledge. Start up the
left-hand of two inset corners, some 20m left of the buttress edge, then
climb the corner right of the rib, which is vegetatious in parts.

12   Hangover   60m   Hard Severe   (1956)
Start at the highest point of Heather Ledge, a few metres left of the
central rib, where a heathery ledge slants steeply up to the left. From
the foot of the ledge a crack springs up vertically. Climb the crack for
10m to a ledge, immediately above which a thin crack cuts through
the overhang. Go up and right then left, passing a jammed spike, and
climb the overhang. Traverse right for 6m to a wide crack and so to
the top.

13   Slanting Ledge   60m   Very Difficult   (1937)
Start at the same point as Hangover. Traverse the steep ledge
leftwards and from its top climb up until forced to traverse right on good
rock. Continue more directly upwards at the first opportunity.

14   Spillikin Route   60m   Severe *   (1934)
Start at the left end of Heather Ledge.
1. 25m   Climb a broad tier of easy rock to a second heather ledge,
above which the rock steepens.
2. 25m   Start 5m right of the highest point of the ledge, and directly
below a short vegetatious chimney on the top section of the wall. Go
slightly left for 10m into a steep recess, then straight up to an edge
below an overhang. Traverse hard right and pull up right into a small
niche with a good belay.
3. 10m   Slightly to the right above the niche climb a short vegetatious
chimney, then continue up the wall on the left. Scramble to the top.

15   Waterslide Wall   60m   Severe   (1946)
1. 25m   Spillikin Route, pitch 1.
2. 35m   Start 2m right of the highest point of the ledge, 3m left of
Spillikin. Go 3m up a slab on small holds, then traverse obliquely left
round the edge to the face overlooking the Waterslide. Climb steep,
exposed rock to a small stance. Continue either by a difficult corner
above or traverse right to easy rock.

SOUTH FACE

The climbs here are secluded, sunny and excellent, and with the obvious exception, quick drying. The following routes lie at the left end of the lower tier, reached by a leftwards scramble from Rock Climb, passing under a distinctive yellow cave in the steepest section of the loose wall above. Eventually the scramble turns up round an edge. The face above is vividly coloured in parts and is characterised (depending on conditions) by the overspill from the upper reaches of Waterslide Gully. About 7m left of this, a distinctive, reddish clean-cut rake leads up to a saddle on the slopes to the left of the face.

Descent
First ascend on steep, unpleasant broken ground. Then go left and fairly soon down, contouring back under the foot of the crag. The descent is tricky and not easily followed, and some may prefer to abseil. The routes are described from right to left.

16   Plumbline   75m   VS **   (1962)
The right edge of this face is a rib, defined on the right by a shallow grassy depression. The route follows the rib on steep, sound, but poorly protected rock.
1. 35m 4a Climb a small corner and continue to a spike belay.
2. 15m 4b Move right to a steep crack and climb to a belay near the neck of Waterslide Gully.
3. 25m Finish by the cracks and slab above.

17   Direct Route   95m   Very Difficult   (1931)
A poor route. Approach by traversing left under the lowest rocks of Central Buttress to a solitary rowan tree growing in the dried-up bed of a stream coming from Waterslide Gully. Climb 55m up loose rock to a small pinnacle, a useful landmark. Turn the pinnacle on the right or left and climb 20m to a grass ledge where there is a choice of routes. Either follow the ledge up and right to a vertical 6m chimney which is climbed to Heather Ledge, or traverse briefly left then go straight up steep rock.
Winter: IV *   (1984)
Take the 6m chimney variation. To descend from Heather Ledge, traverse right and climb down or abseil into the wide gully between the lower part of Central Buttress and D Gully Buttress.

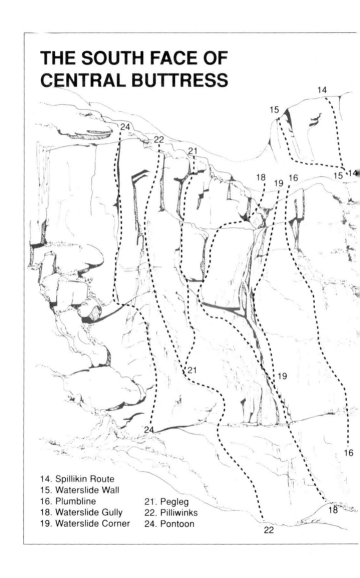

THE SOUTH FACE OF CENTRAL BUTTRESS

14. Spillikin Route
15. Waterslide Wall
16. Plumbline
18. Waterslide Gully
19. Waterslide Corner
21. Pegleg
22. Pilliwinks
24. Pontoon

18   Waterslide Gully   75m   Severe *

(1951)

Dry conditions are necessary. The line of the watercourse when dry is
well marked by white, yellow and black streaks. There is also much
red slabby rock and, 30m up, some right-facing corners.

1. 20m Climb the steep red slabs to an obvious shallow groove.

2. 35m Climb the corner for 10m, then traverse delicately left to easier
ground. Follow the line of least resistance to a belay.

3. 20m Continue to the left end of Heather Ledge.

Winter: 90m   IV **

(1986)

1. 50m Climb ice to a hanging belay near Pegleg.

2. 40m Continue straight up.

19   Waterslide Corner   70m   HVS **

(1970)

This route continues up the corner where Waterslide Gully goes left.

1. 20m As for Waterslide Gully.

2. 20m 5a Follow the groove with increasing difficulty to a peg belay
on the left below a steep corner.

3. 10m 5a Climb the smaller corner on the right for 3m, step right onto
the wall and climb it delicately to an awkward move onto a sloping
ledge.

4. 20m Finish more easily up the groove above.

20   The Veil   180m   V **

(1986)

This is a winter ascent of Waterslide Corner. Although close to Waterslide Gully, the two lines are quite independent. Climb the icefall right
of Waterslide Gully in two pitches (small stance on the right at half
height). A further pitch up a snow bay leads to a prominent vertical
column of ice. Climb this for 8m to easier ground.

21   Pegleg   95m   HVS ***

(1957)

A good, rather bold route whose name becomes all too apparent at
the crux. Start 7m left of Waterslide Gully at a red clean-cut rake.

1. 20m 4a Climb straight up to a ledge and belay.

2. 40m 5a Go up slightly right on steep, waterworn rock and make an
awkward mantelshelf onto a small ledge. Traverse hard left (crux) to
a ledge. Climb the groove above then traverse right to a crack. Follow
this to the top of a large flake.

3. 35m 4a Easier rock leads to a steep crack and so to the top.

22   Pilliwinks   110m   HVS **   (1970)
Takes the prominent black rib between Pegleg and Pontoon, finishing
up the thin corner between them. Start as for Pegleg.
1. 20m 4a Pegleg, pitch 1.
2. 20m 5a Follow Pegleg and belay on the ledge just after its crux.
3. 40m 5a Move left to the rib and climb it for 20m. Move left then up
a wall and step left to a ledge and poor belay.
4. 30m 4c Go back right and climb to the foot of a thin corner. Climb
the corner for 6m, then pull out right and finish up a wall.

23   Gravity and Grace   50m   E2 5c **   (1986)
From the foot of the easy gully just left of the start of Pontoon, scramble
up to a heather ledge at the bottom of a shallow, left-facing corner.
Climb the corner and crack above. Move left below a smooth wall and
climb this rightwards to a thin crack. Up this (fragile poised flake on
left) to reach a left-trending ramp-groove. Follow this to an overhang.
Cross this on the left (crux) to easier rock. A bold pitch.

24   Pontoon   75m   E1 ***   (1959)
Start about 12m up and left of the reddish rocks below Pegleg, some
20m left of Waterslide Gully. An excellent and varied route.
1. 30m 5a Climb the grey wall to a point 5m right of the base of a black
crack splitting the upper wall. Traverse into the crack and belay.
2. 25m 5a Climb the crack to where it narrows.
3. 20m Continue up the crack to the top.

NORTH-EAST FACE OF STOB DEARG

This aspect of the Buachaille is most apparent from the Jacksonville
car park, and comprises from left to right: D Gully Buttress, D Gully,
Curved Ridge, Easy Gully, Crowberry Ridge and Rannoch Wall,
Crowberry Gully and North Buttress.

    The approach routes from Jacksonville and Altnafeadh have al-
ready been described, and above the Waterslide the path zigzags up
towards the foot of D Gully Buttress and then bears right below the
lowest rocks of Curved Ridge to reach, by an easy scramble, the
Crowberry Basin.

    An alternative approach from Altnafeadh follows the path described
previously to its crossing of the outflow of Great Gully. Once across

the gully follow another path which climbs steeply for a short distance on its east side and then makes a rising traverse across the broken lower rocks of North Buttress. This leads to the foot of the steep rocks of the buttress. A little higher the broad grassy ledge at the foot of the East Face of North Buttress is reached, and there is an easy descent from there into Crowberry Gully, which can be crossed to reach the lowest part of Crowberry Ridge

D Gully Buttress is bounded on the left by Central Buttress, from which it is separated by a wide bay backed by a line of chimneys and little gullies, and on the right by D Gully. It forms a right-angle with Central Buttress, the two merging at the top.

Alpen   245m   IV **   (1972)
This follows the line of chimneys and gullies noted above on the left flank of D Gully Buttress. The route trends left to a big snow bay, then zigzags rightwards. Between Central Buttress and D Gully Buttress an easy open gully leads up then left to Heather Ledge. Start halfway up this easy gully at the foot of a wall.
1. 45m   Climb steep turf ledges to the start of a corner.
2. 20m   Continue up the corner to belay in a cave.
3. 10m   Climb the right wall of the cave to the upper chimney.
4. 40m   Climb the chimney then trend more easily left to a small spike belay.
5. 15m Move left to belay below the right-hand of two parallel chimneys (the left-hand one is North Face Route).
6. 40m   Climb the chimney then follow a ramp right to a belay.
7. 40m   Go up left in the now open gully.
8. 45m   Finish up right on the buttress top.

Special K   85m   IV *   (1984)
This route takes the obvious icefall right of a prominent fin of rock at the top of the open gully. Start higher up the open easy gully from which Alpen starts.
1. 40m   Back and foot between rock and ice, then bridge up and climb the icefall to a belay.
2. 45m   Continue in the same line slightly left to easy ground slanting up left to the top of Central Buttress.

The following three routes lie on the east face of D Gully Buttress which forms the right wall of the heathery gully in the angle between

THE NORTH FACE O

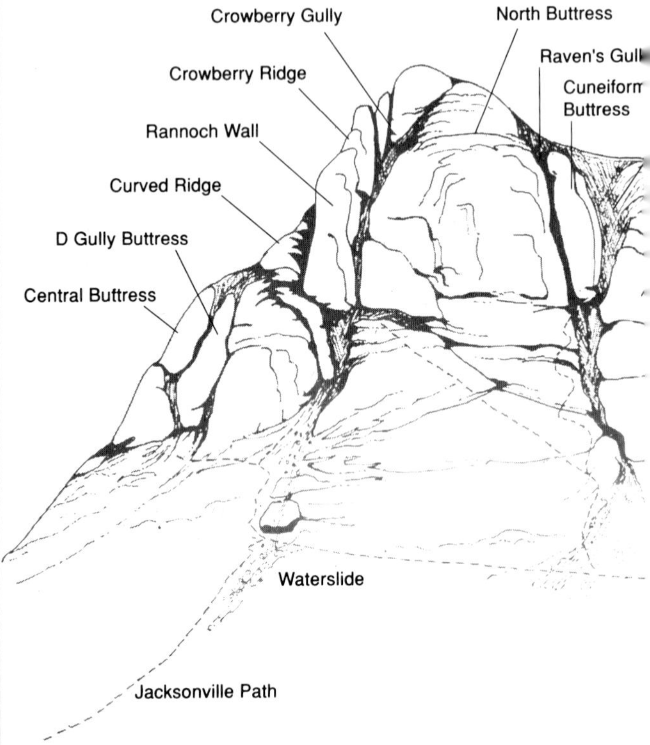

Crowberry Gully

North Buttress

Crowberry Ridge

Raven's Gull

Cuneiform
Buttress

Rannoch Wall

Curved Ridge

D Gully Buttress

Central Buttress

Waterslide

Jacksonville Path

BUACHAILLE ETIVE MOR

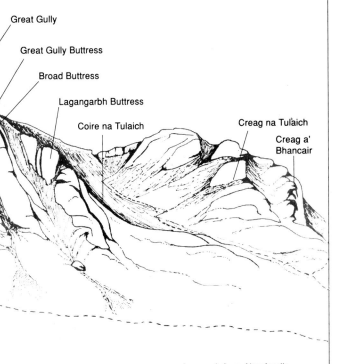

Great Gully

Great Gully Buttress

Broad Buttress

Lagangarbh Buttress

Coire na Tulaich

Creag na Tulaich

Creag a' Bhancair

Approach from Altnafeadh
and Lagangarbh

it and Central Buttress. This gully is the line of Original Route (not described) and is common to Special K and Alpen.

Toast   95m   Very Difficult   (1964)
The route follows the corner on the right at the head of the initial gully of Original Route.
1. 35m Climb the corner for 10m, then traverse right and climb a wall to a heather stance.
2. 20m Easier ground leads to a belay below a left-trending crack.
3. 40m Climb the crack to finish on the crest of D Gully Buttress.

Marmalade   100m   Severe †   (1964)
Halfway up the initial gully of the Original Route, an obvious crack splits the right wall.
1. 35m Climb the crack for 10m via a recess, step left and continue up a shallow chimney to belay on the terrace above.
2. 25m Cross the terrace, and continue up easy rocks towards a chimney on the upper face.
3. 40m Climb the chimney to finish above the crux of D Gully Buttress.

Cornflake   80m   Severe †   (1964)
The route starts from a ledge 10m right of Marmalade. Climb the arete to a stance below the terrace (35m). Complete the arete and cross the terrace to block belays below the obvious upper roof. Move right and up the wall above, then left to a broad ledge and belay immediately below the roof. Move back right and climb the shallow fault between the roof and the diedre on the right to the upper slab. Finish below and left of the crux of D Gully Buttress.

D Gully Buttress   150m   Difficult/Severe *   (1903)
The crux, Hell's Wall, is an unprotected and serious lead, but it is avoidable. Start near the foot of D Gully. The lower section is indeterminate, but the 20m crux wall, about halfway up, is obvious. Climb a slab (avoidable on the right), then after 45m of easy ground the ridge steepens and 25m of good scrambling leads to the crux. The rock is excellent but the holds slope outwards on this pitch. The climbing is harder by the right flank, or can be avoided altogether by a ledge and easy climbing on the left flank. Above the crux there is another 20m slabby wall, climbed on its extreme right edge. Above that the ridge becomes narrow and easy.

Winter: III *

A good route which always provides sport of the mixed variety. The start is vague and entry is best made from the foot of D Gully. Avoid the summer crux by the chimney on the left and a gully leading back right to the crest. The second slabby wall provides the winter crux. At its top traverse right and finish up Curved Ridge. Hell's Wall can be climbed at grade IV.

D Gully   150m   II *   (1898)
Straightforward if banked out, otherwise this is an interesting climb with several short pitches.

Curved Ridge   240m   Moderate **   (1896)
A grand mountain route and a smashing way to the summit. It is also a useful approach to climbs on Crowberry Ridge and Rannoch Wall, and the quickest way off in summer. The ridge starts at the 630m contour in Crowberry Basin (described in the introductory notes to the Buachaille). The climb curves up and under Rannoch Wall through some impressive rock scenery, and ends at a cairn below the Crowberry Tower. In its middle part and towards the top the ridge is no more than a walk, but elsewhere the rocks steepen to give enjoyable climbing with plenty of scope for variation. From the cairn an easy scree gully leads up then rightwards round the base of Crowberry Tower and up to Crowberry Tower Gap. A short scramble out of the Gap leads to the summit slopes.
Winter: II/III ***   (1898)
One of the finest 'alpine' type routes in Glen Coe. It can be climbed under most conditions but if any avalanche hazard exists great care should be taken around the Crowberry Basin and the exposed slopes under Crowberry Tower. Curved Ridge is not a good descent in winter. From the Basin, climb a short steep ice pitch in Easy Gully and gain the ridge. The crest provides the most difficult line, but a gully on its right is an easier alternative. This is not without interest and leads to the final narrow section. Turn this on the left to emerge on a flat rib beneath the cairn. Make an exposed traverse left under Crowberry Tower to the gully which goes up to Crowberry Tower Gap. A good little pitch leads out of the Gap to the summit slopes. A quicker alternative from the cairn at the top of Curved Ridge continues left to a gully which curves up towards the summit.

It is worth noting that in winter the section of the approach between the Waterslide and Crowberry Basin may present a simple route-finding problem and difficulties of about grade I/II. Normally one follows a line to the left of a shallow gully, turning a pinnacle on the left and making an exposed and possibly icy traverse to the right to reach the Basin. It is also possible to approach by scrambling up the lower section of North Buttress from the foot of Great Gully.

The small east face of Curved Ridge lies 30m up to the left of the resting place on Curved Ridge. It is split by a fine vertical crack, which is climbed by **Iron Cross** (35m VS * 1964).

Easy Gully   150m   II *   (1898)
This is the shallow gully between Curved Ridge and Crowberrry Ridge. It gives a pleasant and picturesque outing and can be combined with Curved Ridge. There are usually two pitches.

CROWBERRY RIDGE
This fine ridge lies between Easy Gully and Crowberry Gully. It descends directly below the summit, narrow and easy-angled in its upper half with a considerably steeper lower 90m section. The climbs on Crowberry Ridge are found on (from left to right): the South-East Face (Rannoch Wall), the North-East Face and the North Face. Above the steep lower section the routes on all three faces converge onto the upper easy section, leading in 75m to Crowberry Tower. The 45m Tower looks like an attractive finish, but is loose and disappointing at close quarters. The west side of the Tower is a moderate 12m step leading down to Tower Gap, the top of the Left Fork of Crowberry Gully. A pleasant scramble then leads out of the gap, across the top of Crowberry Gully, and up to the summit slopes.

SOUTH-EAST FACE - RANNOCH WALL
There can be few crags in the country which offer middle grade climbs of such amazing verticality and exposure. Not only are the situations impressive, but the outlook is quite magnificent, giving this aspect of the Buachaille an undeniable charm. The rock is generally very good and quick drying. An early start is worth the effort, for the face receives

ILLUSTRATIONS
Opposite: Buachaille Etive Mor from the River Coupall at Jacksonville.
Next Page: The Chasm, pitch 4.

the sun only until the early afternoon. The routes are described from right to left; all start from Easy Gully, which contains two small pitches. The first six routes lie between the right end of the face and the first (cave pitch) in Easy Gully.

1   Grooved Arete   65m   Hard Severe ***   (1946)
This excellent but poorly protected route follows the edge formed by Rannoch Wall and the North-East Face and then veers right to join the last pitch of Fracture Route. Start at a groove immediately right of the edge. To the right is a prominent 6m chimney leading to the first platform below the North-East Face. Agag's is the cracked groove immediately round the edge to the left.
1. 25m Climb straight up on small holds then move left to the block belay of Agag's Groove.
2. 40m Gain the arete on the right and make a delicate right traverse to regain the groove. This now trends right to a belay below the last pitch of Fracture Route, which leads easily to the ridge.

2   Agag's Groove   105m   Very Difficult ***   (1936)
This great route follows the obvious cracked groove which curves up to form undercut rock leaves on the upper part of the wall. Look for a large detached, rectangular block at the extreme right edge of the face. Start up the crack behind the block.
1. 25m The crack soon becomes a corner which leads to a block belay at the start of a groove.
2. 35m Follow the groove easily up and left to a large block belay.
3. 25m Continue up the groove until a traverse left leads onto the face below a nose. Climb the exposed nose by a narrow groove, then go up and left to a block belay.
4. 20m Move left and continue quite boldly to the top.
Winter: VI ***   (1953)
The difficulty depends entirely on the amount of snow. When truly plastered it will give a sustained and difficult climb, the nose on pitch 3 providing a bold and difficult crux.

ILLUSTRATIONS
Previous Page: Grooved Arete, Rannoch Wall   (Climber, Ken Crocket).
Opposite: Admission, Creag a' Bhancair   (Climber, Paul Laughlan).

3 Curving Groove 80m VS *
(1946)

This takes a bold line between Agag's to the right, and the more prominent groove of Juniper Groove to the left. Start at the first small pinnacle about 6m left of and above the start of Agag's.

1. 40m 4c Go up a few metres until the angle suggests a leftward trend to a position below some overhangs. Two parallel faults break through the overhangs, and should not be confused with the deeper recess of Juniper Groove close on the left. Climb either fault on small holds to a stance. Continue directly to Agag's Groove.

2. 20m 4b/c Climb the slabby wall above by a curving groove then go left into a wide, exposed groove which leads to a comfortable triangular niche, The Haven.

3. 20m A choice of finishes lead to the top. The most elegant goes left to a belay below the overhanging crack on Satan's Slit. The easier groove of January Jigsaw is to the right.

4 Juniper Groove 45m Severe
(1946)

Start about 6m right of the small pinnacle of Curving Groove, at a groove with a small sloping slab near the start. Climb the groove (awkward to start) for 20m, then traverse up and left to a small ledge with a juniper. Step right round a corner, make an ascending traverse right and continue straight up the groove to finish at the block belay below the nose pitch of Agag's.

5 January Jigsaw 85m Severe ***
(1940)

Another magnificent climb, slightly harder and with more route-finding difficulties than Agag's. Start from a small pinnacle on the grass ledge halfway between Agag's and the semi-detached flake in Easy Gully.

1. 30m Climb straight up a crack for 7m. Go up and left by large steps to a big flake, and then hard right along a ledge to a flake belay above the start.

2. 20m Move right and climb a flake and wall to the block belay below the nose of Agag's.

3. 15m From the top of the block, traverse right round an edge into a slanting groove. Follow this to The Haven on Curving Groove, then continue left to belay below the overhanging crack of Satan's Slit.

4. 20m Traverse up and right, swing round an edge into a groove and follow this for a short distance before working left onto a steep wall. From the top of the wall take the last 10m of Satan's Slit or finish up an easier groove on the right.

6 Satan's Slit 85m VS **   (1939)

A varied counter-diagonal to Agag's. Start in the easy chimney left of the large semi-detached flake in Easy Gully.

1. 30m 4a Climb the chimney and steep straightforward rock to some obvious flakes. Traverse left for 6m, then go up and right to belay above the start.

2. 20m 4b Climb up for 6m on small holds, aiming slightly left, then traverse horizontally right for 12m. This bold and delicate traverse ends in Agag's some 12m below the nose.

3. 15m 4a Follow Agag's for 5m, break out right up a shallow scoop and go 10m to a belay and small stance below an overhanging crack.

4. 20m 4c Climb the crack (crux) for 10m and continue more easily to the ridge.

7 Pandava's Progress 80m VS   (1988)

There is a prominent W-shaped overhanging flake halfway between Red Slab and Satan's Slit. Start just right of this flake.

1. 40m 4c Climb right for 4m then up to a ledge at 10m (in Satan's Slit). Climb the curving fault line directly above to a ledge. Climb straight up to a small overhang, pull right, then go up to join Red Slab at its crux. Belay about 15m above this.

2. 40m Climb straight up, crossing Agag's, to the top.

8 A Game of Dice 75m E2 **   (1988)

This excellent route starts left of the W-shaped flake.

1. 45m 5b Climb the obvious left-trending crack with increasing difficulty to gain a left-facing corner above. Climb this and the hanging groove continuation (some loose rock) to easier ground. Continue directly to a belay on the traverse ledge of Red Slab.

2. 30m 4c Climb the deceptive wall above, moving left to finish.

9 Red Slab 80m VS ***   (1939)

Start about 5m above and left of the cave pitch in Easy Gully at an overhanging groove. An old favourite.

1. 20m 4b Climb 10m up the groove, then more easily to a small stance and belay at the bottom left of a rock nose.

2. 30m 4c Step right round the nose, traverse a ledge for 6m and then climb a red slab on small holds (serious for the second). Traverse right round an overhang and continue for a further 6m to a corner. Climb the corner and a short vertical section above (crux) to easier ground.

3. 30m Climb easily to finish about 5m left of Agag's.

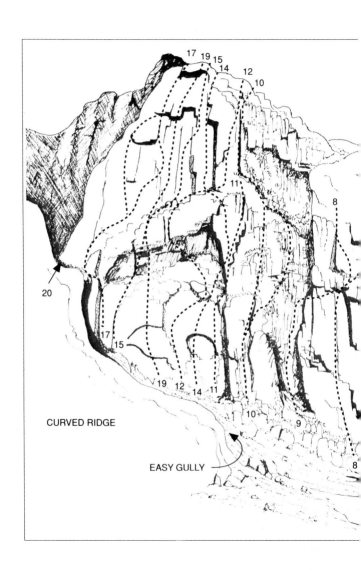

CURVED RIDGE

EASY GULLY

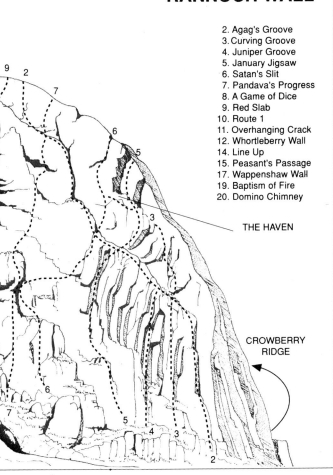

RANNOCH WALL

THE HAVEN

CROWBERRY RIDGE

Winter: VI **   (1988)
A technically difficult and serious climb.
1. 20m Climb the groove to a roof. Move up right into another groove.
Follow this to belay in the obvious niche.
2. 40m Climb an icy groove for 10m, traverse right then climb down
and right for 5m to a rest. Traverse right then make hard moves to the
overlap. More difficult climbing leads up right to a good foot ledge.
Swing right into the obvious corner, then climb this with difficulty (crux)
to a ledge on the right. From there balance climbing leads to a belay
in the last pitch of Agag's Groove. Finish up this.

10   Route I   70m   Very Difficult   (1934)
Towards the upper left of the wall there is a vegetatious line of
weakness, slanting left and developing into an obvious groove. Start
about 15m above the cave pitch in Easy Gully at a short vegetated
chimney with a large, prominent red slab to its left. Climb the chimney
to belay at some more open rocks (15m). Trend right over loose rock,
then take a long slant up a narrow shelf, which ends at an awkward
stance where two sloping slabs are topped by a 4m wall. Climb the
wall, or make a short left traverse round a corner first. Finish by the
long upper groove.
Winter: IV **   (1972)
An excellent and exposed mixed climb, following the line of the
summer route with the 4m wall providing the crux.

11   Overhanging Crack   35m   Severe   (1940)
This route joins Route I just below its crux. Start at the right side of a
red slab 4m left of the vegetatious chimney of Route 1.
1. 25m Climb the slab to spikes very near the chimney.
2. 10m Traverse left to a dirty groove and go up to a crack with an
overhang at its top. Climb this and the wall above to join Route I.

12   Whortleberry Wall   115m   HVS ***   (1946/56)
Start at the left side of the red slab. Quite bold.
1. 25m 4c Climb up then trend right, aiming for the left side of a small
hanging slab (junction with Line Up). Go up and right (crux) to a ledge
and belay.
2. 30m 4c Traverse horizontally left for 5m then gradually up to a
shallow groove, which is climbed to a small juniper ledge. Climb the
left of twin cracks for a few metres, then the right. Easier climbing now
leads to a belay common with Peasant's Passage.

3. 25m 4c Traverse horizontally right for a few metres, go up and right again to a large groove capped by a roof (Line Up). 3m below the roof step right round an edge and cross the face rightwards to a small ledge and belay.
4. 35m 4b Climb the crack directly above to reach easier ground.

13   Plink   75m   HVS *   (1969)
An eliminate route which offers some good climbing. Start as for Whortleberry Wall.
1. 25m 4c Go up for about 6m then left to a shallow groove. Follow this to a left-sloping fault which forms an obvious inverted V (often wet) and traverse left to a ledge and belay on Peasant's Passage.
2. 25m 5a Follow Peasant's Passage for about 6m, then climb straight up the wall and thin crack-groove to a stance and belay where Wappenshaw Wall trends back left.
3. 25m 4c/5a Continue directly above to a narrow ledge below a broken overhang. Make a long step right and continue up the wall above, moving right at the top to easier ground.

14   Line Up   75m   HVS ***   (1969)
One of the best routes of its grade on the Buachaille. Start towards the right side of the red slab, below a prominent narrow overlap.
1. 25m 4c Climb to the overlap and continue directly to the left side of a small hanging slab, common to Whortleberry Wall. Now go right and up (or up and right) to a ledge and belay.
2. 25m 5a Climb the corner above for 5m, step left and continue to a belay at the foot of the roofed corner.
3. 25m 5a Climb the roofed corner to the top.

15   Peasant's Passage   70m   HVS ***   (1952)
Between Whortleberry and the final pitch of Easy Gully there is a shallow corner on the left. Bold.
1. 15m 4c Climb the corner for 5m then swing right onto a rib. Traverse slabs on the right to a narrow ledge and then then move right to a peg belay.
2. 20m 4c Go up and round the edge to a steep wall with a shallow crack. Go slightly left then follow easier broken rocks on right to a stance and belay.
3. 35m 4b Climb the steep corner above to a white spike. Swing onto the rib on the right and continue to the top.

16 Plonk 65m VS   (1983)
Start as for Wappenshaw Direct Start.
1. 25m 4b Climb the corner in its entirety to a ledge and belay.
2. 40m 4c Take a direct line from the ledge to the top.

17 Wappenshaw Wall 70m VS **   (1952)
At the left end of the Rannoch Wall, Easy Gully flattens to form a
stonefield accessible from Curved Ridge. At its lower edge, above the
final pitch of Easy Gully, a corner springs up. Quite bold with a big
route feel.
1. 25m 4b Climb the corner trending right until it is possible to move
down and right along an obvious traverse to a block belay.
2. 35m 4b Make a tricky move leaving the belay and move right under
a big overhang to a rib. Go straight up under a small overhang, then
left past a detached block. Above are two steep grooves. Climb these
then move left onto a shelf. Where it broadens follow an obvious fault
up and right to a belay.
3. 10m 4a Go back left and up a short wall to finish.
Direct Start: 25m   Mild VS 4b   (1955)
Starts below the final pitch of Easy Gully. Climb the right-angled corner
in its entirety to the start of the original route, or at 10m traverse right
to a line of holds which lead back into the corner.
Variation on pitch 2: HVS 5a **   (1955)
From the top of pitch 1 go up and left of the big overhang and make
a direct line up and right to the grooves near the top of Pitch 2.

18 Shattered Wall 55m   Very Difficult   (1952)
Start between the top of the final pitch of Easy Gully and Domino
Chimney.
1. 25m Climb up to a belay well left of a prominent deep groove.
2. 30m Traverse horizontally right into the groove and climb it until
forced right round a corner to easier rock.

19 Baptism of Fire 60m E5   (1987)
A direct, bold route up the left side of Rannoch Wall.
1. 30m 6a From the upper reaches of the gully climb the blank steep
slab between two wet streaks directly (thin and poorly protected) to
easier rock. Then move direct over the bulge, moving right at the lip
to a small ledge.
2. 30m 5c Move up and back left to climb a thin crack and awkward
shallow groove to the top.

20   Domino Chimney 50m   Severe   (1948)
Start 30m above the rock pitch in Easy Gully at the extreme left end
of Rannoch Wall. Climb slabs for about 30m, then the chimney above
by its left wall.
    In winter this forms an attractive column of ice, as yet unclimbed.

21   Rannoch Traverse 225m   VS **   (1970)
By far the most satisfactory girdle on Rannoch Wall.
1. 45m Climb Agag's Groove to the block belay.
2. 45m Go left round the corner and follow the obvious traverse across
the red wall to a belay.
3. 45m Continue traversing up left round the corner to reach a block
and spike belays on Route 1.
4. 30m Traverse horizontally round the corner for 10m. Climb a steep
wall then go left to the second belay on Whortleberry Wall.
5. 30m Continue past the block belay on Wappenshaw Wall to a loose
block in a large groove.
6. 30m Climb diagonally left up the wall to the foot of a small corner.
Climb this and continue to the top of Domino Chimney.

22   High Level Girdle Traverse Severe   (1940)
This route gives a long rising traverse of the whole of Crowberry Ridge.
There are many variations but the following offers the most varied and
interesting line. Start at the foot of the ridge and climb Naismith's Route
to the foot of the steep chimney and make a rising traverse leftwards
to the Upper Ledge on the crest of the ridge. Alternatively, climb the
Direct Route to the same point. (These routes are described in the
following section).
    From the Upper Ledge a rising traverse left leads to the thread belay
in the easy part of Fracture Route. Continue the horizontal line across
the slabs to a ledge on the crest of the ridge, then traverse to The
Haven. Climb left to the belay below the overhanging crack on Satan's
Slit. Continue to a wall opposite the crux nose of Agag's Groove. Cross
this wall and gain the sloping block belay above the crux of Agag's.
Traverse left and slightly down, and continue below some dubious
flakes to a belay at the top of Red Slab, whence easy scrambling leads
to the crest of ridge.

CROWBERRY RIDGE, NORTH-EAST FACE
This narrow face overlooks the approach path. The rock is excellent, quick-drying and the climbs although short are as good as any in the vicinity. From the lower part of Curved Ridge a traverse across Easy Gully leads to a well-marked 6m chimney at the edge between Rannoch Wall and North-East Face. The chimney leads to The First Platform from where the climbing starts. The right half of the face projects well beyond the steeper reddish wall of the left half. A pillar lies against the left half with V-cracks in the wall above; this is Fracture Route. To the right a prominent corner provides the line of Dingle and bounding the right side of the terrace is the Direct Route, the classic route on Crowberry Ridge.

To descend from the tops of the routes described below, two or three possibilities exist. From the short routes described next, the quickest descent is down Crowberry Ridge using one of the easy variations to avoid the crux pitch of the Direct Route. For those continuing up Crowberry Ridge to the Tower, the descent is by Tower Gap and down Curved Ridge (as described previously). It is also possible to traverse left from the crest of the ridge below the Tower and reach the top of Curved Ridge directly. The routes are described from left to right.

23   Symposium   65m   E2 **   (1985)
The thin crack left of Engineer's Crack. Start above the chimney.
1. 30m 5c Climb the crack direct to a small overlap, go left above this to easier ground and belay on the right.
2. 35m Continue up Fracture Route.

24   Engineer's Crack   65m   E1 **   (1951)
A fine sustained pitch. Start 5m left of Fracture Route.
1. 25m 5b Climb a crack to small ledge. Continue up the thin crack above until it is possible to traverse right onto a stance on Fracture Route above the second mantelshelf move.
2. 40m Continue up Fracture Route.

25   Fracture Route   65m   VS **   (1946)
Awkward and strenuous. Look for a pillar lying against the reddish wall on the left half of the face.
1. 15m Climb the easy pillar to a belay.
2. 10m 4c Ascend the left-hand V-crack above for 5m. Now climb a more difficult and sustained section including two mantelshelf moves which lead to a stance and belay.

3. 40m Rather than continuing straight up, a better and more difficult finish can be made by traversing left round an edge and climbing a crack left of the nose.

26   Dingle   35m   HVS **   (1958)
The obvious corner right of Fracture Route. Well protected and quite sustained.
1. 10m Start at a narrow wall and climb to a belay.
2. 25m 5a Climb the corner then slabs on the ridge.

27   The Widow   40m   VS 4c   (1965)
Well below and right of Dingle is a right-angled groove capped by a roof in the side of the ridge. Climb the left arete of the groove and pull over into the crack, which is climbed heading slightly left to the crest of the ridge.

28   Direct Route   225m   Severe ***   (1900)
This is the original route by the famous left traverse from Abraham's Ledge. The Direct Route is described first, then the variations avoiding the crux.
    Start at the right end of the First Platform, near Crowberry Gully, where a 15m pinnacle lies against the face (not to be confused with Fracture Route, some distance to the right).
    Climb a shallow chimney on the left side of the pinnacle to the Pinnacle Ledge at its top, from which a 5m wall leads to Abraham's Ledge (20m). The crux now looms up on the left. Make an exposed left traverse and an upward balance move on sloping footholds to gain a scoop. Go gradually right and climb straight up on large holds to the Upper Ledge, 12m above the belay. Poorly protected. (The Upper Ledge leads to the North Face on the right, and descends obliquely into Naismith's Route.) From the left end of Upper Ledge climb directly up, steeply at first then more easily to easy ground.
    The route is now obvious. The steep section of the ridge ends with a long pitch on fine slabby rock. Easy climbing and a narrow ridge lead in a further 75m to the base of Crowberry Tower. This is climbed direct on its north side without difficulty. The descent off the short side to the Crowberry Tower Gap is vertical but not difficult. There is an easier spiral descent from the top by a ledge on the west flank to reach the Gap.

Variations To The Direct Route avoiding the Crux Traverse

Pinnacle Ledge   Easy
From the top of the pinnacle 5m below Abraham's Ledge, traverse right onto the north face to Naismith's Route. Regain the crest by a rising traverse to Upper Ledge.

North Chimney   Easy
From the right end of Abraham's Ledge descend a short chimney, join Naismith's Route, and return to the crest by Upper Ledge.

Greig's Ledge   Difficult   (1907)
From the right end of Abraham's ledge, climb a little way up the north edge and traverse right to an open corner. At the right edge of the further wall is the start of Greig's Ledge. There is one awkward move traversing round the edge onto the ledge. From its far end climb up left by a rising traverse to Upper Ledge.

Speirs' Variation   Very Difficult   (1938)
From the right end of Abraham's Ledge, climb up and round the north edge into the open corner at the start of Greig's Ledge. Instead of going round the awkward corner, climb straight up to Upper Ledge on very steep rock.
Direct Route, Winter: IV/V ***   (1938/53)
This follows the summer line throughout and will always provide a hard and serious climb. The main difficulties centre around Abraham's traverse and the slabby scoop which follows. The next pitch can be just as hard, if not harder, depending on the amount of ice.

THE CROWBERRY TOWER
The east face of Crowberry Tower overlooks Easy Gully. It is loose and climbable almost anywhere. **Route 1**   (40m   Severe) starts a few metres right of South Chimney and climbs steep rocks to a corner and finishes at the top of the South Ridge. **Route 2**   (40m   Moderate 1901) starts right of Route 1 at the highest point of a shallow gully and climbs straight up to a shallow scoop and finishes a few metres below the summit of the Tower.

The left side of the east face is formed by **South Ridge** (Moderate) which is the bounding rib of Crowberry Tower Gap Gully. In winter it is Grade II/III. Immediately right of South Ridge is **South Chimney** (Difficult 1898) which gives a pleasant winter climb (III 1959).

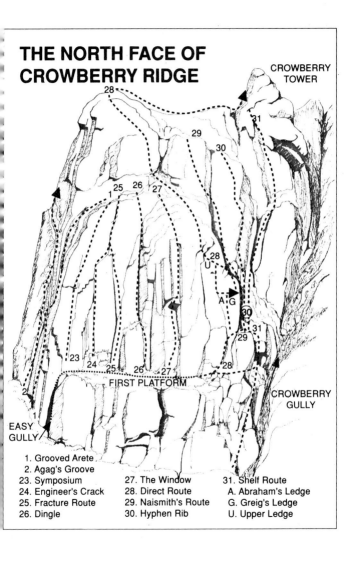

THE NORTH FACE OF CROWBERRY RIDGE

CROWBERRY TOWER

FIRST PLATFORM

EASY GULLY

CROWBERRY GULLY

1. Grooved Arete
2. Agag's Groove
23. Symposium
24. Engineer's Crack
25. Fracture Route
26. Dingle
27. The Window
28. Direct Route
29. Naismith's Route
30. Hyphen Rib
31. Shelf Route
A. Abraham's Ledge
G. Greig's Ledge
U. Upper Ledge

CROWBERRY RIDGE, NORTH FACE
This is the right flank of the ridge, overlooking the lower section of
Crowberry Gully. Nowhere outstanding in summer, but in winter it
provides some of the best mountaineering in Glen Coe. Between the
crest of Crowberry Ridge and Crowberry Gully to its right there are two
long parallel ribs separated by a shallow gully. The gully and right-hand
rib form Shelf Route. The left rib is Hyphen Rib, bounded on its left by
another shallow gully, Naismith's Route. Approach as for the Direct
Route to the right end of the First Platform, then scramble right. The
routes are described from left to right.

29 Naismith's Route   210m   Moderate   (1896)
The original route up Crowberry Ridge. The lower section of Shelf
Route is split by three chimneys. This climb follows the leftmost one.
Scramble right from the foot of Direct Route to the foot of the chimney.
Climb the chimney, which becomes a long, unclean shallow gully with
a series of short pitches. The upper part of the route quits the north
face in favour of the crest of the ridge which is gained by an easy
traverse onto a platform below the long slab pitch. The gully climb may
be continued to join the final part of Hyphen Rib.
Winter: III/IV   **
The easiest line up the ridge, but harder than North Buttress. Approach
via Direct Route to Pinnacle Ledge and then traverse right to the
left-hand chimney of Naismith's Route. This point can also be gained
from the narrows at the foot of Crowberry Gully, but is dependent on
the amount of snow build-up. In the upper section continue up the gully
until it ends on a wide sloping slab. From the top of the slab climb the
short left wall, which overhangs and is hard, to gain the crest. Failing
this, traverse onto the crest from the bottom of the slab.

30 Hyphen Rib   90m   Difficult   (1937)
The left-hand rib. Start in a bay below the chimney of Naismith's Route.
Climb the rib immediately right of the chimney. There is a section of
easy ground above, followed by a succession of short walls. The best
climbing overlooks Shelf Route.

31 Shelf Route   165m   Difficult   (1920)
To the right of the start of Hyphen Rib the middle and rightmost
chimneys converge above the rib dividing them. The rightmost chimney is the Direct Start (Very Difficult 1933). The normal start goes by
the right wall and rib of the middle chimney. The Shelf in its upper part

is loose and dirty and becomes a shallow trough, steepening to a scoop in the angle between the left wall and a small pinnacle on the right. At this point an upward left traverse can be made to the crest of Crowberry Ridge, however the most direct route goes straight up to a square recess under the pinnacle and then by an awkward right traverse below it. (The pinnacle can be climbed direct or on either side). A long groove then leads up to the level section of the ridge below Crowberry Tower.

Winter: IV ***   (1937)

The obvious winter line running parallel to and left of Crowberry Gully. When in condition it is a superb and difficult mixed climb, sensational and highly exposed in its upper part. Start from the First Platform, or if there is enough snow, from the narrows at the foot of Crowberry Gully by a traverse of steeply shelving snow to reach a cave. Climb the right wall and rib of the middle chimney. The route now runs up the trough in the shelf for several pitches to merge into the face above. This is beneath a small rectangular tower. Go right towards Crowberry Gully to a square recess under a pinnacle, beyond which a broad groove hangs over the gully. Climb this to the crest beneath Crowberry Tower.

32   Crowberry Gully   300m   Very Difficult   (1898/1910)

The deeply-cut gully between Crowberry Ridge and North Buttress. The first pitch is a deep cave topped by a huge chockstone, climbed on the right wall. Four short pitches follow. Pitch 6 is the Thincrack Chimney, a constricting chimney leading to a through route. Position in the chimney is best maintained by lung expansion. Those not long-winded can climb slabs on right. The gully forks immediately above. The right fork is the original route, finishing nearer the summit than the left fork. Climb straight up from Thincrack Chimney to a scree slope leading to the Cave Pitch. Climb this by the mossy right wall. A short easy pitch above leads to a point midway between Crowberry Tower Gap and the summit.

Winter: III/IV ***   (1898/1909)

A magnificent climb of great character and beauty. Conditions vary enormously depending on the build-up of snow. There are seldom more than five distinct pitches, most of which can be obliterated by heavy snow. Ideal conditions are not frequent and the gully can be very dangerous due to avalanche. From Crowberry Basin easy snow leads to the narrows. A short pitch may be encountered here. More snow then leads to the first hard pitch, the Thincrack Chimney. This may give 10m of steep climbing but often forms no more than a few awkward steps. The junction is now reached where a steep rib divides the two forks. From a stance at the foot of the left fork make a rising right traverse, which may be hard if the ice is thin, below the rib into the right fork; then another pitch leads to the Cave Pitch. This is nearly always the crux and is climbed by an impressive curtain of ice on the right wall. Snow leads to the final slopes.

33   Centre Rib   40m   Very Difficult   (1956)
Climb the loose and exposed rib dividing the left and right forks.

34   Left Fork   35m   Severe *   (1943)
From the top of the Thincrack Chimney climb a short pitch to a vertical chimney roofed by a large capstone. Climb well inside the chimney to reach a constricted stance of jammed stones. Climb to the cavity below the capstone (crux), traverse out back and foot (gulp!) below the capstone and move round and over it with care, as there are no 'saving' holds above. The situation is impressive. Walk up the narrow cleft beyond to Crowberry Tower Gap.
Left Fork, Winter: IV***   (1949)
The narrow iced chimney leads to a great chockstone, the crux. This is hard but short and well protected. Easy snow leads to the gap.

NORTH BUTTRESS
This broad and massive buttress lies between Crowberry Gully and Raven's Gully. The lower 90m are fairly steep, then the rocks lie back. The buttress is divided into three sections, from left to right The East Face, the easy central section (taken by West Route) and the West Face (Slime Wall).

EAST FACE OF NORTH BUTTRESS
This varied and attractive face has a lot to offer in the VS to HVS grades. It is very quick drying and catches the morning sun. It is really a two-tiered crag which extends right from the foot of Crowberry Gully and is easily identified by the obvious dark recess of Bottleneck Chimney. The base of the crag is skirted by a broad grass ledge, The Terrace. Separating the upper and lower tiers is the shallow grassy Green Gully which curves up left. Higher still the entire buttress is girdled by High Ledge which connects Crowberry Gully and Great Gully.

The routes on the East Face can be reached either by climbing rightwards out of Crowberry Basin, or by an upward traverse from the outflow of Great Gully (where the Altnafeadh path crosses) across the lower broken section of North Buttress. Descent is down the crest of North Buttress by the original 1895 route or any of its variations. The routes are described from left to right.

East Ribs   210m   Difficult   (1905)
At the extreme left end of the East Face of North Buttress the lower and upper tiers are split by wide chimneys. Between the chimneys and Crowberry Gully to the left are the ribs. Not very satisfactory as a summer line, but certainly worthwhile in winter. Start in Crowberry Gully and follow the line of ribs to High Ledge. Variations are endless.
Winter: II/III
An interesting route with the main difficulties at the start.

LOWER TIER

1   North-East Zigzag   85m   Difficult   (1940)
This route and Slanting Groove lie on the easier ground at the far left of the face. Open to many variations. Start from the left end of a narrow raised rock ledge near the left end of the terrace. Go up left and round an edge to a grass niche, then take a short right traverse to a grass ledge. Trend up right to the large block of Slanting Groove and then left to Green Gully. At the top of Green Gully a narrow prominent 20m rib (Judas Rib) forms a flying buttress against the main face. Climb the rib, go slightly right and then up to High Ledge.
Variation: 45m   Very Difficult   (1952)
From the grass ledge above the corner, aim for a prominent detached flake some distance above. Climb the right edge of the flake and follow any line above to Green Gully.
Winter: III/IV*   (1957)
Climb the line of North-East Zigzag to join Slanting Groove upper section and follow Green Gully left to the series of gullies in the area of East Ribs. Difficulties are found mainly at the start.

2   Slanting Groove   100m   Very Difficult   (1940)
About 8m from the left end of the face and 5m up is an area of rough, red rock cut by a crack (Brevity Crack). Start below and left of this at a left-slanting groove. Follow the groove to a small ledge then climb directly to a large block belay. Turn the block on the right and continue

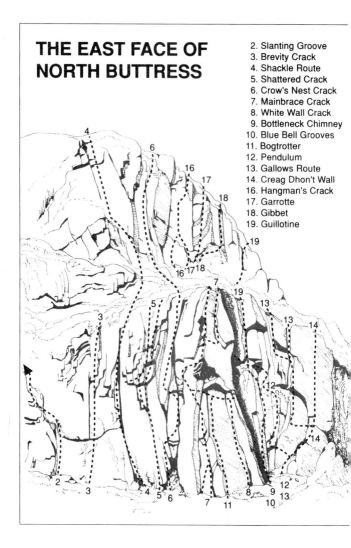

THE EAST FACE OF NORTH BUTTRESS

2. Slanting Groove
3. Brevity Crack
4. Shackle Route
5. Shattered Crack
6. Crow's Nest Crack
7. Mainbrace Crack
8. White Wall Crack
9. Bottleneck Chimney
10. Blue Bell Grooves
11. Bogtrotter
12. Pendulum
13. Gallows Route
14. Creag Dhon't Wall
16. Hangman's Crack
17. Garrotte
18. Gibbet
19. Guillotine

to Green Gully. Just below the top of the gully climb a crack followed by black slabby rock, then trend right by a steep rib to a ledge below a shattered overhang. Avoid this on the left.

3   Brevity Crack   50m   HVS 5a **   (1954)
Start immediately right of Slanting Groove. Climb easily to the crack and a lot less easily up it to a sloping ledge. Continue steeply but without too much difficulty to Green Gully. This pitch can be split by taking a belay in the sentry box of Shackle Route.

4   Shackle Route   75m   Severe ***   (1936)
Start about 10m from the left end of the face beneath a prominent crack. This classic route is low in its grade.
1. 20m Climb the crack for 18m, move onto the left wall and belay in a sentry box just above.
2. 25m Continue up the crack and then easier ground to Green Gully.
3. 30m Directly above is a tall pinnacle-flake with a jammed block between it and the left wall. Either climb the black groove right of the pinnacle, or climb over the jammed block, to a left-slanting groove. A steep wall and easier rock lead to High Ledge.

5   Shattered Crack   45m   VS 4c **   (1946)
The long thin crack 3m right of Shackle Route. Climb the steep wall on good holds, passing a loose flake, towards the block overhangs. Belay below these or preferably traverse left into the sentry box of Shackle Route, or continue. A crack splits the block overhang, climb it on small holds and continue by steep enjoyable climbing to Green Gully.

Right Crack Variation   VS   4c *   (1949)
Climb the block overhang by a thin crack to the right of the original line.

6   Crow's Nest Crack   85m   VS ***   (1946)
Where the crag turns round to the north an edge is formed. A few metres right of this and about 10m left of Bottleneck Chimney a crack springs up from a grassy overhung recess, giving the line of this excellent sustained route. Start 2m left of the recess, just right of Shattered Crack, at the middle of a small flat ledge.

1. 45m 4c Climb up for 3m and continue slightly right for 7m. Make an awkward move at a corner and traverse right into the narrow crack. Six metres up this make a long step left below a small roof onto a slab. Climb the slab then regain the crack where it is divided by an overhanging nose. Follow the left-hand crack to Green Gully.
2. 40m 4a At the lower right end of Green Gully there is a tall pinnacle-flake with a jammed block between it and the left wall (Shackle Route). From the black groove to the right go up and right to climb an obvious crack to High Ledge.

7   Mainbrace Crack   50m   HVS 5a ***   (1955)
Another Buachaille classic. Start 3m right of the grassy overhung recess of Crow's Nest Crack at a groove beneath a crack splitting the overhang above. Climb the wall right of the groove to the crack, then surmount the overhang with difficulty to gain a groove. Quit the groove to traverse up and left to a more open groove. This leads to a short left traverse and a small stance (possible belay). Climb the wide crack above then traverse right to a small ledge below an arete. Climb the arete in a great position to finish.

Direct Finish: HVS *   (1970)
Follow the open groove on the original route to where it goes left, then go straight up to beneath an overhang. Gain a foothold on the right edge (hard) and climb the steep delicate groove above. Move slightly right and finish up a steep wall on good holds. This originally required a piton for tension. Rumours of a free ascent have never been confirmed.

8   White Wall Crack   50m   E1 **   (1955)
The left-bounding wall of Bottleneck Chimney is distinctly white. Immediately left again is a corner behind a large boulder.
1. 35m 5b Climb the corner crack (thin) and mantelshelf onto a small ledge. Step right onto a rib and climb to a ledge (possible belay). Traverse left round an edge and continue the traverse for 6m to an open groove. Follow the groove (Mainbrace Crack) which leads to a short left traverse and a belay.
2. 15m 4c Climb the wide crack above for about 5m, then traverse right to a small ledge below an arete (as for Mainbrace Crack). Make an awkward step down, traverse right to a rib and continue to Green Gully.

9 Bottleneck Chimney 40m   Hard Severe **
(1941)

The obvious, dark, bottle-shaped recess about 6m from the right end of the terrace. A good route, quite strenuous and well protected. Climb the crack to the overhang of the Bottleneck. Traverse right by high handholds, exit through the neck and climb easily to Green Gully.

10 Bluebell Grooves 40m   E4 *
(1958)

A difficult and serious climb which has retained its reputation as one of the nastier leads on the Buachaille.

1. 5b Climb the undercut groove immediately right of Bottleneck Chimney to a small grass ledge.

2. 6a Traverse right for a few metres to an overhanging groove. Climb this using holds on the left wall and continue steeply to a ledge and belay.

11 Bogtrotter 25m   E2 5c *
(1977)

The shattered arete between White Wall and Mainbrace cracks. Climb the strenuous arete on dubious rock with awkward and unconvincing protection. Finish by a traverse right to the neck of Bottleneck Chimney, gained from a ledge below the overhang on White Wall crack.

12 Pendulum 40m   E2 5c *
(1955)

Steep and intricate climbing with spaced protection. Use the same start as Gallows Route at a point about 4m below its traverse. Traverse briefly left to a crack. Climb this awkwardly, then the right side of a small slab to a sloping ledge, then traverse left to a stance. Above and right is a large flake. Gain this with difficulty, go up then left across Bottleneck Chimney. Finish by climbing a fault on the left wall leading to Green Gully.

13 Gallows Route 25m   E1 5c **
(1947)

The Terrace ends on the right of a broad nose projecting from the face. Immediately right of the corner so formed is a shallow chimney which provides the start of this legendary chop route.

Start from the top of the chimney. Descend 3m and traverse left for approximately 3m to reach a steep scoop with difficulty. Climb the scoop, surmounting the overhang on the left, and a second scoop turning the overhang on the right. A third scoop is climbed until a left traverse leads to better holds and a stance and belay. Scrambling leads to Green Gully. It is also possible to go left after the second scoop to an open groove which is climbed straight to the top (1950).

14   Creag Dhon't Woll   20m   E5 6b ***   (1987)
This climbs the attractive compact wall right of Gallows. A difficult and
fingery test piece. Start from the top of the chimney on Gallows.
Ascend the white groove to a good rest below a thin crack. (Friend 1
and RP1 in hidden undercut on right). Make awkward moves up to an
RP2 placement then more hard climbing leads to a slot (RP5, Friend
half). Continue with difficulty up a crack to finish.

15   Girdle Traverse   100m   HVS   (1967)
Start just right of North-East Zigzag at the left end of the crag.
1. 40m Climb a faint diagonal fault until a right traverse leads to the
sentry box on Shackle Route.
2. 20m Cross Shattered Crack and Crow's Nest Crack until a steep
groove can be descended for 3m (as for Mainbrace Crack). Continue
right to belay above the first pitch of White Wall Crack.
3. 40m Step across Bottleneck Chimney to a ledge with a small
juniper. Traverse right, step down to a smaller ledge, then move round
the corner into the scoop of Gallows just above the first roof. Climb
the scoop to a ledge and traverse right (crux) to a mossy groove. Climb
the groove to a block belay.

UPPER TIER

16   Hangman's Crack   30m   Mild VS 4b **   (1941)
The obvious clean-cut corner. Start by scrambling to a belay at its foot.
Go up and slightly right, make an awkward mantelshelf and move left
into the corner. (This point can be reached directly with more difficulty).
Follow the corner until a long reach is made onto the right wall. Steep
climbing leads to the top.

17   Garrotte   30m   VS 5a **   (1955)
Good climbing up the obvious crack in the slab 3m right of Hangman's
Crack. Depending upon one's ability to jam, ascend the crack with
more or less difficulty to an awkward bulge. A further 10m leads to a
grass ledge. Continue via the overhang above and finish up easy
ledges.

18   Gibbet   30m   HVS 5a **   (1955)
From the first bulge on Garrotte traverse delicately right into a steep
groove. Start this by an awkward move and continue to top.

19   Guillotine   30m   HVS 5b   (1955)
Start about 10m right of Gibbet below an overhanging wall with a thin crack. Climb this (peg) and make an awkward move onto a small shelf at 7m. Trend left up the groove above to finish.

20   North Buttress (West Route)   300m   Moderate *   (1895)
The original route up the North Buttress and the second on the Buachaille. A quote from an account of the first ascent has a strangely familiar ring to it. 'It was a disgusting morning. The rain was falling dismally, and the whole mountain was concealed in mist'. Start at the centre of the buttress. Climb up to the steepest section, then traverse right and climb up, keeping close to Great Gully. A prominent leftward sloping chimney is a feature of the route.

   The buttress can be climbed equally well by other variations of the original route. The prominent and fairly continuous line of shallow chimneys up its centre ends in 150m on High Ledge, from which easy scrambling leads to the top of the buttress and the summit of the Buachaille.
Winter: III/IV ***
This fine route can be climbed under almost any conditions and will always provide plenty of interest. From the point where the Altnafeadh path crosses the foot of Great Gully there are two approaches to the start of the climb. The first ascends the easier lower section of the buttress, aiming for the prominent line of chimneys splitting the middle section.

   An alternative approach can be made by continuing along the path to the foot of the Waterslide and up from there to the lower reaches of the Crowberry Basin, from where a rising right traverse leads to the foot of the chimneys. After about 150m the chimneys lead to easier-angled ground, with the occasional awkward step. The outlook is superb.

NORTH FACE OF STOB DEARG

The North Face of the Buachaille includes all the cliffs to the right of North Buttress. The crags fall naturally into two regions, the Great Gully group and the Lagangarbh group. The Great Gully group consists of, from left to right: Slime Wall, Raven's Gully, Cuneiform Buttress, Great Gully, Great Gully Buttress and Great Gully Upper Buttress.

During the summer this part of the Buachaille provides some of the finest climbing in Glen Coe, if not the country. In a good winter the Great Gully area is transformed into a magnificent amphitheatre of high standard ice and mixed climbing. Despite its low altitude, good conditions, although not so long lasting as other areas in Glen Coe, are more frequent than people think.

Approach by either of two routes. After about 20 minutes the path from Altnafeadh crosses the great slabby rift of Great Gully, unmistakable even in thick mist. In winter, however, it is sometimes confused with easier gullies further west. The first route involves a scramble up the rocks well right of Great Gully, contouring into the gully below Great Gully Buttress, above a big pitch in the gully. The second route, not so good, starts at the intersection of the path with Great Gully, and climbs the slopes just to the left, contouring into the gully just below Slime Wall. This takes about 50 minutes.

To descend, traverse right immediately above the finish of Raven's Gully into Great Gully, then down this, keeping close under Cuneiform Buttress. A better alternative, especially when there is snow in the gully, is to go right and descend slabby rocks on the crest of a ridge below Great Gully Upper Buttress. There is a tricky slab at the bottom leading to grassy ledges and traces of a path going down under Great Gully Buttress. In winter Great Gully provides a quick descent, but in avalanche conditions it should be avoided at all costs. If in doubt go to the top of the mountain and descend by Coire na Tulaich.

WEST FACE OF NORTH BUTTRESS - SLIME WALL

Despite the passage of time this superb and atmospheric cliff has retained its reputation as one of the most intimidating climbing grounds in Glen Coe. Its name, however, is something of a misnomer, as the rock is excellent, compact bubbly rhyolite which is free of vegetation. Protection is not always plentiful, which, coupled with the daunting air and sloping holds, makes many of the climbs feel harder than their grade would suggest. Slime Wall receives little sun and requires several days of good weather to dry. It is worth noting that many of the weeps dry out after midday during sunny weather.

The left section of the crag is in two tiers, the lower climbed by Pluto and Belial. Both lead to ledges beneath the smoother upper tier; this faces north-west, and is climbed by the obvious Bloody Crack. Marking the outer edge of this tier and the left-hand boundary of the main wall is Doom Arete. The main wall is more continuous and is bounded on the right by Raven's Gully and in its upper part by the Great Cave. It presents a series of slim corners, walls and grooves, the most obvious being the two parallel lines of Bludger's Revelation and Lecher's Superstition, with the prominent hanging groove of Shibboleth further up to the right. An obvious ramp and curving groove close to and on the left wall of Raven's Gully provides the line of Guerdon Grooves; the steeper lines of Apparition and Apocalypse are to the left. Routes are described from left to right.

1 Plutocrat 80m Severe   (1966)
This and the next three routes climb the left section of the lower tier. Start 30m below Pluto beneath the left edge of the steep wall.
1. 25m Climb a groove to a block belay on the right.
2. 30m Continue by a steep edge to a grass terrace.
3. 25m Finish by the edge above.

2 Pluto 50m Severe   (1940)
Start at a cairn 45m below the foot of Raven's Gully, level with a large detached block in Great Gully. The route follows a line of weakness to the right of a large tower set against the face.
1. 10m Step up to a slab, traverse left under a bulge and gain a grass platform. Climb a narrow chimney formed by a big detached flake to another grass platform.
2. 40m Climb a corner and crack to a triangular ledge (crux). It is often greasy and can be avoided on the right. Now climb a short overhang and steep rocks to finish, or traverse left and climb a shallow groove.

3 Belial 50m Very Difficult *   (1940)
Start 20m below the foot of Raven's Gully.
1. 15m Climb up trending left to a grass stance.
2. 35m Continue direct to gain and climb the right-hand of two parallel chimneys, which finishes below the upper tier.

4 Misty High 105m V **   (1979)
This fine route is based on the line of Belial. Climb the icefall and the right-hand chimney. Ascend easier ground to a short chimney and go under the chockstone to North Buttress. Follow the icefall on the right for 90m to easier ground.

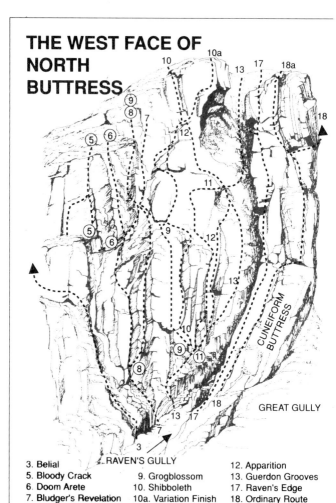

THE WEST FACE OF NORTH BUTTRESS

RAVEN'S GULLY

GREAT GULLY

CUNEIFORM BUTTRESS

3. Belial
5. Bloody Crack
6. Doom Arete
7. Bludger's Revelation
8. Lecher's Superstition
9. Grogblossom
10. Shibboleth
10a. Variation Finish
11. Apocalypse
12. Apparition
13. Guerdon Grooves
17. Raven's Edge
18. Ordinary Route
18a. Central Chimney

5   Bloody Crack   40m   E1 5b **   (1956)

This is on the upper tier. The start can be reached by climbing the lower tier or, more in keeping, by the original Bludger's Route, (see Bludger's Revelation Pitch 2), or simply by scrambling up North Buttress. Climb the strenuous right-hand crack to a ledge. Continue up the crack to finish.

6   Doom Arete   75m   E1 **   (1956)

Above and right of the finish of Belial is a block and an easy, right-sloping ledge about 7m right of Bloody Crack. A very exposed and poorly protected climb.

1. 30m 4c Follow the ledge round the corner then climb up and right a few metres. Move left and up a steep right-slanting ramp to a ledge.
2. 25m 5b Step back along the ledge and climb a steep wall aiming left for the edge, and so up to a shallow corner. Start up the corner then step left (crux) and continue to ledges.
3. 20m 4b Climb the wall above for a few metres, traverse right to a crack, follow this to a ledge and then a corner to the top.

7   Bludger's Revelation   130m   HVS ***   (1952/56/57)

This combination, with a vital link pitch, provides a superb and highly enjoyable outing. Revelation can be climbed separately by approaching via the first pitch of Doom Arete. Start at a corner below the left-hand of two parallel grooves on the left side of the main face, about 10m down and left of Raven's Gully.

1. 20m Climb to a belay at the foot of the groove.
2. 25m 5a Climb a detached flake right of the groove, step left into it then continue on good holds to a ledge. (The original Bludger's Route traverses left round the edge, continues across the wall for a few moves then descends with difficulty to a large recess. The chimney on the left leads to the terrace).
3. 30m 4c Move left to the edge, climb up for 2m, traverse left into a vertical crack and follow this to a ledge and corner. Move round the edge onto the wall and ascend excellent slabby rock to finish by a move left to the belay at the top of pitch 1 of Doom Arete.
4. 35m 4c Swing down and right into a steep groove and follow this for 6m. Traverse right (hard) to a flake crack using undercuts, and keeping a cool head swing into the crack and climb to below the overhang. Avoid this on the left, then climb up to a ledge and belay.
5. 20m 4a Follow the crest of the large flake to the right and finish more easily.

8   Lecher's Superstition   120m   E2 ***   (1959/62/68)
Another combination with a more distinct crux, taking the parallel
groove right of Bludger's Revelation and incorporating Lecher's Direct.
Start as for Bludger's Revelation.
1. 20m Climb to the belay at the foot of the groove.
2. 25m 5c Often wet. Climb the detached flake to the foot of the
groove. From the top of the flake step left onto a steep wall and pull
onto the arete (crux). Return right to the groove, climb it for 15m then
step left to belay above pitch 2 of Bludger's.
3. 35m 5b Step right and follow the prominent crack to the belay at
the top of pitch 1 of Doom Arete. A great pitch.
4. 15m 5b Climb the groove above the belay for 10m, then go up and
right to an awkward corner stance, 3m left of Revelation flake.
5. 25m 4c Climb up and left to an obvious crack which leads to easier
ground and the top.

9   Grogblossom   115m   E4 **   (1978)
The hard and quite serious slim groove left of Shibboleth.
1. 25m 4b Shibboleth, pitch 1.
2. 40m 6a Trend left across the wall to enter a groove beneath a small
overhang (old peg). Climb this awkwardly to easier ground before
launching up the overhanging wall above. This leads to a good ledge
and poor peg runner. Climb the right edge of the groove to a bulge
which teasingly bars access to easier ground. (Protection of doubtful
quality can be arranged here in quantity!). Go left and climb a scoop
with difficulty to a belay on the flake of Revelation.
3. 40m 4c Go up and left to a black mossy groove. Climb this for 15m
(old peg), move right and finish up Revelation flake.

10   Shibboleth   155m   E2 ***   (1958)
An all-time great, taking the prominent groove almost directly above
the start of Raven's. Start 6m down from the mouth of the gully.
1. 25m 4b Climb a series of right-trending slabby grooves to a ledge
and flake belay.
2. 25m 5c From the right end of the ledge climb the obvious crack for
4m, traverse left for 3m then go up and right (often wet) to enter the
groove. This leads to a small ledge and belay.
3. 20m 5a Continue up the groove. Step right, following the obvious
continuation, then go left to a small stance.
4. 30m 5b Trend delicately right across an exposed wall to a small
isolated overhang. Go back left across shallow grooves to a slabby

scoop, then right and up to a ledge and belay below an overhanging wall. It is also possible to climb a hanging corner above the left side of the isolated overhang.

5. 20m 5a Follow the shallow groove above to the right end of a ramp. (The True Finish goes right from here).

6. 35m 4b Continue up the wall, then trend right up grooves to a platform. Finish by a short overhanging corner.

Shibboleth True Finish   50m   E2 ***   (1959)
A very sustained and bold undertaking. Probably Smith's greatest climb. Start from the belay at the end of pitch 5.

6. 25m 5b Traverse right to a good spike, step up and right to enter a bottomless groove. Climb to a ledge on the right.

7. 25m 5c Traverse the wall on the right (strenuous), just above the Great Cave, to the recess at the bottom of the crack springing from the cave roof. Climb the crack.

11   Apocalypse   155m   E3 **   (1969)
This intricate, bold and serious climb finds a way up the wall on the right of the rib right of Shibboleth. Route-finding problems have caused several epics.

1. 25m 4b Shibboleth, pitch 1.

2. 40m 5c Climb the corner above for 3m, step right into another corner and climb it to a jug under a small square-cut overhang. Traverse left to a black groove, climb this for 3m then traverse right to a smaller groove. Climb this and the bold and difficult bulging wall to slabby rock. Step left to a stance.

3. 30m 5c Step left then climb up and right to a crack. Climb this, then trend up and right to flakes and a peg. Traverse horizontally right to descend slightly to the recess and grass ledge shared with Apparition, pitch 3.

4. 25m 5b Climb up to and climb the diagonal crack in the steep wall above to a slim ledge. Continue directly up steep walls, moving slightly left to the right end of the ramp of Shibboleth, pitch 5.

5. 35m 4b Shibboleth, pitch 6.

12   Apparition   145m   E1 ***   (1959)
A superb climb.

1. 30m 4c Climb the first pitch of Shibboleth. From its belay, traverse 3m right round an awkward square-cut edge to belay.

2. 45m 5b Climb the prominent V-groove directly above, step left into

a parallel corner and climb this to a square-cut roof. Pull over into a steep groove and follow this to a ledge. Climb the slab on the right to belay below a grass ledge in a recess.
3. 35m 5a Follow Apocalypse to the slim ledge. Traverse left along the ledge (peg runner in a crack above midway) to join the slim groove and ramp of Shibboleth pitch 5.
4. 35m 4b Finish up Shibboleth.

13   Guerdon Grooves   160m   HVS *   (1948)
A worthwhile excursion with character and atmosphere, skirting the steep main face on the right.
1. 30m 4c Apparition, pitch 1.
2. 45m 4c Climb the groove right of the steeper groove of Apparition. As soon as possible move slightly left and traverse right into a groove overlooking the gully. Climb the groove, which runs rightwards and parallel to the gully. The groove ends at a projecting nose; climb a crack on its left to a slab and so to a small grass ledge.
3. 40m 4b Traverse right across a grassy corner into a fault with an overhanging top. Climb the fault until an easy traverse leads to a belay near Raven's Gully.
4. and 5. 35m Easy grooves lead to a large terrace level with the top of the gully.
Winter: VII ***   (1984)
Follow the summer route to the flake belay in Raven's Gully. The traverse on the first pitch is hard. The second pitch is technical and serious, the hard section being a left traverse to a grassy ramp at about one third height, and the slab leading to the belay (peg runner used in initial groove). The traverse and overhanging fault of pitch 3 are reasonable; belay at the top of this section. Pitch 4 differs from the summer line. The slab is relatively straightforward. Above however, a steep verglased wall bars access to a snow-filled crack and rib, which leads to easier ground. This whole section is both difficult and serious. After the rib trend right to a groove and climb down to the flake belay in Raven's Gully. Two pitches in Raven's Gully lead to an overhanging chimney crack in the wall on the left. This provides a difficult finish.

14   Raven's Gully   135m   HVS 5a ***   (1937)
A difficult and distinctive climb with character and atmosphere. A route for the connoisseur of Scottish gullies. A spell of drought is desirable but not essential. Climb the first three pitches to a belay in a cave underneath a huge chockstone completely blocking the gully. Climb

strenuously up the smooth and exposed left wall (crux) until it is possible to reach a high handhold above the slot between the chockstone and the wall. Belay well up the scree slope above. (Possible escape to the right at this point). Pitch 5 (4c) takes the narrow chimney with a jammed block then climbs a deceptive groove in the left corner. Pitch 6 (4c), The Bicycle Pitch, is climbed on small holds up the left wall (perhaps the crux if wet). Above Pitch 8 a huge crag arches the gully, which higher up bristles with splendid caves and overhangs. At the top of Pitch 8, a rib and shelf rise steeply against Slime Wall. Traverse left round the foot of the rib into grooves running parallel with the gully. Climb 45m of easier rock to a grass platform at the edge of the gully, above the caves of the Direct Finish. Finish by a narrow and holdless (gasp!) 3m chimney on the right, or (phew!) by traversing left across slabs and up a 12m chimney and groove.

Direct Finish: 50m   E1 5a ***   (1948)
Instead of traversing left at the top of Pitch 8, continue straight up the gully to chockstones and caves. The first is taken on the right, then traverse onto the left wall and gain a dark cave. Bridge up strenuously until rock shelves allow a left traverse under a huge chockstone to a grass ledge, which leads to the normal route at the penultimate pitch.
Winter: V ***   (1953)
A magnificent climb. Normally there is a pitch leading to the cave belay beneath the chockstone of the summer crux. Climb the left wall, followed by snow leading to a narrowing of the gully with a chockstone above. Another two difficult pitches lead to the gully fork. Climb snow and ice grooves left of the rib to the platform on the gully edge. Climb the chimney on the right, or traverse left and finish up ice grooves.
Winter Direct Finish: V ***   (1970)
Held in great respect by the few repeat ascensionists.

15   Nightmare Traverse 75m   E2 †   (1956)
Start 4m below the start of Doom Arete.
1. 35m Traverse across an arete and to the left of a small overhang. Move right round a corner, and so across to a flake and belay.
2. 35m Climb the rib above until a hard right traverse can be made to small ledges. Climb a crack for 3m, then climb to the top of a steep wall at a small spike. Tension down from a peg under an overhang to a flake belay.
3. 5m Climb the crack above to a small ledge.
4, etc. Finish up Guerdon Grooves.

16   Girdle Traverse   130m   E1 †   (1956)

Start up the wall left of the crack left of Bloody Crack.

1. 20m Climb the wall, then step across the crack to a ledge which is followed to a flake belay.

2. 10m Go right along the ledge to a corner with a small triangular grass ledge a little higher. Belay just above.

3. 10m Traverse right round a very exposed corner and continue past a crack, then up to a small ledge. Move right to huge flake belays.

4. 20m Go gradually up and right to a sloping ledge and a block.

5. 20m Traverse right to a grassy corner, then climb to a belay below a large cave.

6. 30m Step down and follow a line of weakness beside Raven's Gully to a belay in a corner well up Guerdon Grooves.

7. 20m Climb up and right to finish.

CUNEIFORM BUTTRESS

This buttress is separated from Slime Wall by the narrow slit of Raven's Gully. Its north face is narrow and faces down Great Gully, and a more extensive area of good rock higher up to the right forms its west face. The north face sees little sunshine and tends to be vegetated; it is therefore ideally suited to winter climbing. The real potential for summer climbing here is yet to be explored. Climbs are described from left to right.

17   Raven's Edge   140m   VS **   (1964)

A climb with great positions and rock scenery. Start at the foot of Raven's Gully. The stunning situations on pitch 5 are the main attraction.

1. 30m Climb the left edge of the buttress until about 10m above the crux chockstone of Raven's Gully, at a large block belay below a vertical wall.

2. 25m 4c Climb the wall then traverse left to a prominent corner. Climb this to a ledge.

3. 25m 4c Continue up the corner to a platform.

4. 30m Ascend easily to a thread belay below the big roof on the extreme left edge of the buttress.

5. 30m 4b Traverse left under the roof to emerge in a very exposed position on the right wall of Raven's Gully. Climb the deep crack to the top.

Direct Finish: 30m   HVS 5a *   (1970)
From the thread belay at the top of pitch 4 climb the steep wall on the
right, then a chimney and twin cracks to finish.
Winter: V   ***   (1984)
Generally follow the summer line but avoid the open book corner of
pitch 3 by taking the rib on the right.

18   Ordinary Route   135m   Very Difficult   (1930)
Start at the lowest rocks near the foot of Raven's Gully. Follow the line
of least resistance to a broad grassy terrace. From its right end climb
a short but steep pitch and then follow grassy grooves to another broad
ledge under the vertical upper third of the buttress. Traverse right
round an exposed edge onto the west face. Climb an obvious shelf,
then turn towards the centre of the cliff. The last section from the broad
ledge gives a good finish.
Winter: IV   **   (1957)
A good climb, following the summer route throughout. The main
difficulties are at the summer crux and at the west shelf near the top.

19   The Central Chimney   35m   Severe   (1934)
This is a poor direct finish to the Ordinary Route. From the broad ledge
under the vertical upper third of the buttress traverse left to and climb
the loose, prominent chimney.

20   The Long Chimney   135m   Severe   (1955)
Follow the Ordinary Route to the broad grassy terrace. Now traverse
hard right and climb the long, obvious shallow chimney.
Winter: IV **   (1957)
Follow the summer line.

21   Backing Out   190m   Hard Severe *   (1969)
At the left end of the west face there is an inverted V-shaped corner.
Start 4m left of this.
1. 40m Move up and left over the edge of the buttress onto slabs.
Climb these by a crack and a shallow corner to belay beneath smooth
walls.
2. 35m Move right, then up the wall to sloping ledge. Follow the ledge
right round the edge (crux) and continue right, passing a square-
topped block. Make an awkward step to stay on the ledge line, then
go up to a platform with a large block.
3. 35m Step off the block, then trend right to the foot of a broken corner

right of the top part of The Long Chimney. The corner slopes up and right over a steep wall.
4. 40m Climb the corner to belay on a large ledge.
5. 40m Continue up the buttress to finish.

22   Snowba's   125m   VS **   (1968)
Start roughly in the centre of the west face to the left of an obvious corner and approximately 30m left of a damp chimney.
1. 30m 4c Climb an overhang and layback onto a slab on the left. Continue bearing left, bypassing a large ledge leading off right, to belay on a ledge below a greasy corner leading diagonally right.
2. 30m 4c Climb the corner and move right on ledges, passing bulging walls to an overhung corner. Climb the corner, move right to a small ledge, then go up and across a mossy wall to a ledge.
3. 40m 4b Climb a corner and jumbled blocks to easier ground leading to the foot of a large corner.
4. 25m 4a Ascend the corner to finish.

23   Lift Off   90m   HVS **   (1969)
Start just right of the unclimbed corner in the centre of the west face.
1. 25m 5a Move up the wall and follow a groove rightwards to belay beneath a corner.
2. 35m 4b/c Climb the corner and wall above, passing a nose on the left to belay on a ledge.
3. 30m Continue to the top of the buttress.

24   Cuneiform Corner   60m   IV *   (1979)
This short but steep route follows the obvious icefall which forms in the corner right of Snowba's and leads to the traverse ledge going right into Great Gully.

25   Cuneiform Corner Continuation   180m   III *   (1983)
A complete route leading to the summit of the Buachaille. After the first pitch of Cuneiform Corner, belay on a large platform. Continue up right via steep corners and groove for 45m to a small ledge and belay. Climb a steep but short black wall on ice smears for 25m, then continue by two or three rope lengths to easier ground.

26   Overhanging Groove   65m   Severe   (1955)
The west face terminates where a small buttress abuts against it. Near the small buttress a corner leads into a groove.

1. 15m Climb the corner to a belay below an overhang.
2. 10m Traverse left and down to a crack, climb the overhang (crux), and go up to a small cave (thread belay).
3. 40m Continue up the groove, avoid the overhang by the right wall and finish up easy slabs.

27   Great Gully   360m   I/II   (1894)
This massive gully dominates the north side of the Buachaille. Other than providing access to the Great Gully group of climbs, it is of little interest in summer. Early in winter several pitches of water ice may provide sport, but these generally bank out later in the season to give a straightforward snow climb. There is usually a pitch where the gully kinks right under Cuneiform Buttress. Great Gully is a notorious avalanche trap and should be avoided at all costs should such conditions prevail.

GREAT GULLY BUTTRESS
This buttress stands on the right of Great Gully, roughly at the same level as Cuneiform Buttress and Slime Wall. Its east face boasts routes as good as any in Glen Coe. Climbs are described from left to right. Descent is by a scramble down to the right.

1   Trident Crack (Direct Start)   45m   Hard Severe *   (1955)
Near the left end of the face a right-angled grassy groove can be seen above a 12m slab. The slab is split by three thin fissures.
1. 20m Climb the thin fissure and slab to a large grass ledge. Continue by the wide crack right of the right-angled grassy groove to a stance and belay common to August Crack.
2. 25m Step down, traverse right for 6m, then move up a steep fault with some loose flakes. Finish up slabs.

2   August Crack   50m   VS *   (1955)
The leftmost of the three parallel cracks. Start 10m down and right of the start of Trident Crack at a grass ledge.
1. 30m 4a Climb to a ledge below a thin crack. Traverse 5m down and left to a thin crack which is climbed to a ledge and belay. The thin crack can also be gained from directly below.
2. 20m 4b Climb the steep fault running slightly left to the top.

3   July Crack   50m   HVS 5a **   (1958)
Climb the first pitch of August Crack then the thin crack above. An excellent sustained pitch.

4   Playmate of the Month   50m   E3 6a **
The obvious and impressive thin crack between June and July Cracks.
Start as for June Crack. Move left and climb a thin crack to reach a
steep wall. Surmount this (crux) and climb the crack to easier rock.

5   June Crack   60m   VS **   (1948)
The first pitch is common to Ledgeway and Direct Route. About 10m
from the right end of the face there is a 10m rib topped by a grass
ledge. Start at a groove immediately right of the rib.
1. 10m Climb the groove to the grass ledge.
2. 20m 4c From the left end of the ledge climb up and slightly left to
a prominent crack. Climb the crack, embarking on the left wall, to a
small rock shelf.
3. 30m 5a Above, the crack overhangs. Either climb the nose on the
right for a few moves or climb the crack direct (harder but well
protected). Continue up the crack to easier ground.
Winter: V   (1984)
Follow the summer line, going directly up at the crux corner.

6   Augley Crack   50m   HVS *   (1990)
This route follows a curving crack in the wall to the right of June Crack.
1. 10m As for June Crack.
2. 40m 5a From the middle of the ledge climb straight up to join Direct
Route. Follow this until a traverse left above an overhang gains the
base of the crack. Follow this to the top.

7   Direct Route   45m   Hard Severe **   (1946)
Start from the left end of the ledge at the top of pitch 1 of June Crack.
High in its grade and poorly protected.
1. 20m Climb up and slightly left for about 5m, then make for a
right-sloping shelf. Step up onto the shelf and continue up the fracture
above to a grass ledge and large pointed flake belay.
2. 25m Climb a short steep wall left of the flake and enter a long line
of weakness which trends slightly left to the top.
Winter: V **   (1979)
A short but steep climb. In a good season it holds much ice. Follow
the summer line.

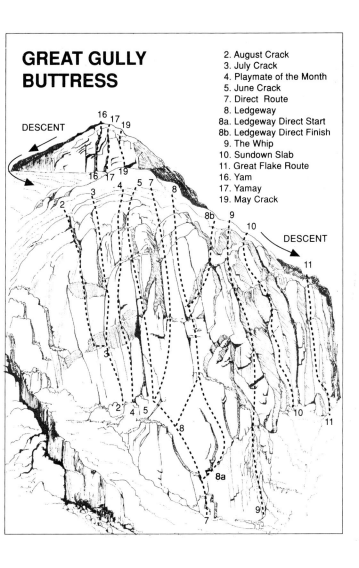

GREAT GULLY
BUTTRESS

2. August Crack
3. July Crack
4. Playmate of the Month
5. June Crack
7. Direct Route
8. Ledgeway
8a. Ledgeway Direct Start
8b. Ledgeway Direct Finish
9. The Whip
10. Sundown Slab
11. Great Flake Route
16. Yam
17. Yamay
19. May Crack

DESCENT

DESCENT

8   Ledgeway   45m   Hard Severe **   (1952)
Another line in the Direct Route mould, starting at the June Crack ledge.
1. 20m From the left end of the ledge, traverse right and up to a shallow, white-scarred fault. Follow this to a bulge, pass it on the left and go up left to the pointed flake belay of Direct Route.
2. 25m Climb the flake and then the crack and open groove above to the top (hard).
Direct Start: 40m   VS 4c **   (1956)
Steep and poorly protected. Start just right of and lower than the original start. Follow a fault to join the normal route at the white-scarred section.
Final Variation: 25m   Severe *   (1957)
Instead of traversing left to the large pointed flake belay, climb the obvious crack which springs up from the right end of the grassy ledge.

9   The Whip   75m   E1 **   (1966)
Start just left of the right end of the main face, 10m right of Direct Route.
1. 35m 4c Climb directly to a small overhang, turn this by a groove on the right and climb to a grass ledge.
2. 15m 5b Climb up to and ascend the brown groove (often wet) to spike belays.
3. 25m 4c Traverse left to a gangway then finish directly.

10   Sundown Slab   50m   Severe **   (1967)
Start below and left of the flake of Great Flake Route under two grooves. Climb the left-hand groove. Go left by delicate slabs and open grooves to the top.

11   Great Flake Route   45m   Very Difficult   (1947)
Start below the flake, which stands out clearly just right of the edge formed by the east and north faces, and climb a 5m arete. Continue up a pillar bordered by cracks and finish up grooves.
Winter: III/IV   (1985)
Start about 6m right of the edge of the east face.
1. 25m Climb iced slabs and a groove to the start of Great Flake Route.
2. 45m Climb the summer route via iced cracks.

12   Sunset Groove   40m   Very Difficult   (1947)
Just left of Sunset Rib is a groove leading to an obvious short slab below another groove. Follow this line and continue to the top.

13   Sunset Rib   30m   Very Difficult   (1947)
Near the right end of the narrow north face is a thin, grey rib right of a smooth groove. Climb the rib then easier rocks.

14   Girdle Traverse   120m   HVS **   (1966)
Exposed pitches with good climbing from bottom right to top left.
1. 20m 4a Climb just left of watermarked rocks to blocks and belay.
2. 15m 4c Move up to the corner on the right and climb to a grass ledge and belay.
3. 35m 4c/5a Traverse left along a horizontal crack. After 20m climb up, then cross Direct Route and climb a crack to a belay.
4. 25m 5a Traverse left by the lip of the slab, crossing the lines of June, July and August cracks to a notch on Trident Crack.
5. 25m Finish by the wall and crack on the left.

GREAT GULLY UPPER BUTTRESS

This fine little buttress lies some distance above Great Gully Buttress. It presents a short, steep face which is in fact the east face of Broad Buttress. Immediately right of the face is the exit to Narrow Gully. The climbs are described from left to right.

15   Happy Valley   30m   E1 5b **   (1969)
The steep and strenuous wide crack about 10m left of Yam.

16   Yam   40m   E1 5b**   (1963)
The prominent chimney-crack splitting the centre of the face, with a difficult move over the roof at 15m.

17   Yamay   40m   E2 5b **   (1968)
A steep, well-protected pitch which takes the prominent crack and corner between Yam and May Crack. Climb to a small roof, traverse the wall on the right and climb the corner above.

18   Yamay Variation Start   E2   5c **   (1981)
Climb the crack 5m right of the normal start to join the original route at the base of the groove.

19   May Crack   35m   VS 4c**   (1952)
From a detached block 5m right of Yamay climb the crack until a long reach gains better holds. Continue to the top.
Winter: V   (1985)
Follow the summer line.

20   Facade   40m   Severe *   (1957)
Right of May Crack is an open corner. Start up the wall immediately
right of the corner. A weird route.
1. 20m Climb up to a long horizontal fault below overhangs.
2. 20m Aim right for a breach in the form of a vertical groove. Climb
the groove and trend left on the steep wall above to finish.

21   Bent Crack   40m   Very Difficult   (1954)
At the right edge of the face there is a prominent crack with a rightward
twist near the top. Climb it.

22   Bent Crack Rib   40m   Very Difficult   (1954)
The rib immediately right of Bent Crack.

LAGANGARBH GROUP

This group includes (from left to right): Narrow Gully (an obvious,
trench-like grassy gully), Broad Buttress (split by a deep groove higher
up), the West Face of Broad Buttress, Broad Gully, Staircase Buttress
and Lagangarbh Buttress. The area has a pleasant atmosphere and
is relatively quiet. Its various aspects allow climbing all day in the sun
(should the sun be shining). In winter Narrow and Broad gullies provide
pleasant Grade I/II climbs, but tend to be avalanche prone. Staircase
and Lagangarbh buttresses are at the right end of the North Face of
the Buachaille. The West Face of Lagangarbh Buttress overlooks
Coire na Tulaich. To the left of the larger Lagangarbh Buttress there
are two parallel ribs, and above and to the left of these is the distinctive
stepped formation of Staircase Buttress. Left again and separated by
a grassy slope is the West Face of Broad Buttress. Access to all the
buttresses is by a scramble up the rocks below Lagangarbh Buttress.
This avoids the dire heathery slope to the left.

BROAD BUTTRESS

The west face of this quick-drying, two-tiered crag catches the afternoon sun, and it is easily reached from Staircase Buttress. To descend,
scramble down the right-bounding rib of the gully right of the buttress,
or continue up and then over the top of Lagangarbh Buttress. It is also
possible to scramble down Broad Buttress itself. The first four climbs
are on the lower buttress, and are described from left to right. The last
route is on the upper part.

Ephemeron Gully   340m   III/IV **   (1985)
Hard under the West Face, left of Broad Gully, a sinuous line of
grooves gives, under icy conditions, five ice and three mixed pitches.

Pedlar's Groove   40m   Severe   (1954)
Start below and left of Hawker's Crack, at the bottom left end of the
face.
1. 15m Step up, then traverse left and continue steeply to a belay.
2. 25m Step down and right and climb a groove immediately left of
Hawker's Crack, and below the corner of the face, to the top.

Hawker's Crack   30m   Severe †   (1954)
The obvious crack near the left end of the face.
1. 10m Climb the crack via an awkward move to a belay.
2. 20m Continue up the crack.

Paladin   45m   VS †   (1964)
The crack right of Hawker's Crack.
1. 15m Climb the crack to a ledge and spike belay.
2. 30m Continue straight up the crack (crux) to the top.

Meson   40m   VS †   (1968)
Start below and left of a prominent square-cut overhang in the centre
of the face. Climb a crack to a small spike belay beneath an obvious
corner. Climb the corner and continue to the top.

STAIRCASE BUTTRESS
The rock is sound and the climbing varied. There is a cave on the left
flank of the crag above the lowest rocks. The left arete of the cave is
taken by East Chimney Variation. Pedestal Arete is immediately left of
and a little higher than this and is separated from it by a gully which
narrows to a chimney.

Pedestal Arete   75m   Severe *   (1955)
Climb numerous blocks and pinnacles 'alpine style' to a gap beyond
a high gendarme. Cross the gap and traverse delicately left to the left
edge. Climb the edge for about 3m, traverse diagonally right across
the face and continue up to a broad grass ledge. Pull up the short right
wall and go to the triangular stance at the left edge of the final wall.
Finish round to the left up the very exposed short chimney.

Original Route   90m   Very Difficult   (1947)
Climb heather to the cave, then exit onto the right wall. Make two left
traverses into the gully. Follow the left branch of a chimney, then leave
it by the left wall and climb to a grassy terrace overlooking the gully
on the left. Continue to the top.

East Chimney Variation   Very Difficult   (1952)
Start on an arete below and left of the cave. Climb a small chimney to
a detached boulder, then traverse left into the gully. (This is the second
of two traverses mentioned in Original Route). Now climb the chimney
immediately above to the grassy platform. Continue up Rehabilitation
Route.
Winter: III   (1955)
Follow the arete of East Chimney Variation, then traverse right to
Rehabilitation Route, which provides the crux.

Rehabilitation Route   90m   Severe   (1952)
Start at the lowest left-hand rocks. Low in the grade. Go up a wide
crack and move right on slabs to a large platform. Now go up the wall
facing the gully on the west side to a ledge, then climb a crack and
slabs to a distinctive grassy platform. The platform is partly separated
from the wall by a miniature gap. Traverse up and right on the wall
beyond the gap and move round the edge to the open corner and a
line of weakness above. Climb this or, better, the steeper rocks to the
left to reach a large, prominent easy-angled diamond-shaped slab. Go
up to and climb a short steep wall and scramble to the top.

Bag   60m   VS   (1966)
On the right of the buttress there is a prominent vertical arete.
1. 20m Climb the arete on its left side to a block belay.
2. 40m Continue along a narrow ledge on the right and straight up the
crest over a bulge on the right (crux) to the top.

Blaeberry Rib   55m   Very Difficult   (1950)
Climb the right-hand of the two parallel ribs left of Lagangarbh Buttress. The left-hand rib is disappointing.

LAGANGARBH BUTTRESS

The most westerly buttress on the North Face of the Buachaille. It is
bounded on both sides by grassy gullies and comprises a fine East
Wall, a two-tiered north-easterly facing crest and a West Face which

overlooks Coire na Tulaich. A prominent feature of the front face of the buttress is the line of Lagangarbh Chimney. Descent is by grassy gullies on either side of the buttress.

The following climbs (described from right to left as approaching up the gully) are on the east face. This catches the morning sun, so an early start is worthwhile.

Sassenach Groove   60m   VS 4c **   (1947)
Climb the impressive and sustained groove which starts about 15m up the gully.

East Face   45m   Severe   (1947)
Halfway up the gully there is a prominent cave in the wall of Blaeberry Rib. Start opposite the cave and below the obvious slab of Bollard Slab. Make a short right traverse and climb to a grass ledge and spike. Traverse right and down to the recessed area right of Bollard Slab. Climb a short wall left of a shallow chimney with a chockstone, and continue by an obvious chimney to the top.

Bollard Slab   40m   Severe **   (1952)
An elegant but poorly protected pitch. Start as for East Face but climb the crack direct to ledge and block. Now climb the attractive slab above to near its right edge, then its upper part slightly leftwards on small holds. Climb the wall above or a groove to its left. An easier variation goes right from the block to a groove between two overhangs. Climb the groove and the slab where convenient.

Nameless Wall   35m   Severe   (1952)
Start 10m left of Bollard Slab at the left edge of a steep wall. Climb up, traverse right and follow the thin crack above.

Nameless Groove   35m   Very Difficult   (1953)
The groove immediately left of Nameless Wall.

Crest Route - Left Edge   115m   Severe *   (1936/56)
This enjoyable combination climbs the two tiers of the north-east crest. Start from a ledge 10m up, gained from the left.
1. 35m Follow the rib near the left edge of the wall on good rock. There is a delicate move a few metres up.
2. 35m Scramble to the terrace.
3. 25m It is possible to escape right up enjoyable easy rock. Alternatively go to the left end of the terrace where the buttress edge springs

up steeply and climb the slab and groove above to cracked blocks which are turned to the right.
4. 20m Easier climbing leads to the top.

The next four routes are on the west face of the buttress.

Lagangarbh Chimney   60m   Difficult **   (1930)
An excellent route. The chimney starts about halfway up the gully on the right of the buttress. The last 15m is the crux.
Winter: II/III **
The chimney often contains ice and gives a good route for a short day.

Pang   45m   VS 4c   (1956)
Start about 30m right of Lagangarbh Chimney beneath two parallel cracks. Climb the right-hand crack, then the left one to a rock bay. Climb the steep arete on the left to a large slabby ledge and continue to a thin crack topped by a spike. Climb the crack.

Infected   100m   III   (1989)
Follow the obvious right-slanting groove, just left of the ice smear which forms halfway along the shelf below the broken buttress below Lagangarbh Buttress. A good climb for bad weather.
1. 25m Follow the groove right to easy ground, belay 3m back.
2. 30m Go up to and climb the obvious icefall.
3. 30m Move right up a small wall then right again to easy ground.
4. 15m Climb the small icefall, moving right at top.

The Dial   60m   Very Difficult   (1966)
This is the large foreshortened slab situated below and to the right of Lagangarbh Buttress. It appears to be climbable almost anywhere.

COIRE NA TULAICH

This large north-western corrie of the Buachaille lies directly above Lagangarbh, and is popularly known as the Lagangarbh Corrie. It gives the easiest route to the summit and is the most certain winter descent route. From Lagangarbh take the path to the Buachaille and in about a hundred metres, its right branch, which goes straight into the corrie and up its west side. The path ends at a scree slope at about 700m. Continue up the scree towards a narrowing gully, best avoided by a scramble on its east bank, to emerge on the col at 870m. The slopes on the right lead to the lower top of Stob Coire nan Tulachain while those on the left go east by a well-worn cairned path to the summit of Stob Dearg.

There are crags on both flanks of the corrie, the best one being Creag a'Bhancair. Just above it is Creag na Tulaich, and high up on the left lies Flem Wall, probably the least coveted of the Buachaille crags. Elsewhere, numerous small crags appear to offer some enjoyable climbing. During a cold snap much fun can be had on the many icefalls which form low down on the left of the narrows leading into the corrie. In summer these crags provide climbing on clean, compact rock.

FLEM WALL

This crag of steep, clean, sound rock lies within 30m of the summit of the Buachaille, and is most conveniently reached by climbing towards the summit from the top of routes on the West Face of North Buttress, Raven's Gully or Cuneiform Buttress. The main feature is a centrally placed broad sloping ledge, the Balumph, topped by a large corner, well seen even from the road. The crag faces north-west and appears to suffer from almost permanent weeps. Very little is known about these climbs, which may be unrepeated. The routes are described from left to right.

Sgub   55m   VS   (1966)
Below and well to the left of the Balumph is a short arete with a cairn at its foot. Follow the line of most resistance to the top.

Seek Tochil   90m   Severe   (1966)
About 30m right of Sgub, though still left of the Balumph, is a cairn and arrow. Zigzag up the wall by shelves, flakes, and ledges to the left extremity of the Balumph, then climb the imposing rib directly above, first by a corner on the left, then go right to the crest and follow this to the top (exposed and wet).

Shasmakelmanov   75m   VS   (1966)
Takes the most direct line on the cliff. Start below the right end of the small roof directly below the Balumph.
1. 30m Climb a prominent shelf leading up right, then move out left onto the wall and up to the Balumph.
2. 30m Climb the prominent corner and the rib on its right to a ledge on the right, then continue up the corner to a sloping ledge.
3. 15m Finish up right and belay round the summit cairn! How seriously one takes a description like this, is of course entirely up to you!

The crag at the top right of Coire na Tulaich has a number of routes on good clean rock. All were climbed in 1966. **Awrong** (75m Very Difficult) takes the large central crack on the crag. **Nobad** (90m Very Difficult) takes the wall to its left and **Awrite** (75m Severe) the wall to its right. **Soso** (45m Very Difficult) climbs the crack in the centre of the steepest part of the red crag above and to the left of Nobad, easily reached by a left traverse along a terrace from the top of Nobad. Below the rim of the corrie on the right, above and left of the crag of Soso, there is a small, rounded buttress. **Dinnaeken** (45m VS) starts from the lowest rocks and climbs an overhanging wall direct to a sloping platform, then the steep wall above. **Uhuh** (30m Severe) is a pleasant route which follows the well-defined crest of the small buttress to the right of the buttress of Dinnaeken.

CREAG A' BHANCAIR   (Map Ref 215 551)

This superb crag harbours one of the most continuously steep rock walls in Glen Coe. It lies at an altitude of 450m on the west flank of Stob Coire na Tulachain, which is the west bounding ridge of Coire na Tulaich. The climbs contrast between the difficult and bold traditional routes, and the bolted 'sport' climbs of Tunnel Wall. Although lacking the power and steepness of their limestone counterparts, they are renowned for their boldness and sustained big pitch feel. This is ideally suited to the 'stamina merchant' or that well-known crag scavenger - the Flash Vulture. The bolted climbs have been given French grades in addition to their E grades, but beware, this is not a place for those accustomed to the normal European frequency of protection.

The crag is quick-drying and catches the sun from mid-afternoon onwards. Though perhaps a bit cold, it is not unheard of to climb here in March and April, although May and June are the best months. By July the mighty midge is quietly but persistently making its presence felt. The approach is obvious, up the main path towards Coire na Tulaich and then right on faint tracks to the foot of Tunnel Wall.

The rising traverse line of Carnivore bisects the crag. In the centre of the main section a diagonal crack springs up and right from a bulge about 15m up the Direct Start to Carnivore. To its right the reddish-pink and almost circular Tunnel Wall is obvious. Right again is the left-facing corner of Outlandos, from which stems a series of impressive curving overlaps. Risk Business takes the lower of these. Further to the right the crag slants up, easing in angle and taking on a less daunting air. A prominent, left-trending crack and chimney provides the line of Piranha, which marks the right-hand extremity of the crag.

A number of the newer climbs have fixed lower-off points. PLEASE DO NOT REMOVE THEM. If descending from the top, traverse south-west on rough slabs, then continue right to vague shallow gullies which lead down to slopes going back to the foot of Tunnel Wall. The climbs are described from left to right.

1   The Chimney   5m   Very Difficult   (1934)
A vegetated line near the left edge of the crag leads to 5m of rock just below the top.

2   Carnivore   160m   E2 ***   (1958/62)
A classic route and the first to breach the central wall. The first pitch is serious and sustained with much traversing. Either a competent second or a very conscientious leader is recommended if the second is to avoid the all too frequent inspection of the grass slope below. The line described takes in the Whillans' 'Villain's Finish', which is more in keeping with the standard of the route. The original finish is described later. Start approximately 10m right of the left end of the crag at a bulge below a right-trending weakness.
1. 45m 5b Pull over the bulge and trend right on good holds to a thread runner (seek and ye shall find). Now climb a tricky little wall and continue to a small ledge at the start of the traverse (peg and krab sometimes *in situ* for a back rope). Follow a descending line of weakness and continue to a point beneath the left end of a long ledge. Climb steeply onto this and walk right to a belay.
2. 20m 4b Climb the green slabby scoop on the right to a ledge.
3. 20m 5a Climb ledges and an obvious line of weakness to a right-slanting crack. Climb the crack to belay on a shelf beneath a black overhung recess.
4. 25m 5c The Villain's Finish. Climb the recess and boldly layback the crack above to the base of a slim groove. Attain a standing position with difficulty and continue easily to a ledge.
5. 50m Easier climbing leads to ledges and the top.

3   The Original Finish   110m   E3 ***   (1958)
Starting from the stance after pitch 3.
4. 20m   6a Traverse right across the slab, take a horizontal crack beneath overhangs and at about 6m climb the overhang. Continue right with difficult moves to a cave belay.
5. 15m 5c Using undercuts (often wet), continue the traverse to a grass ledge.

CREAG A'BHANCAIR

Abseil

1. The Chimney
2. Carnivore Direct Finish
3. Carnivore Original Route
6. Waltzing Ostriches
7. Le Monde
8. Celtic Dawn
9. Carnivore Direct Start
10. Romantic Reality
11. Admission

12. Fated Path
13. The Tribeswoman
14. The Railway Children
16. Outlandos
18. The Risk Business

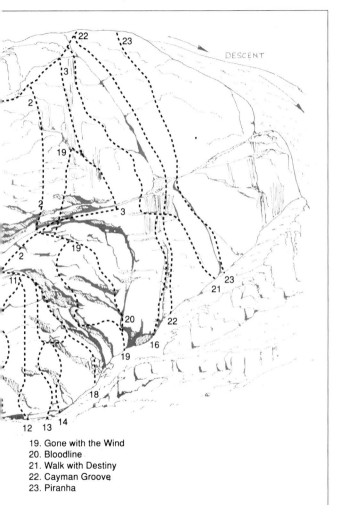

19. Gone with the Wind
20. Bloodline
21. Walk with Destiny
22. Cayman Groove
23. Piranha

6. 25m 4c Traverse left and up for 10m, move left under a bulge and across to a grass ledge. Climb the wall above to a small ledge.
7. 50m Easier climbing leads to the top.

4   Meat Beater   35m   E3 5c *   (1986)
Follow Carnivore to the start of the traverse. Move up and right. Make an awkward move up then finish up the headwall on good holds.

5   Twilight Zone   40m   E6 6b **   (1987)
This climbs the wall left of Waltzing Ostriches, cutting through Carnivore and the second pitch of Le Monde, to finish up the cleaned white streak. Start at a small bulge directly beneath a gap in the overhang. Climb the groove boldly to a serious section through the bulge (Rock 2 placement) to join Carnivore traverse (fail-safe protection). Up the steep wall above to the top of the ramp on Le Monde, then directly up until it is possible to hand traverse right on spikes to the bottom of a cleaned streak. Ascend the wall above with some technical moves at the top, then the slab above to an *in situ* belay.

6   Waltzing Ostriches   20m   E6 6a *   (1986)
Another serious route. The first weakness right of Carnivore is the initial groove of Le Monde. Traditionally characterised by a hole in the ground (although it has been superseded by more recent additions). Just left is an obvious pedestal. From the top of the pedestal climb steeply just right of some black rock to a jug in a scoop (protection). Continue steeply and away from the sole runner to the base of a slim groove. Start this with an awkward move, better holds then lead to the Carnivore traverse. Move right and abseil off.

7   Le Monde   50m   E5 *   (1976)
Good climbing, better than its appearance would suggest.
1. 25m 5c Climb the groove on good holds and, where it fades, move right and up to a thin horizontal break. Dubious protection can be arranged here, the last before the Carnivore traverse. Climb the scoop and bulge above with difficulty (rock slightly suspect). Step left then go straight up to a belay on Carnivore.
2. 25m 5a Follow the obvious slanting flake on the left to a peg belay beneath a roof. Abseil off, or continue, ape-wise, through vegetation and occasional rock above.

8   Celtic Dawn   25m   E5 6a **   (1987)
A beautiful pitch up the wall to the right of Le Monde. Protection is only just adequate. Climb the right-hand, more prominent groove right of

Le Monde. Move left at its top to good holds in a niche at about 10m (Friend 1, RP2) then up to an obvious hole. Exit right through the bulge onto a green slab (peg). Move right to a small overlap and climb the steep wall above on good holds.

The next obvious feature is a right-slanting crack which springs from a bulge about 15m up.

9 Carnivore Direct Start 25m E4 6a * (1980)
A good pitch which could do with some traffic to keep the bulge clean. Protection improves as height is gained. Start beneath the line of the crack at a bulge below a circular recess. Gain the recess, step up then slightly left to a bulge barring access to the crack above. Climb this using an assortment of techniques to an uncomfortable rest. The excellent final bulge leads with some more difficulty to a ledge and belay on Carnivore.

10 Romantic Reality 85m E7 *** (1984)
The superb headwall above the right end of Carnivore's first pitch.
1. 25m 6a Climb Carnivore Direct Start.
2. 30m 6b Climb the short overhanging wall to a slab beneath a narrow overlap. Turn this on the left (Friend 2 in undercut, RP2 just above) and ascend the wall above with difficulty to a series of ramp holds going right. Follow these with more difficulty (crux) to a pocket and protection. Move up and left to a tiny groove leading to the curving overlap. Turn this by using the rib on the right, boldly and blindly climb to a jug in the middle of the wall. (Poor wires behind the hold). Make an awkward move to gain the next bulge above and then go left to a small ledge and nut belays.
3. 30m 5b Climb the awkward mossy wall on the right to finish.

11 Admission 40m E6 6b (F7c) *** (1987)
This takes a series of scoops and bulges up the left side of the wall. Not as sustained as Fated Path, but with harder sections. Start about 6m left of Fated Path on the left side of a small bulge. A selection of Rocks 1-7 are needed for the top section. Move up and directly past a bolt to a small ledge. Climb up and right through the bulge to a stopping place (Friend 2). Climb the excellent 'truckin' wall above to reach the left end of a small overhang. Move right underneath this and surmount it to gain an obvious diagonal crack. Follow this right with a tricky move to join the final section of Fated Path.

12   Fated Path   40m   E6 6b (F7c+) ***   (1986)
This magnificent pitch is very sustained and at times very runout,
particularly between the second and third bolts. Start in the middle of
the wall at the left side of a block in the initial overhang. Move left from
the block and then directly up (bolt) until it is possible to swing right
into a shallow groove (bolt). Traverse right and then up to a small
overlap with good holds above (bolt). Climb the wall above past three
pegs (in each of the three obvious horizontal breaks) to a hard section
before the final less overhanging finish. Take a few large RPs and
medium Rocks for the final section.

13   The Tribeswoman   45m   E6 6b (F7c+) ***   (1990)
Start just right of Fated Path. Gain the obvious right-trending rail via
undercuts (bolt). Boldly clip the second bolt and move up and left to a
niche. Step right and ascend, with a cool head, the superb wall to a
horizontal break (Friends 2 and 1). Finish up The Railway Children.

14   The Railway Children   45m   E6 6b (F7b+/7c) ***   (1987)
Probably the most varied of the three routes following the obvious line
of weakness on the right side of the wall. Start at a block overhang
just where the crag starts to curve up to the right. Climb to a bolt
beneath an overlap at about 7m. Clip the bolt above the overhang and
make a difficult move to gain easier ground going right to a second
overlap. Climb this (bolt) to a good shake-out in the recess. Go left
round the bulge (peg) and traverse left to another peg. Now climb a
difficult section above (two peg runners) to easier ground. (Rocks 1,
4, 8 required for the easier upper section).

15   Uncertain Emotions   25m   E5 6b (F7b) ***   (1986)
This is really a softer option to The Railway Children, though nevertheless an excellent pitch with a bold final headwall. From the
shake-out turn the bulge on the left as for The Railway Children and
then go back right into the middle of the wall. Go straight up on good
but hidden holds to a lower-off on Risk Business.

16   Outlandos   70m   E2   (1981)
This is the corner on the right margin of Tunnel Wall, broken by a
grassy ledge at half-height. Start at a tree.
1. 45m 5b Climb a corner until a move right over a bulge (old peg)
leads into the main corner line. Climb this to the grass ledge then
continue to its top. Move out right to a belay.

2. 25m Climb the wall above to the grass rake. From there it is possible to walk off or follow either Cayman Groove or Walk with Destiny.

17   Up with the Sun   120m   E6 ***   (1991)
A direct uncompromising line, filling the obvious gap cutting through Risk Business. Start 6m down and left of the tree at a prominent triangular foothold.
1. 50m 6b Climb left and up on cleaned edges to a thin crack. Make difficult moves right through a bulge to better holds, then up right to the peg on Risk Business. (Three ropes were used on this section, with side runners on the tree and in Uncertain Emotions). Follow Risk Business to just before its belay, then climb a shallow groove in the arete, past overlaps, to pull onto the capping wall with difficulty. Continue more easily to belay below Carnivore pitch 4.
2. 20m 6b Move out left to a prominent undercling and climb direct with difficulty to a mysterious old sling. Step left then up to the roof, then traverse diagonally left to the belay at the top of Risk Business pitch 3.
3. 50m Climb easily to the top.

18   The Risk Business   120m   E5 ***   (1980)
The obvious counter-diagonal to Carnivore provides a modern classic. Start at a tree at the foot of Outlandos.
1. 25m 6a Climb up and left to a poor peg and place a Friend 2 under the overlap. From the peg, either traverse horizontally left or step down first and then go left to better holds and protection. Continue up until an exposed left traverse leads to a ledge and peg belays below a prominent groove.
2. 15m 5c Climb the unprotected groove to a ledge on Carnivore.
3. 30m 6a Move left then up a short wall to a ledge below a small overhang. Pass this on its left and climb a short groove to another small overhang. Pull over leftwards in a very airy position and continue up a groove to a ledge.
4. 50m Continue more easily in the same line to the top.

19   Gone with the Wind   75m   E6 ***   (1984)
This superb route climbs the hanging pink slab and bulges above The Risk Business (not to be confused with another overlap below) and then cleaves a direct line through the original traverse of Carnivore.
1. 45m 6b Climb the corner of Outlandos and traverse left to good holds at the start of the pink slab. Arrange protection in the groove

above, then follow a difficult descending traverse to a crucial foothold above the lip of the overlap below. In an intimidating position go left across a groove to a good hold and nut placement at the foot of a slightly bigger groove. Move up to a slightly better position and arrange an assortment of dubious wires. Ascend to the bulge above and climb this with difficulty (poor peg) to the easier upper section. Trend slightly left, then arch back right to a small ledge and peg belay on Bloodline.
2. 30m 6a Go left on the hanging slab (Bloodline) then break up and slightly right to the Carnivore traverse. Continue steeply up the scooped groove, make a difficult move to exit right to easier ground and continue to a grass ledge. Easy steep climbing leads to the top.

20   Bloodline 95m E3 **   (1984)
A good route taking the obvious diagonal crack above the start of Gone With the Wind.
1. 45m 5c Climb the corner and break out left to climb the crack. This leads steeply onto the upper wall. Now weave a line up and left, at times quite boldly, to a peg belay.
2. 25m 5c Traverse the hanging slab on the left and continue up and round into Carnivore.
3. 25m 5c The Villain's Finish.

The following routes start up and right of Tunnel Wall.

21   Walk with Destiny 100m E2 **   (1978)
A fairly sustained climb up the less steep right-hand section.
1. 40m 5b Follow Cayman Groove until it is possible to move left to a crack system. Follow this with little deviation to a grass ledge. Walk left to the right end of the Carnivore traverse.
2. 20m 5b/c Climb the wall and bulge above to a horizontal break. Climb the bulge above the break and continue to a ledge.
3. 40m 5a Climb the obvious shallow groove and continue up the wall to a ledge and belay. This pitch is unprotected.

22   Cayman Groove 70m E1 *   (1959)
Start 7m left of the obvious wide crack, beneath a corner. A good first pitch.
1. 40m 5b Follow the slim corner and awkward crack, step right at the top and up the wall to a ledge and belay below a chimney.
2. 30m 4c Climb the chimney to the top.

23   Piranha   70m   VS *   (1959)
The obvious wide crack.
1. 30m 4c Climb the crack and traverse left to ledge and belay.
2. 40m Continue up the wall above.

24   Reptile   70m   Severe   (1975)
1. 35m From the top of a large pedestal at the right end of the crag, climb a crack and a chimney to a ledge.
2. 35m Continue to the top.

25   The Flying Scotsman   100m   III/IV   (1988)
This follows the obvious vegetated chimney line bounding the left side of the steep central section of the crag. Follow the rightward-rising ramp (left of and above Carnivore) to a cave and chimney. Traverse right out of the cave, climb a steep wall and move back left above the chimney. Continue up the gully to a large block belay on the right. Finish up the wall above by an ice pillar and finally up easier ground.

CREAG NA TULAICH

This nice wee crag is just above and set back slightly from Creag a' Bhancair. It is well worth a visit in its own right. From the tops of both Creag a' Bhancair and Creag na Tulaich rocky spurs descend into the lower reaches of Coire na Tulaich. Approach up a broad grassy corridor thus formed between the two spurs. Descent is down the west side.

East Route   45m   Moderate   (1947)
Start at the south end of the east face, just left of the cairn of Arrowhead Groove. Climb a square-cut corner followed by the line of least resistance to the top.

Arrowhead Groove   45m   Very Difficult   (1947)
Start just right of the left end of the face, below a rock arrowhead perched on a platform 10m up. Climb a groove to the arrowhead, traverse left and climb easily to the top.

Dwindle Wall   45m   HVS 5a *   (1958)
This follows the line of a faint ramp trending right across the face. Start below a fault at an overhang near the left edge. Climb the steep fault and the delicate slab above.

Too Cold for Comfort   45m   E3 5c **   (1984)
This follows a pale streak to the left of Easy Going, starting slightly
down and to its left. Climb directly up the wall with slowly improving
protection in the three horizontal breaks. Continue up thin cracks and
short walls to the top.

Easy Going   45m   E2 5b **   (1977)
The obvious left-facing groove. Start by scrambling to a small tree
beneath the groove. Where the groove peters out, move up then left
to a small block overhang. Go left again to better holds on a narrow
ramp. Follow this rightwards (unprotected but not hard), then climb to
a large ledge and belay just below the top.

Crest Route   60m   Moderate *   (1934)
A pleasant route up the right edge of the face.

The Bidean nam Bian Massif

Bidean nam Bian (1150m) the highest peak in Argyll, is the culminating point of a large and complex massif comprising nine satellite tops, four main ridges and three great corries. The summit ridge of Bidean stretches from An t-Sron in the north-west, over the shapely peak of Stob Coire nam Beith to Bidean itself, and then out to Stob Coire Sgreamhach in the south-east. A long ridge extends north-east from Stob Coire Sgreamhach to terminate in a blunt nose overlooking Glen Coe; this is Beinn Fhada. Running parallel to it, and further west are the twin ridges of Gearr Aonach and Aonach Dubh which radiate from perhaps the finest of Bidean's satellites, Stob Coire nan Lochan. This peak, which is only 35m lower than Bidean itself, stands one kilometre north-east of the main summit. These three long ridges all terminate abruptly in steep, blunt noses: The Three Sisters of Glen Coe. Three principal corries lie between these ridges and the main ridge. From east to west they are Coire Gabhail (The Lost Valley), Coire nan Lochan, and Coire nam Beith.

Surprisingly the summit of Bidean is the only Munro. This should not deter the mountaineer from exploring the delights of the 'lesser hills', for to approach Bidean solely for the purpose of standing on its summit is a pity indeed. Bidean's ridges offer some rewarding high-level walking, particularly in winter. Suggested starting routes with a mountaineering flavour, which might be used as approaches to other climbs, are Sron na Lairig (II) on Stob Coire Sgreamhach, The Zig-Zags (I) on Gearr Aonach, Dinner-time Buttress (I) on Aonach Dubh and Summit Gully (I/II) on Stob Coire nam Beith. None of these are recommended descents.

The climbing in this massif is described under the following headings: Stob Coire Sgreamhach and Beinn Fhada, Gearr Aonach, Aonach Dubh, Stob Coire nan Lochan, Bidean nam Bian, Stob Coire nam Beith and An t-Sron. The roadside crags of the Glen Coe Gorge, The Bendy and Allt Doire Beith are described in the Outlying Climbs section. The small crags west of Glencoe village will be described in the forthcoming SMC Highland Outcrops guide.

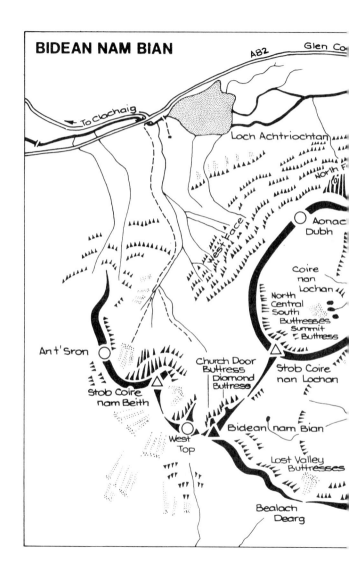

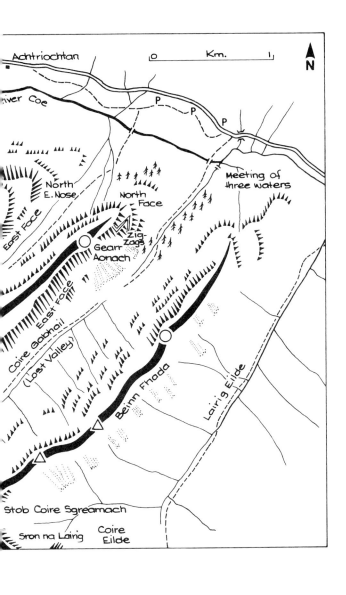

STOB COIRE SGREAMHACH AND BEINN FHADA
1070m   (Map Ref 155 537)

Stob Coire Sgreamhach is the shapely peak at the south-west end of the Beinn Fhada ridge. Its west face has an alpine character and offers a number of easy (I/II) routes which provide elementary route finding exercises. A direct line taking in all the obstacles, and finishing at the summit cairn, provides a highly enjoyable outing with steps of grade III. There are a few climbs on the north flank of the south-east ridge of Stob Coire Sgreamhach. Approach from the Glen Coe side of the Lairig Eilde at a signposted footpath to Glen Etive (188 563). A long but easy walk of about four kilometres leads to the corrie. Alternatively start at Dalness in Glen Etive.

Sron na Lairig   300m   II ***   (1934)
The prominent subsidiary ridge descending north-east into the Lairig Eilde gives an excellent outing with a remote and alpine feel. The broad lower part, with a central gully with a spur on each side, is open to much variation. Higher, the route takes a well-defined crest, similar in parts to the Aonach Eagach. This is usually gained by a snaking line on the left side; harder variations on ice exist to the right.
    To the left of Sron na Lairig, high up under the main south-east ridge, are two short parallel ribs. On their left is a prominent shallow gully which runs the full length of the face. A short steep grade III climbs the gully between the two ribs. Right of Sron na Lairig, under the summit buttress, an easy grade I gully climb leads up to join the arete of the normal route.
    The best descent from the top of Sron na Lairig is to go south-east to a col (164 528) and then north into the Lairig Eilde. Alternatively, continue over the summit of Stob Coire Sgreamhach to the col at the head of the Lost Valley, but note that the broad gully descending north-east from this col can be corniced and is subject to avalanche.
    Beinn Fhada (927m), the eastmost of the Three Sisters, is the fine ridge terminating in a blunt nose of shattered rock overlooking the Meeting of Three Waters. There is not much to interest the climber, although the hillside above the Lost Valley has some potential; indeed, a number of climbs have been done here in both summer and winter. The prominent arete at the foot of these crags, as they turn the corner into the Lost Valley, is **Big Al's Arete**, E2 5b. After a prolonged cold

spell a number of icefalls form on the east face and although most have been climbed, only the most prominent one has been recorded.

The Bubble   60m   III/IV *   (1982)
The prominent icefall, easily seen from the road, which forms low down on the right side of the north-east face towards the north face. Climb it in two pitches to finish up a short groove.

High on the north-east side of Beinn Fhada there is a steep little face, possibly the same crag that contains The Bubble. **Kak** (80m Very Difficult 1965) starts below an obvious groove and climbs straight up its centre.

The north face comprises the blunt nose of shattered rock overlooking the road. A diagonal fault runs up left from beneath the face; midway up is a detached pillar.

Triple 'C' Special   55m   HVS 5a   (1978)
Christine's Cracked Cranium (!).
1. 30m From the base of the pillar take a central line up the buttress going left at the base of the obvious arete. Follow a grassy fault to a tree.
2. 25m Continue up the fault to the rear of the pinnacle, climb a crack to a platform, then move left and up to the top.

The entrance to Coire Gabhail (The Lost Valley) is sharply defined by the steep frontal noses of Gearr Aonach and Beinn Fhada. Most of the climbing in the corrie, especially in summer, is on Gearr Aonach, both on the frontal nose and on its east face. At the head of the Lost Valley on the summit ridge of Bidean lie the two Lost Valley buttresses.

The approach begins by crossing the River Coe by a footbridge (173 564) just below The Meeting of Three Waters. A well-made path climbs up the right side of the wooded gorge of the Allt Coire Gabhail. The path levels out at the deeply cut entrance to the main gorge. Here another path branches off right up a rocky bluff towards the nose of Gearr Aonach. The path to the corrie continues through the gorge to a large boulder opposite the slabby Sentry Crag. Ahead is a formidable barrier of jumbled boulders and trees formed by a huge landslip from Gearr Aonach. Cross the river and by-pass the boulder field easily around its left side to a magnificant viewpoint of the well named Lost Valley. A short descent leads to the flat valley floor. There is a huge boulder at the start of the valley, the Lost Valley Boulder, which sports several problems.

If the best path is missed, one is plunged into the midst of the boulder field. Entertaining though this may be, especially when breaking trail in the dark through deep snow, the chance of dropping down a hole is best avoided! However, it may be necessary if the river is in spate. It is also possible to by-pass the boulder field up on the right.

Beyond the boulder field a remarkably different picture stretches ahead; a long flat plain has accumulated behind the landslide. Throughout this flat section, unless in spate, the river runs underground. Hemmed in by towering walls, the atmosphere of peace and seclusion is very noticeable. At the far end of the flat section the path rises up the right side of the upper gorge to the obvious col at the head of the Lost Valley, the Bealach Dearg.

WEST FACE OF BEINN FHADA

The hillside dropping into the Lost Valley holds a number of crags, all approachable from the Lost Valley or the Beinn Fhada ridge. Descent from the ridge into the Lost Valley is possible, but it is safer to drop into the Lairig Eilde to the east, taking care of rocky outcrops. Do not attempt to descend from the nose at the termination of the ridge.

SENTRY CRAG (Map Ref 170 558)
This is the slabby crag beside the Lost Valley path on the east side of the stream, just before the boulder field at an altitude of about 300m. It is slow drying.

Sentry Slabs Direct   100m   VS 4c   (1989)
Start at the lowest point of the lowest tier at a clean pink slab between two prominent water streaks. Climb an easy slab to a black bulge. Go over this, then up slabs to the top of a ramp which slopes down left. Climb the extreme right of the wall behind and continue directly up bulging slabs until an obvious traverse leads right to a tree. Climb a short, pink wall to easy ground.

Screw   80m   Very Difficult   (1960)
1. 25m Starting towards the left end of the main face, go up easy slabs to an overlap and tree. Traverse 6m right, surmount an overlap and continue to easy slabs. There is a steep wall beyond.
2. 25m Take the line of least resistance on the right, then move left to an overhang.
3. 30m Move right and up slabs to the top.

Smiley's Indecision   50m   E1   (1990)
Start near the centre of the slab, above and diagonally right of a short
steep wall.
1. 25m 5a Climb easily diagonally left to the leftmost and turfiest of
two cracks. Climb the slab between the crack and the left arete until
moves can be made right to the belay of Showcase.
2. 25m Move left and continue the same line to easy ground. Descend
by abseil, or by easy slabs and walls to the terrace.

Showcase   50m   HVS   (1987)
1. 25m 5a Follow Smiley's Indecision to the two cracks. Climb the
right-hand one straight up to a belay.
2. 25m 4a Continue direct to the top. Abseil descent.

Eugallt   45m   HVS   4c/5a   (1989)
Follow Smiley's Indecision for a few metres until a hard traverse right
can be made into the centre of the slab. Climb up and very slightly
right to a good runner at 12m, then continue boldly to the top.

White Spiral   90m   Severe   (1960)
Takes the smooth mass of slab at the right end of the main face.
1. 25m Easy at first, the slab steepens to force a kind of spiral line to
a heather patch. Traverse 3m left to a small stance.
2. 30m Climb up right to a steepening. Traverse left to a tree.
3. 35m Easier slabs lead up right to the top.

After a cold spell a number of icefalls form here, which give several
good pitches. Easier ice on the right provides good introductory
climbing. One route has been recorded.

Bop Till You Drop   105m   IV *   (1981)
The steepest central icefall.
1. 30m Climb to a small ice cave and rock belay.
2. 30m Go up and right to a small tree.
3. 45m Move horizontally left onto vertical ice, then straight up to a
fallen tree.

ECHO CRAG (Map Ref 170 552)
Directly above the Lost Valley Boulder two shallow gullies slant up the
hillside. Echo Crag lies high up on the ridge near the top of the
right-hand gully. It is so named because a double echo can be obtained
from Gearr Aonach and the Aonach Eagach.

Echo Crag Route   60m   Very Difficult   (1945)
Start near the left-hand corner, right of a small gully which separates
the route from a smaller, beetling crag. Climb up near the corner, take
in a steep slab on small holds and make for a triangular recess, belay.
Go obliquely right to climb a 6m crack leading to easier ground and
the top.

WEST FACE BUTTRESS (Map Ref 166 546)
This crag lies high up the hillside, at about 700m, directly above the
southern end of the flat section of the Lost Valley, from whence it is
reached. It can also be gained from the ridge to the north-east. A
narrow, twisting chimney provides a useful landmark. The gully on the
right of the crag provides an easy route (I/II).

The Midge   120m   II/III   (1969)
Climb the buttress crest to the left of the narrow twisting chimney at
the left side of the crag. From a wide snow ledge it is possible to gain
and finish up a gully on the left.

The Wasp   120m   III **   (1969)
The narrow, twisting chimney gives a good route. It is climbed in two
pitches with hard moves at the top of each. Easier ground leads to the
top.

The Cleg   120m   III/IV   (1969)
From near the start of The Wasp follow a diagonal line up right. The
crux is a narrow hanging scoop.

   Somewhere on this cliff may lie **Greez** (75m Severe 1965), which
climbs the slabby wall left of a prominent grassy corner which splits
the west face above the Lost Valley gorge.

NORTH-WEST FACE BUTTRESS (Map Ref 161 542)
Although called the North-West Face, this cliff lies further south on the
Beinn Fhada Ridge than the West Face, beneath the summit of Beinn
Fhada. It can be reached from the flat valley floor by going up right,
or by continuing up the Lost Valley path beyond the upper gorge until
it is possible to head up left towards it. The face can also be reached
from the ridge.

Broken Lip Gully   175m   II *   (1969)
From a snow bay at the left side of the buttress follow a chimney-gully line which runs parallel with Main Buttress.

Main Buttress   200m   II   (1969)
From the lowest rocks take a direct line up the buttress, going slightly right after the first pitch to climb a short snow gully. Break left onto the buttress and finish by a variety of lines.

The Direct Route   75m   Very Difficult   (1949)
Start at the lowest rocks. Climb easily to a 25m pitch on good holds up a vertical wall, then a right traverse across an outward sloping slab to finish by a left traverse. A wide step from a detached block gains a wide undercut crack which leads past a chockstone to a finish up two short walls on good holds.

Twine Climb   180m   II *   (1969)
Climb the chimney-scoop line right of Main Buttress, then traverse left on snow to take a parallel line to the top, just right of that route.

Starting some 20m right of and 15m above Direct Route, **South West Rib** (Moderate 1949) climbs an avoidable steep nose to the crest of the rib, then trends right with left traverses between pitches. Keep fairly close to the right edge of the buttress.

Quintet   135m   III *   (1969)
Climb the snowy corridor which cuts diagonally across the face from left to right. Start a short way up the obvious ramp. Climb an iced chimney to a block belay. Continue to a narrowing section of the gully, then bridge up and right over the edge to the true corridor. An awkward section leads to easier ground.

The Ramp   210m   II *   (1969)
Climb the obvious ramp running up right to the crest.

At the southern end of the flat section of the Lost Valley is the **Upper Gorge**, Severe (1942). This provides a number of pitches leading to a conspicuous high waterfall, where an exit is made up the 45m very friable right wall.

The Black Crack   50m   Severe   (1959)
Climb the prominent black crack on a buttress just left of where the ground begins to rise again, left of the upper gorge.

SOUTH-EAST RIDGE OF BIDEAN NAM BIAN

The south-east ridge of Bidean drops from the summit for just over one kilometre to the Bealach Dearg at the head of Coire Gabhail, and then rises a short distance to Stob Coire Sgreamhach. On the north-east side of the ridge between Bidean and the bealach there are two conspicuous buttresses overlooking the head of Coire Gabhail.

LOST VALLEY MINOR BUTTRESS (Map Ref 149 538)

The smaller and left-hand of the two buttresses lies just to the north-west of the Bealach Dearg at the head of the Lost Valley. Facing north-east at an altitude of about 900m, this crag readily comes into winter condition. The approach to it continues up the path in Coire Gabhail beyond the upper gorge towards the col, then goes up right (allow about 2 hours).

Descent is possible by either of the gullies left of the crag (I), which are separated by a rocky rib, or the gully to the right of the crag (I), which may have a large cornice. Alternatively, follow the ridge east to the col at the head of the Lost Valley (151 537). There is likely to be a small cornice. If the slope is doubtful due to avalanche danger, continue over Stob Coire Sgreamhach and down its south-east ridge to a col (164 528), then descend into the Lairig Eilde.

1   Left Edge Route   80m   III   (1959)
Near the left edge of the buttress is an obvious gangway.
1. 40m Follow the gangway up left to below a short corner.
2. 40m Climb the corner to the top.

2   Left Wall Route   90m   Severe   (1955)
Starting left of and below the obvious chimney, climb to a platform, then traverse right to near a chimney. Go left and up on pock-like holds, then climb a bulge followed by steep lichenous rock.

3   Chimney Route   80m   III/IV *   (1959)
The obvious chimney provides several interesting chockstone problems. In summer it is a vile Very Difficult (1955).

4   Minor Issue   80m   IV *   (1988)
Climbs the corner-groove line left of the buttress edge between Chimney Route and Central Scoop.
1. 15m Climb the corner-groove to a ledge.

2. 20m Move left and climb a corner to a small block, step right and follow a groove to easy ground.
3. 45m Easily to near the top.

5   Central Scoop   75m   IV *   (1969)
The chimney-corner just up and right from Minor Issue is followed to more open buttress climbing.

6   Right Edge   130m   III/IV **   (1959)
The main central corner and ramp line leading up right beneath the headwall gives a fine varied route with some good situations.
1. 40m Ascend the chimney past a chockstone, then go up an icy groove to a belay in the corner.
2. 45m Move up to the headwall either via the corner or by its slabby right wall, then traverse awkwardly up right to the edge. Care should be taken in arranging protection.
3. 45m A shallow gully leads to easy snow slopes and the top.

7   Minor Adjustment   115m   IV **   (1989)
This is the obvious groove and corner just up the gully from Right Edge, a direct line joining that route after its upper traverse.
1. 45m Climb the steep groove to a small ledge and spike, then follow a ramp steeply up left around the edge to ledges. A short traverse right leads back to the corner; belay 3m higher.
2. 25m Continue up the corner, then move right and climb a short groove to step right below a small roof. Follow the snow ramp to a short wide crack and climb this to a belay.
3. 45m Easier ground to the top.

8   Grannies' Groove   70m   III
The right branch of the gully right of the crag has a steep scoop which sometimes has an overhang, taken on the left.

LOST VALLEY BUTTRESS (Map Ref 148 540)

This, the right-hand and larger of the two buttresses, is divided by a great central groove into an easier-angled left half and, set back at a higher level, the steeper right half. Approach as for the Minor Buttress, or, from the top of the upper gorge, follow the right bank of the deeply-cut stream which descends from the col between Bidean and Stob Coire nan Lochan. This leads over two steepenings to a level section which continues to the slopes (possibly avalanche-prone)

THE LOST VALLEY BUTTRESSES

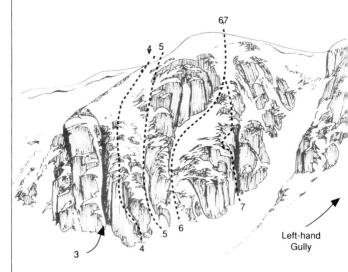

3. Chimney Route
4. Minor Issue
5. Central Scoop
6. Right Edge

7. Minor Adjustment
10. Sabre Tooth
11. Delusion
12. Directosaur

15. Pterodactyl
17. Neanderthal
18. Savage
19. Barracuda

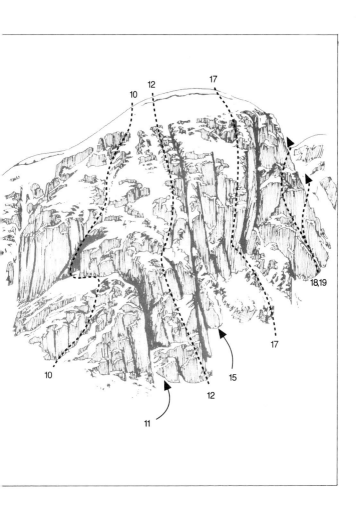

beneath the crag. The buttress can also be reached from the col between Bidean nam Bian and Stob Coire nan Lochan, or via the Zig-Zags on Gearr Aonach followed by skirting Stob Coire nan Lochan.

Descent Gully to the right of the crag (see below) provides a way down; from the top of the buttress head north-west along the ridge a short way, passing the top of Right-hand Gully. There is a convenient boulder (146 540) which can be used if an abseil is required to break through the cornice. This gully can be prone to avalanche. The alternative is to use any of the descents from the Minor Buttress, described above.

9   Left-hand Gully   120m   I
This gully, running up the left side of the buttress, is bounded on the left by an indefinite rib of rock. It provides straightforward climbing, but has a steep corniced exit.

10   Sabre Tooth   120m   III/IV *   (1969)
Towards the right-hand side of the left half of the buttress there is a prominent vertical corner. Start up left from this corner. Climb to a snow bay, break out right, gain the terrace and then traverse left to a steep, shallow corner (which is also approachable by a traverse from the left). Climb the corner to a line of grooves which lead to the top.

11   Delusion   120m   Very Difficult   (1966)
The prominent vertical corner. Scramble to its base. Climb the left wall by cracks and huge flakes to a belay in the corner 6m below its top. Climb a chimney, then walk left along a terrace until the corner of Sabre Tooth can be followed back up right. Grassy grooves lead to the top.
Winter: IV *
As for the summer line, a harder version of Sabre Tooth.

12   Directosaur   160m   V **   (1989)
A good route based on Tyrannosaur, but taking a much more direct line up the right-hand edge of the left half of the buttress, with only the short corner of that route in common. Start at the lowest rocks below the edge.
1. 45m Climb the shallow groove just left of the edge, step left and move up to a ledge leading back right to the edge. Ascend a steep

flake crack on the left, then easier ground to below the Tyrannosaur corner.
2. 30m Climb the corner, then follow grooves up the right side of a huge block-like feature and continue up to its top.
3. 35m Move across right and climb a short groove to regain the crest. Snow grooves now lead to the upper rocks.
4. 50m Continue up the snow grooves to the final slopes.

13   Original Route   120m   Severe   (1942)
Takes the right-hand edge of the left half of the buttress. Start under the edge.
    Climb 12m on grass to a prominent patch of moss. Go slightly left for 12m on a steep, delicate slab to a small ledge on the buttress crest. The smooth bulge above is the crux and leads to easier climbing on good rock to the top.

14   Tyrannosaur   150m   V *   (1969)
Start about 10m up from lowest rocks of the right edge. Climb a shallow chimney, then the thin continuation crack slanting slightly left over the buttress edge to a snow bay. Climb the steep corner, then follow grooves up the left side of a huge block-like feature to easier grooves which lead to the top.

15   Pterodactyl (Moonlight Gully)   105m   V *   (1964)
The great central groove of the buttress. The upper section is a narrow gully, guarded by a 2m overhang. Start from the highest point of the snow bay beneath the line. Follow the steep corner to a stance beneath the overhang. Climb the crack on the left with aid (on the rare occasions that the icicle on the right forms it can be climbed free). The narrow upper gully leads more easily to the top.

16   Moonlighting   120m   V **   (1988)
Takes an obvious line right of Pterodactyl. Start at the top of the bay beneath a groove.
1. 35m Gain the groove and climb to a ledge at the foot of a wall.
2. 35m Climb the steep flakeline up on the left, moving left at its top to the edge overlooking Pterodactyl, then up and right to a shallow groove leading to a short wall.
3. 50m Move into the gully of Pterodactyl and follow this to the top (all the more appreciated when climbed by moonlight!).

17   Neanderthal   120m   VI ***   (1987)
An improbable line up the huge corner about 30m right of Pterodactyl.
Superb climbing in an impressive situation.
1. 20m Easily up a gully, then its left wall to a ledge.
2. 15m Traverse right and climb chute to belay at the cul-de-sac.
3. 20m Move out right until it is possible to move up to a roof and gain
the base of the corner. Climb this to a small ledge.
4. 25m Continue up the corner to the right side of a square roof, then
move left beneath this to cracks in a recessed wall. Climb the cracks
over a small roof and through the final eaves by the narrow slot which
is clearly visible from below, lurking on the skyline. Belay by large
blocks a short way above.
5. 40m Up the short corner to easy snow slopes and the top.

The Primordial Soup Kitchen (HVS 5a 1987), is a loose and vegetated line starting just right of Neanderthal. A low-angled arete leads
to a steep wall. Move right, take a flake in the left wall of a small corner
then move right to climb the right side of the obvious monolith.

18   Savage   80m   V **   (1988)
Climbs the obvious monolith on the wall right of Neanderthal, gained
from the left-trending ramp starting from the edge of the buttress.
1. 20m Follow the ramp up left to a belay at the foot of the monolith.
2. 10m Attack the corner-crack up the right side of the monolith. Belay
on its top if successful!
3. 50m Climb stepped walls and grooves directly above until further
progress is barred, then traverse right and around the buttress edge
to a shallow groove. Climb the groove, then the rib just left of the
steepening on Barracuda and step right to finish as for that route;
chockstone belay a little higher.

19   Barracuda   80m   V **   (1988)
Takes the obvious steep crack springing from the left-trending ramp.
Start as for Savage. The easiest of the harder routes hereabouts.
1. 10m Follow the ramp past a groove to belay beneath a crack.
2. 20m Climb the crack to the buttress edge and belay 5m higher in
a shallow gully.
3. 50m Follow the gully directly, over a steepening, to the top.

20   Dislocation   85m   III   (1969)
Starting 15m up from Barracuda and the right edge of the main face,
this route follows a groove trending slightly right to a snow patch, then
finishes up a shallow broken chimney.

21 Trilobite 60m   II/III *   (1969)
Follow Right-hand Gully to the point where it starts to narrow opposite
a ramp running steeply up right, and climb the steep groove which
runs up the face.

22 Right-hand Gully 100m   I/II
The gully bounding the right side of the buttress, steep with a big
cornice, it often contains a small ice pitch.

23 The Ramp 100m   I/II
Follow Right-hand Gully to where it narrows opposite Trilobite, then
take the ramp running steeply up right.

24 Descent Gully I
Separated from Right-hand Gully by a rocky rib. Straightforward with
a small (usually!) cornice.

25 Short Gully 30m   II
The narrow gully-chimney in the rocks right of Descent Gully.

GEARR AONACH

691m   (Map Ref 163 557)

This, the middle of the Three Sisters, is the north-east ridge of Stob
Coire nan Lochan. The north face presents a remarkable dome of
steep rock overlooking Glen Coe. To the left of the dome is the
North-East Face whilst further up the Lost Valley lies the East Face.
The quickest approach to the ridge is a series of traverse ledges, the
Zig-Zags, running up broken ground between the nose and the
North-East Face. The Zig-Zags are fully described in the North-East
Face section. The only recommended descent in winter is to head
south along the ridge into Coire nan Lochan and to come down the
east side of the waterfall issuing from the corrie.

EAST FACE (Map Ref 162 554)

This face overlooks the flat section of the Lost Valley, from whence it
is easily gained. The lower face is criss-crossed by horizontal ledges.
The upper half is formed by a steep continuous wall, rising over 100m
from a broad grassy alp to meet the summit ridge. This is the Mome
Rath Face, which is defined by the long, left-trending gullies of Lost

Leeper on the left, and Rev Ted's on the right. These two gullies, or a route up the lower walls between them, allow access to the face. In winter the face does not come into condition often since it faces south-east and is at an altitude of only about 600m, but when it does a number of excellent ice lines form, all of which have a tremendous outlook. In summer the face is slow to dry.

Descent is possible down the grassy buttress left of Lost Leeper, or more safely down easy slopes further south, or down the Zig-Zags. However, the surest and the safest descent, especially in winter, is via Coire nan Lochan. The routes are described from left to right.

At the extreme left end of the face there are four main gullies, the leftmost three being hidden until one is almost directly beneath them. Approach from the path rising up the hillside beyond the flat section of the Lost Valley.

1   Gully C   245m   I
A useful winter descent, this is the long, shallow couloir at the extreme left before the cliffs fade out entirely. There can be a few short pitches.

2   Gully B   245m   II
This, the second-last of the four main gullies, is straightforward except for one large chockstone pitch.

3   Gully A (Right Fork)   245m   III/IV **   (1964)
The first gully encountered once the path starts to rise at the southern end of the Lost Valley. A steep, initial pitch leads to the bifurcation where the steep ice scoop on the right leads to easier climbing up the gully. In summer this fork is Very Difficult (1955).

From the bifurcation the Central Branch (IV 1969) continues directly up a steep ice scoop. The Left Branch (IV 1970) starts as a steep ice pitch slightly left of the main gully.

4   M   65m   Severe †   (1966)
Low down to the left of Lost Leeper Gully is a wall, capped by an enormous roof. This route starts 10m left of the roof.
1. 40m Climb a grassy crack up right to a ledge, traverse right to surmount a bulge, then trend right to a break in the roofs. Climb the roof using a peg and belay below a prominent chimney.
2. 25m Climb the chimney, breaking out right to finish.

5   Lost Leeper Gully   300m   III **   (1969)
Rising from the end of the flat section of the Lost Valley, this shallow, indefinite gully bounds the left side of the Mome Rath Face. In winter

it provides interesting route finding with, higher up, the possibility of some ice pitches. Belays in the main part of the gully are poor, and it is avalanche prone.

The following routes lie on the short walls under the grassy alp beneath the main face. The largest of the walls is split by two cracks. Left of this, adjacent to Lost Leeper Gully, is a smaller wall split by a prominent crack.

6 Goldfinger 50m Hard Severe   (1964)
The prominent crack on the small wall next to Lost Leeper Gully.

7 Slimcrack 60m Severe   (1965)
The left of two cracks on the largest wall.

8 The Burning 60m E1   (1990)
Start mid-way between Slimcrack and the left edge of a brown streak on the clean wall to its right.
1. 30m 5a Climb the wall fairly directly to a belay.
2. 30m Continue up the easier wall above.

9 Batura Wall 60m HVS   (1989)
Start immediately left of a large brown streak of rock on the clean wall a short way left of Flake Groove.
1. 30m 5a Climb directly up through an obvious break in the wall just left of the brown streak to a small ledge below a bulge at 15m. Climb up right to brown rock until a short traverse left can be made above the bulge. A crack leads to a belay.
2. 30m Finish up easier rocks.

10 Flake Groove 70m Very Difficult *   (1967)
The right-hand crack, a right-trending cracked groove, is often wet.
1. 25m Climb the groove past a pinnacle to a ledge. The pinnacle demands great care.
2. 10m Traverse left across the exposed wall, then move up to a small stance with a thread.
3. 35m Go left up slabs and walls. Scramble to the top.

A variation (Severe) which is more often dry starts up the groove's edge, enters it higher up and continues to a ledge before finishing directly up walls.

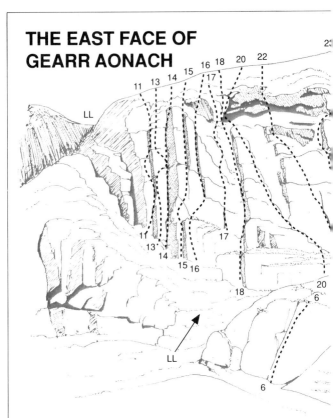

THE EAST FACE OF GEARR AONACH

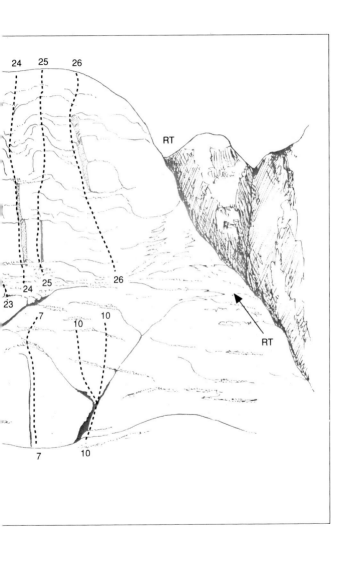

MOME RATH FACE (Map Ref 162 554)

The grassy alp beneath this face does not quite extend to the left end of the face. Summer routes on the left side offer fine climbing and begin from Lost Leeper Gully.

In winter a large number of ice-streaks can form on this wall and there are some excellent routes. A prominent icicle fringe forms on the upper overhangs.

The left edge of the face is defined by a prominent deeply recessed diedre, the line of Rainmaker. Smersh, and the routes to its right as far as Rev Ted's Gully, start from the alp.

11   Persuasion   60m   HVS 5a   (1958)
Start at the left end of the face, at a fault 10m left of the deeply recessed diedre. Climb the fault to a crack, step left up a gangway and gain a ledge. Move up to a large flake and overhang, then climb to a crack and continue on good holds to finish.

12   Demoniser   105m   VS †   (1977)
It is not certain how this route relates to others in this area. Start at a large flake at a recess in the middle of the Persuasion buttress.
1. 40m Climb the obvious crack.
2. 30m Climb direct to an overhang.
3. 35m Traverse right into a groove, then up easier ground.

13   Sundance   90m   VS 4c *   (1980)
Climbs the wall between Persuasion and Rainmaker. Start below a short chimney on the wall immediately left of the deep recessed diedre.
1. 35m Climb the chimney, go up and left behind blocks to the left edge, then follow short walls to a large ledge on Rainmaker.
2. 35m Above are two roofs. Follow the chimney of Rainmaker for a few metres, then traverse left between the roofs and continue up the wall on good holds.
3. 20m Finish either on the wall above or left and up the corner of Persuasion.

14   Rainmaker   60m   Hard Severe ***   (1958)
Takes the deeply recessed diedre about 10m right of Persuasion.
Winter: V ***   (1980)
1. 45m Climb the shallow chimney left of the main corner (Sundance), then continue up ice-smears to an ice belay left of the icicle recess.

2. 45m Climb the chimney through the recess, avoiding the corner on the left. Regain the corner for the final 10m. Belay on a rock rib to the right.
3. 15m Ice, then easy snow leads to the top.

15   Snowstormer   85m   HVS 5a **   (1974)
An attractive route, closely following the exposed edge overlooking Rainmaker. Start on a steep wall, 10m below Rainmaker, at patches of white lichen.
1. 25m Climb a small overhung corner to an awkward move left onto a slab. Pass a second overhang by the arete on the right. Climb more easily to belay below a slanting slab.
2. 30m Climb the slab or traverse left to the edge and move up. Climb the corner to below a steep wall.
3. 30m Start the wall on its left edge, go up and right into a corner, then up to a bulge at 10m. Pass the bulge by a left traverse to a niche on the left edge, and so to easier ground.
Winter: V ***   (1984)
Climb the first summer pitch direct to a belay on a small pedestal above the obvious V-notch. Icy corners directly above lead to a belay under a small overlap overlooking Rainmaker. Easier to the top.

16   Smersh   120m   VS 4b   (1965)
Start at the left end of the alp, a few metres right of the left edge, below a loose chimney. Climb a wall (45m) then a groove (20m) then traverse right beneath a bulge (15m). Climb an overhang at its right edge, move left over the main bulge and up a wall to finish.

17   Slithy   120m   Severe   (1967)
Start at extreme left end of the alp at a cairn. Above is a rib with, on either side, a shallow groove.
1. 20m Climb up and left to the left-hand groove which leads awkwardly to a ledge.
2. 25m Follow the cracks above.
3. 30m Continue up the fault to a bulge then go left to an obvious chimney.
4. 45m Climb the chimney and exit left to a grassy bay, then finish by a big flake and easier ground.

18   Outgrabe Route   115m   Very Difficult   (1954/66)
A direct start and variation finish to Mome Rath Route. About 25m right
of the left extremity of the alp, a light grey shelf of rock slants up and
left. Start 10m left of this, below two obvious cracklines.
1. 35m Climb to a recess and go left up a short slab-corner to the
left-hand crack. Follow this to a stance by a large block.
2. 30m Continue to a flat grassy eyrie at the foot of a steep, exposed
chimney (Mome Rath Route) left of large overhangs.
3. 50m Climb just left of the chimney to the top.
Winter: V ***   (1980)
A more direct and virtually independent line from that of the original
Mome Rath Face Route. Climb Outgrabe Route directly to the gully-
chimney fault and follow this in two pitches, keeping left of the icicle
fringe on the second.

19   Newsholme's Groove   140m   V   (1986)
The broad groove between Snowstormer and Mome Rath Route. It is
not known how this relates to earlier routes; it may be the same as the
previous one. Climbed when the cliff was in very icy condition.

20   Mome Rath Route   135m   Very Difficult **   (1954)
Start up the light grey shelf of rock which slants up and left, some 25m
right of the alp's left extremity. Climb the shelf to a flat grassy eyrie at
the foot of a steep exposed chimney, on the left of large overhangs
three quarters of the way up the face. The chimney leads to the top.

21   Mome Rath Face Route   150m   V ***   (1969)
The original winter route on this area of the face, climbed the same
day as The Wabe. It takes the left-slanting shelf to break out left from
the summer line about 20m up the steep chimney. Move left into
another chimney. Climb this a short way to a bay on the left, then finish
up the short steep corner-chimney of Slithy.

22   Jabberwock   105m   VS *   (1966)
This route lies under the main overhangs and demands dry conditions.
Immediately right of Mome Rath Route is a steep wall with a thin crack,
prominent from directly below. Climb the crack to a peg belay (35m).
Continue up the crack, then across slabs and up a short groove to a
good ledge. Go up a steep corner-crack on the left until it is possible
to swing onto the nose on the left. Continue up the wall to the top.

Winter: V **   (1984)
The obvious icefall between Mome Rath Route and The Wabe, taking in the icicle fringe at the top.

23   The Wabe   135m   Very Difficult **   (1954)
Start a few metres right of the grey shelf of Mome Rath Route. Climb a flake and groove to a stance below a small overhang. Go over this, steep but on good holds, to a slab, then right to a stance in a corner. Traverse left onto the wall and climb up to a large square block under overhangs. Traverse right and up a recessed panel, just right of the overhangs, to a stance on the rib to the right. Cross left to a slab above the overhang and go straight up to the top.
Winter: V ***   (1969)
An excellent and exposed route following, with minor deviations, the fine icefall descending the summer line, to the right of the icicle fringe. Start a few metres right of the summer line. Climb a wall to a ledge then head up left to a small stance just below a prominent nose; flake belay. Turn the nose on the left, immediately above an overhang, and go up the corner on the right to the pedestal below the right edge of the icicle fringe. Move right and climb the icefall through the recessed panel to a stance on the rib to the right. Go diagonally right, then back up left to finish.

24   Whimsy   120m   Severe   (1966)
In the centre of the face, about 10m up, is a large grass ledge. Rising from this is a rib split by a wide crack. Just left of the rib is a corner-crack, well seen from directly below. Climb the corner-crack in two pitches to belay below a steep wall with twin cracks. Climb the right-hand crack until it bulges, then move left into the other one. Easier climbing leads to a belay in a recess. Continue to the top.
Winter: IV **   (1984)
Climb the icefall which approximates the summer line.

25   Annie's Route   120m   HVS 5a   (1967)
1. 25m   Climb the wide crack just right of Whimsy.
2. 20m   Ascend the wall above, then traverse right to a groove.
3. 30m   Go up the right wall of the groove, over a bulge, then left into a crack. Follow this for 10m, then go left to a large stance.
4. 45m   Go back right into the crack and follow it to easy ground.

Right of Annie's Route the face becomes more vegetatious and broken before meeting a long left-slanting gully.

26   Mimsy   95m   Very Difficult   (1960)
Near the right end of the alp there is a right-slanting grassy groove.
About 6m right of this is a crack. Climb the crack, then broken rocks
to a grassy platform and nearby bushes. Follow the line of a shallow
gully and emerge left. Climb an exposed crack and continue to the top
by broken ledges and a steep 20m section.

27   Rev Ted's Gully   300m   II/III **   (1960)
The long, obvious gully slanting left up the full height of the face. The
lower reaches are straightforward and can be used to approach the
Mome Rath Face. From the junction in the upper cliffs there are several
options. Best is the iced chimney just left of an icefall, or the icefall
direct. There is also an easy right branch leading to a bay and another
steep chimney, interesting but awkward. From the bay an escape right
can be made, thus reducing the entire route to grade I/II. Avalanche
prone.

   To the right of Rev Ted's Gully the terrace continues. Above it a
series of grassy walls hold no summer interest, but in a good winter
an ice-ribbon, visible from the road, falls the height of the face. There
are eight routes on the hillside between Rev Ted's Gully and the
North-East Face at the mouth of the corrie.

28   Frostbite Wall   200m   IV *   (1969)
The obvious ice-ribbon which falls the height of the face is started by
a right traverse from its foot, then back left to gain it some 45m up by
a ledge. The ribbon then leads directly to the top.

29   Frostbite Groove   200m   IV   (1969)
Start up Frostbite Wall and climb to where it traverses back left across
an obvious ledge. Climb the iced chimney-groove going up slightly
right. After one pitch, break out left over an ice bulge to an ice-scoop.
Climb this and a small chimney to the top.

30   McArtney Gully   155m   II/III   (1969)
This gully, the second encountered on emerging from the boulder field
at the foot of the Lost Valley, takes the face right of the ice-ribbon of
Frostbite Wall and is gained from just left of the start of Ingrid's Folly.
The lower half is straightforward and the upper section, which can be
approached from either end of the mid-way terrace, takes an obvious
right-facing corner. Several pitches lead to a steepening, where a
chimney, then a diagonal groove, and finally the corner lead to the top.

31 Lady's Choice 160m III   (1969)
This route lies on the big wall to the right of McArtney Gully and starts at an obvious pale block. A grooveline curves up to the right, then back left to finish in a steep chimney with a chockstone.

32 GSWC Memorial Route 180m II   (1970)
The right edge of the buttress between McArtney Gully and Ingrid's Folly. A good introduction to the poorer routes in the Lost Valley!

33 Ingrid's Folly/Peregrine Gully 300m II/III **   (1960)
This long recessed gully system running the full height of the face is the first gully encountered on emerging from the boulder field in the Lost Valley. An entertaining combination of routes. Follow the gully of Ingrid's Folly with some amusement, including a through route, to the easier upper gully. An easy finish can be made up this, but further entertainment can be obtained by traversing up left into the shallow fault of Peregrine Gully. This provides further pitches of caves and chockstones. Avalanche prone.

34 John Gray's Buttress 300m II   (1968)
Take the easiest line up the long grassy buttress just right of Ingrid's Folly. A good freeze and heavy snowfall are required.

35 The Graduate 170m III/IV *   (1969)
This route takes the prominent, large right-facing corner which forms the left side of the huge recess from whence the Lost Valley landslide came. It is not often in full condition although it can provide steep turfy climbing after a hard freeze.

NORTH-EAST FACE (Map Ref 167 559)

This reasonably quick-drying face is at a height of about 420m, not far above the path into the Lost Valley. It extends rightwards from the stone shoot which fans into the boulder field. To its right are the Zig-Zags, then the nose of Gearr Aonach. About one kilometre from the road, after crossing a stile, the path into the Lost Valley levels out at the entrance to the lower gorge. Take the small path up a rocky bluff on the right, then follow grassy slopes up left to the lowest rocks where the first Zig-Zag runs out right. Please keep to the paths to help avoid further erosion.
    The face is divided by ledges, with the easier-angled right half being separated from the steeper left half by the obvious chimney-fault of

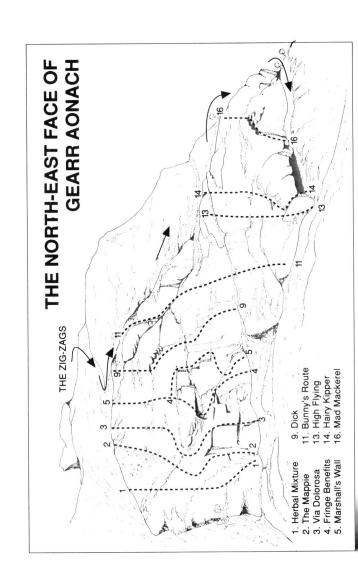

THE NORTH-EAST FACE OF GEARR AONACH

THE ZIG-ZAGS

1. Herbal Mixture
2. The Mappie
3. Via Dolorosa
4. Fringe Benefits
5. Marshall's Wall
9. Dick
11. Bunny's Route
13. High Flying
14. Hairy Kipper
16. Mad Mackerel

Bunny's Route. A short walk up left gains the steeper section, recognisable by a wide crack leading to a line of curving overhangs. Descend by walking off right to the Zig-Zags. It is also possible to abseil from various trees. The routes are described from left to right.

1   Herbal Mixture   70m   Hard Severe *   (1957)
Start below the left end of the overhangs, 10m left of the wide crack.
1. 30m Climb up and left by heather grooves to a ledge at 15m, then up and left again to a ledge in a corner.
2. 40m Go up slightly right to a ledge at 12m, then up and left across the final steep wall (poorly protected) to easier ground.

2   The Mappie   80m   VS **   (1959)
Start 5m left of the wide crack, below a thin, clean crack.
1. 40m 4c Climb to the obvious fine traverse line. Move left for 12m, climb up, then back right to a stance and spike belay above the start. Runners placed on the latter section can lead to an embarrassing lack of rope. It is possible, though harder, to leave the traverse line sooner.
2. 40m Climb the wall above to finish.

3   Via Dolorosa   100m   HVS **   (1964)
Start below the wide crack, just left of a yellowish recess.
1. 50m 5a Climb the crack to overhangs, then traverse 6m left. Go up for about 15m and move back right to a stance. It is possible to belay beneath the overhangs.
2. 10m 5a Go right to a belay.
3. 40m 4b Climb the wall above and finish up a short crack.

4   Fringo Bonofito   30m   E5 6b   (1988)
Starting just left of Marshall's Wall, this route climbs the centre of the wall through two roofs. Go easily up the fault, then left to a small ledge. Climb the wall left via a thin crack, veering to the left edge where sloping holds lead to a roof. Pull directly over, then go up to the large upper roof. Traverse right along the sloping ledge below the roof, to its right end (poor RPs). Pull over the lip (poor rurp on left), then up with difficulty to a ledge. Abseil off.

5   Marshall's Wall   80m   E2 *   (1960)
Start just right of an overhung recess where a line of weakness runs leftwards up a red wall. A hard route for its time, it still retains some of its boldness.
1. 20m 5b Move up to thin cracks and follow these up left to a steepening. Traverse above the bulge on the right and step down to

an awkward stance in a recess; peg and nut belay. If particular care is taken with the ropes, pitches 1 and 2 can be run together.

2. 20m 5b Traverse 3m right, pull onto a ledge, then traverse boldly right for another 3m to a small ledge. Climb up and back left to a grass ledge; peg and nut belay.

3. 40m 4c Step left, then climb to ledges and finish up a short undercut corner.

6 Eyes of Mica   30m   E4 6a   (1988)
Start just right of the diagonal fault of Marshall's Wall. Climb the wall to a horizontal crack. Pull over the bulge, then go left into the recess of Marshall's Wall. Climb the thin crack and wall above to the right end of the final steep wall with a long reach to better holds. Possible abseil descent.

7 Bosco   75m   VS †   (1969)
Start 5m right of Marshall's Wall at a grassy bay.
1. 20m Climb the wall directly by a rib and a crack to a ledge.
2. 20m Trending right, climb the wall to a huge block, then climb the arete behind to a block belay on Tom.
3. 35m Trend left, then go straight up to easier rock.

8 Tom   85m   VS   (1965)
The obvious left-trending corner to the right of Marshall's Wall.
1. 25m Climb straight up into the corner and up to a tree.
2. 25m Make a rising traverse left until it is possible to go straight up to ledge and block.
3. 35m Traverse up and right to the edge of the wall overlooking the chimney-fault of Bunny's Route, then go straight up to finish.

9 Dick   85m   HVS   (1965)
Straightens out Tom.
1. 25m As for Tom to the tree.
2. 25m Climb straight up a blocky crack to its conclusion.
3. 35m Climb the wall to the overhang which is taken directly on improving holds to finish above.

10 November Wall   45m   Severe   (1952)
Gained by a traverse from Marshall's Wall, this route starts directly below the chimney-fault of Bunny's Route. Climb a short chimney slanting left for about 6m, then slightly right for another 6m. Traverse left and follow a shallow groove to a ledge. Climb a wall to a ledge right of the big overhang. Finish up Bunny's Route (on the right).

The following routes lie on the lower right-hand section of the face where the first section of Zig-Zag goes out right. The left margin of the face is taken by the chimney-fault of Bunny's Route.

11   Bunny's Route   95m   Very Difficult *   (1952)
Start some 50m left of the lowest rocks. Climb walls in two pitches to the terrace. Above, climb a fault leading up and left into the prominent chimney and follow this to the top.
Winter: III *   (1967)
Though not often in full condition this provides a fine little route, useful if there is avalanche danger elsewhere. Approach the chimney-fault by a series of short walls, avoiding the first two by snow gangways just left of Harry.

12   Harry   135m   VS   (1965)
High up, to the right of the chimney of Bunny's Route, is a steep buttress recognisable by an inverted T-shaped overhang. Start beneath this, 30m left of the lowest rocks. Climb a series of steep walls and ledges, heading towards the right end of the overhang (90m). Climb a vertical groove for 15m (crux) to a platform, then go up left to finish up steep, exposed, rough rock on the crest.

13   High Flying   80m   Very Difficult *   (1966)
Start at the lowest rocks where a small buttress is separated from the face by a shallow gully.
1. 30m Climb the small buttress, descend into the gully and belay at a short corner.
2. 25m Climb cracked wall to ledge beneath a prominent cube of rock.
3. 25m Continue up the steep wall just right of the cube on good holds to the terrace.

14   Hairy Kipper   60m   Very Difficult *   (1966)
A few metres along the first Zig-Zag, scramble up a shallow gully to a crack on the right wall at 6m.
1. 35m Climb the crack, traverse right and slightly up for about 12m; good positions. Follow cracks to a ledge below a block recess.
2. 20m Climb the right corner of the recess to the terrace.

15   The Zig-Zag Roof   25m   E1   5b   (1979)
The roof above the first Zig-Zag. Start below a grassy bulge. Climb to a good hold just right of a loose block. Swing up right, then follow the left side of the arete just above two small trees. Traverse off or continue by Hairy Kipper.

16 Mad Mackerel 60m   E1   (1990)
This lies some distance to the right of Hairy Kipper. Start beside an obvious dirty corner with a roof at 6m.
1. 35m 5a Climb to a roof and undercling to its right end. Step round right into the bottom of an obvious groove and climb this to a good stance on the left of the groove.
2. 25m 5a Follow a groove to the overhanging wall above. Pull through and up, then climb broken ground to a sapling belay.

The following three routes lie on a small face some 60m directly above the finish of Hairy Kipper. There are three prominent parallel cracks, all Very Difficult, 45m (1966). From left to right these are; **Leg Stump**, **Middle Stump** and **Off Stump**.

17 The Zig-Zags 200m   Easy/I
The easiest approach to the ridge and also a means of descent is by the broken ground between the North-East Face and the nose on the right. From the entrance to the lower gorge of the Lost Valley there is a path leading up, then left to the lowest rocks of the North-East Face at the start of the broken ground. Traverse up and right below overhanging rock walls. Go up past a tree, then back up left to the foot of the wall above and climb a short chimney step. Make a long traverse left beneath broken walls, then go up and back right to where the shelf opens out (cairn). Go up, then left beneath a small wall to the ridge.
    In descent reverse these directions. A small cairn marks the start, on the right when heading north, at the termination of the ridge. In winter crampons are likely to be a necessity and care should be taken, especially under heavy snow when the ledges can form windslab. Conditions may dictate that the descent is pitched. This is not a recommended winter descent and it will usually be safer to descend from Gearr Aonach by traversing its ridge south-west to reach Coire nan Lochan.

NORTH FACE (Map Ref 166 561)
This imposing face lies at 420m on the right side of the frontal nose of Gearr Aonach. It is easily reached by heading up right from well below the Zig-Zags. Grassy slopes lead around then up to the sloping terrace beneath the crag. A prominent ledge, the junction of the andesite below with the rhyolite above, girdles the face. Descent from the top of the face is by the Zig-Zags. The first few routes lie left of the main mass of rock on the scrappier left-hand portion of the face.

Routes are described from left to right.

1   Easy Route   180m   Moderate   (1898)
At the left end of the frontal face, where the cliff begins to bend round towards the Zig-Zags, there is an area of pleasant rough rock which allows a scrambling route to the ridge.

2   White Rhino   135m   IV/V   (1988)
Start from the girdle ledge, accessed from the first traverse ledge of the Zig-Zags, below a recessed chimney. Tree belay.
1. 45m Climb a long diagonal left-slanting rake.
2. 40m Continue on this line to a small snow patch, belay below an open groove and capped, indistinct gully.
3. 50m Climb the groove to a recess below an overhang. Move out left over a wall and slabs to the top.

3   Trumpeting Elephants   130m   III   (1988)
Start as for White Rhino and climb the recessed chimneyline.

The division between the steep vegetated left portion of the face and the cleaner area of steep rock to the right is marked by a vertical corner-fault rising above the girdle ledge. This is just above a large prominent roof low down on the left of the crag. An obvious thin chimney starts from the girdle ledge and slants up and right out of the corner-fault.

4   Chimney and Face Route   135m   Severe *   (1949)
The obvious thin chimney which slants right from the girdle ledge is guarded by some unpleasant ground to its left. Once gained it gives three pitches on good rock. After reaching the upper terrace the direct continuation is avoided for easier ground on the right.
Winter: V **   (1988)
Start in the shallow gully formed between the main crag and the turfy face on the left. Climb easily to beneath a huge roof and traverse the ledge left around an edge to belay.
1. 35m Climb steep heather up slightly left, then back right to follow a ramp to a shallow gully. Belay below a large recess.
2. 45m Climb across the rib on the right to a thin chimney. Follow this past a constriction to another steepening and belay above.
3. 20m Continue up the chimney to the terrace.
4. 35m Above is a vague right-trending groove. Move left and follow it to where it bulges. Move across right and up past a tiny sapling to easier ground leading up left to above the fault. Tree belay.

On the left side of the main mass of rock, about 45m left of the highest part of the face, there is a small vegetatious buttress with a grey slabby tongue of rock at its base. The right flank of this buttress is bordered by a shallow grassy fault.

5   Preamble   140m   Severe **   (1957)
Start below the grey tongue, 10m left of an obvious boulder.
1. 25m Climb the tongue to a small chimney left of the fault.
2. 25m Continue up the chimney to the main girdling ledge.
3. 30m Follow the line of a black groove.
4. 30m Continue on this line to a slabby ledge. Traverse left into the chimney of Chimney and Face Route and climb to a large grass ledge.
5. 30m Climb the wall 10m right of Chimney and Face Route.

6   Perambulator   170m   HVS *   (1980)
The second route to climb the convex upper wall, just left of The Kneepad. It takes a diagonal line across the face to climb the rightmost of three chimneys high up on the face. Start behind an obvious boulder where a shallow grassy fault slants up right.
1. and 2. 70m Follow the fault to the girdling ledge.
3. 10m Traverse right to the skyline (as for The Kneepad).
4. 25m Climb the wall on good holds, move up and left into a corner, then follow this to a block below the chimney.
5. 25m 5a Ascend the chimney over a bulge, then the steep crack above to a tree on the left.
6. 40m Easier rock leads to the top.

7   The Late Late Show   155m   HVS   (1967)
Takes the lower rocks just right of Perambulator. Start at a groove above and just right of the boulder. Only the first pitch is hard, the remainder taking steep walls with good holds but poor protection.
1. 25m Enter the groove from the left, climb it a for few metres, exit right and go up a steep wall. Surmount a bulge and cross a slab to a small left-slanting ramp; peg belay.
2. 25m Climb the ramp and steep wall beyond to easier ground leading to the girdling ledge.
3. 50m Follow a system of cracks and grooves immediately right of the black groove of Preamble to a slabby ledge; peg belay.
4. 25m Climb the steep black wall on the right. Continue to a stance.
5. 30m Easy ground to finish.

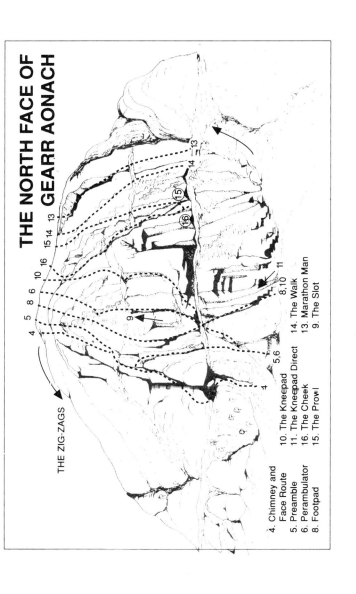

THE NORTH FACE OF GEARR AONACH

THE ZIG-ZAGS

4. Chimney and Face Route
5. Preamble
6. Perambulator
8. Footpad
10. The Kneepad
11. The Kneepad Direct
16. The Cheek
15. The Prowl
14. The Walk
13. Marathon Man
9. The Slot

8   Footpad   165m   VS   4c   (1972)
Start up the first two pitches of The Kneepad.
3. 20m Climb the clean shallow corner above to a small cave.
4. 25m Go left 5m, climb a chimney and step left at its top to a peg
belay on the slabby ledge of The Late Late Show.
5. 25m Traverse right and climb the wall rightwards to a ledge.
6. 40m Climb the wall to the top.

9   The Slot   165m   VS   4c   (1980)
The leftmost and widest of the three chimneys high on the face. Gain
the girdling ledge by any of the three previous routes.
3. 25m Two small adjacent corners lie on the wall above. The cleaner
left-hand corner is taken by Footpad. Climb the right-hand corner to a
cave below a chimney.
4. 40m Climb the chimney, passing a roof and moving onto the left
wall, then the edge. Follow the groove above to ledges, then move
right to belay.
5. 45m Easier rock leads to the top.

10   The Kneepad   165m   HVS *   (1959)
The first route to break through the large, convex upper wall. Good
situations higher up. Just left of the highest point of the face, about
10m left of a great curving diedre, is an arete with an overhanging
nose below. Left of the nose is a steep slabby corner. Start below the
nose and scramble to a belay at 6m.
1. and 2. 55m Climb the wall above at a short arete about 6m left of
the nose, trending up right then up left on slabby rocks to the girdling
ledge.
3. 30m Traverse the ledge rightwards to a large cave.
4. 35m 5a Turn the roof on the left by an oblique crack, pass a
chockstone and gain the lip of the overhang. Move right to an overhung
bay, climb the overhang by a crack on the right and gain a small
platform. Move right and follow steep grooves for 30m.
5. 45m Easier climbing to the top.

11   Direct Start   E1   5a   (1961)
Takes the great curving diedre right of the normal start, joining The
Kneepad at the end of pitch 3. Often wet with some dubious rock. Start
beneath the diedre.
1. 25m Go up the wall on the left, then traverse right to flakes.
2. 35m Climb the diedre. Traverse left onto an arete to finish.
3. 35m Follow the arete to the large cave of The Kneepad.

The remaining routes are on the wall round the corner from the highest point of the face. All start from the right end of the girdling ledge, reached by scrambling up scrappy, vegetatious Very Difficult ground; take care. In winter this forms an icefall. The routes are described from right to left. Meander excepted, the climbs are on excellent rock with good positions.

12   Meander   80m   Very Difficult   (1959)
A poor route. From the right end of the ledge climb the wall for 40m to a large grass ledge. Turn the grey nose above by a groove on the left and continue to the top.

13   Marathon Man   95m   Severe **   (1978)
Start 10m left of the right end of the ledge below a steep black wall marked by grooves and cavities.
1. 45m Climb straight up to a ledge.
2. 40m About 10m above is a left-trending gully with a rib of steep clean rock on its left. Climb to the rib, step onto it from the left and climb it directly on perfect rock to a ledge and flake.
3. 10m Step left and climb the awkward wall above to easier ground. Scramble to the top.

14   The Walk   80m   Difficult **   (1957)
A pleasant route, although the approach is harder than the climb itself. Start some 10m along the ledge, immediately left of Marathon Man and follow obliquely the line of two grass bays to the top.
Winter: IV **
Follow the summer line.

15   The Prowl   75m   Very Difficult **   (1959)
Start 30m along the ledge at a recess beyond a large rowan tree. Climb a chimney to a small bay. Leave the bay by a crack on the left and follow the line of the crack to the top.

16   The Cheek   90m   Severe **   (1968)
1. 5m Climb The Prowl to the small bay.
2. 20m Move left round the steep corner, then go diagonally up and left to a small ledge on the edge of the wall. Traverse round left horizontally then down to a groove. Climb this to a block.
3. 20m Climb the chimney above directly to a ledge.
4. 45m Finish more easily up a wall of fine rock on the left.

17   Agoraphobia   245m   VS 4c *   (1967)
This route, a high level girdle, is continuously and spectacularly exposed. Unfortunately it does not maintain its standard. Climb Easy Route to the grass ledge above the first band of red rock. Follow the ledge rightwards to a point 10m before a prominent black cave. Climb up diagonally right, then slightly down above the roof of the cave past a shallow chimney to a sloping shelf (35m). Move along the shelf, cross a steep wall by a diagonal crack, then continue up the shelf to a tree on the skyline (45m). Walk and climb horizontally right for two pitches, then finish diagonally right for three pitches on excellent rock.

18   Ziggy   190m   II   (1988)
Traverse under the north face to a very shallow gully. Climb the gully and the short ridge above (overlooking Avalanche Gully), then the open buttress above trending right.

The Lower North Face is the small crag lying beneath the grass slopes leading to the North Face. There is one route, **The Knowles Spence Route (**VS, early 70s) which takes a short hard groove up the middle of the face, reached by a traverse from the left.

NORTH-WEST FACE
The hillside running up towards Stob Coire nan Lochan holds a number of routes, begining with the prominent gully whose outflow crosses the path. These routes are reached from the car park at 168 569 by taking the path up towards Stob Coire nan Lochan.

Avalanche Gully   600m   III/IV **   (1960)
The prominent stream and gully to the right of the nose, running virtually the full height of Gearr Aonach. The lower part crosses the path about five minutes walk from the bridge over the River Coe. The gully slants right; where it forks, in both the lower and upper reaches, the right branch should be taken. There are some steep pitches which can be turned. Higher up, the gully runs out into broken ground overlooking Farewell Gully. Although it takes time to come into full condition, all that is required is a good freeze. The lower stream can provide some six or seven pitches on water-ice which, when combined with the Upper Left Fork, produce a first-rate long climb.
Variations:
The Lower Left Fork (IV) gives a hard short climb to finish on an open ledge exiting left.

The Upper Left Fork (IV) has a short pitch to start, then goes under a big chockstone to a steep pitch, rarely in condition. Above, a further pitch is usually climbed on the left to easier snow, then the top. It is possible to escape out left or onto the easy buttress on the right.
North-West Gully (Severe 1955) probably follows the Upper Left Fork of Avalanche Gully.

Sidewalk 60m   Severe *   (1972)
This starts some 90m up Avalanche Gully at a steep smooth wall on the left side. The wall borders the left side of the steep Lower Left Fork. Start by a boulder near the right end of the wall at a point of weakness.
1. 25m Gain a ledge, sidle left, then layback a crack to a tree.
2. 35m Climb the wall on the left on good rock.

Farewell Gully/Grand Finale   150m   II/III *   (1969)
This is the next obvious gully as one goes up the path in the lower part of Coire nan Lochan. It meets Avalanche Gully at the top. It is easily gained from the path and can give three pitches before easing off into the upper slopes. Care should be taken after heavy snowfall.

UPPER WEST FACE BUTTRESS (Map Ref 158 555)
This face lies at an altitude of about 650m beneath the highest point on the Gearr Aonach ridge. The routes are easily accessible and come into condition fairly rapidly after heavy snow. From the point where the Stob Coire nan Lochan path goes beneath a series of small outcrops the buttress and its easy access gully become clearly visible high up on the slopes of Gearr Aonach. The routes are described from left to right.

Ciotach Route   90m   II/III   (1959)
This lies higher up the easy access gully, out on the left and follows an icy section rising to the ridge; variation possible.

Rescue Team Gully   75m   II/III *   (1966)
This is the steep but short iced chimney directly above, and is essentially the left-finishing branch of the easy approach gully. There is a through-route chockstone at its foot and two good pitches.

Jim's Gully   75m   II/III   (1968)
The central branch via an icefall, above which it is easy.

999   120m   III **   (1969)
The right branch is followed by the most obvious line with caves,
chimneys and chockstones providing entertaining short steep pitches.

SUNSET WALLS (Map Ref 156 554)

High on the approach path to Stob Coire nan Lochan at an altitude of
650m, this small north-west facing wall of compact, waterworn rock
has a pleasant outlook. It is level with, and not far left of, the foot of
the waterfall which issues from the head of the corrie. Although slow
to dry, the rock is excellent and holds abound, even if runners do not!
In winter some fine icefalls can cascade over the wall. Highest and
wettest at its left end, the crag diminishes in height rightwards. Routes
are described from right to left.

Sunstroke   30m   HVS 5a *   (1990)
At the point where the crag increases in height there is an obvious
wide crack. Climb straight up the wall just to its left into a groove, then
up to the top.

Sunnyside Up   30m   E1 5a *   (1990)
Starting just left of Sunstroke, climb the wall passing two grass ledges
to enter a groove. Step right and up to finish.

Sunset Strip   40m   E1 5c *   (1990)
Moving down to the point where the wall is at its highest,there is a thin
crack in the centre between two lines of weakness. Easily gain the
crack and climb it to a ledge, step left, then continue to the top.

ILLUSTRATIONS
Opposite: Neanderthal, Lost Valley Buttress (Climber, Rab Anderson)
Next Page, Left: Hairy Kipper, NE Face of Gearr Aonach (Climber, Ans Khan)
Next Page, Right: Crocodile, NE Nose of Aonach Dubh
                                        (Climbers, Jim Melrose and Jerry Handren)
Facing Page 167: Unicorn, Stob Coire nan Lochan (Climber, Bob Richardson)

AONACH DUBH

892m   (Map Ref 150 559)

This, the most westerly of the Three Sisters, presents on its three faces much of the best and most varied climbing in the group.

EAST FACE

The climbs on the east face fall into four groups; The Lower North-East Nose, The Lower Walls, The Main Face, and the Far Eastern Buttress. Approach via a footbridge over the Coe (166 566), just under a kilometre below the Meeting of Three Waters. The path is obvious, fairly dry, and goes up then contours round Gearr Aonach into the glen below the cliffs. It is best to cross the river just above a little gorge, only about 100m below the lower walls. Avoid the temptation to cross lower down. The closest climbing is about 30 minutes from the road, making it one of the most accessible cliffs in the area. There is a wide spectrum of climbing on good, mostly sound rhyolite. A few of the routes have had winter ascents but these demand almost freakish conditions. They may be useful when higher ground is under very heavy snow or avalanche prone.

LOWER NORTH-EAST NOSE *(Map Ref 159 562)*

This south-east facing crag overlooks the valley at an altitude of 400m. The best approach is to scramble up right from just below the lower walls. A very steep wall on its east flank is prominent, being pale and smooth. The most obvious line is the curving corner near the left end, taken by Boomerang. To the left is a smaller, darker wall, the two separated by a steep rib. Right of the pale wall is an inset chimney, best seen from the north. Further right the rocks become easier but the approach more difficult. The routes are described from left to right.

On the smaller dark wall left of the rib are a number of relatively inconsequential routes. **Slaver** (65m VS 1965) climbs the dark wall approximately centrally, and may be related to **The Wellie Boys** (70m VS 1983) which climbs to a small niche, passes this by grooves to the left, then traverses left to a groove which leads to the top.

1   Impulse   75m   HVS *   (1990)
An excellent climb with good holds but scanty protection up the wall
left of Turnspit. It is probably related to The Wellie Boys in its lower
part. Start 10m left of the right arete of the wall.
1. 50m 4c Climb directly to a small grass ledge with a small prominent
overhang above, then take the red wall to a left-slanting slabby groove.
At the top of the groove step right to climb a line of cracks. Just below
the top of the wall step right to finish up the arete in a fine position.
2. 25m Scramble to the top.

2   Turnspit   60m   VS *   (1961)
Follows, for the most, the right edge of the dark wall. Start in the grassy
gully a few metres up from the right edge.
1. 30m 4b Climb the steep wall, move right into a groove on the edge
and follow this to a poor belay.
2. 30m 4c Continue up the groove, move out onto the left wall, pass
a creaking flake and climb the wall to top.

3   Guinness   55m   HVS   (1978)
Starts at a corner 7m left of Little Boomerang.
1. 25m 5a Climb the corner for 6m then move left onto the arete.
Continue for a few moves then go back right across the top of the
corner. Climb up then right to belay in Little Boomerang under an
overhang.
2. 30m 4c Climb the overhang and the groove above to the top.

4   Little Boomerang   65m   VS   4c   (1955)
Climbs the right corner of the steep rib. Slow to dry. Start below the
obvious wide crack. Climb to the crack, passing a small chockstone,
till a long step left can be made. Continue over a bulge to easier rocks
and scramble to a spike belay. Continue up the crack for 35m, belay
on the left. Go up and right to a bulging crack and so to the top.

5   Girdle Traverse   75m   E1   (1967)
Start about halfway up Little Boomerang.
1. 10m Traverse right between the two lowest overhangs, cross the
steep wall and descend to the belay in Boomerang.
2. 15m Reverse the crux of Boomerang and follow the obvious
descending fault across the white wall to the belay on Freak-Out.
3. 10m 5b Crocodile, pitch 2.
4. 40m Climb a short crack, cross Original Route and go up and right
to the top.

6   Stormtrooper   40m   E3 6a   (1978)
Climbs the steep wall and overhangs between Little Boomerang and
Boomerang. Start below the righthand of two cracks. Climb the crack
to the first overlap, go slightly left into a broken crack and climb this,
trending right (loose rock) to the centre of the wall. Continue to a small
ledge below the roof, climb its left side, traverse right through overhangs then climb the wall to belay on Boomerang. Finish up this.

7   The Chant of Jimmy Blacksmith   30m   E5 6a   (1987)
The arete to the right of Stormtrooper gives blind, improbable climbing.
Climb the crack a short way, then break out right to an undercut on
the arete. Climb the wall to a small horizontal crack (Rock 1 in crack,
RP3 in flake on left), then up into the groove (poor blade runner)
continuing to the arete. Make a hard move past a fingerlock (crux) then
easily finish on the ledge of Boomerang. Finish up this.

8   Boomerang   90m   HVS *   (1955)
The prominent, left curving corner at the left end of the wall.
1. 30m 5b   Climb the wall, sometimes using the crack, to a ledge.
Continue over a steepening (crux), and make a long step left to a
ledge.
2. 30m 4b   Continue more easily to belay in a small recess.
3. 30m   Finish up a grassy crack.

9   Freak-Out   75m   E4 ***   (1967/79)
One of the Glencoe Greats, taking the central crack line up the pale
wall, cutting through obvious niche at half-height. Scramble up the
lowest rocks to a ledge and tree belay below the crack.
1. 20m 5c   Climb the wall to the crack. Follow this to the obvious right
traverse to a small ledge and assorted belays.
2. 30m 6a   Regain the crack and climb it to a poor rest under the roof.
Pull over on good holds then make a few powerful moves to a slightly
more relaxed position. Sustained but more reasonable climbing leads
to an inverted flake under the final roof. Taking care to enjoy the full
impact of the situation, pull out right to easy ground.
3. 15m   Climb the wall above to the top.
If the initial crack of pitch 2 is wet, it is possible to climb direct from the
stance to a hollow, downward-pointing flake (Friend), then move left
with difficulty to the crack immediately below the roof (6a).

AONACH DUBH
NORTH-EAST NOSE
AND LOWER WALLS

1. Impulse
2. Turnspit
6. Stormtrooper
7. Chant of Jimmy Blacksmith
8. Boomerang
9. Freak-out
10. Crocodile
11. Revengeance
12. Spacewalk

17. Lady Jane
19. Sir Chancealot
21. Grochan Grooves
23. Double Exposure
24. Lament
27. Blockbuster
28. The Challenge
29. Sticky Fingers

10   Crocodile   70m   E3 **   (1977)
Start 5m right of Freak-Out at a left curving line of overhangs.
1. 20m 5c Climb steeply to the overhangs then pull out left to a small ledge. The shallow groove above leads to the belays of Freak-Out.
2. 10m 5b Climb the groove on the right for 6m, then traverse right round the edge of the wall to a ledge below an obvious groove.
3. 40m 5c Climb the groove with difficulty until a hard move left leads to easy ground.

11   Revengeance   55m   E6 **   (1981)
The wall right of Crocodile, starting from the same point. A mean route for bold technicians.
1. 25m 6b Climb the crack in the bulge rightwards to join Spacewalk. Follow this to its junction with Crocodile. Step right and up the wall to a small overlap (good Stopper 2 at right end of overlap in thin diagonal crack; RP4 in slot to right). Step right again and continue up the wall (crux) to the ledge at the end of pitch 2 of Crocodile.
2. 30m 5c From the top of cracked blocks climb the wall just right of the groove and enter its upper part. This leads to an overhang which is climbed direct to finish.

12   Spacewalk   50m   E5 ***   (1978/80)
A good companion route to Freak-Out, with one very hard move and less convincing protection. Start down and right of Crocodile, directly below a crack in a steep wall.
1. 25m 5c Climb the crack, then go up and slightly right to roofs. Climb out left then quite boldly across the wall to join and follow Crocodile to the Freak-Out belays. A superb pitch.
2. 25m 6b Climb the groove on the right to a small roof (small wires behind loose flakes). Step left and make a desperate move, past an *in situ* RP, up a short groove (no, it isn't a jug). Continue up then right to the top.

13   Original Route   90m   Severe *   (1934)
A route of 'character', the grading is nominal. At the right of the crag the wall is inset, forming a chimney hidden from below though conspicuous from further north. Climb easily up ledges and chimneys to a large stance below the main chimney. Above an overhung recess is the chimney proper, containing many jammed flakes and chock-stones. The start is desperate and leads to a short section only 20cm wide. Above, embracings of rattling flakes lead to thankful release on easier ground.

Several routes have been made right of Original Route, beginning with SMC and Creag Dhu parties in 1956. The rock is mostly scruffy and the climbing unlikely to excite. **Venison Dagge**r (75m VS 1976) starts just right of Original Route, climbs a small chimney crack then a rib and then the obvious open corner. **Novity** (90m Very Difficult 1965) is the next obvious line right of Original Route; a corner groove near the prow of the nose. **Sinus** (90m Very Difficult 1971) climbs the rib just right of Novity.

THE LOWER WALLS

These are the long, low line of dark cliffs which lie lower than, and between, the main east face and the north-east nose. The routes are described from left to right, taking the lefthand, lower wall first. At its left end are bands of overhanging grooves. The first route takes the wall and arete immediately right of the furthest left corner.

14   Daredevil   30m   E1 5b   (1978)
Climb the corner and at 6m move across the steep wall on the left and follow a thin crack to a ledge. Continue up the left side of the arete above to the terrace.

15   Baldrick   30m   E3 5c   (1990)
Start up Daredevil, then move right and up via thin cracks to the arete. Continue more easily to the top.

16   Exellerator   25m   HVS 5a   (1978)
Start at a wet crack about 5m left of Lady Jane. Climb the crack and gain the groove on the left at 5m. Follow the groove to the overhang which is climbed to easier ground.
Winter: IV/V   (1986)
An impressive ice smear may form in some winters.

17   Lady Jane   25m   E2 5b ***   (1977)
A brilliant pitch up the steep wall right of the obvious wet crack. Often possible when adjacent routes are wet. Climb the wall to a right curving crack, follow this then up to the horizontal break just left of the wet streak. Step right and up (dryness not essential) then quite boldly left and up past a tiny overlap (crux) to a tree on the break. Walk off left.

18   Mr Bates   25m   E3 5c   (1988)
A direct version of Lady Jane, starting just to its right where a short ramp slopes up left. Move up and make difficult moves over the bulge

until it is possible to step right to a horizontal break. Move up to the base of a short flange, break on right, continue to just below Lady Jane, step right to a ledge and pull up to the end of the horizontal break. Finish as for Lady Jane.

19 Sir Chancealot 45m   E2 **   (1978)
Climbs the centre of the wall right of Lady Jane, heading for a tree in the horizontal break. Start midway between the black streak right of Lady Jane and a shallow, stepped corner which leads to the tree.
1. 25m 5b Climb the wall more or less directly, taking a small overhang on the right to an awkward thread belay in a cave.
2. 20m 5c Climb the roof just right of the belay (strenuous) to good holds. (If the leader falls, the second is liable to incur injuries on being rammed into the roof of the cave!). Easy ground above.

20 Blast-Off 50m   E1   (1978)
Start 5m left of Grochan Grooves.
1. 25m 5b Climb the bulging wall on left trending holds then go directly up the wall to a rounded ledge. Follow a crack line to the horizontal fault and tree belay.
2. 25m Move left 6m to a large overhanging corner. Climb the corner then the wall above to the terrace.

21 Grochan Grooves 50m   Severe   (1952)
Left of the lowest rocks is a well defined groove, the most prominent feature of the wall. Climb the shattered groove (often wet) to a small ledge at 20m. Continue up the wall, trending right then up to a grass platform and a tree. Starting right of the tree, climb a 6m wall to a small ledge. Traverse right to a slab and so to a recessed corner. Climb the corner and finish at a rowan tree.

   At the lowest point of the cliff the wall turns round and up for a stretch, before bending north again to give a short righthand section parallel to, but higher than, the lefthand rocks. The righthand section is bounded on its left by a dripping, slimy chimney (the winter line of Heart of Glass). The next three routes lie on the middle stretch of wall.

22 Tartan Slab 35m   Difficult   (1969)
Some 5m right of the lowest rocks is a corner with small, multicoloured slabs. Start below the corner.
1. 10m Climb to a large block belay.
2. 25m Climb a greasy slab, then traverse grass ledges left to the tree belay on Grochan Grooves. Finish up this.

23   Double Exposure   70m   VS *   (1978)
Start as for Tartan Slab.
1. 25m Climb the corner for 15m, break out right and go up to belay under a roof.
2. 45m 4b Go up and left a few metres, step onto a steep wall, move right, climb to a block then follow the groove on the left. Easier rocks lead to top.

24   Lament   60m   Very Difficult **   (1951)
High in its grade, an excellent steep route with good holds just where needed. Some 20m up and right of the lowest rocks is a small ledge a few metres above the ground.
1. 35m Gain the ledge, climb a corner trending slightly left, and at the top pull out right (crux). Climb straight up for 20m, move right and up, then follow a shallow groove to belay in a recess.
2. 25m Climb straight to the top.

25   Paul Rodger's Wake   135m   III/IV   (1984)
Start just right of Lament and climb directly on ice for three pitches. The wall just right of Lament gives a 50m Severe on good rock.

26   Heart of Glass   105m   IV *   (1979)
This climbs the chimney up and right from Lament.
1. 30m Follow ice steps to a good cave on the right. Traverse left then back right, go up steeply to a recess and belay.
2. 30m Traverse left and climb a ramp to a recess on the left of the obvious ice boss. Go up and right then directly up the ice pillar to a belay on the left.
3. 45m Traverse left and follow the ice flow to the top.

27   Blockbuster   55m   HVS   (1978)
This route climbs the arete left of The Challenge.
1. 4c Climb the obvious groove on the arete to a belay.
2. 4c/5a Follow the crack through the overhangs to a pulpit. Continue, trending slightly right to the top.

28   The Challenge   45m   E3 **   (1978)
The right-bounding rib of the wet chimney, which is the line of Heart of Glass. A serious route, with protection only after the crux and an ankle-bending penalty clause. Start at a cave.

1. 20m 6a Climb the overhang to a small ledge, then traverse up and right across the wall to a ledge and belay.
2. 25m Step left and climb the obvious left-trending ramp. Finish up the wall.

29 Sticky Fingers 45m   E2 5b *   (1978)
Start 3m right of The Challenge. Climb the overhung groove breaking through the overhangs to a ledge on the wall to the right. Climb to the stance on The Challenge. Move left 3m then up a steep groove to the top.

30 Layla 25m   HVS 5b   (1978)
Start 7m right of Sticky Fingers. Climb a bulging wall to a side pull, then aim for a finger crack on the right.

The main part of the East Face consists of The Barn Wall, 180m of easy rock to the left of a great curving fault (The Bow), and the right-hand section which is divided by a wide, grassy Terrace. The Bow crosses the Terrace at its left end. Below the Terrace, the rather broken Rowan Tree Wall lies to the left of the finer Weeping Wall (named after its distinctive black streaks). The cliff above the Terrace and to the right of the Bow is the Terrace Face. Near the foot of the Bow, about the middle of the face, stands a small outcrop with perched boulders and the ubiquitous rowan trees. This marks a useful stopping place, as the curving fault above provides a useful route to and from the Terrace.

Descent:
To return to the foot of the crag following routes on the Terrace Face, walk rightwards (north) to gain the top of a shallow gully formed by an eroded intrusion dyke hard against a short steep wall. Scramble down the outside of the first section of the gully, then enter the second section and continue down this to gain the open hillside. Turn down past the north-east end of the Terrace Face to gain the Terrace. Continue down The Bow. Its bottom steep section may be avoided by traversing left (facing in) to reach easier-angled rock. This descent brings one back to the start of the climbs.

An alternative and easier descent if one intends to go down the corrie is to go left (south-west) from the top of the crags to reach easy ground and then descend south-east down easy slopes between Barn Wall and Far Eastern Buttress.

BARN WALL (Map Ref 157 558)

This is formed in one steep mass, crossed by innumerable small ledges. It gives pleasant easy climbing almost anywhere.

31   Barn Wall Route   150m   Moderate   (1947)
Start at the highest point of the foot of the wall and climb by the line of least resistance.
Winter: III   (1965)
Follow the summer line.

32   The Bowstring   180m   Difficult *   (1947)
Start about 25m above and left of the stopping place, and 30m directly below a chimney. Climb 25m to a slab beneath a vertical wall. Go right to a corner and climb this to a grass ledge. Now trend left and up to the chimney which is followed for 6m. Continue on either side of the chimney. The rock is excellent.
Winter: III   (1971)
Follow the summer route throughout. The crux is the corner and the ensuing chimney.

33   Lower Bow   75m   Moderate   (1947)
The lower part of The Bow, which leads to the Terrace, provides a useful descent and also a pleasant climb for beginners. The only difficulties are on the first few moves. Start directly opposite the stopping place. Climb the long shallow groove, the most obvious weakness in the wall.

34   Rowan Tree Wall   75m   Very Difficult   (1947)
This route climbs the short stretch of wall between the Lower Bow and a vegetatious corner some 30m to its right. About 10m right of the Lower Bow is a clean wall with three cracks and a small pock hole. Climb any of the cracks, the right-hand one being the most difficult. The rocks lie back after 20m and scrambling leads to the Terrace.
Winter: IV   (1983)
Climb the summer line on good ice.

WEEPING WALL (Map Ref 157 558)

To the right of Rowan Tree Wall the rock is smooth, marked only by streaks and faint grooves. Right again the face turns up and ends at a deep inset chimney, Drain Pipe Corner. A further narrow wall lies right of this before the rocks merge into the hillside. Routes are described from left to right.

35   The Fly   60m   E3 *   (1977)
Start at a crack below the centre of the clean wall to the right of the
vegetatious corner which marks the right-hand side of Rowan Tree
Wall.
1. 40m 5b Climb the crack to a ledge. Proceed with caution up the
wall above, past a scoop and then slightly left by a difficult move; the
consequences of a fall don't bear thinking about. The upper section is
easier. Belay on the terrace.
2. 20m Climb the easy wall above.

36   Spider   60m   HVS ***   (1957)
An excellent route at the lower limit of its grade. Right of The Fly a
shallow, cracked depression lies just left of the dark brown streaks
formed by waterslides. Start below the depression.
1. 35m 5a Gain a good ledge then climb the steep wall for 10m and
traverse right into the groove which borders the left edge of the
waterslide. Follow the groove for 5m then move left to a crack, which
leads (crux) to a narrow ledge. Continue to a broad ledge.
2. 25m Easier climbing leads to the Terrace.

37   Solitude   75m   E3 ***   (1977)
A brilliant pitch which just merits its grade, either for the guile required
to protect it, or for the commitment if you can't. Take two sets of micro
wires. Start as for Spider.
1. 50m 5b Climb the initial wall of Spider. From the right end of the
ledge climb a short corner on the right to a higher ledge and a large
block. Move boldly up the wall above, slightly right, to the base of short
diagonal crack running out left. Follow this then climb with continued
interest on superb rock to a large ledge.
2. 25m Finish up the easy wall.

38   Short But Sweet   70m   E2 *   (1981)
Another very bold lead on excellent rock, climbing the centre of the
wall between Solitude and Quietude.
1. 50m 5b Climb the lower wall to the right end of the grass ledge
containing the block of Solitude. Climb the wall, starting past two
obvious finger pockets, then up and right to a slight overlap. Step left
and up the steepening wall, with final tricky moves about 2m left of the
finishing corner of Quietude.
2. 25m Climb the easy slab.

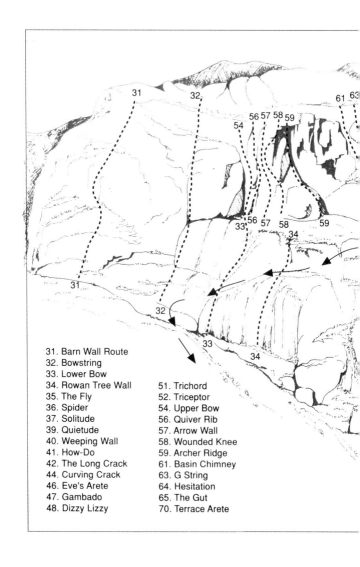

31. Barn Wall Route
32. Bowstring
33. Lower Bow
34. Rowan Tree Wall
35. The Fly
36. Spider
37. Solitude
39. Quietude
40. Weeping Wall
41. How-Do
42. The Long Crack
44. Curving Crack
46. Eve's Arete
47. Gambado
48. Dizzy Lizzy

51. Trichord
52. Triceptor
54. Upper Bow
56. Quiver Rib
57. Arrow Wall
58. Wounded Knee
59. Archer Ridge
61. Basin Chimney
63. G String
64. Hesitation
65. The Gut
70. Terrace Arete

THE EAST FACE OF
AONACH DUBH

39   Quietude   60m   HVS *   (1977)
This route climbs a slightly left-trending line up the middle of the dark
brown waterslide belts, finishing up an obvious short right-facing
corner. Start about 25m right of the left edge of the face, below an
obvious black cracked overhang.
1. 20m 4a Climb the wall to a ledge below the overhang.
2. 40m 5a Climb the diagonal crack leftwards to a ledge. Continue up
and left via cracks to finish up a short corner.

For the following routes a useful point of reference is the large
detached block at the foot of the face, some 10m left of the right edge.
The individual features of the routes are best seen when standing
back.

40   Weeping Wall Route   105m   Severe **   (1947)
Look for a cracked fault beginning halfway up the wall and trending
slightly left, adjacent to the right edge of the waterslide belts. Start just
left of the detached block.
1. 15m Climb to a belay in a recess below the fault.
2. and 3. 90m Climb the steep fault above, trending slightly left to a
bulge with a small block above. Pull over the block and take the line
of least resistance on parallel grooves above to easier rocks and the
Terrace.

41   How-Do   60m   Severe   (1968)
Start at the detached block.
1. 25m Climb the conspicuous fault, trending left to a short bulge.
Belay on the ledge above.
2. 35m Climb the fault above by walls and grooves to the top.

42   The Long Crack   90m   Severe *   (1953)
The prominent feature of the route is a long crack which begins in the
middle of the wall right of the waterslide belts and goes diagonally right
for 3m then straight up almost to the Terrace. Start just right of the
detached block at a fault which goes through a small bulging wall at
10m.
1. 30m Climb to the bulge, then take the fault to a ledge.
2. and 3. 60m Above and right is the crack. Climb it using the wall on
the right, awkward. Continue more easily to the top.
Winter: V **   (1989)
Follow the summer line in two pitches to a tree. Abseil off. It requires
a heavy plastering of snow; ice is unlikely.

43   The Straight Climb   50m   VS   4b *   (1991)
Good though somewhat eliminate climbing taking a direct line between
The Long Crack and Curving Crack. Start midway between these two
routes. Take a straight line to the rowan at the top of the wall, passing
the midway rowan on its left. Sparsely protected, but on accommodat-
ing holds. Abseil descent.

44   Curving Crack   90m   Severe **   (1952)
Start at the clean wall some 8m left of the right edge of the face. Climb
to a ledge at 10m, continue to another ledge and tree belay. Climb the
crack above then a steep wall to easier rocks. This route may be the
same as **Wall and Crack Route** (90m Severe 1951).

45   Wall Climb   50m   VS   4c   (1991)
The wall just to the right of Curving Crack. Start at a slim corner 5m
left of the right edge of the face. Climb this to a ledge, continue to the
next ledge, then step right to a vague line and climb the wall to the
top. Move easily up, then left to the rowan at the top of The Long Crack.

46   Eve's Arete   70m   Very Difficult *   (1969)
Climbs the extreme right edge of Weeping Wall. A poor first pitch is
redressed by a superb traverse on the second. Start at the lowest
rocks at the edge of the face.
1. 20m Climb to the right end of a grass ledge, 10m right of Curving
Crack.
2. 15m Traverse slightly up and right to the arete and a ledge on the
right. You definitely get your money's worth on this one. A recent
rockfall removed a block belay. (Many seconds seem to go too high
on the traverse, must be the instinct for survival..)
3. 35m Climb the arete to a tree.

47   Gambado   55m   E2   (1977)
This takes the line of Dangle, an old aid route. Start from a shelf left
of Drain Pipe Corner, below the roof.
1. 15m 5b Climb up right from the shelf onto a steep wall, then trend
right and over the overhang, stepping left to a ledge.
2. 30m Climb a left-trending fault through a bulge to a ledge.
3. 10m Finish up easy rocks.

48   Dizzy Lizzy   45m   E3   5b/c   (1977)
Climb the arete right of Gambado.

49   Drain Pipe Corner   60m Severe *   (1951)
Beyond the right edge the rocks turn up and terminate at a deep inset
chimney. This lies under a steep narrow wall on the right. It gives an
excellent sustained route, slow to dry.
Winter: IV *   (1965)
Follow the summer line with much difficulty.

50   Adam's Wall   70m   Severe   (1954)
Start as for Drain Pipe Corner.
1. 30m Climb the first 20m of Drain Pipe Corner. Traverse onto the
right wall to a belay below a crack.
2. 20m Climb the crack, steep but with good holds, to belay on the
fault ledge at a large jammed block.
3. 20m Go 3m right and climb the overhang strenuously (crux).
Scramble to the Terrace.

51   Trichord   65m   HVS *   (1978)
This sustained route climbs the steep face to the right of Drain Pipe
Corner, crossing Adam's Wall at the large jammed block. Start 3m right
of Drain Pipe Corner.
1. 25m 5a Climb a short wall trending left to a small arete, then go up
right to a ledge at 7m. Follow a faint crack line to flakes on the left,
continue directly to a large horizontal fault and traverse right to belay
before a tree.
2. 20m 4c This pitch climbs the right trending and overhanging ramp
above. Start up a short steep corner to gain the ramp, continue through
overhangs moving rightwards to a large ledge. Traverse left to belay
at a large block.
3. 20m 4c Above and left is a large roof. Climb this at its widest point
to the ledge above. Continue more easily to the top.

52   Triceptor   65m   E5 *   (1978)
A route no insurance company would look at; the unprotected crux is
10m above a nasty landing. Start 6m right of Drain Pipe Corner.
1. 30m 6a/5c Gain a narrow ledge at 5m, move up then hand traverse
left a few moves (hard). Move back right and up, then follow an obvious
mossy groove line to a ledge. Walk right 5m to a tree.
2. 20m 5c Start just right of the tree, climb up about 8m, step left,
climb up about 3m, then move left to easier ground. Belay on the ledge
above. Some loose rock.
3. 15m 5a Start at a small cairn just left of two cracks. Climb directly
to a bulge, step right to a wide mossy crack and up to easier ground.

53 Impresario 65m   HVS   (1969)
Start 7m right of Drain Pipe Corner.
1. 20m Climb up the right edge of the steep wall to the first terrace.
2. 20m 5a Climb the thin crack on the right to an overhang, step right, then go up very steep broken grooves to the second terrace.
3. 25m Take the easiest line over the overhang, and finish easily.

Above and to the right of Impresario, at the top of a basin, a stepped icefall has been climbed (III, 1974).

TERRACE FACE (Map Ref 157 558)
This face is above the Terrace and right of The Bow. The best climbing is found at either extremity, on good rock. Some way up the centre of the face is a marked concavity, The Basin, recognisable by distinctive up-curved rocks. The routes are described from left to right.

54 The Upper Bow   60m   Very Difficult   (1946)
This is the continuation of the great curving fault of The Bow. Above the Terrace it forms a deep chimney, usually wet.

55 Shiver 75m   III/IV *   (1965)
The large icefall which occasionally forms about The Upper Bow and Quiver Rib. Take Quiver Rib for about 10m, traverse left to the centre of the icefall then climb it directly to the top.

56 Quiver Rib   60m   Difficult ***   (1947)
At the left end of the Terrace is the dark and damp chimney of the Upper Bow. This route climbs the rib and wall just right of the chimney.
1. 30m Climb the rib to a stance below a steep wall.
2. 30m Above, a narrow groove trends left up the steep face. Follow the groove on good holds; there is a hard move just above the belay.

57 Arrow Wall   70m   Very Difficult **   (1953)
This route, hard for its grade, climbs the steep wall to the right of Quiver Rib. Start midway between Quiver Rib and the arete on the right, below a groove on the wall above.
1. 35m Climb the wall, move slightly right at a bulge at 12m, continue up then left to a ledge. Belay on Quiver Rib.
2. 35m Directly above is a very steep and narrow black groove (left of which the wider groove of Quiver Rib slants up left). Climb the groove on excellent holds to the top.

58   Wounded Knee   70m   Severe **   (1991)
A harder, drier alternative to Arrow Wall, this route climbs a shallow
groove on the front face parallel to, and left of the arete between Arrow
Wall and Archer Ridge, then takes the imposing headwall above. Start
midway between Arrow Wall and the arete on the right.
1. 30m Climb a steepening groove to a ledge; belay on the left.
2. 40m Step left onto the steep wall. Move up and left a few moves
then traverse right across the bulging wall to the edge. Continue on
good holds to the top.

59   Archer Ridge   70m   Very Difficult ***   (1947)
This classic climb completes the quartet of good routes on this crag.
It takes the blunt arete right of the Upper Bow chimney. Start at the
lowest rocks, where the ridge is somewhat rounded.
1. 25m Follow the crest to a good stance just to its right.
2. 20m Directly above on the crest is a steep corner-groove, with a
steep rib to its right. Climb up and slightly right under the steep wall
for 7m, move up and back left to the crest, then continue to a stance
in a corner.
3. 25m Move right a few metres, then up a crack to the final steep
wall. Climb this at an obvious breach and continue more easily to a
belay.

60   Archer Ridge Direct   55m   Severe *   (1954)
This harder route climbs the ridge directly, missing out the two right-
slanting sections of the original.
1. 25m Archer Ridge, pitch 1.
2. 30m Climb the steep corner-groove on the crest, often wet. Follow
the ridge to a formidable bulge, move left below it and go up then back
right to the steep exposed crest which leads to the top.

    Further right the rocks turn in and lead to more broken ground. The
following two routes are found at the left side of the Basin.

61   Basin Chimney   75m   Very Difficult   (1947)
Start from the Terrace below the lower left-hand corner of the Basin.
Climb straight up to the Basin by the line of a waterslide. The chimney
starts from the top left-hand corner of the Basin as a narrowing grassy
gully. Climb loose rock, move up to the left past a tree and enter the
chimney. Climb it to the top.

62   De Vreemde Stap   40m   HVS   (1978)
This is a direct entry to the Basin, useful for access to the routes above.
Start about 10m right of the Basin Chimney.
1. 25m 5b Climb a shallow groove until a wide step right and up is
required to gain the continuation of the groove.
2. 15m 4c Continue up a left-trending crack to the Basin.

63   G String   75m   Severe   (1955)
Make for the Basin below the distinctive jagged overhangs. This route
keeps left of the overhangs. Traverse up and left into a groove at 10m.
Go up the groove to a large grass ledge and belay at 21m. Step round
left into a steep groove and climb this to a grassy recess. Finish up
the crack at the back of the recess.

64   Hesitation   60m   HVS **   (1966)
Above the Basin is a distinctive pink slab with overhangs above and
upcurving grooves on the right. This route takes a line up the left of
the slab and finishes through a large roof above. Gain the Basin by a
choice of routes. Belay above and left of the trees. Above is a slabby
scoop, left of which is a shallow but obvious groove.
1. 45m 4c Climb the groove then move up and right to a ledge at 35m.
Climb diagonally right into a large groove topped by a huge roof. Small
stance.
2. 15m 5a Climb to the roof, traverse left 5m, break out right (crux)
via an overhanging groove and finish on a large ledge.

65   The Gut   75m   VS *   (1956)
A good line, marred by some dubious rock on the first pitch. Start just
right of Hesitation, below the slabby scoop.
1. 35m 4c Climb the scoop, delightfully delicate, passing an overlap
at 5m and a bulge at 12m. Climb diagonally left then up to a ledge, go
up and traverse right to the small stance of Hesitation.
2. 40m 4b Climb the groove for 5m, step right to a ledge, traverse
right about 5m and then go up and right on a steep wall to the top.

66   Gutrot   50m   E1   5b
Start right of The Gut at a short groove behind a tree.
1. 25m Climb the groove until bulges force a move out left to a slab.
Climb the slab trending left to a belay on The Gut.
2. 25m Climb the steep wall above The Gut traverse, trending left to
a mossy rib which is climbed to the top.

67   Stitch   35m   VS 4c   (1973)
Start right of The Gut past the trees at the end of the Terrace where a
blunt arete rises above a sapling. Climb the wall to a shallow break in
the bulges, which are climbed on awkward jugs. Easier rock leads to
an exposed left traverse past a block overhang whose steep left wall
is climbed on sloping holds. Use a small foothold under the overhang
and pull up to the rounded ledge above. Easier rock to finish.

68   Basin Traverse   75m   Difficult   (1947)
Gain the Basin by following broad zigzag ledges on its right. From the
Basin three outward-sloping ledges run right to the north edge of the
face. Traverse the middle ledge to its end and climb up the edge to a
large slab. Follow the lower rib of the slab left to an arete and climb
the flank that overlooks the Basin.
Winter: III   (1971)
Follow the summer route. The traverse is the only awkward section.

   Level with the descent route from the east face, and a little way up
the glen, the upper cliff throws down a buttress to a grass terrace
angled between two walls. The following route follows this buttress
and offers a convenient continuation up the hill. The grass terrace is
at the far right of the upper cliff, whose main face is invisible from the
walk-off path.

69   Buttress Route   70m   Difficult   (1960)
Start at a small cairn at the top of the grass. A white patch is on the
left-hand wall, and an overhung gully and a grassy gully descend from
left and right respectively.
1. 35m   Climb the buttress on the left, avoid an overhang at 6m and
belay at the second terrace below a rowan.
2. 15m   Continue up the arete, belay at the third terrace.
3. 25m   Continue by easy scrambling or, better, walk a little right to the
end of grass terrace and climb the right wall of the gully.

70   Terrace Arete   45m   Severe **   (1954)
Excellent rough rock. At the extreme right-hand end of the Terrace,
where the descent path turns towards the Terrace, a steep arete rises.
Start just right of the arete. Climb to a ledge at 5m (nut runner low
down), then make a delicate step left onto the arete proper. Continue
to a recess and finish directly up a groove and a short wall.

71   Girdle Traverse of Terrace Face   180m   VS *   (1969)
Start just left of the Upper Bow.
1. 35m Climb grooves to a belay.
2. 40m Continue up grooves for 12m, then traverse right to cross the grooves of Quiver Rib to a belay near the arete.
3. 20m Go round the arete, then right and up to belay in a corner below the last pitch of Archer Ridge.
4. 40m Traverse right under the leaning wall, go round the corner and continue to the next arete. Now go down and round to a ledge on G String. Climb the wall for 5m and belay on the traverse of The Gut.
5. 45m Continue up The Gut, then climb a big groove for 3m, go right round the edge and traverse down to a small ledge. Continue horizontally across a bottomless groove and under a huge detached block to finish.

72   Two-Step Arete   70m   VS *   (1991)
Behind the chimney-gully of the descent route, about a rope's length away, is a well-defined arete. To reach it, either turn left up the hillside from the foot of the gully, or climb the wall above the gully and scramble over. Belay on a large tree at the foot of the smooth wall and below the arete.
1. 30m 4b Climb a short wall to a ledge at the foot of arete. Start up the wall, move left to the arete and climb this to a ledge.
2. 40m Pull up left to the steep continuation of the arete and finish by easing ground.

73   Cross-Over Wall   40m   E2   (1991)
Climbs the smooth wall left of the start of Two-Step Arete.
1. 20m 5b Gain the obvious slot in the wall, move up, then left and back up right into the centre.
2. 20m 5b Start just right of the upper arete, climb up then rightwards to the top.

FAR EASTERN BUTTRESS (Map Ref 154 556)
This cliff lies above and to the left of the main part of the East Face, ten minutes walk past Barn Wall. Much of the rock is excellent and the cliff offers an increasingly rare commodity, a quiet day in the hills. It has a high central section, rising steeply above the lower slabs. To the left is more broken ground, with a ramp running up and left. To the right is a cracked wall, bounded on the right by an obvious chimney

crack. Right again is a wall, starting about 15m up, with two parallel cracks running up and right. The arete on the right is taken by North-East Nose. Up and right from this is Hole and Corner Gully, well seen from the approach, while further up the hill again is the smaller upper buttress.

Descent from the main buttress starts by an easy but exposed traverse rightwards (north) above the finish of Hole and Corner Gully, leading to easy ground round the edge. A longer but uncomplicated alternative, especially in winter, is to continue up then left (south) to descend past the left end of the crag.

The routes are described from left to right. Well to the left of and above the foot of the main face the rocks turn in, with a clean wall overlooking a broken gully. The first route takes the clean wall.

74 Rough Slab   50m   Severe **   (1962)
Start at a groove on the right wall of the broken gully. Climb the groove past a large block to a good ledge below small overhangs. Traverse right slightly and break through the overhangs by a groove. Leave this and swing round left onto a steep clean slab and so to the top.

75 Buckshee Groove   50m   Severe   (1962)
Start some 12m lower down the gully from Rough Slab, at an undercut nose. Climb the nose, follow the grassy groove on the left past a small tree to a corner crack and climb this to a belay behind a huge boulder. Traverse left under overhangs and climb a groove to a ledge below a steep wall; climb this on the left and finish by a small niche.

76 Orient Express   85m   IV *   (1991)
Takes the thin iced chimney up the left side of the main mass. Start just left of an obvious corner.
1. 45m Climb easy-angled ice left of the corner, belay on a ledge on the right.
2. 25m Move up left and climb the steep iced chimney to a ledge.
3. 15m Continue up ice to a large boulder.

77 Left Edge   90m   Moderate   (1948)
Follow the line of least resistance near the left edge of the main face. Good rock, few belays.

78 Blister   105m   Severe   (1970)
Start 6m left of Nirvana Wall. Climb the wall and follow the edge of the ramp in two pitches to an obvious chimney-crack system. Follow this to the top.

79   Eastern Promise   75m   E1 **   (1991)
A fine route taking the arete and thin crackline left of Nirvana Wall.
Start at the base of a grassy groove.
1. 50m 5a Move up the grassy groove a short way and pull onto its
right wall into a thin crackline. Follow this and the arete to a block belay
below the upper wall.
2. 25m 5b Step down right, then climb the thin crack up the middle of
the wall past the right side of a block to the roof. Pull through this
rightwards, then back left above it and continue to the top.

80   Nirvana Wall   75m   Severe **   (1966)
Start about centrally, where the crag reaches its maximum height. A
thin crack goes the full height of the crag, cutting through the final roof
on the right. Begin near the left end of the bulk of slabby clean rock,
where the thin crack begins next to thin streaks of quartz. Climb it in
three pitches.

81   Yen   70m   Very Difficult *   (1966)
Start 5m right of Nirvana Wall. Climb smooth slabs to below a steep
cracked wall. Move right and climb the wall (crux) to a grassy ledge.
Climb a groove to the top.
Winter: IV *   (1991)
Approximates the summer line. Start at the lowest rocks.
1. 40m Move right along the base of the crag then follow easy ground
to an obvious chimney. Traverse up left to belay at a short corner.
2. 20m Climb the corner and cracks to a ledge beside the gully.
3. 40m Step left and continue up the groove.

82   Turkish Delight   55m   HVS *   (1991)
This route climbs the arete left of Satori. Excellent rock, though a bit
contrived.
1. 15m Scramble to a stance at the foot of a chimney-groove.
2. 40m 5a Pull onto the wall and follow the arete to the top.

83   Satori   55m   VS **   (1990)
Climbs the left-hand of two parallel and right-trending cracks on the
wall right of an obvious chimney-groove.
1. 15m Turkish Delight, pitch 1.
2. 40m 4b Step onto the wall, move right then up to a block at the right
end of a small roof. Climb this moving left and continue up a crack.

84   Shibumi   55m   VS **   (1990)
The right-hand crack.
1. 15m Turkish Delight, pitch 1.
2. 40m 4b Go right to good footholds before the corner. Follow the obvious crack to easier ground at the top of the corner. Climb the edge to the top.

85   North-East Nose   90m   Very Difficult   (1946)
The arete formed by the east and north-east faces. Scramble up then take the line of least resistance, with one awkward move near the top.

86   Hole And Corner Gully   30m   Moderate   (1946)
The deep gully at the right edge of the buttress. There are two pitches, the second being an interesting cave.

87   Farewell Arete   80m   Very Difficult *   (1990)
The right wall of Hole and Corner Gully forms an arete. Climb this, with a step left at 6m, then continue up superb rock to a ledge and belay. Continue up the same line for two pitches.

88   Triangle   50m   Very Difficult   (1966)
Thirty metres right of and up from Hole and Corner Gully there is a triangular cavity with a large flake at its apex from which a deep crack rises vertically. Climb the flake and crack past an awkward constriction to a platform belay. Finish by the obvious right-slanting groove.

NORTH FACE

This is the massive dark face rising steeply above the middle part of Glen Coe and Loch Achtriochtan. Like the west face, its lower slopes are vegetated andesite, unsuitable for rock climbing. Sloping across the face from middle left to top right is a prominent ledge system, especially distinct in its upper half, where it is known as Sloping Shelf. An alternative name might be Shifting Shelf as its slabby nature and easily accumulated snow tends to make it a very high avalanche risk. Avoid it during and after snowfall or in a thaw. Even when clear of snow, icy sheets may require crampons. Above the Shelf, which marks a geological boundary, the rock is rhyolite, which provides steep and impressive climbing. The most obvious feature of the face is the great black slot of Ossian's Cave. This has lured unsuspecting climbers into its leafy glade since its first ascent in 1868. Left of the cave, a prominent gully slants down right through the lower part of the face. Further left again is a buttress with several good winter routes; it is level with the north-east nose. In its lower part it sports a belt of trees with continuing vegetation above. This buttress is the Lower Cliff.

The best approach is from the footbridge across the River Coe at 166 566, just under one kilometre below the Meeting of Three Waters. Head up and right to the ledge system leading eventually to Sloping Shelf. The only awkward section in summer is in crossing a gully which lies further left than the slanting gully mentioned above. A second and more direct path climbs steeply up the left side of the slanting gully; it can be reached quickly across the river if the latter is fairly dry.

The Shelf continues up and right below the upper cliffs to reach the base of Deep-Gash Gully. It then passes to the right of a 60m buttress and continues upwards until it runs out on easy ground above the west face. It is recommended as an excursion in its own right through marvellous and impressive rock scenery.

One other important feature of the north face is the large ledge known, somewhat sarcastically, as Pleasant Terrace. This runs across the upper face from Deep-Gash Gully to above and right of Ossian's Cave. It provides the descent from the routes on the upper face.

The climbs are described from left to right, beginning with the routes on the Lower Cliff.

1   Slake 90m Severe   (1971)
Near the middle of the cliff there is a large amphitheatre with a steep right wall bounded on its left by a curving corner. Gain the foot of the corner above a band of grey rock and climb it in three pitches with cave belays. Seldom dry.

When seen from below, there is an obvious Y-shaped feature on the buttress. The right branch is taken by Darwin's Dihedral. Further right the buttress is split by twin gullies which start about 100m up the face. Venom climbs the left-hand gully, White Snake the right-hand one.

2   Darwin's Dihedral 240m V ***   (1981)
Climb the obvious icefall and large right-facing corner to the left of the gully of Venom.

THE NORTH-EAST FACE OF AONACH DUBH

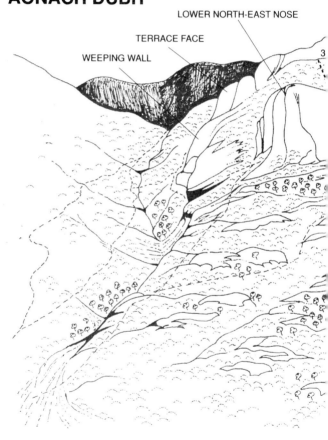

LOWER NORTH-EAST NOSE

TERRACE FACE

WEEPING WALL

3

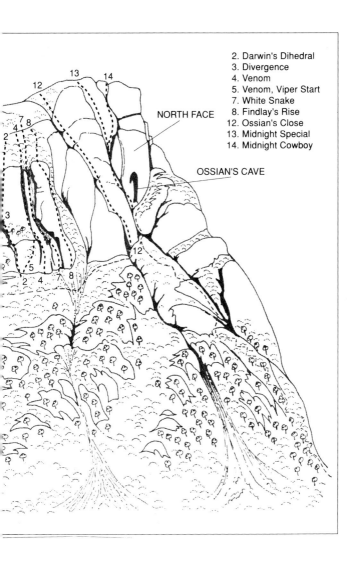

2. Darwin's Dihedral
3. Divergence
4. Venom
5. Venom, Viper Start
7. White Snake
8. Findlay's Rise
12. Ossian's Close
13. Midnight Special
14. Midnight Cowboy

NORTH FACE

OSSIAN'S CAVE

3   Divergence   170m   IV   (1984)
This route takes the left branch of Darwin's Dihedral. Take that route
until its crux pitch is reached. Climb the buttress on the left of the ice
to the upper basin. Take the left branch, which is a deep chimney (55m
from a tree belay to the top).

4   Venom   300m   IV/V *   (1979)
The left-hand of twin gullies, starting about 100m up the face. Start
beneath an icicle on the initial wall. Gain a shallow chimney and climb
it to a tree-covered ledge. Traverse left to another chimney, which
leads to the gully. Continue up, turning two large roofs on the right.

5   Venom, Viper Start   120m   IV/V **   (1979)
This route climbs the icefall and less obvious chimney to the left of the
original start. The chimney leads more directly to the left-hand gully,
avoiding the traverse of the arboreal ledge. An abseil descent can be
made through the trees, followed by an ascent of the normal line (a
full day for the energetic).

6   King Cobra   280m   V/VI   (1986)
1, 2 and 3. 120m Climb the Viper Start to Venom.
4. 25m Climb Venom (the chimney-gully) to the point where an ice
seep comes down the very steep left wall.
5. 35m Climb the ice seep (thin) to a stance under the roof right of
icicles.
6. 60m Traverse left to an icicle, climb this and a left-trending ramp
above to a further steep groove. Up this to a block belay.
7. 40m An easier iceflow leads to the top.

7   White Snake   360m   IV *   (1979)
The right-hand of the twin gullies. Climb the obvious icefall to a huge
roof, bear left and continue up the right-hand gully.

8   Findlay's Rise   150m   IV *   (1978)
The obvious icefall which usually forms by mid-winter, given sufficient
freezing. Climb the ice direct and continue up the buttress, occasionally awkward, sometimes desperate.

9   Two Shakes   250m   III   (1984)
The buttress right of Findlay's Rise. Start up the diagonal gully running
right from a snow basin below and right of Findlay's Rise. Move onto
the buttress on the right and take a diagonal line to a terrace. Go right
30m and climb the headwall by a turfy V-groove.

10   Abomination   120m   Severe   (1956)
This route climbs the buttress left of Waterfall Wall, passing an area
of brightly coloured moss at mid-height. Gain the buttress from the
right about 15m above its base. Traverse left after an awkward corner
to the left edge of a large open corner and climb the edge to a belay
at 30m. Turn the overhang on the left to a grass bay and exit by a flake
crack. Traverse right to an open corner, climb this for 7m, then its steep
right wall to the mossy area about 60m up. Vegetation then scrambling
on very rough rock follow for the remaining 60m.

11   Waterfall Wall   120m   Severe   (1955)
This route climbs the left wall of Ossian's Close, the well-defined gully
which cuts down through the upper face, and is the gully left of the
more prominent slanting gully which descends below Sloping Shelf.
To approach, climb the first short pitch of Ossian's Close from Slanting
Ledge then move left onto the wall at a cairn. Climb up and left for
10m, make an awkward step left at a peg runner and continue for 25m
to a belay. Continue to a large detached block, traverse right for 10m
on a rock shelf then go up to a sloping ledge. Climb a short wall to the
right and continue to near the top of the buttress by a long pitch. Finish
up easier rocks.

12   Ossian's Close   150m   III *   (1979)
The obvious deep gully left of Ossian's Cave. The difficulties are
confined to the lower part. Climb an initial steep pitch just above the
traverse path to the enclosed gully and move up to a large chockstone.
Climb this on the left wall and belay in a cave. Climb steeply out of the
cave to the upper, easy gully. The climb can be finished by taking the
Grade II buttress on the left.

13   Midnight Special   270m   IV/V **   (1970)
The obvious line sloping steeply up leftwards to the left of Ossian's
Cave. Start just above and to the right of the point where the two
approach paths meet. Climb to a depression (steep), then follow the
line up left.

14   Midnight Cowboy   360m   V **   (1973)
The obvious gully running straight up the cliff to the left of Shadbolt's
Chimney. Start between Midnight Special and Shadbolt's Chimney.
Climb iced walls and a chimney for about 60m. Follow the deepening
gully with a long 50m ice pitch (crux). A number of shorter pitches lead
to the top.

15   East Wall Climb   165m   Very Difficult   (1894)
Start from Sloping Shelf up a rock and grass recess left of the deep-cut
Shadbolt's Chimney. The middle part approaches very close to the
shallow part of the Chimney, then trends away left. There are several
chimneys, one vertical with a chockstone.

16   Shadbolt's Chimney   210m   Severe *   (1908)
Despite much loose, slimy and vegetatious rock, this route has distinct
character. Start a few metres left of Ossian's Ladder, below a deep-cut
chimney. Climb the chimney and difficult rock, sometimes by back and
foot (45m). Move right onto the buttress and climb turfy ledges to a
grass platform. The chimmney then resumes with a steep 10m pitch,
overhanging at the top. Climb it direct, or avoid it on the outer left wall,
to emerge into a grassy amphitheatre. The direct line continues for
60m by a wide trap gully, The Corridor, which is harder than it looks.
When the slabs in its bed become unbearable, escape by rotten ledges
on the left wall. The Corridor may be avoided on the outside right wall.
Winter: IV **   (1955)
On the first ascent the rocks were icy but not snow-plastered. The main
difficulties are in the initial chimney, the 10m pitch, and The Corridor,
which was quitted for the left wall.

17   Corridor Wall   75m   Severe   (1956)
An alternative finish to Shadbolt's Chimney, avoiding The Corridor.
Climb Shadbolt's to the grass amphitheatre. About 15m below The
Corridor is a steep wall on the left with two vertical grooves. Climb the
right-hand groove for 7m, go left round a nose into a recess and belay.
Climb the right rib of a small chimney above, step left and continue up
easy slabs to a large grassy ledge. A corner above has a jammed flake.
Climb the flake and after 10m of steep climbing scramble to the top.

18   Ossian's Ladder   60m   Difficult   (1868)
The Ladder is the route into Ossian's Cave, the great black slot which
is very prominent from the road. Start from Sloping Shelf, directly
below the Cave. Climb loose, vegetatious ground to the cave floor. The
vegetation is luxurious but the floor slopes up at 45 degrees. The
ascent is not recommended; there have been several bad accidents
here involving inexperienced parties and loose rock.

19   Flip-Out   85m   E2 *   (1967/77)
This route takes the crack in the left wall of Ossian's Cave, starting
just above the top of Ossian's Ladder. Interesting, gargoyle-like rock

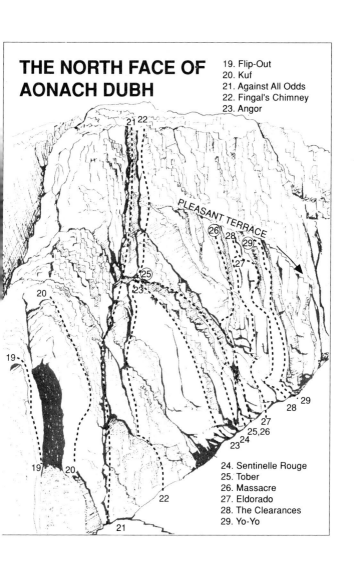

THE NORTH FACE OF AONACH DUBH

19. Flip-Out
20. Kuf
21. Against All Odds
22. Fingal's Chimney
23. Angor

PLEASANT TERRACE

24. Sentinelle Rouge
25. Tober
26. Massacre
27. Eldorado
28. The Clearances
29. Yo-Yo

scenery, though not a clean route.
1. 45m 5b Follow the crack fairly directly. Near the top move up and left to a ledge and peg belay (abseil point if wished).
2. 40m Pleasant scrambling to Pleasant Terrace.

20   Kuf   120m   HVS 5a   (1963)
The white wall right of Ossian's Cave. Climb Ossian's Ladder to below the wall, then climb it (some unsound rock) to a large flake and peg runner. Traverse right then climb the steep crack on the edge of the buttress (two peg runners). Climb easier cracks to Pleasant Terrace.

21   Against All Odds   150m   VI **   (1988)
The prominent winter line just right of Ossian's Cave, between Kuf and Fingal's Chimney. Excellent and very hard climbing. Start just left of the weakness at a tree.
1. 30m Move up right and tension to a bendy sapling in the fault line. Climb the overhanging fault on tufts to a niche at 25m. Exit right and move up to an in-situ nut belay.
2. 30m Surmount a short wall on the right and the next overhang in the corner. Continue on tufts just right of the corner line to gain a ramp coming in from the right (from the base of the chimney pitch of Fingal's Chimney). Continue for 10m to a ledge.
3. 30m Above is a very steep section with minimal tufts. Climb up on ice smears and tufts right of the wide crack until beneath the main overhanging section. On the first ascent three pegs were used to reach the next tufts which led steeply to snow. Move up to belay at the foot of a snow-filled chimney slanting up to the left.
4. 45m Climb steep thin ice and tufts (in the line of the lower pitches) with little protection to less continuous difficulties and a snow slope ending 15m below Pleasant Terrace.
5. 15m A ramp on the left leads to the left end of Pleasant Terrace. Take easy slopes on the left to open slopes, or descend Pleasant Terrace.

22   Fingal's Chimney   180m   VS *   (1955)
To the right of Ossian's Cave two narrow chimneys cut the big wall. Fingal's Chimney, the right-hand one, is clean-cut and begins about 30m up and right of the lowest rocks right of Ossian's Cave. Above, vegetatious ledges run left across the face. At the right end of the ledges is a pinnacle.
1. 15m Climb the right edge of the pinnacle to a block belay.

2. 30m Go up beneath an overhang, traverse left then down and across to a ramp. Follow cracks to poor belays near the chimney.
3. 35m Climb the narrow chimney past loose blocks to a sentry box.
4. 10m Go up the wall on the right to below an overhung cleft.
5. 10m Climb the strenuous cleft (crux).
6. 20m Climb the deep chimney to a broad ledge.
7. and 8. 60m Go deep into the dark cave, climb out awkwardly over the roof, then follow the chimney past a rocking stone to Pleasant Terrace. Continue in the chimney, now deep and easy, to the top. This last section was originally climbed as **West Chimney** (1935).
Winter: V ***   (1969)
A classic line giving four hard pitches. It is not often in condition and holds little ice. The initial pitches provide the major difficulties, with hard mixed climbing.

Above and to the right of Fingal's Chimney the wall turns up and the rock improves. At the far right end is the dark recess of Deep-Gash Gully. About halfway along the wall, where the cliff is at its steepest, is a great vertical corner, the line of Yo-Yo. Left of this the wall has two obvious breaks, taken by Angor and Tober.

23   Angor 65m HVS   (1966/80)
The leftmost of the two breaks in the wall left of Yo-Yo. Look for an undercut triangular slab below a short overhanging chimney and slab corner running up and left.
1. 30m 5a Gain the right edge of the slab, traverse left and climb the chimney bulge. Continue to belays in an overhung recess.
2. 35m 5a Go left then up right over a bulge to a rake which leads into Fingal's Chimney. A direct finish climbs the obvious crack (HVS 4c).

24   Sentinelle Rouge 75m E3 *   (1980)
The obvious red slabby wall left of Tober. Start at the next obvious break below and left of Tober.
1. 40m 5c Traverse left to beneath the roof, turn this on the right and enter a groove which is followed until a line can be taken up the slabby wall on the right to a left-rising overlap. Follow this, then ascend the wall to an awkward belay under a downward-pointing flake.
2. 35m 6a Above and right are two steep hanging grooves; traverse right and climb the right-hand one (hard) and continue to a belay on Tober.

25   **Tober**   150m   VS *   (1965)
This route follows the prominent break left of Yo-Yo, an open corner
with a red slabby left wall.
1. 35m   Climb a slab leftwards, then a short wall to the overhangs
where a short traverse leads to a little groove. Climb this and move
right into another groove which leads to a stance.
2. 35m   Cross to a ledge on the right, then go up left to regain the
groove. Follow this to exit left across slabs. Belay at the foot of a grass
rake.
3, etc. 80m   Climb a rib and slabby grooves above to join Pleasant
Terrace at Fingal's Chimney. Walk 10m right to finish up an obvious
line. A variation start (1966) climbs the two overhanging flakes above
the initial slab and continues up a loose groove to belay above the first
pitch.

The next set of routes lie on the steepest section of the face. The
dominant line is the great corner of Yo-Yo, which seems to overhang
in two planes. There are three routes on the wall to its left.

26   **Massacre**   120m   E3   (1977/80)
Start at the foot of Tober.
1. 20m 5b   Go up and right to a niche below a large loose roof, climb
this and continue up left to a ledge.
2. 20m 6a   Climb the flake and awkward groove above, then continue
to a slanting crack and ledge.
3. 40m 5b   Follow the crack up and left, pull over a bulge and climb
up and right (as for the Barrier Pitch of the Girdle). Climb a mossy
groove to a ledge.
4. 40m   Climb the darker mossy corner above, move left to another
corner and climb this to the top.

27   **Eldorado**   125m   E5 ***   (1977/80)
A very strenuous climb. An obvious, thin crack cuts the wall left of
Yo-Yo. About 5m further left is a fainter crack line, broken by small
bulges. Start just right of this crack.
1. 20m 5c   Climb up and left into the crack and follow it to a ledge. As
this pitch is loose and verdant, it is better to approach from The
Clearances by the obvious line.
2. 40m 6b   Climb the wall to the overhang, launch into the short corner,
then step left above the roof; poor rest. Climb the groove and crack
above, passing another small roof by a desperate move to better holds

where the angle eases. Move up slightly left to a crack which is followed to a terrace and awkward belays.
3. 40m 5c Climb the groove just right of the arete (the second most obvious groove left of The Clearances), steep and bold, until it is possible to traverse right to the poor belay on The Clearances.
4. 25m 5a Climb the rib to Pleasant Terrace.

28   The Clearances   105m   E3 ***   (1976)
This fine route climbs the very steep wall left of Yo-Yo.
1. 40m 5c Climb the slabby breach leading left through the lower bulges, then go left on a slab until it is possible to go right to a thin ledge (peg runner). Continue directly up the wall (bold) past a poor peg, then step right into a crack which leads with interest to a ledge.
2. 40m 5c Climb the left wall of the open corner above to an *in situ* nut runner. Step right under the roof, pull over and continue to a small ledge and poor belay.
3. 25m Continue more easily to the top.

29   Yo-Yo   90m   E1 ***   (1959/60)
The great corner of the cliff, and another of the Glencoe Greats. Start below the corner at an undercut flake. The first pitch contains some superbly delicate and technical moves, the second pitch is physical, and some have fallen off the third through tiredness.
1. 40m 5b Step left onto a steep slab and go up and left for 6m then up and right into the corner. Climb this to a shelf and belay on the left.
2. 20m 5a Climb the corner and chimney to a belay above the main overhang.
3. 30m 5a Climb the crack with minor deviations on the left (ignore the left-trending ramp just above midway) to Pleasant Terrace. Two continuation VS pitches have been added, climbing straight up from the Terrace by a grooved arete and corner.

30   The Cough   75m   E1   (1971)
On the wall right of Yo-Yo is a large shallow cave, often wet. Start at the right-hand end of the cave.
1. 30m 5b Climb up and left to the top of the cave. Move left onto the wall (peg runner) and climb it, then move left to a ledge.
2. 10m Climb the short corner on the right and continue to a ledge.
3. 35m Climb the right-hand crack above, with a deviation left and back again into the corner near the top, to Pleasant Terrace.

31   19th Nervous Breakdown   75m   E1 †   (1966)
A few metres right of the cave of The Cough is a wide undercut crack containing a jammed block. Start below and right of this where a large boulder lies embedded in the scree.
1. 30m 5b Climb the loose corner for a few metres then go up and left to a small ledge. From its left end descend 3m (peg runner) and traverse the red wall to the jammed block in the wide crack. Climb the crack to a niche and belay.
2. 20m Go left from the niche to a large ledge, then climb the gangway on the left of a big V-notch to a poor stance.
3. 25m Climb the steep chimney-crack on the right (one wedge for aid) to Pleasant Terrace.

32   Yak   50m   E1 †   (1966)
The deeply-indented, prominent V-groove near the top of Sloping Shelf, a few metres right of 19th Nervous Breakdown. The groove has mossy walls and loose chockstones.
1. 25m 5a Climb the groove to a ledge and belay.
2. 25m Climb the square corner on the left to Pleasant Terrace.

33   Pleasant Terrace   270m   Moderate   (1935)
This cuts across the face from Deep-Gash Gully on the right to Shadbolt's Chimney on the left. It is useful for access to the routes described below and also as a descent from climbs on the face described above. In its lower reaches it is distinctly unpleasant. Start from Sloping Shelf at the large recess under Deep-Gash Gully. To the left a wide shallow fault runs halfway up the face. Climb its right flank for 15m, then traverse across to the left flank. A chimney now leads to the right end of the Terrace, which is a path to its left end. Finish by the easy final chimney of Fingal's Chimney, or by traversing left into a grassy amphitheatre to finish up the Corridor of Shadbolt's Chimney.
Winter: II/III *   (1969)
Gain the right end of the Terrace as above (75m). Continue for three easy but spectacular rope-lengths before finishing by the upper part of Fingal's Chimney.

34   Way In   90m   VS †   (1967)
Takes the crag above Pleasant Terrace, left of Rabbit's Hole and above Clevedon Way.
1. 25m Climb a broken corner to a belay on a loose pinnacle.
2. and 3. 65m Go briefly up then right over a slab to another corner; belay above an overhang. Walls and broken ground lead to the top.

35   Rabbit's Hole   110m   VS †   (1967)
The obvious deep gully, capped by chockstones, above the access
pitch to Pleasant Terrace.
1. 30m Climb the central chimney crack for 7m, traverse right into
another crack and then go up to belay in the Hole.
2. 25m Continue to a dark cave.
3. 10m Negotiate a huge chockstone on aid to a stance. Continue up
and out to a chockstone belay.
4. 45m The gully now opens out; escape up easy rocks on the left.

36   Stook   120m   VS 4c   (1959)
This poor route follows the steep, open, left-facing corner above the
first section of Pleasant Terrace, about 30m left of Deep-Gash Gully
and just right of Rabbit's Hole. Approach by the start of the Terrace.
1. 35m Climb a rotten rib and a steep wall to enter the corner. Climb
this to a stance.
2. 25m Continue up the corner.
3. and 4. 60m Finish by walls and grooves.

37   Fall-Out   125m   VS   (1968)
Start at the prominent prow split by a narrow chimney some 20m right
of Stook.
1. 35m Climb the chimney to a belay.
2. 10m Continue in the chimney to a ledge. Move right to another
chimney.
3. 40m Climb the chimney on its left wall, exiting beneath a chockstone by a squeeze, then bridge across the chimney. Move left to a
crack, climb to a ledge then to a small chimney, which is followed to
an overhang. Pass this on the right wall to belay above.
4. 40m Continue more easily to a wall with a diagonal crack. Climb
the crack and the rock above to the top.
Winter: VI ***   (1988)
Start directly below the chimney at the foot of Deep-Gash Gully.
1. 30m Climb a corner and a short wall to belay just right of the
chimney.
2. 25m Move left and climb the chimney to belay beneath a huge
chockstone.
3. 25m Continue in the chimney to a good ledge.
4. 20m Move right along the ledge, then up to another chimney (it
may be better to belay here). Climb the chimney and belay at the base
of a short chimney-crack.

5. 40m Go up and left to easier ground, follow this back right then climb grooves and short walls to a ledge. Move up left to easy ground.

38   The Twarf   120m   VS   (1984)
Right of Fall-Out a short chimney leads to V-grooves. Climb the left groove, then take a choice of routes. The difficulties are short-lived, but the rock is better than that on neighbouring routes.

39   Clevedon Way   50m   Severe   (1956)
At the right end of Sloping Shelf, just left of the recess below Deep-Gash Gully, a left-slanting crack lies on the wall above.
1. 10m Climb the crack until a move left can be made to a small stance and belay.
2. 20m Continue by a rib on the left for a few moves, regain the crack and continue by steep ledges to the left to reach an insecure ledge and belay.
3. 20m Cross to a corner on the right, climb it for a few moves and follow the rib to the right of Pleasant Terrace.

40   Deep-Gash Gully   40m   VS *   (1951)
The gully at the right end of the upper face.
1. 10m Climb the first section on the right by back and foot.
2. 10m Start on the right, then go up the back of the cave by tunnelling and crawling through a small hole to a ledge.
3. 10m Climb the right wall by an overhang, crux. (It is possible to reach a hole in the cave roof to fix a thread runner)
4. 10m Start by crawling, feet first, through a small hole to reach a grass ledge. Now climb a short corner and scramble up the gully bed to a belay on the right wall at the end of the climbing.
Winter: IV   (1957)
Follow the summer line, using aid from the thread runner at the summer crux.

Alcoholics Arete   (40m   Very Difficult   1952) follows the arete immediately right of Deep-Gash Gully on poor rock.

41   The Girdle Traverse   300m   E2   (1962)
A traverse between Ossian's Cave and Deep-Gash Gully. The first section has some poor rock; it may be better to avoid it by starting up Tober. Start by climbing Ossian's Ladder.
1. 20m From above the tree belay at the mouth of the cave go right

and slightly up to a peg runner, then step down and across a loose chimney and climb a clean rib to a ledge.

2. 10m Go up and right to the top of a short groove to belay below the chimney section of Fingal's Chimmney.

3. Descend a grass ledge and traverse round an edge on loose rock to below a jagged roof.

4. 15m Climb a shattered bulge on the right, go right round a clean rib and cross a slab to a recess above a grass tongue.

5. 35m Traverse a delicate wall on the right and climb a crack to the point where it bends left under a roof.

6. and 7. Find a way up and right to a semblance of a break in the overhanging barrier running up and left across the whole cliff.

8. 20m 5b The crux Barrier Pitch. Cross the bulging wall past peg runners, then move up and right to a stance on an edge.

9. 25m Follow the steep staircase on the right to slabs, then descend a shelf slightly rightwards to belay at the top of pitch 1 of Yo-Yo.

10. 15m Climb Yo-Yo for 6m then cross the wall on the right to the arete. Descend to slabs.

11. 25m Follow steep grooves on the right to bulges. Continue to the foot of a large inset V-groove.

12. 35m Climb the V-groove then a shallow diedre on the right. Step right round the arete and climb the wall above to a large ledge.

13. 35m Traverse right and step off cliff.

The following winter climbs take the impressive mixed ground above Loch Achtriochtan. Route-finding ability is a prerequisite, as is, obviously, a hard freeze and a low snowline. Perhaps useful when higher cliffs are being weather-beaten.

42 North Face Route   600m   III *   (1982)
An enjoyable route which takes a central zigzag line to the obvious girdling shelf. From there follow snow slopes rightwards to Dinner-time Buttress. Much turf and numerous tree belays.

43 North-West Face Route   450m   II *   (1971)
Takes a line up the right side of the face.

44 Mr Softee   V *   (1983)
The impressive steep icefall high on the face, gained by wandering up the lower face. The icefall offers high-angle climbing with a long vertical section on pitch 2.

WEST FACE

The West Face of Aonach Dubh flanks the entrance to Coire nam Beith, and dominates the lower reaches of the glen. It is best seen from the old Glen Coe road near the Clachaig Inn. This complex face requires some description. It is divided vertically by six gullies, forming distinct buttresses. It is further divided by two horizontal ledges. The lower narrow ledge is called Middle Ledge, while the upper, broader ledge is known as The Rake. Each buttress is thereby in three tiers. The lowest tier, below Middle Ledge, is composed of layers of decaying andesite and vegetation, and has no climbing value. The middle tier, between Middle Ledge and The Rake, is steep rhyolite and provides most of the climbing, while some additional routes are on the good and more open rocks of the upper tier rising above The Rake.

The gullies are numbered from 1 to 6, left to right. The main mass of the middle tier, between Gullies 3 and 4, is further split by two scoops. The most prominent gully is No.2, which runs up to the col between Aonach Dubh and Stob Coire nan Lochan. Even in bad weather it is difficult to miss this gully which has a wide re-entrant. To its left are Dinner-time Buttress (originally A Buttress) and No.1 Gully. To its right are No.2 Gully Buttress, B Buttress, No.3 Gully, C Buttress, C-D Scoop, D Buttress, Amphitheatre Scoop, E Buttress, No.4 Gully, F Buttress, No.5 Gully, G Buttress, No.6 Gully, and Chaos Chimney. Situated above and between the middle tiers of buttresses D and F is The Amphitheatre, a large basin of pinnacled and spectacular rock scenery.

The approach to all the climbs on this face begins where the main road crosses the River Coe close to the junction with the old road (leading to Clachaig Inn). Climb a stile at the south-west corner of the bridge and follow the path towards Coire nam Beith. Strike off left below the lowest waterfall, cross the stream and gain the lower slopes of Dinner-time Buttress. No.2 Gully is easily crossed at this point, giving access to the grassy lower tier of B Buttress or any of the gullies further right. Climbs on buttresses B to F are best gained by climbing the lower tier of B Buttress then traversing right along Middle Ledge. Access to the gullies in winter is from directly below. Dinner-time Buttress gives access to No.2 Gully Buttress and climbs further right on the upper tier, The Rake being easily gained from the upper section of No. 2 Gully.

The various buttresses and gullies end on stony slopes below the ridge between Aonach Dubh and Stob Coire nan Lochan. In normal

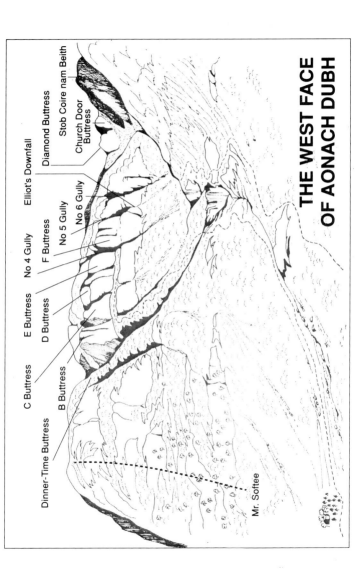

THE WEST FACE
OF AONACH DUBH

Dinner-Time Buttress

B Buttress

C Buttress

D Buttress

E Buttress

No 4 Gully

F Buttress

No 5 Gully

No 6 Gully

Elliot's Downfall

Church Door Buttress

Stob Coire nam Beith

Diamond Buttress

Mr. Softee

conditions the best descent route, both in summer and winter, goes north-east to the lowest point of this ridge at the top of No.2 Gully. Go down the easy, upper section of No.2 Gully and where it steepens below Middle Ledge traverse right (north) onto Dinner-time Buttress. The rocks of both gully and buttress are thereby avoided. In bad or dangerous conditions it is better to make for the lochans in Coire nan Lochan and descend by the path down this corrie. If time is short, The Rake provides an easy escape route, leading left into No.2 Gully.

The gullies are not recommended in summer. No.1 Gully is easy but poor, and the others have difficult wet sections which have prevented complete summer ascents. In winter, several give good climbing. The routes are described from left to right (The Amphitheatre is under a separate heading).

1   Dinner-time Buttress   180m   Easy/I
The leftmost buttress, between gullies 1 and 2. There is a long approach up easy grass and scree. The only rock is a 45m stretch high up, easily avoided by entering No.2 Gully. A useful access route (see above).

NO.2 GULLY BUTTRESS (Map Ref 146 558)
The steep little buttress lying above the left end of The Rake, between Dinner-time and B buttresses. No.2 Gully is wide and easy at this point. To reach the buttress, scramble up Dinner-time Buttress and where it steepens enter No.2 Gully. The buttress is directly ahead; a grass shelf cuts across it at mid-height.

2   Oz   70m   VS †   (1964)
The grooves in the centre of the face left of Rose Innominate.
1. 25m Climb the groove until it overhangs, then climb right to an arete which is followed until a swing across into the next groove can be made. Climb this to a small ledge (thread runner), then up an over-hanging, wedge-shaped crack to a block belay on a large heather ledge.
2. 20m Trend right to an overhang which is climbed, then go left to a ledge and belay.
3. 25m Follow a rising line, first right, then left, to the top.

3   Rose Innominate   45m   HVS **   (1951)
Left of the lowest rocks is a slabby pillar of rough clean rock, split by a thin crack.

1. 25m Climb the crack to a small ledge. Continue up the crack (crux) to a block at the top of the pillar and a belay above.
2. 10m Step right to a grass ledge. Climb the slightly overhung crack in the corner to an overhung ledge and small cave. Move left to a belay under the overhang.
3. 10m Climb the groove and finish up easy rocks.

4   Rose Late   60m   Difficult   (1953)
Begin at an obvious easy scoop at the lowest rocks. Climb the scoop to a terrace below the overhang on Rose Innominate. Traverse left along the terrace round the edge onto the north face to a right-angled recess. Climb its left edge and step right over the apex to a noticeable clean-cut crack which is climbed to another terrace. Traverse left, climb the right edge of a wall and scramble to the top.

5   Steptoe   60m   VS *   (1971)
Start 10m right of Rose Innominate at a deep chimney-groove whose right wall is formed by a pinnacle. An easy and well protected route on good rock.
1. 30m Climb the groove, move left onto the arete and back right by a crack in a slab to belay on a grass ledge.
2. 20m Move right below an overhang, then back left to a ledge below a second overhang. Climb this to a rock bay with a loose flake.
3. 10m 4a Climb the groove on the right, then easier rocks to the top.

6   The Verger   90m   Severe   (1971)
On the right of the buttress, about 20m right of Rose Innominate, is an impressive arete crowned with pinnacles. This is an illusion however, as one can walk off it in its lower half. About 60m up, the ledge common to all routes is reached below a corner. Traverse 5m left and climb a wall to the top.

B BUTTRESS (Map Ref 145 557)

This lies between gullies 2 and 3. The climbing is concentrated on the 90m middle tier. The upper rocks, which rise 120m above The Rake in two steps, have been climbed by several lines with some good pitches, but only one route has been recorded. Exploration can be enjoyed here. The first four routes described are on the north face, overlooking No.2 Gully. It is loose in places and care should be taken.

7 Left End   60m   Very Difficult   (1958)
From the left end of the north face climb a series of clean walls. The crux is where a traverse to the left edge is necessary near the top.

8 The Shake   105m   VS †   (1964)
The most obvious feature of the buttress is its central rib, well seen in profile when ascending the lower reaches of Dinner-time Buttress. The Shake starts at a short corner below and just left of a deep crack which splits the lower part of this rib. Climb right then left to overhangs. Surmount these to easier ground, then continue up right to a block belay. Move up and right to a chockstone belay (20m). Follow the open groove above to easier ground (30m). Continue to the top.

9 Bumblebee   115m   Very Difficult **   (1972)
On the right flank of the central rib, starting about 30m above the lowest rock, is a system of grooves leading to a final crack. The route gains these fairly directly, starting right of the deep crack in the rib, and follows the grooves and the final crack to the top. The rock is excellent and the grooves section gives a fine pitch.

10 The North Wall   105m   Severe   (1964)
The first part is in common with Original Route (45m Severe 1940s) which provides an alternative approach to the routes on the west face. Approach by No.2 Gully and start 10m above the gully bed at the middle of the wall. Choose a zigzag line of least resistance, which will not be found easily. Sound steep rock, with narrow ledges and sufficient belays, leads to the top.

11 Silent Running   120m   IV/V   (1986)
An ice smear forms on the north wall of the buttress where Dinner-time Buttress joins No.2 Gully. Gain the smear by a ramp from the right. It provides one long pitch.

12 Direct Route   135m   Severe **   (1948)
When approaching Middle Ledge, B Buttress is seen to be crested by triple pinnacles which cluster on its right-hand section. The long vegetatious groove of Cyclops runs down the buttress to the left of the pinnacles; Direct Route takes the face on its left. Start at a vertical rib 10m left of the long groove. A prominent feature of the route is a mass of red rock just above mid-height.

1. 35m Climb the corner on the left of the rib and continue to belay on slabs below a wall.
2. 40m Move right, climb a steep wall then take the line of least resistance to the top of a grass rake which plunges down left.
3. 40m Move straight over a bulge and continue by slabby rock.
4. 20m Continue to the top.

13 Cyclops 105m III/IV *   (1970)
A long vegetatious groove runs down the buttress to the left of the pinnacles. Climb the groove to easier ground. Take a chimney line above to pass through an eye in the buttress formed by an enormous chockstone behind the pinnacles. Continue up easier rocks on the buttress crest.

14 The Pinnacle Face 90m Very Difficult **   (1932)
Some 15m from the right end of the face the steepest rocks are bounded on the left by a chimney slanting up and left. This is just right of the groove of Cyclops. Climb the chimney, (crux at the top) to a ledge and belay. Step right then climb trending right to a belay in a short chimney. The right-hand pinnacle is now above, with a cracked wall on its right. Climb the wall on good holds to easier ground. Scramble to the top. The starting chimney may be avoided by easier rocks at the right edge of the buttress.
Winter: III/IV *   (1971)
Start 10m right of the chimney, just left of the buttress edge. Follow an awkward slab up and left to the crest which is climbed for two pitches to a steep wall. Climb the wall on the right to easier ground and The Rake above.

15 No.3 Gully 300m II/III   (1934)
The gully right of B Buttress. It is shallow and indefinite, except where it crosses the middle tier. There is a continuation gully above The Rake.

16 The Smear 90m III   (1969)
The icefall which develops on the left wall of C Buttress. Start from No.3 Gully above Middle Ledge. A short steep ice wall leads to a long left-slanting ice gangway, bulging at the top. Easier climbing then leads to the top of middle tier.

17   C Buttress   150m   II   (1969)
The buttress right of No.3 Gully. From Middle Ledge start up a very narrow gully, then traverse to a narrow ledge which leads to the buttress crest. After a short steep face the upper half of the buttress lies back. A right-hand variation (30m IV 1986) starts up the right wall of a scoop between the normal route and C-D Scoop, then trends left to join the original line. In summer the buttress is Moderate.

18   The Screen   75m   IV *   (1965)
The icefall which forms over the lowest tier right of No.3 Gully. It provides a direct start to C-D Scoop, the combination of the two giving a good outing. Climb ice to an icicle recess and traverse right then left above the icicles to the final steep ice runnel.

19   C-D Scoop   150m   II **   (1965)
The gully right of No.3 Gully, rising above Middle Ledge, can be climbed on its own or following an ascent of The Screen. From Middle Ledge two short ice pitches lead to The Rake. A good finish, giving one further pitch, is by the hidden right branch of the gully on the left, which is the continuation of No.3 Gully above The Rake.

20   The Lid   60m   Severe †   (1964)
Just right of C-D Scoop is a large roof. Climb a short steep wall to a ledge at 5m. Continue up and out past three roofs (on aid) then follow a brown fault to the top.

21   D Buttress   150m   II/III   (1969)
This buttress is squat, broad and undercut. It is bounded on the left by C-D Scoop and on the right it is separated from E Buttress by Amphitheatre Scoop. Start from Middle Ledge, 6m right of C-D Scoop. The route is obvious and leads via a right traverse onto the crest, which is easy. In summer the route is Moderate.

22   D Buttress Final Tier   90m   II   (1969)
Starts from The Rake and follows a shallow gully fault above the left end of the middle tier. There is a short ice pitch near the foot then easy snow leads to a chockstone finish.

23   The Flute   60m   IV   (1979)
The obvious chimney line right of The Screen leads in two pitches to a tree belay on the right. Easier ground then leads to Middle Ledge.

24   Amphitheatre Scoop   75m   Very Difficult   (1900)
The scoop divides D and E buttresses and is the most direct approach
to the north side of The Amphitheatre. It is usually wet and slimy, and
is approached from Middle Ledge.
Winter: IV **   (1966)
The first 45m climbs a very steep ice column in the back of a corner
in two pitches divided by a belay on a pedestal on the left wall. Above,
the angle eases and the upper gully leads to The Rake, where an easy
continuation slants left to the top.
Direct Start: 65m   IV ***
The obvious icefall on the lower tier gives one of the best routes on
the face when combined with the normal route.

E BUTTRESS (Map Ref 144 555)

This great buttress lies on the left of No.4 Gully below The Amphitheatre. It has two distinct faces; the west face is above Middle Ledge,
and the south-west face soars above No.4 Gully. Left of the west face
is Amphitheatre Scoop. Approach by Middle Ledge; at the point where
it suddenly turns in and down into No.4 Gully the secrets of the buttress
are revealed, with the formidable wall of the south-west face above.
There is a triad of classic routes - The Big Top, Trapeze, and Hee-Haw
- with modern, hard routes in between. An obvious landmark of the
south-west face is the huge corner taken by Trapeze. The routes are
described from left to right.

25   Original Route   70m   Severe *   (1958)
From the foot of Amphitheatre Scoop, walk right round an edge to the
point where a shallow scoop can be seen to the left of the buttress
crest.
1. 10m Go up to an overhang and belay.
2. 20m Traverse left and climb a steep wall to a slab. Move up the
slab to a grassy scoop.
3. 40m Traverse right to the crest and scramble up excellent rock to
the top.

26   Consolation   80m   VS *   (1962)
Right of the crest a large spike marks the start of a heathery groove.
Climb the groove to belays below twin cracks. Gain the right-hand
crack and follow it to a recess below an overhang. Move left round a

rib to a belay at the foot of a little chimney. Move up then left for 10m to a good belay. Pleasant slabs are followed by scrambling.
Winter: V **   (1980)
Follow the summer route. A rest point was taken at the shelf at the foot of the right-hand crack. The first ascensionists descended via The Rake and No.2 Gully, following the tracks of a smart Glen Coe hare...

27   Blind Pew   60m   HVS †   (1967)
Start as for The Big Top.
1. 35m Go up and left for 15m as for The Big Top, then go straight up a corner to a mossy ledge. Traverse the ledge rightwards, then go up to an awkward stance and belay.
2. 25m Move out on an undercut flake to a ledge on the left, climb the wall (3 pegs, 1 sling) to the overhang, traverse right beneath it, step round the edge then across to belay midway up pitch 2 of The Big Top. Finish as for The Big Top.

28   The Big Top   160m   E1 ***   (1961)
This route starts up the west face, crosses the exposed edge to the south-west face, then makes a rising traverse across it. Start at a block below the right edge of the west face. One of the ten best routes in the area.
1. 35m 4c Go up and left for 15m, climb a slabby corner and then up and right to a belay on top of a large flake.
2. 35m 5a Climb the bulging arete on the right and continue by a crack on the edge of the arete to an easing of the angle.
3. 45m 5a Move right to a diagonal line of slabby grooves (overlooking the slab of Trapeze) and climb these until it is possible to move left to a short crack. Climb this to a large ledge.
4. 45m 5a Climb a monster flake on the right to a wall. Move left up the wall (old peg runner) then right and traverse right across a groove to a slab. Climb the slab and a wall and finish up a broken groove to the top. There have been fatal accidents on this pitch due to bad leader falls; there is a good runner in the groove just before the slab.

29   Salome   25m   E5 6a   (1987)
A useful alternative first pitch to Prophet of Purism, following a more direct line up the left side of the very steep wall, close to the left arete. Slightly less death-defying. Start on the large platform just above the

rowan tree below the wall, where a large flake sits at the base of the route. Step off the flake and follow two thin parallel cracks running vertically up the wall until forced to make a thin move out left to an obvious diagonal handrail. Follow this left (Friend 2 halfway along) and make some committing moves to large flakes where the handrail fades. Gain the recess up on the right and exit directly on poor rock and poor protection to an impasse. Move diagonally left to the arete and belay at the base of the large flake on The Big Top, as for Prophet of Purism. Finish up either route.

30   Prophet of Purism   135m   E6 *   (1981)
Zigzags a way up the big wall between The Big Top and Bannockburn. Start on the rake of Trapeze, about 5m from the foot of the corner.
1. 30m 6a Traverse left and climb a right-facing corner. Move left across the wall to a small hanging groove, step down to an obvious traverse line and follow this to a recess on the left side of the wall (avoid the obvious traverse down and left). Continue up the overhanging wall, then go diagonally left to the arete of The Big Top. Belay at the foot of the flake crack. A very serious pitch.
2. 35m 5c From the top of the flake step down and move right to a thin diagonal crack. Follow this to a delicate thread and ascend to just below a ledge on The Big Top. Step down and follow the obvious traverse line to a large flake, move back left and up a groove, then move left from its top and up to a belay on Bannockburn.
3. 30m 5a Climb twin grooves to the huge flake of The Big Top.
4. 30m 5b Climb the open corner to the peg on The Big Top, continue up the steep undercut groove above and move right to finish up an easy right-angled corner.

31   Bannockburn   130m   E4 *   (1977)
This supersedes the old aid route Tightrope (1966). After starting up Trapeze, the route takes the wall to the left; pitches 2 and 4 are poorly protected. Start near the left edge of the face.
1. 15m Scramble up grassy rakes to the foot of the corner.
2. 35m 5b From a ledge 6m up the corner, step left to an obvious flake crack. Climb this and traverse left along a break to a ledge halfway along pitch 3 of The Big Top.
3. 40m 5b Climb the wall above to a terrace.
4. 40m 5c Climb the left-hand of the two grooves above and finish by an easy groove.

32 Trapeze 150m   E1 **   (1958)
Climbs the very obvious corner, then takes a winding line up the slabs
and overhangs above. Start near the left edge of the face.
1. 15m Scramble up grassy rakes to the foot of the corner.
2. 20m 5b Climb the corner, strenuous, to below an overhang.
3. 40m 4c Turn the overhang on the left and follow the easy corner to
slabs, continuing to a mossy bay.
4. 5m Traverse right to a well-defined platform.
5. 40m 5a Leave the platform on the left and climb a steep wall to a
ledge and corner above. The wall is both steep and delicate. (The
Direct Finish takes the obvious corner above). Turn the corner on the
right and make an ascending traverse right to a groove and crack.
Climb these to a slab beneath an overhang and traverse right to a
rocky bay.
6. 10m Climb a right-slanting groove and a short crack to the top.
Direct Finish: 30m   HVS 4c *   (1965)
Start from the top of the initial steep wall on pitch 5. Climb the clean
corner, which the original route turns on the right, then easier climbing
leads to the top.

33 Sideshow 180m   E1 5b †   (1966)
Start about 15m right of Trapeze under a steep wall defined on the left
by a short chimney.
1. 35m Climb the wall trending right to a ledge, then more easily by
a series of short walls leading to a ledge and belay.
2. 10m Move onto the upper wall and at 6m traverse right to a steep
crack leading to a corner and belay.
3. 20m Climb the corners above to the foot of the upper slab.
4. 50m Climb the steepening above by a small groove, then go direct
to the top of the slab.
5. 20m Traverse right to a large platform, then climb the steep wall
on the left (as for Trapeze).
6. 25m Climb the corner of Trapeze Direct Finish, turn the bulge on
the left and belay on a slab.
7. 20m Finish up easy slabs.

34 Performance 120m   E2 *   (1980)
At the point where the crag meets No.4 Gully a grass ramp leads up
left towards the corner of Trapeze. Start 7m up the ramp at a line of
holds trending right just right of a shallow chimney-crack.
1. 30m 4c Follow walls and grassy ledges trending right to a grass

AONACH DUBH
E BUTTRESS

28. The Big Top
29. Salome
30. Prophet of Purism
31. Bannockburn
32. **Trapeze**
32' **Trapeze Dir Finish**
37. Hee-Haw
38. The Fly Man

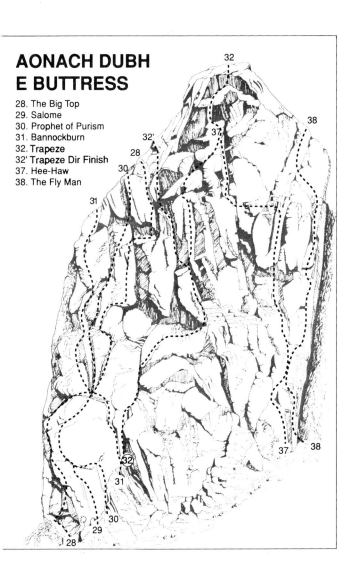

ledge beneath a shallow groove in the arete right of Trapeze.
2. 25m 5b Climb the groove for 6m, then move out to the right arete (peg runner) and climb the shallow groove to holds leading up right to a stance and belay 3m left of a grass ramp.
3. 35m Move slightly right and climb the mossy streak until it is possible to move left onto easier spiky rock. Climb to the right edge of the slab of Trapeze and follow this to a stance before the short traverse.
4. 30m 5b Climb the overhangs directly above the stance and 5m higher move left on spiky rock to a right-slanting line leading to the top.

35 The Tumbler 115m HVS †   (1967)
Start 6m left of the original buttress start of Hee-Haw.
1. 25m Climb the groove for 5m, traverse left across the steep wall and go up to a large grass ledge and belay.
2. 40m Climb the small flake pinnacle on the right, step left onto the wall and go up to belay on Trapeze below the steep wall.
3. 35m From the right side of the edge climb up right and continue up the overhanging wall to a groove-crack system. Follow this to join Trapeze pitch 5 at the slab beneath an overhang.
4. 15m Continue up Trapeze to the top.

36 Hamburg 100m E2 **   (1984)
The obvious crack below the direct finish to Hee-Haw, gained via the wall below. Start as for The Tumbler.
1. 20m Climb diagonally up left to grass ledges 6m below and left of the Hee-Haw stance.
2. 25m 5b Climb the short steep wall and continue up the easy right-slanting flake to its top. Step left and up to loose blocks (peg runner). A difficult pull straight up on dubious holds leads to better holds and a belay ledge below the crack.
3. 25m 5c Gain a narrow ledge below the crack and climb it to a junction with Hee-Haw at the groove of the direct finish. An excellent and strenuous pitch, though usually wet.
4. 30m 5a Finish up Hee-Haw Direct Finish.

37 Hee-Haw 135m E1 *   (1959)
This very steep and impressive route climbs the wall above and right of Trapeze. Scramble up the gully for about 50m to a point directly

beneath the right-hand of two imposing hanging cracks on the right-hand section of the buttress. At the foot of the wall projects a small steep buttress. The original line took a steep groove on this small buttress to start, but this is somewhat artificial as easier variants can be found up its flanking ribs. On the other hand, it does have most of the clean rock found on the route.

1. 25m 5b Climb the groove, or a choice of easier lines to the grass ledge.
2. 25m 4b Climb a crack in a corner for 6m and so up a steep wall to a detached block below a prominent crack.
3. 25m 4c Climb the crack, which overhangs, to a point below a large overhang. Go up right by a steep wall to a ledge.
4. 40m 4c Traverse left to a steep groove which is followed to its conclusion. Go left to a small stance on a slab.
5. 20m Climb the slab and finish by an overhanging crack near the top of the buttress.
Direct Finish: 30m   HVS 5a
The steep groove above pitch 3 of Hamburg.

38   The Fly Man 70m   E2   (1976)
Start in the gully to the right of Hee-Haw where a fault splits the gully wall. The route is spectacular, but loose and lichenous.
1. 15m 5a Climb the fault to the top of Hee-Haw pitch 1.
2. 40m 5b Swing onto the rib and gain the obvious flake. Climb this and continue past two small ledges until it is possible to move right round the arete to a small ledge below a thin crack. Climb the crack to a flake belay.
3. 15m Climb the wall above to the top.

39   The Girdle Traverse 225m   HVS †   (1967)
Start on the nose of the buttress at the foot of Original Route.
1. 40m Scramble up right to a slab above an overhang, then traverse 30m horizontally right, descending two overhanging corners, to join The Big Top above the slabby corner on pitch 1.
2. and 3. 90m Continue up The Big Top until an easy traverse right leads to Trapeze slab at mid-height.
4. 30m Cross the slab at that level to a ledge.
5. 15m Climb straight up to the platform on Trapeze pitch 4.
6. and 7. 50m Finish up Trapeze.

The following three routes are on the small crag which lies above and right of E Buttress, splitting No.4 Gully in two. Scramble up the gully to the small steep buttress whose crest is split by the chimney crack of Stickleback. The routes lead to The Amphitheatre. To escape from its clutches either finish up a route there, or traverse right across the face of F Buttress by grassy ledges (care needed).

40   Serenade   90m   VS **   (1977)
The slab on the left flank of the crag. Start below the left-slanting break in the overhangs topping the left flank.
1. 45m Climb slabby rock to an obvious corner, climb this (often wet), move right slightly and follow the obvious line up and left to belay in a niche in the right wall.
2. 45m Step back left, follow the ramp up left to a hidden corner, then climb this and pull over the roof at the top.

41   Stickleback   90m   HVS *   (1959)
The chimney-crack splitting the crest of the buttress. Start on the left flank of the buttress.
1. 25m 5a Climb an easy slab to beneath an overhang. Traverse right to the buttress edge, make an awkward move round the edge to an amusing stance at the foot of the crack.
2. and 3. 65m Follow the crack to the top.

42   Stumblebum   115m   E1 †   (1966)
Start as for Stickleback.
1. 25m As for Stickleback to the amusing stance.
2. 20m Continue up Stickleback to the point where it swings up. Move under a roof, then right to a stance below overhanging crack in a corner.
3. 25m Climb a crack to a roof, move round a corner to the right and up an overhanging groove to a poor stance and belay.
4. 45m Continue up the crack to a roof, move left onto an open face and climb a crack to scrambling ground.

43   No.4 Gully   300m   III/IV *   (1952)
The prominent broad gully draining The Amphitheatre. In a good winter it can give several difficult ice pitches below Middle Ledge. Otherwise, start from Middle Ledge and climb up beneath the south-west face of E Buttress to the crag which divides the gully. Here the gully trifurcates. An easy ramp leads left and up to join The Rake. This ramp is both an escape route leading to No.2 Gully and the normal descent route from

the top of E Buttress. The gully proper, however, narrows to a deep cleft on the left side of the Stickleback crag and leads eventually to the left side of The Amphitheatre. Finish up to the left. The right fork, to the right of Stickleback crag, remains unclimbed.

44 E4F5 Route   135m   Moderate   (1898)
Start below the bottom tier of E Buttress. Climb vegetation to Middle Ledge and traverse into No.4 Gully. Climb the gully to The Rake and traverse across F Buttress to No.5 Gully. Climb the upper part of the gully by a knife-edge arete in the centre.

45 Christmas Couloir   240m   III/IV **   (1965)
Approach by Middle Ledge. The couloir climbs an obvious rake above and right of the bed of No.4 Gully and just left of F Buttress. At the Stickleback crag climb a steep section right of the buttress; this is right of the unclimbed right fork of No.4 Gully. The steep section is the crux and is often heavily iced. Above this the route continues up the right side of The Amphitheatre, leading to three obvious finishes. The direct one is the most difficult.

46 Christmas Eaves   90m   III/IV
This is a variation to Christmas Couloir. Take a central line when opposite the base of the ramp leading to The Rake and climb it into a corner. Move up right and regain Christmas Couloir on the main snow slope.

F BUTTRESS (Map Ref 143 554)
This is to the right of No.4 Gully. The clean slabby wall above the gully gives several short routes. On the west face there is a prominent narrow chimney in the middle of the buttress (**The Vent,** 75m Severe 1956). This can be reached by a horrible traverse along the continuation of Middle Ledge, or climbed as an integral part of the winter route Southern Death Cult.

47 Nirvana   50m   VS   (1976)
There is a grassy gully at the foot of the clean slabby wall on the opposite side of No.4 Gully from the start of Trapeze. Start at the upper left of the face where the gully narrows.
1. 35m Climb up past a prominent cavity and gain a ledge on the right. Move right along the ledge and climb a crack which curves up and left to finish in a small bay directly above the start.
2. 15m Scramble to the top.

48   Pocks   60m   Severe   (1965)
The clean pock-marked slab opposite the start of Trapeze. Start left
of a prominent flake. Go up to a ledge at 12m, move up and traverse
slightly right then up and right again to a grassy ledge. Climb the short
steep crack above (one peg). Scramble to the top.

49   Gazebo   50m   HVS †   (1977)
Gain the wall near the start of the grassy gully.
1. 40m (3 pegs and 2 nuts for aid). Climb up and left until forced to
make a long step right. Move up and back left to a ramp leading to a
small ledge (2 nuts). Move across and then up to easier rocks. Belay
in a niche right of Pocks.
2. 10m Move up and left to finish up the last few moves of Pocks.

50   Southern Death Cult   150m   V **   (1984)
A direct line up the centre of F Buttress. Start at a recess 15m left of
No.5 Gully.
1. 30m Follow the overhanging fault diagonally right via vegetation to
a hanging stance under the right-hand end of the roofs.
2. 40m Climb through the roof on icicles into a snow bowl. Exit right
to a shallow cave below a rock barrier.
3. 35m Climb up and left to a weep of ice cutting through the bulge
and groove. Continue up an easy slope past trees to the upper rock
band. Belay below the iced chimney of The Vent.
4. 45m Climb a vertical icicle in the chimney and the overhanging
groove above. Continue up snow to a large chockstone cave.
5. An easy gully leads to the top.

51   Original Route   270m   Very Difficult   (1935)
Start at the base of the waterfall from No.5 Gully. Climb up left to a
subsidiary gully. Follow a steep slab and a grassy buttress with trees
to the Needle's Eye, a 10m chimney roofed by a boulder just left of
No.5 Gully. Above, an arete joins the south ridge of The Amphitheatre.
Winter: III/IV   (1969)
Start just left of the variation start to No.5 Gully and take the easiest
line to Middle Ledge. Above, climb the buttress via the Needle's Eye.

52   No.5 Gully   300m   III **   (1969)
Start up an obvious short, shallow slanting gully to the left of Elliot's
Downfall. Where this steepens, move up and right to a ridge left of the
gully bed and below the deep chimney of the Needle's Eye. Traverse

right into the gully where a steep ice pitch leads to the easier upper section. There may be a further 45m ice pitch here at an easier angle.

53   Elliot's Downfall   105m   V ***   (1979)
The pillar of ice which occasionally forms the Direct Start to No.5 Gully. Climbed in one long pitch of 45m and two easier pitches to join No.5 Gully. It is notoriously subject to collapse.

54   G Buttress Chimney   IV   (1969)
The obvious chimney in the small buttress between No.5 and No.6 gullies. It is approached by climbing No.6 Gully then moving left.

55   No.6 Gully   240m   IV ***   (1951)
This is the rightmost gully on the west face, and it comes into condition most winters. Normally two ice pitches lead to the crux pitch, a large icefall at the level of Middle Ledge. There is a small stance about 15m up the icefall, otherwise a long pitch ensues. At the top of the gully there is a small bay and a choice of finishes. A fast way off is to traverse right into Coire nam Beith, but only if conditions and visibility allow.

56   Chaos Chimney   135m   III *   (1969)
The chimney-gully system right of No.6 Gully, ending about halfway up the face. Start from the foot of No.6 Gully. Two short ice pitches lead to a 25m pitch in the narrows. Two further pitches lead to the top.

57   Squaddie's Climb   130m   II/III   (1980)
An ice flow which often forms on the ground right of Chaos Chimney.

58   Middle Ledge Traverse   II/III   (1969)
A winter traverse of Middle Ledge, following the obvious line.

THE AMPHITHEATRE (Map Ref 144 554)

The Amphitheatre is a miniature hanging corrie between the upper tiers of E and F buttresses. Good rock scenery. The North Ridge, bounding The Amphitheatre on the left, is narrow and impressive. The North Ridge and Bell's Pinnacle on its immediate right are approached from The Rake at the top of E Buttress. The remaining routes are best gained by ledges running across the east flank of F Buttress. These ledges also provide an escape route for parties climbing the Stickleback crag and wishing to descend. Routes are described from left to right.

59   North Ridge   60m   Moderate *
This attractive little ridge of excellent, rough rock is best gained by an
easy scramble from the upper rocks of C or D buttresses, or by a
traverse along The Rake.
Winter: 90m   II/III *   (1969)
Equally attractive in winter, the ridge gives a good finish above The
Rake for the middle tier routes to the left of No.4 Gully. It starts above
and slightly right of the easy upper gully of Amphitheatre Scoop.

60   North Ridge, South Wall   60m   Severe **   (1959)
Climb a series of short steep cracks on the right flank of the ridge,
about 6m from the crest, on excellent rock.

61   The Slot   90m   II   (1969)
Start from The Rake above E Buttress and follow the slope right of
and below North Ridge. This becomes a shallow gully, with an awkward cave pitch. Above this, exit by a deep crevasse on the left.

62   Bell's Pinnacle   45m   Difficult   (1932)
This pinnacle, which is immediately to the right of North Ridge, is not
(despite its name) a true pinnacle. Start up a gully under North Ridge.
Climb up vegetatious rock on the left to the west arete. Traverse right
to a corner and continue by a ledge on the far side until a higher ledge
leads back left to an exposed edge. Climb this excellent arete to the
top. A short easy neck leads to the main crag and to an easy gully
leading to the upper slopes.

63   Central Ridge   60m   Very Difficult   (1935)
This ridge buttresses the centre of the Amphitheatre wall. The lower
part is a fine arete leading to the wall.
1. 40m Climb up the knife-edge to a stance below a chimney.
2. 20m Gain the chimney by an exposed wall. The chimney is the crux
and has some unsound rock. Climb a big chockstone and continue on
easier rock. More pleasant climbing follows to the top.

Winifred's Pinnacle is a feature in the right corner of The Amphitheatre. The 60m west side is steep, loose and unclimbed. It can be
climbed either from the neck connecting the pinnacle to the main face
(15m Easy), or from a point about 15m below the neck on the north
side (30m Difficult 1900). The North-West Arete (40m Very Difficult
1954) starts where the north flank and the west face converge, and
follows the arete formed thereby.

64 Rear Exit   50m   Very Difficult   (1953)
This little buttress is part of the main face at the rear of The Amphitheatre, immediately behind Winifred's Pinnacle.
1. 30m From the gap between the Pinnacle and the buttress climb to
a recess, then traverse right to an arete which leads to a belay.
2. 20m Finish up easier vividly coloured rock.

STOB COIRE NAN LOCHAN

1115m   (Map Ref 149 549)

Stob Coire nan Lochan, the finest attendant peak of Bidean, stands
proud one kilometre north-east of the main summit. The long ridges
of Gearr Aonach and Aonach Dubh run northwards from it, defining
the north-east corrie, before finally plunging down into Glen Coe itself.
The corrie has a superb outlook and is an idyllic spot, with several tiny
lochans backed by tall columnar cliffs and deeply-cut gullies. In full
winter garb its beauty is further enhanced.

The height of the corrie floor (780m), coupled with its northerly
aspect, makes it the most reliable winter climbing area in Glen Coe.
Accordingly there is a variety of excellent routes of all grades. Since
the cliffs take little drainage from above there is not much ice, but the
corrie now boasts a number of fine and very hard snowed-up rock
routes. There are a few summer routes, some of which are good. The
rock is andesite, generally more columnar and cracked than rhyolite,
and this combined with the frost shattering of winter means that there
is a fair amount of loose rock, particularly on terraces and ledges, and
on the whole of the Pinnacle Buttress. Nevertheless, due to its height
and the fine outlook, the rock climbing is well worth sampling,
especially since the snow lasts most of the year, adding an alpine
flavour. Unless verging on insanity, none of the gullies are worthy of
summer attention.

The easiest approach starts from either of two large laybys on the
main road in Glen Coe. Cross the bridge over the river at 166 566,
then a long steady haul up a well-trodden path on the Gearr Aonach
side of lower Coire nan Lochan leads to the lip of the upper corrie
(allow an hour and a half). Alternative approaches are via the Zig-Zags
of Gearr Aonach or Dinner-time Buttress on Aonach Dubh.

The topography of the corrie is straightforward. On the left the bulk
of Summit Buttress lies beneath the summit. To its right is the uncom-

plicated slope of Broad Gully, then Forked Gully, South, Central and North buttresses and finally Pinnacle Buttress. The buttresses are divided by narrow gullies, the most prominent being SC Gully between the tallest cliffs of South and Central buttresses.

Descent in summer or winter is quickest by Broad Gully. A good safe alternative is to follow the rim of the corrie north-west then northwards, taking care of the deeply cut gullies, to easy ground beyond Pinnacle Buttress on the ridge leading to Aonach Dubh where a short easy slope leads into the corrie bowl. Note that the steep slopes below the crags accumulate large amounts of fresh snow after a south-westerly blizzard, so beware of windslab avalanche danger. The routes are described from left to right.

SUMMIT BUTTRESS (Map Ref 150 550)

This lies directly beneath the summit. On the left it is broken and easy whilst on the right it is steep and crossed by diagonal ramps and shelfs. There is an easy Grade I face route up the left side of the easier ground.

1   Boomerang Gully   210m   II *   (1949)
A pleasant route up the obvious curving gully immediately left of the steepest rocks. There is often an ice pitch where the main gully turns upwards to the right. At that point the left branch (II) leads onto the face.

2   Boomerang Arete   210m   III   (1956)
Traverse right onto the buttress opposite the entrance to the gully, then go up a short wall and grooves to a large ledge. Turn the steep wall above on the right. The next steep section is climbed by a chimney on the right, which sometimes forms an ice pitch.

3   Yankee Go Home   180m   III   (1982)
Start some 45m left of Scabbard Chimney at a right-slanting ramp.
1. 50m Climb the ramp to a ledge, traverse left and climb a hidden gully.
2. 45m Ascend the rocks above to a snowfield going left. Belay just above a groove leading right.
3. 40m Climb the groove to a right-slanting snowfield. Belay at a crack at the top of a ramp.
4. 45m Move up left to climb a left-facing corner to easy ground.

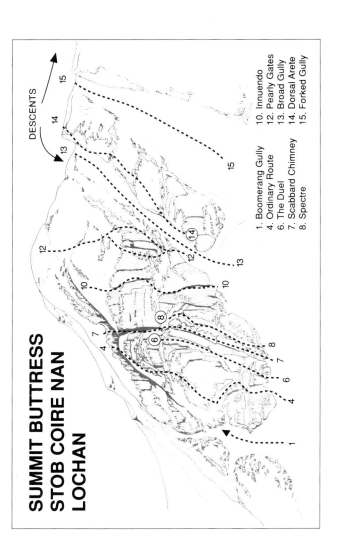

SUMMIT BUTTRESS
STOB COIRE NAN
LOCHAN

DESCENTS

1. Boomerang Gully
4. Ordinary Route
6. The Duel
7. Scabbard Chimney
8. Spectre

10. Innuendo
12. Pearly Gates
13. Broad Gully
14. Dorsal Arete
15. Forked Gully

4   Ordinary Route   130m   IV **   (1971)
Start just left of the obvious line of Scabbard Chimney.
1. Climb straight up to a snow shelf and move left to a corner.
2. Climb the corner past a block, then follow a snow shelf up left
beneath the main buttress. (Easy snow escape to Boomerang Gully).
3. On the steep wall to the right, gain then climb the obvious long
right-leaning groove and crack system and stepped ledges to the top.
The summer route approximates this line (Very Difficult 1931).
Variation: 50m   V **   (1986)
From the point where there is an easy escape into Boomerang Gully,
an awkward short wall on the right leads to a ledge system. Traverse
this rightwards, including a mantelshelf to a higher level, to reach a
block belay in a sensational position. Climb the tapering groove above
(sustained) then a short ramp and a blocky chimney leading back left
to easier ground.

5   En Garde   90m   HVS 5a †   (1980)
This route takes the upper of two well-defined ramps rising up the right
side of the buttress above Scabbard Chimney.
1. 35m The Duel, pitch 1.
2. 40m Follow the ramp and climb a crack to an overhanging chimney.
3. 15m Climb the overhanging chimney.

6   The Duel   90m   HVS †   (1967)
The lower ramp. Scramble to the foot of a steep slab left of Scabbard
Chimney.
1. 35m Climb slightly rightwards by cracks and grooves. Pass through
a break in the overhangs and climb the slab above by its right edge
until a step down right can be made onto the lower ramp.
2. and 3. 55m Continue up the groove above, gain a chimney-crack
with difficulty and follow this to the finish.

7   Scabbard Chimney   120m   Severe   (1954)
The most obvious feature of the buttress is a chimney slanting up right
under the steep right flank.
1. 20m Climb a short chimney then grass to a crack. Climb the slab
on the right of the crack to a stance.
2. 30m Climb the crack and a chimney to a sentry box.
3. 10m Above, the chimney narrows and forms a short crack in the
roof of the recess. Climb the crack, gain the rib on the right and climb
back left to the crack which leads (crux) to a large block belay.

4. 30m Continue more easily to a shoulder overlooking Broad Gully.
5. 30m Climb columnar rocks on left of the narrow gully on the left.
Winter: V ***   (1956)
Although an excellent natural winter line, there is likely to be little ice.
Normally the crack left of the slab on pitch 1 is taken and thereafter
the chimney is followed throughout, with the exit from the sentry box
providing the crux. From the shoulder the easy gully leads to the
summit.

From the belay below the easy gully of Scabbard Chimney a long
abseil into Broad Gully gives a quick approach to the following route.
The abseil sling can be collected on the way past.

8   Spectre   120m   IV **   (1958)
A fine companion to Scabbard Chimney, separated from it by a rock
rib and taking the steep shelf some 12m right of that route. Climb a
broken wall to a point directly below the first true chimney section of
Scabbard (20m). Above and right a 12m slab leads to a ledge which
is followed to the right for 6m to a point where an awkward descent
gains the long shelf. Above, an icy bulge is followed by an icy groove.
Climb a steep slab and a bulge to an easing and continue to a broad
ledge leading to the narrow gully of Scabbard Chimney.
Alternative Start: IV   (1985)
1. 50m Climb the shelf below the original start. Continue up a chimney
and the shelf above.
2. Step up left and cross a slab to join Spectre.

9   Double Entendre   IV   (1989)
Further up the side wall overlooking Broad Gully is an obvious chimney
groove. Start some 10m left of and below this. Hard for its grade.
1. Move up and right along a slabby ramp, then make a hard move
left. Go up right to belay at a spike almost in Innuendo.
2. Move 2m left and gain a groove just left of the arete of the steep
tower. Go up the groove to belay in the gap behind the tower.
3. Move up to a good flake runner, then right up a slabby ramp. Belay
on a block under the obvious hanging block 15m above.
4. Move up and right on more broken ground with better protection to
an obvious off-width chimney-crack. Squirm up this, moving right at
the top. Belay 10m higher.
5. Move right and over an awkward bulge to easier ground.

10   Innuendo   150m   IV **   (1969)
This is the obvious chimney-groove on the side wall overlooking Broad Gully, right of and below the final gully of Scabbard Chimney. Start level with the foot of Dorsal Arete.
1. 35m Climb the chimney-groove to a ledge on the left.
2. Continue up to an overhung bay.
3. Exit from the bay by an awkward chimney on the right and climb easily up rightwards to below the upper wall.
4. Traverse right beneath a hanging chimney until steep cracks lead back left into the chimney above the overhang. The chimney leads to easier ground.

11   Langsam   200m   II *   (1969)
Start up the gully from Innuendo. Follow the snow slope to under a rock wall. There is now a choice; either (i) traverse left on steep snow, then up right to a short gully and so to the top, or (ii) on the right, climb the chimney under the wall and continue the traverse to ascend steeper snow up left (crux) to easier ground.

12   Pearly Gates   150m   II   (1966)
Start in Broad Gully where the steep walls of Summit Buttress fade out. An obvious notch or gateway is visible above. Climb a line of ramps for 45m to the notch, then pass through the 'gates' into a shallow snow fan leading to the top.

13   Broad Gully   150m   Easy/I
An easy access and descent route which should be avoided in avalanche conditions. An alternative safer descent takes the main ridge down north-west then northwards past the tops of the buttresses and gullies of the corrie.

14   Dorsal Arete   120m   II **   (1951)
Starting from Broad Gully, this excellent route takes the rib between it and Forked Gully. Climb a groove in two pitches to a good ledge. Above, the arete becomes more defined and very narrow, with steep sides falling away on both flanks. This section is often avoided by a rising traverse on the left flank leading to the final wall. Belays are good.

ILLUSTRATIONS
Opposite: Stob Coire nan Lochan
Next Page: S C Gully, Stob Coire nan Lochan

15 Forked Gully 135m II/III
To the right of Dorsal Arete, the upper section of this gully is split by a 60m rock rib, producing two forks. The Left Fork is normally steep but straightforward snow. The Right Fork is harder and may contain a small ice pitch.

16 Twisting Grooves 130m III/IV (1962)
A line of diedres on the broken buttress left of Twisting Gully, starting 30m to its left.
1. 25m Climb the first corner to a small snow patch, then continue up a crack with an overhanging chockstone at its top.
2. 30m Climb diedres to a snow patch above the first pitch of Twisting Gully.
3. and 4. 55m Climb snow to the bottom of a chimney.
5. 20m Climb the chimney to broken rocks leading to the top.

SOUTH BUTTRESS (Map Ref 147 550)

This, the left-hand of the two tallest buttresses, is between Twisting and SC gullies. At its base a narrow grass ledge runs right beneath steep rocks, around the crest, then under a soaring cornerline and a steep pillar towards SC Gully. At the left end of the narrow ledge is a very steep deeply-cut chimney; on its right, before the crest is turned, is another deep chimney, starting some 20m up, taken by Tilt. The soaring cornerline is taken by Unicorn, and the steep pillar by Scansor. A short way up Twisting Gully a broad ledge cuts across the left side of the buttress towards the deeply-cut chimney; this was used by the original route on the buttress. An upper terrace runs left from the top of the corner on Unicorn to stop at a huge fin of rock in line with the deep chimney at the foot of the buttress.

17 Twisting Gully 150m III *** (1946)
One of the classic Scottish winter routes, taking the gully on the left of the steeper rocks. The line is by the original Left Fork with the harder Right Fork described in combination with Moonshadow. Climb to a deep recess where the gully forks (good belay on left wall). Above, a

ILLUSTRATIONS
Previous page: Central Grooves, Stob Coire nan Lochan
(Climber, Murray Hamilton)
Opposite: Looking up Glen Etive from Pause on the Trilleachan Slabs.
(Climber, Philip McAra)

17. Twisting Gully
18. Moonshadow
20. Chimney Route
22. Tilt
23. Inclination
24. Unicorn
25. Scansor
26. S C Gully
27. East Face Route
28. Central Grooves
29. Central Buttress
30. Satyr

SOUTH & CENTRAL BUTTRESSES
STOB COIRE NAN LOCHAN

crag splits the gully into its two forks. Climb the chimney on the left to where it steepens, gain a ledge on the vertical left wall (crux) and traverse left along this to the crest. Above is an awkward mantelshelf followed by some 30m of snow, a small pitch, then easy ground to the final snow fan and a choice of steep exits.

18   Moonshadow   150m   III **   (1958/72)
The first section of this good, sustained combination is the **Right Fork of Twisting Gully** (1958). The prominent right-trending corner on the left flank of South Buttress provides a fitting finish. If necessary, the Right Fork can be continued to rejoin Twisting Gully.
1. 30m Climb Twisting Gully to the point where it forks.
2. 40m Move right and climb the chimney on steep ice to belay 12m above an ice bulge.
3. 35m The corner starts on the right wall. Climb the wall to a thread belay in the corner.
4. 45m Continue up the groove past a chockstone to the top.

19   Ledge Route   150m   Difficult   (1934)
This is the original route on South Buttress. It climbs Twisting Gully to reach a broad horizontal ledge which is traversed rightwards to a chimney and a finish above.

20   Chimney Route   125m   V ***
The steep chimney at the left end of the narrow grass ledge gives a first-rate climb. The first ascent is unknown, but it has been climbed a number of times, either in mistake for Direct Route or Tilt, both of which start further right.
1. 25m Climb steeply up the chimney
2. 45m Continue up, then slightly right on turfy ground to the left end of the upper terrace.
3. 25m As for Tilt. A wall and a V-groove lead to the crest.
4. 30m Easy to the top.
   On pitch 2 it would be possible to head straight up into the wide chimney of Inclination. This is separated from the upper terrace by a huge fin of rock.

21   Direct Route   150m   Very Difficult   (1941)
Start along the narrow ledge beneath the chimney of Tilt, which starts some 20m up. Just left of the crest of the buttress is a pinnacle-flake. Climb the flake and a groove to a platform. Head up towards the

chimney, traverse left below it, then continue up left to a large grass platform below a great wall. Traverse left across a deep groove, then climb a dirty chimney to the top of the wall. Now go up over grass and climb a corner-crack on the left until a traverse left can be made into a gully leading to the top.

Winter: V **   (1972)

Details are vague, but it appears that the route takes the summer line, moving left at early difficulties, then up and back right to the upper terrace. Finish up the wall and V-groove of Tilt.

22 Tilt 140m VS **   (1966/7)

Start 2m right of Direct Route, immediately left of the crest.

1. 40m 4b Climb cracks and ledges to the foot of the chimney, then climb this to the crest.

2. 25m 4c Follow the groove above and once above an overhang move right onto the wall and climb to a huge flake.

3. 20m 4c Climb grooves to the upper terrace.

4. 25m 4c Move left along the terrace. Climb a wall to make an awkward entry into a V-groove chimney and finish up this.

5. 30m Easy to the top.

Winter: VI***   (1980)

Excellent sustained climbing, low in the grade, following the summer line.

23 Inclination 145m VI ***   (1991)

This route uses the original start to Tilt on the right of the crest, then takes the wall on its left to finish up a chimney. Belay at the start of Tilt.

1. 20m Move right to gain and climb a right-slanting, stepped groove up the right side of the crest to a ledge and large block.

2. 20m Move up the ramp on the left, step very gingerly up right onto a small block and torque up cracks in the wall to a chimney. Climb this and easier ground above to join Tilt on the crest. Chockstone belay.

3. 20m The unlikely looking wall on the left. Move up left to a foothold, then climb the wall to finish up a short groove.

4. 45m Climb the wide fault above (Chimney Route), but go left and up into a wide chimney whose right side is formed by a huge fin of rock. Climb the chimney to belay on top of a boulder choke.

5. 40m Move up left and onto a large chockstone, then up right to easier ground, the crest, and the top.

24 Unicorn 125m E1 ***   (1967)
The huge monolithic corner which soars up near the right edge of the buttress. Start beneath the corner. Low in the grade. A classic.
1. 35m 5a Climb the corner for 6m, then move right onto and climb the rib for 5m before re-entering the corner. Continue to a stance.
2. 20m 5a Continue up the corner.
3. 40m 5a Climb wide crack in the corner to shattered ledges.
4. 30m 5a Carefully climb over loose rock to a chimney. Climb this for a few feet then swing out right onto the wall. A few steep moves up this lead to the top.
Winter: VII **   (1985)
A modern desperate. On the first pitch the corner was climbed direct (1 nut for aid, 1 aided rest). Pitches 2 and 3 followed the summer line (1 aided rest on each). Due to darkness the final pitch was avoided. Traverse left for 15m beyond a bottomless corner, then climb a back-and-knee chimney with a difficult entry, probably Tilt.

From the top of the third pitch of Unicorn it is possible to abseil back down the line to climb Scansor (any slings found should be left), thereby ticking off two routes and avoiding having to pick one's way across the minefield of loose rock twice to get to the final chimney common to both. Your feet will appreciate not having to do the descent twice!

25 Scansor 120m E2 *   (1972)
An overated route taking the pillar right of Unicorn. Loose and mossy. However, the positions and the setting are worth the strain. Start at the foot of Unicorn.
1. 45m 5b Climb the groove right of Unicorn over suspect blocks and flakes to a ledge on the edge. Step up left and steeply climb a crack until level with a small roof on the left. Traverse right across the wall to the edge and go awkwardly up to a good belay.
2. 25m 5b Awkwardly gain the upper ledge on the left. Move up the wall until it is possible to reach right and climb onto the left end of a ledge. Traverse right to its end (peg runner), then pull up into a groove and go up right to a large stance and shelter from falling rock.
3. 20m 4c Cautiously climb the groove on the right to ledges, then up and left across alarmingly loose ground to belay on Unicorn.
4. 30m 5a Finish up the chimney and wall of Unicorn.

26 SC Gully 150m III ***   (1934)
Cleaving a line through impressive rock scenery between the tallest
cliffs of South and Central buttresses, this is one of the classic gully
climbs of Glen Coe. Normally there is a short ice pitch near the start.
A second pitch continues up steep snow in the narrowing gully to a
cul-de-sac. The next pitch, the crux, takes the icefall curving its way
up the right corner. Gained by an awkward right traverse onto a ramp,
the icefall, which may be some 20m high, leads to the easy upper
section of the gully. A long runout may be required to reach a belay.
More snow leads to a corniced exit. In summer the gully is loose and
definitely not recommended (Difficult 1931).

CENTRAL BUTTRESS (Map Ref 147 551)

This buttress is between SC and NC gullies. The face overlooking SC
Gully presents a series of steep grooves and cracks. The buttress
crest, formed by columnar rocks, has an obvious small roof 5m up.
Just left of the crest is the prominent diedre of Central Grooves. To the
right of the crest a steep smooth wall has a crack on its left, the line
of Satyr. Further right is a small bay, the start of Ordinary Route,
bounded on its right by a projecting spur leading to the buttress edge
overlooking NC Gully.

On the east face of the buttress overlooking SC Gully there are two
obvious parallel chimney systems. The left-hand one terminates at the
headwall and the right-hand one, to which direct entry is barred by
steep walls, continues to easy ground on the crest. East Face Route
climbs the lower half of the left-hand chimney then gains the right-hand
one to finish up it. The left-hand chimney has been climbed with some
aid to ledges below the headwall, but a complete ascent is awaited.

27 East Face Route 130m V **   (1982)
1. 20m Climb the left-hand chimney then move left to a pedestal.
2. 15m Move back right and climb past the left end of a roof in the
corner to good belays in a shallow recess.
3. 30m Move across the wall on the right, make a hard swing around
the arete, then go up and right to enter the right-hand chimney system.
4. 45m Climb the chimney past a steepening to belay on its left wall.
5. 20m Move right to the crest. Finish up Ordinary Route.

THE BUTTRESSES AND GULLIES OF STOB COIRE NAN LOCHAN

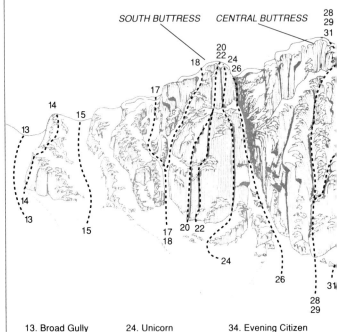

SOUTH BUTTRESS *CENTRAL BUTTRESS*

13. Broad Gully	24. Unicorn	34. Evening Citizen
14. Dorsal Arete	26. SC Gully	36. Para Andy
15. Forked Gully	28. Central Grooves	39. Crest Route
17. Twisting Gully	29. Central Buttress	42. Pinnacle Buttress
18. Moonshadow	31. Ordinary Route	Groove
20. Chimney Route	32. NC Gully	43. Pinnacle Buttress
22. Tilt	33. People's Friend	North-East Face

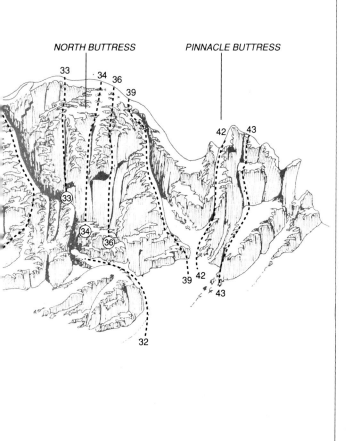

NORTH BUTTRESS

PINNACLE BUTTRESS

33
34 36
39

42 43

33
34
36

39 42
43

32

28   Central Grooves   130m   VS 4c **   (1960)

The obvious diedre which springs from near the toe of the buttress. Start just right of the diedre.

1. 30m Climb up and left into the corner and follow it to small ledges.
2. 25m Continue up the corner until it opens out onto mossy ledges.
3. and 4. 50m Follow the grooves above, passing left of a conspicuous overhang to finish on a broad terrace.
5. 25m Easy to the top.

Winter: VI ***   (1983)

A magnificent climb, one of the best in the country. Climb the initial 5m direct and follow the summer line throughout.

29   Central Buttress   135m   VI ***   (1981)

Viewed from a distance an elongated S-shaped line cleaves the buttress starting from its toe. Another superb route.

1. 30m Central Grooves, pitch 1.
2. 20m Traverse right, climb the wall to a corner and follow this to a ledge on the crest.
3. 40m Climb the short wall above, then follow easier ground up and right to the edge. Move right and climb a pinnacle to a small snowfield.
4. 45m Climb the chimney above and break out right just below the top to reach Ordinary Route. Follow this to the top.

30   Satyr   100m   E1 5a †   (1973)

Start just right of the buttress crest, below a crack.

1. 30m Climb the crack to a ledge and hanging block. From a peg on the right move left to a ledge and across to a higher shelf on the crest.
2. 30m Climb a groove and move over loose blocks slightly right to a cave under a pinnacle-flake.
3. 40m Move left, climb the crest by a crack and go up a further crack to the flake top (peg runner above on the left). Mantelshelf and climb the right twin groove past overhangs to a grass ledge and V-groove leading to easier ground.

31   Ordinary Route   150m   III ***   (1907)

An excellent open route with fine situations. Start in the small bay some 10m right of the crest where an angle is formed between the main face and the projecting spur on the right. Climb mixed ground, then a groove, moving right at its top to gain the edge overlooking NC Gully. Follow the edge to a tower, visible from below, and turn this on the right by a short chimney. Continue by a series of short, awkward walls. In summer this route is Moderate.

32   NC Gully   180m   I/II **
The gully between Central and North buttresses. Normally a straight-forward snow climb with a small cornice, it can sometimes form a short pitch. A good introduction to gully climbing.

NORTH BUTTRESS (Map Ref 147 552)

The rightmost of the three main buttresses. The rock is not as good as on the others, but when bonded together by snow and ice there are some fine routes. A tower with a prominent roof halfway up is obvious. On its left, overlooking NC Gully, is the cornerline of Evening Citizen, whilst on its right are two groovelines, then the crest taken by Crest Route. The face then turns to form the North Face overlooking North Gully.

33   People's Friend   105m   V/VI   (1985)
The grooveline left of Evening Citizen. Direct access to the groove is barred by a short wall, so start at the foot of NC Gully.
1. 35m Climb a groove and traverse left beyond Evening Citizen to a stance below a 3m pinnacle and directly above the NC Gully chock-stone.
2. 20m Climb the pinnacle to a groove capped by a small recess. Enter the recess with difficulty and exit via its top left corner (very committing).
3. 50m The sharply-defined groove above is started with difficulty and climbed, gradually easing to the top.

34   Evening Citizen   95m   IV **   (1971)
The obvious cornerline left of the roofed tower. Start in NC Gully, then climb the corner chimney and up steeply to the crest.

35   Fawlty Tower   75m   E3 *   (1983)
This route climbs the obvious roofed tower to reach a knife-edged arete. Scramble up a grassy groove for 20m to a ledge below the roof.
1. 30m 5c Climb the steep thin crack and wall above to the roof. Traverse right, pull over and go up a slab until an obvious traverse back left leads to the arete.
2. 45m 5a Follow the arete directly to the top of the tower. Scramble to the top.

To the right of Fawlty Tower are two grooves. In the past the larger left-hand one has been assumed to be East Face and the slimmer right-hand one to be Intruder. However, since the left-hand groove climbed direct is at least HVS and highly dangerous, it is likely that East Face and Intruder coincide. Descriptions for both are given for the inquisitive to sort out! The two winter routes up these grooves do not coincide and are greatly superior to their summer counterparts.

36   Para Andy   90m   V **   (1988)
The large corner-groove to the right of the roofed pillar, notable for some sensational exposure above the big roof.
1. 35m Climb directly up to the groove.
2. and 3. 55m Climb the groove until squeezed against a roof (some dangerous blocks), then traverse left and mantelshelf. Belay on the ledge on the front face above the big roof. Pass the short wall immediately above by going left and back right to a crack line in the centre of the face. Climb this until moves left lead to a ledge and blocky arete leading to the top of the tower. In summer a line approximating to this is VS (1987).

37   Intruder   100m   V **   (1988)
The slimmer right-hand groove right of the Tower. Start at the lowest rocks.
1. 15m Move up left passing the start of Financial Times and climb to the base of the groove.
2. 25m Climb the groove (passing two pegs with difficulty) to a flake, then continue to a ledge at the foot of the Financial Times flake.
3. 35m Gain the groove up on the left and climb this to the top of a pinnacle (Financial Times comes into the groove where it deepens). Move up, then right to climb a short groove and go right to belay by an obvious perched block.
4. 25m Easily to the top.

East Face (Severe 1947) takes a steep groove almost in the centre of the buttress to the right of a prominent roof. It starts a few feet right of a grassy hump and climbs 15m up dirty rock to a platform below the groove. The groove is loose in its upper part. **Intruder** (Severe 1966) takes a thin groove between East Face and Crest Route which continues as a crack on the upper wall. It is unsure how these relate to the previous two winter routes.

38 Financial Times   135m   IV *   (1981)
Takes a line near the crest of the buttress. A good route though somewhat superseded by its better neighbours. Start at the lowest rocks.
1. 40m Move up to gain then follow a right-slanting groove in the lower rocks to a pedestal belay by large blocks.
2. 25m Climb up, then left to the edge. Go up a flake-crack and pull round to a ledge in the centre of the face below a large pinnacle.
3. 10m Climb the pinnacle, starting on its right.
4. and 5. 60m Gain the groove of Intruder round on the left, and follow that route to the top.

39 Crest Route   110m   IV ***   (1985)
A fine little route taking the crest between the east and north faces. Originally known as the Toffee-Button Ridge, it approximates the summer line (Very Difficult 1957). A good introduction to modern snowed-up rock climbing. Start at the lowest rocks.
1. 35m Move right, then up broken stepped ground to a short wall where Financial Times comes in from the left. Climb the crack to a pedestal.
2. 30m Climb the flake-crack above, then go right across a slab (Financial Times goes up left towards the frontal face) and climb a groove to the crest. Step left at a large spike to a ledge level with the pinnacle on Financial Times.
3. 20m Regain the groove-crack and follow this directly up the crest to belay by an obvious perched block.
4. 25m Easy to the top.
Variation to pitch 3 (1985): After regaining the groove, return left round the crest and climb the thin crack just to its left.

40 North Face   90m   III   (1956)
The groove running up the right side of the buttress. Start at the lowest rocks. Move up right to a snow ledge in North Gully. Climb to a recess well up the face. From the left end of a ledge climb a steep groove, then go left to a nose and so to easier ground.
    The line is loose, horribly so in summer (Moderate 1931).

41 North Gully   75m   I/II
This separates North Buttress from Pinnacle Buttress. It is steep, occasionally contains a small pitch and can be heavily corniced.

PINNACLE BUTTRESS (Map Ref 147 553)

This, the rightmost crag in the corrie, is notable for its spectacular pinnacles and the overall instability of the rock, especially in summer.

42   Pinnacle Buttress Groove   60m   II/III *   (1958)
Follow a steep groove on the North Gully flank of the buttress, just left of a prominent arete. Start on the right near the foot of North Gully. A good short route in icy conditions. It is not known whether this is the same as the earlier route **Right Chimney** (II 1950) which takes the iced chimney right of North Gully. The crux is the final pitch.

43   Pinnacle Buttress, North-East Face   60m   III   (1967)
Start at the lowest rocks. Climb up right, then left up a short groove to a steep wall. An icy corner-crack on the right leads to a ledge and then a higher ledge. From the left end of the upper one an awkward chimney leads to the top. This approximates to the summer line, which is an unsavoury Very Difficult (1953).

44   Juggler   60m   Severe   (1966)
Takes a line up the prominent steep arete split by a crack in its lower half. Climb the crack and a chimney to a detached pinnacle on the right. Go over a block on the left and make a huge stride to gain a hidden groove. The key foothold is (or perhaps was) a delicately poised block! Finish up a system of cracks.

45   The Jester   10m   Severe   (1966)
The most spectacular pinnacle, well seen from the lower part of Central or North buttress. Approach from foot of North Gully by a grassy rake. Climb an overhanging crack on the short side to a ledge on the east side and swing up to the north side. Amusing.

46   Pinnacle Gully   60m   I
The easy rightmost gully of the corrie.

BIDEAN NAM BIAN

1150m   (Map Ref 143 542)

The entrance to Coire nam Beith, the great north corrie of Bidean, is flanked on the left by the West Face of Aonach Dubh and its continuation southwards to the West Face of Stob Coire nan Lochan, and on the right by An t-Sron. Above and behind An t-Sron is the great pyramidal cone of Stob Coire nam Beith, left of which lies the West Top of Bidean. Further left at the head of the corrie, Bidean nam Bian itself presents two distinctive summit buttresses: Diamond Buttress on the left and Church Door Buttress on the right.

The approach to the corrie begins as for the West Face of Aonach Dubh. At the junction of the main road and the old road leading to the Clachaig Inn go over a stile at the south-west corner of the bridge over the River Coe and follow the recently improved path which winds up on the west of the stream. Above the waterfalls the path levels out and soon reaches a fork in the streams. Cross the right branch and head up left to the main corrie floor (allow about 90 minutes). The path following the right branch of the stream continues to a col on the ridge between Stob Coire nam Beith and An t-Sron, the Bealach An t-Sron. This is the easiest way up Bidean and also the surest descent route in winter.

On the left of the lower part of the corrie are some broken slabby rocks, the continuation of the West Face of Aonach Dubh, which make up the West Face of Stob Coire nan Lochan. The path continues to the right of the stream through marvellous scenery below Stob Coire nam Beith to a higher shallow basin, then up slopes to another shallow basin. Diamond and Church Door buttresses are directly ahead up the boulder-slope, whilst up on the right, through a gateway formed by a rock sentinel and the shoulder of Stob Coire nam Beith, lie the slopes beneath the West Top of Bidean. These highest buttresses are about 2 hours from the road.

As noted above, the rocks of the West Face of Stob Coire nan Lochan (141 553) are really the extreme right end of the West Face of Aonach Dubh. They are most readily approached from the path up Coire nam Beith. There are two crags: a smaller, steeper face on the left and a larger, slabbier one on the right. There are two routes on the right-hand crag, both Difficult (1948). One starts at the left base and goes straight up and diagonally by cracks for 65m. The other starts

35m to the right, at the foot of a subsidiary buttress. Climb easily at first, then more steeply over a spike by a narrow ledge, mantelshelf, climb an easy slab and a detached pillar, and turn an overhang below the top. In winter an icefall can form on the right; this has been climbed but details are not available.

The splendid summit buttresses of Bidean, Diamond Buttress and Church Door Buttress, are separated by Central Gully. To their right the cliffs below the West Top of Bidean also provide some excellent climbing. The approach is as described above. There are a number of descents:

(i) the slopes from the col between Bidean and its West Top, underneath Church Door Buttress.

(ii) the north-east ridge of Bidean to the col (146 545) between Bidean and Stob Coire nan Lochan, then down into Coire nam Beith (beware of avalanche danger).

(iii) over the West Top to the col (140 543) between Bidean and Stob Coire nam Beith, then beneath the cliffs of the West Top into the corrie.

(iv) over Stob Coire nam Beith and down its west ridge to the col at the Bealach An t-Sron (135 547) where easy slopes lead north into Coire nam Beith.

In dangerous snow conditions the last alternative is by far the safest. In poor visibility refer to the more detailed description given in the Stob Coire nam Beith section.

The crags and their routes are described from left to right.

DIAMOND BUTTRESS (Map Ref 144 544)

This, the left-hand of the two summit buttresses, is bounded on its right by Central Gully, at the foot of which is Collie's Pinnacle. It lies at an altitude of about 920m and faces north-west. The rock is andesite, in places loose and often wet and slippery, and it cannot be recommended in summer. However, in winter's icy grip there are some worthwhile routes. The buttress appears to be seamed with cracks and grooves, but the rock is deceptively steep and many of them lead to cul-de-sacs. Two obvious ledge systems girdle the buttress, one at mid-height and one near the top.

1   North Route Direct   210m   III *   (1955)
This climbs the left edge of the buttress. Start below an obvious scoop at the lowest rocks at the left end of the face. The steep scoop swings up right onto the face, and eventually overhangs where it splits a

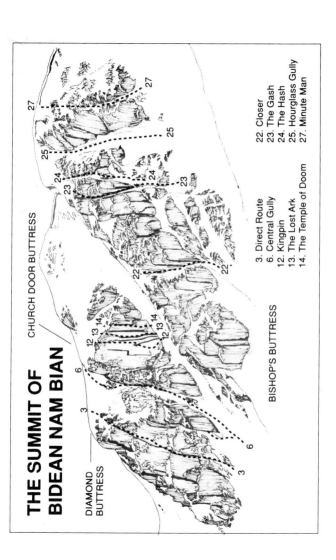

THE SUMMIT OF
BIDEAN NAM BIAN

DIAMOND BUTTRESS

CHURCH DOOR BUTTRESS

BISHOP'S BUTTRESS

3. Direct Route
6. Central Gully
12. Kingpin
13. The Lost Ark
14. The Temple of Doom

22. Closer
23. The Gash
24. The Hash
25. Hourglass Gully
27. Minute Man

projecting spur. Climb the arete on the right, then make a short, steep horizontal traverse round an edge into another scoop. Snow-covered slabs and an awkward crack lead to a platform above the overhang of the first scoop. A long traverse left now leads back to the crest, which leads easily to the top. The original **North Route** (Difficult 1930; II 1955) skirts around the left edge of the buttress by a series of chimneys and scoops. Easy escapes are possible to the left.

2   Diamond Route   255m   V   (1986)
This climbs the left side of the lower face then the upper face by its right side. Start in a bay midway between the foot of the buttress and Collie's Pinnacle, below a left-trending ramp.
1. 40m Gain the ramp and follow it, then go further left.
2. 30m Go up steep ground to belay just below a short V-chimney.
3. and 4. 65m Avoid the chimney by an awkward move right, then go straight up. Continue to the upper girdling ledge.
5. 60m Follow the ledge rightwards to its end.
6. 25m Climb a short difficult chimney to an arete.
7. 35m Easier ground to the top.

3   Direct Route (Summer)   150m   Severe   (1931)
Start directly beneath the summit, midway between the foot of the buttress and Collie's Pinnacle. The general trend of the route is obliquely right to avoid large holdless slabs, then obliquely left to a pinnacle in the centre, and finally straight up. The pinnacle is visible from the start. Climb broken loose rocks to a chimney behind a detached block. Go rightwards for 30m, then back left to a huge mossy projecting block directly above the start. Above the block, go up exposed vegetatious rock to a little chimney on the left, on top of which is a good platform at the base of the pinnacle. Climb the pinnacle by its left-hand corner (hard; possible escape left from its top). Continue up steep easy rocks to a mammoth overhanging block, clearly seen from below. Gain the block from behind, face the rock and make a sensational stride across the abyss to a wall. Above, climb directly by walls and chimneys. A spell of dry weather is desirable for this route.

4   Winter Route   250m   V   (1983)
This appears to follow more closely the summer line of Direct Route than does the winter Direct Route. Start in a bay midway between the foot of the buttress and Collie's Pinnacle at a left-trending ramp.

1. Follow the ramp for about 10m until it is possible to break up and right on steep mixed ground to a snow slope. Climb this to a rock wall.
2. Step left and descend a few feet. Climb slabby ground to a corner at the base of snow basin. Break out right by a steep groove on the right wall, then belay.
3. Follow easier ground to the middle girdling ledge.
4. Climb a groove above.
5. Continue up a groove to the upper girdling ledge on the left.
6. Traverse 30m left along the ledge to the foot of a short wall.
7. Climb up and left across the wall to easier ground.
8. and 9. Continue leftwards to the ridge.

5   Direct Route   (Winter)   150m **   (1959)
Although called the Direct Route, this takes a line further right. Follow a system of grooves up and right to the right-hand end of the middle girdling ledge. Continue by more grooves, up then right to emerge on the right-hand edge not far below the summit.

COLLIE'S PINNACLE (Map Ref 143 544)
This is the large, squat pinnacle at the foot of Central Gully, dividing it into two lower forks. There are a number of ways to its top. **The Short Side** (10m Easy 1894) starts from the neck connecting the pinnacle to the gully. **The South Side** (Easy) starts from the right branch of the gully, just above the pitch. **North Chimney** (35m Difficult 1920) starts below the pitch in the left fork. Climb the chimney to an oblong chockstone. Pass this on the right wall to a platform, huge flake, a wall and a chimney. **North Crack** also starts above the pitch in the left fork. Go up the lower and larger of two cracks. **The West Face** (45m Very Difficult 1931) is the crack to the left of the right fork.

6   Central Gully   180m   I/II **   (1894)
The gully separating Diamond and Church Door buttresses, divided at its foot by Collie's Pinnacle. In summer it is an easy scramble up scree. In winter it gives an interesting and scenic approach to the summit of Bidean. There are two routes. The first (Grade I) starts right of the Pinnacle and continues directly to the top. There should be no complications given enough snow. The second (Grade II) starts left of the Pinnacle, where there can be a short pitch. About 75m above the Pinnacle take the right fork.

CHURCH DOOR BUTTRESS (Map Ref 143 544)

This, the right-hand of the two summit buttresses of Bidean, was christened by W.Tough from its appearance when seen end on. Around the turn of the century a steady stream of pilgrims were in attendance upon the crag. Immediately right of Collie's Pinnacle a wide spur projects from the buttress, dividing it into two faces; the East Face overlooking Central Gully and, to its right, the impressive West Face. The rock is andesite and, as one might expect, the East Face and the frontal projecting spur are made up of pinnacles, flakes, huge boulders and deep fissures. The West Face, however, is quite different. It is uniformly steep and seamed with grooves and cracks of very rough rock, some of the best that Glen Coe has on offer. At a height of about 950m with an expansive view over Ben Nevis, the Mamores and the Grey Corries, it is a marvellous place on which to climb.

EAST FACE

Go up the right fork of Central Gully as far as the neck of Collie's Pinnacle. Opposite is the obvious chimney of Crypt Route leading to the right end of the Arch, an exposed ledge on the vertical front face formed by two huge jammed boulders. On the right, Flake Route climbs a flake-crack and traverses the Arch.

7   Crack-line   120m   HVS 5a †   (1968)
The steep wall left of Crypt Route. Start 6m left of the chimney, at a groove with twin cracks.
1. 35m Climb the groove to a ledge on the right and continue by cracks to a peg belay 12m below the Arch.
2. 35m Take the grooveline slanting to the left end of the Arch. At 15m swing left into a steep groove, follow this to its end, then step left onto a mossy slab leading to a corner and belay.
3. 10m Climb by cracks on the right wall of the corner to belay at the top of Raeburn's Chimney on Flake Route.
4. 40m Climb the face, or grooves on the left, to the top.

8   Crypt Route   135m   Very Difficult ***   (1920)
For this atmospheric and unusual route a headtorch is recommended. Start below the obvious chimney. Climb the chimney for 20m to a rock corridor cutting into the buttress innards. Go to the dark end of the corridor. There is now a choice of routes:
    The Tunnel Route goes through a narrow passage in the left wall into a chamber (total darkness). Another tunnel leads to a second

chamber from which a long, very narrow tunnel runs up to a hole (45cm in diameter) in the face of the cliff, some 6m under the right-hand end of the Arch. From the hole in the face climb moderate slabs to a hole in the lower right end of the Arch.

The Through Route climbs up the cave-like end of the corridor to a second and smaller cave. Make a direct exit, which is sensational and overhanging. The top of a chockstone provides a good hold. Beyond is a grass ledge, then a jumble of boulders, a cracked block and the Arch.

The Gallery Variation (1952) follows The Through Route to the second cave, then climbs into another chimney in the same fault leading to a third and smaller cave. Enter the Gallery above this - an eyrie 2m wide, just over 1m high and 6m long. Descend just over 1m from the Gallery floor then, facing out, traverse 15m right to where it is possible to climb up into the floor of the Arch. All three variations finish up Flake Route.

Winter: IV ***   (1960/84)
The Tunnel Route, The Through Route and The Gallery Variation have all been climbed. An entertaining outing by any route.

9   Flake Route   130m   Very Difficult **   (1898)
The original line up the buttress, and that only after several attempts by the leading climbers of the day. It was so resistant to their efforts that the crux was prospected from above, the easier lower parts having been climbed several times before. On the first ascent Bell and Raeburn tossed a coin for the lead. Bell led to the Arch, then Raeburn led on the crucial chimney. Foiled at first by blocks in the chimney, he returned, a higher block tempting them to throw a stone over it, tied to a piece of string. This failed, Raeburn removed his boots and tried again - Bell recorded 'I went forward to the end of the ledge to try and field him if a slip should occur, while Napier jammed himself in a hole in the ledge, worked Raeburn's rope over a small hitch, and anchored me. This time Raeburn was successful, and wild cheers broke out...'

Some 10m right of Crypt route an enormous flake is split from the buttress by a crack. Climb the crack to a col behind the flake. Alternatively, go up the other side of the flake having first traversed around it some 15m lower down the gully. From the col, step awkwardly up and right, then go straight up broken ground until a left traverse can be made to the Arch. Cross the Arch to climb a shallow chimney (Raeburn's Chimney), the crux. The grooves and walls above lead to the top.

Winter: IV **   (1942)
Follow the summer route. Good in its own right, but outshone by its better neighbours.

WEST FACE
This uniformly steep and impressive face is right of the projecting spur. There are some very fine rock routes, but the altitude and scarcity of sunlight enforce a slow drying regime. A long dry spell is required and the long walk up will be amply rewarded. The first two routes lie on the left of the face, both starting just up from the lowest rocks in a bay formed by the angle between the projecting spur and the face itself. In the middle of the face a long pillar projects slightly. On its left is a grooveline, Kingpin, and on its right another grooveline, Lost Ark.

10   West Face Route 135m   Severe   (1937)
Start at the innermost part of the bay formed on the right of the projecting spur. Above is the chimney of West Chimney Route. The outer face of the bay's left wall rises vertically for 12m to a bulge. Above the bulge a shallow cleft springs vertically, this is the vital link connecting the bay to the crest. Climb up and through a narrow crack between the buttress wall and a detached pinnacle. Traverse a ledge leftwards to the outer edge of the buttress above the bulge and below the cleft. A small, steep slab leads to the cleft. Climb the left wall of the cleft, then turn and climb the right edge to a broad mossy ledge. Climb a short wall, then easy rock to join Flake Route below the Arch. Finish up Flake Route.

11   West Chimney 180m   IV ***   (1969)
Start in the bay formed on the right of the projecting spur. The line is the obvious chimney. A classic, entertaining outing. The summer route (Very Difficult 1955) is definitely not recommended.
1. 45m Gain the ramp-chimney line and follow it under a Damoclean chockstone, then up over two others into a bay at a cul-de-sac.
2. 15m There is a tunnel up on the left; find it, then burrow in and up to emerge mole-like onto a ledge. This may expend considerable time and effort. Those of a masochistic nature may wish to wear their sacs!
3. 40m Move back to the chimney, then follow it up and under a chockstone to its top. Traverse left across ledges and boulders, then step down to a fine belay on the Arch. Don't fall down the hole!
4. and 5. 80m Finish up Flake Route.

12 Kingpin 105m E3 *** (1968/77/78)
One of the best high mountain rock routes in Britain, taking a direct line up the left side of the long pillar which projects slightly from the centre of the West Face. Start some 20m right of West Chimney, below a short crack and a short hanging chimney.
1. 20m 6a Climb the crack to a slab. Move left and up to a steep groove. This gives a few difficult moves before it is possible to swing right and up to a poor stance at a groove junction.
2. 20m 5c Climb up right and follow a black groove to a tricky mantelshelf onto a small ledge below the short hanging chimney. Enter the chimney by an awkward move and at its top step left to a small ledge and belay.
3. 30m 5b Move back right and climb the sloping ramp in a superb position to a small hooded recess. Exit slightly left, then up to a ledge. Continue up to the foot of a prominent corner.
4. 35m 5b Climb the corner to the roof, then swing spectacularly right to a ledge. Climb cracks then easier ground to the top.
Variation Finish: 35m 5c (1982)
A better finish. Follow the corner of pitch 4 to the roof. Step left, continue up the corner to its top and swing right to the original finish.

13 The Lost Ark 85m E4 *** (1983)
The obvious groove and corner system up the right side of the pillar right of Kingpin. Start at the foot of a white-speckled groove.
1. 40m 6a Climb the groove for 20m to a small overlap on its left wall. Move up and left onto the arete, then up this for 5m (crux) to pull back right and up to ledges. Traverse right a few feet and up to the overhang. Pull right across the roof to an old peg runner and climb to a good ledge. Belay at the foot of a long corner.
2. 45m 5b Step right to climb a crack for 6m, then its right wall for a further 12m. Move back left and ascend the easy groove to join Kingpin at the top of the pillar. Climb the groove above to the top.

14 Temple of Doom 75m E3 *** (1984)
The third in a trio of very fine routes takes the obvious V-groove and hanging, stepped-corner system right of Lost Ark. Start at the second groove right of that route; the first peters out after 15m.
1. 30m 6a Climb the groove, then up a hard wall to ledges.
2. 45m 5c Step right to climb a crack for 6m, then step back left and pull over to the foot of the stepped-corner system. Climb this to its top and follow the continuation crack for a short way until it is possible to step into a corner on the right. A few moves up this lead to the top.

15   Inquisition   55m   VS †   (1968)
This, the original description, is hard to follow. Towards the right end
of the face there is a prominent white groove left of large overhangs.
Start below this in a recess.
1. 25m After a few metres move right to a steep smooth groove. Climb
this (peg runner), traverse right for 12m, move up and right into a
groove, then follow this to a small overhung ledge and peg belay.
2. 25m Swing out right and up a small groove to a wall. Climb the wall,
stepping right at some jammed blocks and continue more easily to a
grass ledge with a jammed block belay.

16   The Gangway   60m   II   (1969)
Follow the left-slanting chimney and ramp above the West Face to the
crest and continue straight up to top.

WEST TOP OF BIDEAN

This top, 1141m, is only slightly lower than Bidean itself. The north and
west faces of its north-east ridge are andesite, with the exception of a
tiny section of agglomerate. On the left the rocks merge with the scree
slopes below Church Door Buttress. On the right a small basin under
the west face can be gained from the main ridge, or by heading up
right from the foot of the boulder slope leading up to Church Door
Buttress. Entry to the slopes running up below the face is guarded
by Zero Buttress on Stob Coire nam Beith to the right and a small sentinel
of rock some 20m high on the left. The lowest rocks form a prominent
small and compact buttress, Bishop's Buttress. The cliffs extend up
right to the obvious feature of Hourglass Gully, then to the summit
rocks themselves.

BISHOP'S BUTTRESS (Map Ref 142 544)
When viewed head-on from below, Bishop's Buttress appears as a
steep three-sided tower. There are four routes, three on the north face
and one on the north-west face. In poor visibility the rock sentinel
guarding entry to the slopes beneath the West Top can be mistaken
for Bishop's Buttress, which is some 100m higher. Although the ledge
girdling the buttress can be gained from the right, the recommended
approach and descent is by traversing across from the foot of the West
Face of Church Door Buttress. Routes are described from left to right.

17   Anniversary Arete   50m   E1 **   (1991)
The prominent arete up the left side of the frontal north face.
1. 35m 5b Gain the crack in the right side of the arete and follow it to
pull out left onto the edge. Climb the edge until forced left and continue
a short way, then pull back right to good holds above a small roof.
Continue to the top of the arete, pull onto a mossy ledge, gain the
ledge above and traverse right to the bay on The Crook.
2. 15m 4b As for The Crook.

18   The Crook   50m   HVS *   (1968)
The prominent crack running centrally up the north face.
1. 35m 5a Climb the crack on excellent rock to a right-sloping ledge
and follow this past a small recess into a bay. Climb a left-slanting
groove, then a short wall and move up left into a bay occupied by a
rocking block.
2. 15m 4b Stand on the block and climb a corner, then pull out left to
a mossy platform. *In situ* nuts (1991) facilitate abseil descent.

19   Mitre   65m   VS   (1968)
Start at a crack 3m right of The Crook.
1. 25m Climb the crack for 6m, traverse up and right to the edge of
the buttress, then go past a small recess and crack to a prominent
groove.
2. 35m Climb the groove, step left at its top, move up, then step back
right into a bulging groove. Climb this and continue to a corner; peg
belay.
3. 5m Climb the left wall of the corner.

20   Ambush   75m   VS   (1968)
This route is on the west face. Start some 12m right of the buttress
edge at an obvious line of weakness.
1. 10m Climb a crack to a hole and go straight over twin jammed
blocks to a stance.
2. Move right to a corner and go up to a sloping mossy ledge. Continue
up a groove for 25m and move round to a large triangular stance.
3. Climb direct to a terrace and finish up a wall on the left.

Right of Bishop's Buttress is a deep narrow gully, then a steep
buttress bounded on the right by a prominent chimney. Two major
features of the steep buttress between the gully and the chimney are
an obvious corner high up overlooking the gully and a very large
overhang on its right.

21   Twilight   75m   E2   (1984)
Climbs the steep buttress between the gully and the chimney, going
up the wall left of the large overhang to traverse left into the main
corner. Start just right of the lowest part of the buttress at a small
undercut wall.
1. 45m Climb the wall, then continue easily up to a mossy ledge at
12m. Move round right onto the wall and follow the obvious line until
level with the base of the big overhang. Climb the short corner on its
left and step left to a ledge. Traverse 6m left (watch the rope drag) to
the right-hand corner. Climb this for 6m to an uncomfortable belay.
2. 30m Continue up the corner, step right at its top and continue
upwards near the arete to the top.

22   Closer   75m   IV **   (1982)
The prominent steep chimney right of Twilight with an icefall below it.
1. 40m Climb the icefall to gain the chimney, then follow this over
bulges and chockstones to a cave recess.
2. 35m Continue over bulges and chockstones to the top.

   Moving up the basin, broken ground crossed by ledges slants up
beneath the face towards the entrance of a deep easy gully, Hourglass
Gully. To its left is an obvious V-shape formed by two narrow gullies.
The left-hand one, The Gash, is the more prominent.

23   The Gash   120m   III/IV **   (1959)
Gain the gully by a rising traverse left from Hourglass Gully, or more
directly from below. A ledge on the right provides a good stance. Climb
the steep runnel over several bulges to a large overhanging chockstone. Turn this on the left to reach a cave below a second chockstone.
A right traverse now leads to easier ground or, if you are of a burrowing
nature, find an intriguing through route up snow in the back of the cave
to a squeeze exit.

24   The Hash   120m   II/III   (1971)
Formerly known as Caradhras Cleft, this is the right fork of The Gash.
It is a shallow groove-chimney line and is gained either directly from
below or by a rising left traverse from Hourglass Gully. Climb the
groove directly. At one point it narrows to form a bulge.

25   Hourglass Gully   120m   I *   (1966)
The easy gully splitting the cliffs below the summit gives a steep but
normally straightforward snow climb with perhaps one or two steps.

26   Dubiety   110m   IV **   (1987)
This route is on the steep right-hand retaining wall of Hourglass Gully.
Start some 30m up the gully. A steep iced corner-chimney on the right
leads awkwardly to a poor stance and a good thread belay on the right.
Climb the iced corner directly to finish at the summit.

27   Minute Man   120m   IV *   (1983)
The obvious groove in the buttress on the right of the entrance to
Hourglass Gully. Move up to then over the roof barring entry into the
groove and continue to a belay. Continue up the groove system by the
line of least resistance to the top.

STOB COIRE NAM BEITH
1107m   (Map Ref 139 546)

Stob Coire nam Beith, the north-west top of Bidean, is the shapely
peak which dominates the view from Glen Coe over Loch Achtriochtan.
It is a huge conical mass of andesite some 350m high, riven with
buttresses and gullies generally set at an easy angle. There are a few
worthwhile summer climbs, and the peak is of more interest for its long
winter routes. None of the gullies are worth summer attention.

Approaching from Glen Coe up the Allt Coire nam Beithach, the
most obvious feature is Summit Gully. This runs up left of the right-
hand skyline, starting from just left of the lowest right-hand rocks. On
its right is West Buttress, of which the main face lies higher up,
overlooking a subsidiary corrie. Left of Summit Gully is a buttress
formed by The Pyramid and, above and to its left, the bigger, steeper
Sphinx. Left of these buttresses the shallow North-West Gully wanders
up and left to the convergence of buttresses 1 to 4, well below the
summit.

No.4 Buttress is bounded by North-West Gully and, on its left, by
the prominent narrow cleft of Deep-Cut Chimney. Left of this is No.3
Buttress, the highest and broadest on the mountain. Its principal
features are the crack at the right-hand edge, overlooking Deep-Cut
Chimney (the line of Crack Climb), and in the centre the shallow but
continuous Central Gully. Buttresses 3 and 2 are separated by a
narrow zigzag rake, but the distinction between them is not obvious.
No.2 Buttress sits slightly higher and is bounded on its left by Arch
Gully, not visible from the approach.

The cliffs left of No. 2 Buttress lie back and form a very large bay. Arch Gully runs up the right side of this bay. Left of Arch Gully is No.1 Buttress, whose left-bounding gully is easy and leads to the left-hand recess of the large bay, where a broken gully leads up left. Beyond this, the final mass of rock below the shoulder of the mountain is known as Zero Buttress.

The approach is as described for Bidean nam Bian, up the Allt Coire nam Beithach. The floor of the corrie beneath No.4 Buttress is about 90 minutes from the starting point in Glen Coe at the Clachaig road junction.

To descend from the summit, go down the ridge west, then north-west for about half a kilometre to a level part of the ridge at the Bealach An t-Sron (135 547). In poor visibility this descent can be confusing, especially when approached from Bidean. At the summit cairn of Stob Coire nam Beith a ridge drops gently northwards, appearing to offer a descent, however it actually drops down towards the steep side of the mountain. Instead, go west from the cairn past the head of Summit Gully, which is only a few metres from the summit. The west ridge drops quite steeply at first, then turns north-west and levels off to become sharply defined. A short distance further the Bealach An t-Sron is reached at the head of the subsidiary corrie on the north-west side of Stob Coire nam Beith. It is possible to descend north-east into the corrie from there, in summer down scree, in winter down a fairly easy-angled snow slope.

Descent can also be made from the point of convergence of buttresses 2 to 4 by heading south-east towards Bidean, traversing across the upper easy part of Arch Gully, then crossing easy ground above No.1 Buttress and Zero Buttress to drop into the basin which runs up beneath the West Top of Bidean. Easy slopes lead down to the corrie. This is useful if time is pressing.

Routes on the north face of Stob Coire nam Beith are described from left to right in order of buttresses.

ZERO BUTTRESS

This is the projecting buttress at the left end of the shoulder which extends east from the main mass of rock forming the upper cone of Stob Coire nam Beith. It lies at the entrance to the high corrie below the cliffs of the West Top of Bidean.

1   The Corridors   150m   III/IV *   (1969)
The face of the buttress is cut by two shallow square-cut gullies, the first ending at a ledge some 45m up and the other starting from this ledge a little further right and leading through to the top. These provide the line, steep and sustained for the first 90m. Climb the first corridor, often only filled with powder snow, to the ledge at 45m. Move right and climb the second corridor which should give two pitches, one at the entry and a 10m runnel tapering to a bulge below the final easy-angled section. Walk off left.

Direct Start: IV   (1977)
Climb steep ice on the right of the first corridor directly to the second one.

Alternative Start: IV   (1985)
Climb a narrow chimney between the normal and the direct starts.

No.1 BUTTRESS
Adjoining Zero Buttress and defined on its right by Arch Gully, this buttress is split into two tiers by a broad horizontal shelf. In winter the lower tier appears as a rock island.

2   Broken Gully   150m   II/III   (1966/67)
The thin gully running up the buttress. Climb up left to gain the gully proper at a recess above the rock island. Follow the gully for 30m to the point where it is split by a rib. Take the shallow right branch until an easy left traverse leads to the top of Zero Buttress. The left branch is steeper and holds more ice.

3   No.1 Buttress   150m   II/III   (1958)
Climb the chimneyline up the rock island, just left of Arch Gully, to the broad shelf. Continue up the tier above by a series of short icy pitches, some variation possible. In summer this is Easy (1931).

4   Arch Gully   240m   II/III *   (1933)
This gully is between buttresses 1 and 2. It is set back and hidden until the lowest rocks have been turned. The Arch is a huge chockstone in the lower section which generally banks out. Above, the gully narrows to form three chimney pitches, the first of which often banks out. Above these follow easy slopes to the summit or traverse off left. Not recommended in summer (Difficult 1900).

Nos. 2 AND 3 BUTTRESSES

These lie between Arch Gully and the prominent thin cleft of Deep-Cut Chimney on the right. No.3 Buttress, the highest and broadest buttress on the face, is separated from its neighbour up on the left by a not very obvious narrow zigzag rake.

5   No.2 Buttress   180m   II/III *   (1958)
Start on the left side of the buttress. Follow the line of a chimney. An ice and rock traverse at 30m is the crux. This leads to a snow slope on a chimney arete 45m higher. Take the succeeding two rock steps directly. In summer this is Easy (1931), with much rambling possible.

6   No.3 Buttress, Left Wall   300m   Very Difficult   (1939)
Approach up a triangular mass of rock below the two buttresses. From a grassy platform above, to the left of wet rocks under a large patch of green moss on No.3 Buttress, climb a right-angled corner on the right. Continue up the line of least resistance on unbroken rock which gradually eases.

7   No.3 Buttress, Centre Route   450m   II/III   (1945)
Starting left of the lowest rocks, the route zigzags up the succeeding tiers. The angle eases after 60m. In summer this is Easy (1931).

8   Central Gully   450m   III/IV ***   (1958)
One of the best winter climbs on the mountain, taking the shallow gully up the centre of No.3 Buttress. A natural ice trap. A large icefall can form at the start. From just left of the lowest rocks climb the left side of the icefall (the right side is an optional start) to gain the gully. Follow this with continual interest up several steep pitches to easier ground.

9   Crack Climb   120m   Difficult **   (1912)
This takes the prominent crack and groove at the right edge of No.3 Buttress, overlooking Deep-Cut Chimney. Start at the apex of an obvious cone of scree at the foot of the buttress. Climb a rounded rib and the first part of the crack to a ledge (40m). Continue up the rib on the right (crux, hard and unprotected) and climb the easier crack above to a grass ledge (30m). Go up right of the crack to avoid a small cave, then traverse 10m right. Climb a vertical wall on small holds. After a further 30m the angle eases and the climb joins Centre Route.
Winter: III **   (1958)
A sustained route. The vertical wall will always be difficult, although an escape right can be made into the amphitheatre of Deep-Cut Chimney. Above the wall follow easier ground to the top of No.3 Buttress.

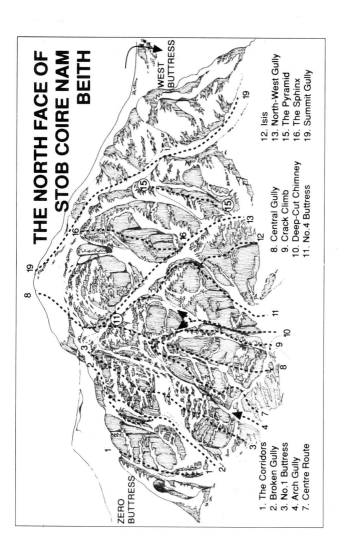

THE NORTH FACE OF STOB COIRE NAM BEITH

1. The Corridors
2. Broken Gully
3. No.1 Buttress
4. Arch Gully
7. Centre Route

8. Central Gully
9. Crack Climb
10. Deep-Cut Chimney
11. No.4 Buttress

12. Isis
13. North-West Gully
15. The Pyramid
16. The Sphinx
19. Summit Gully

ZERO BUTTRESS

WEST BUTTRESS

10   Deep-Cut Chimney   150m   Very Difficult   (1936)
The prominent narrow gully dividing buttresses 3 and 4. The gully
proper ends 120m up in a small amphitheatre, but the climb continues
for 30m by a left or right fork to join any of the routes on the left, where
one can either traverse off left or continue by 200m of easy scrambling
to the top. Start just right of an obvious cone of scree. The first 30m
are straightforward. At 45m there is a cave pitch, often a waterfall. At
this point there are two routes to the amphitheatre.
    The Direct Route climbs the cave pitch on the right wall, then a
steep chimney, then up a central rib to slabs in the amphitheatre.
    The Amphitheatre Route avoids the two principal pitches in the
gully by a steep rib on the left wall. Above the level of the cave there
is a difficult 20m pitch and then easier climbing to the amphitheatre.
    The amphitheatre is backed by a steep crag. This may be turned
on the right by an easy route to join No.4 Buttress. The direct route
takes the left fork, a long steep crack. Climb up the left wall and then
move back into the crack, which widens for a short distance into a
chimney. Above the crack, the route joins No.3 Buttress.
Winter: III/IV ***   (1939)
A classic climb, in its time one of the hardest winter routes in the Central
Highlands. The pioneers made extensive use of an unusually short
axe in the confines of the chimney. Normally three or four short ice
pitches lead to the amphitheatre. The true line is then by the left fork,
which will be difficult if thinly iced. The right fork allows an escape to
easier ground. To finish, either follow 200m of easier ground to the
summit or contour the upper part of Arch Gully and traverse off left.

No.4 BUTTRESS

This is the broad-based buttress between the cleft of Deep-Cut
Chimney and the long shallow North-West Gully. The lowest rocks are
fairly steep, but 60m up the angle becomes much less and easy rocks
continue to the point where this buttress converges with Nos. 2 and 3
about 200m below the summit of Stob Coire nam Beith.

11   No.4 Buttress   450m   II *
A good introduction to snow-bound rock, though allowance should be
made for its length. Start at the foot of Deep-Cut Chimney. An open,
right-slanting gully leads up and round into North-West Gully. From
the top of this gully move back left onto the buttress and so to the top.
In summer this, or a line to its right, is Easy (1931).

12   Isis   60m   VS 4c *   (1959)
Start just up left from the lowest rocks of the clean wall between the
slanting gully of No.4 Buttress and North-West Gully, at the foot of an
obvious groove with a pedestal 3m up on the right wall.
1. 25m 4c Climb the groove to a grassy ledge.
2. 20m 4c Climb the steep flake-crack to a recess below the final
crack. Alternatively, move left across slabs, climb a steep wall and
follow a gangway back right until above the flake.
3. 15m 4a Climb a short crack and easy ground to a suspect flake.
Winter: V **   (1991)
A hard modern snowed-up rock route which follows the summer line
via the flake-crack. Short, sustained and technically absorbing. Descend by the slanting gully of No.4 Buttress or by abseil.

13   North-West Gully   450m   II/III **   (1906)
Sometimes mistaken for Summit Gully, this is the shallow gully which
starts right of No.4 Buttress and just left of the ridge formed by The
Pyramid. It wanders up and left to the convergence of the four
buttresses well below the summit. The scenery is good and there is
usually at least one pitch, even by the easiest start. If the very steep
initial ice pitches left of the normal start are included, the gully can
attain Grade IV. From below The Pyramid go up and left into the gully
where easy snow leads up past The Sphinx to a fork.
   The left fork continues without difficulty to the convergence of the
buttresses. From there, either continue to the summit or traverse left
across the upper section of Arch Gully to easy ground.
   The right fork leads up on the left of the upper part of The Sphinx
for 80m to a second fork (the little buttress splitting the gully here is
The Mummy). At this junction the left fork is better and may give a short
pitch leading up to the shoulder. A steep wall left of the shoulder gives
the crux of the climb. Easier climbing above leads to the summit. Not
recommended in summer (Difficult 1931).

14   Cleftweave   390m   II/III *   (1972)
Start as for North-West Gully, then follow a series of gullies which wind
up immediately left of The Pyramid to a snowfield overlooking Summit
Gully. A short steep ice wall on the left leads to another gully system.
Follow this to a small amphitheatre, move up into a short gully on the
right and climb an ice pitch to exit onto the summit slopes.

THE PYRAMID AND SPHINX BUTTRESSES

On the right side of North-West Gully are two buttresses, set one above the other, which form a ridge on the left of Summit Gully. The lower buttress, which is markedly wedgelike, is The Pyramid and the upper one is The Sphinx. The Mummy is a steep obelisk of rock lying immediately left of, and higher than, The Sphinx.

15   The Pyramid   90m   Difficult *   (1946)
A prominent cone of turf points to the lowest rocks above the start of North-West Gully. Follow the north ridge to the top. The climbing is mostly Moderate, on excellent rough rock. There is an awkward mantelshelf at 40m. Higher still is an airy wall near the left edge.
Winter: III *   (1958)
Follow the summer route.

16   The Sphinx   135m   Difficult *   (1946)
Approach by the lower part of North-West Gully. On the north face, about halfway up, there is a long black cave. Start below and slightly left of this by a shattered wall. Climb to a small basin under the cave. Traverse right to a platform under the perpendicular upper rocks. A chimney some 20m above is the obvious breach. Climb high-stepped walls to reach the chimney, then enter a little recess 3m up to the right. Escape seems impossible, but a pinnacle-flake on the right-hand edge is the solution. Grasp its top edge and swing into space. Beyond, 75m of excellent rough rock lead to the top.
Winter: III/IV **   (1958)
The summer route gives a sustained climb.

17   Direct Route   145m   Severe   (1967)
Start some 30m below the normal route on the Sphinx by a groove near the prow of the buttress.
1. 20m Climb the groove, go up left and take the groove on the right to a grass ledge.
2. 25m Directly above is a prominent groove. Climb up to its right into a short subsidiary groove leading onto the upper right wall of the main groove. Go up this delicately to a ledge and continue up to a big ledge below the crux of the normal route.
3. 30m Follow the normal route up high-stepped walls to a chimney, enter the recess up on the right and swing out right.
4. 30m Traverse diagonally right to the foot of a big corner.
5. 20m Climb the corner, which initially overhangs (crux).
6. 20m Continue directly to the top.

18   The Mummy   60m   Very Difficult *   (1966)
This climb takes a central line up the prominent steep obelisk of rock
splitting the right branch of North-West Gully. It lies immediately left
of, and higher than, The Sphinx. It is easily reached by a left traverse
from below the final wall on The Sphinx. Climb the first groove until it
is possible to move left to a good ledge and belay. Go up the cracks
and grooves above to finish.

19   Summit Gully   450m   I/II *
This is the big gully starting from a point just left of the lowest right-hand
rocks and trending up left to a point a few metres from the summit
cairn. It starts to the right of the ridge formed by The Pyramid and
should not be (though it often is!) confused with North-West Gully
which starts to the left of The Pyramid. From the corrie lip below,
Summit Gully appears the only deep and obvious gully on the mountain. The gully combines length with good scenery. There may be a
short ice pitch near the foot. Despite occasional forks, the route is fairly
obvious. High up, a cave pitch seems to bar the way. This often
provides a reasonable pitch, otherwise turn it on the right. Much higher,
a prominent rock rib forms an island in the gully.

WEST BUTTRESS
To the right of Summit Gully is West Buttress, the rightmost on Stob
Coire nam Beith. There is one route up the crest and three higher up
on the west flank overlooking a subsidiary corrie.

20   Adagio   400m   IV *   (1969)
The obvious narrow and steep gully up the crest of the buttress. Easy
snow leads to a steepening with a thinly-iced left wall. Climb the corner
on the right and make a left-rising traverse round the corner to twin
ice chimneys. Climb the left-hand chimney for 6m, move into the one
on the right above a bulge and climb to easier ground. The continuation
follows the main gully, keeping left, to a cave pitch which is climbed
direct. The gully leads out onto the top of the buttress where the
right-bounding ridge of Summit Gully leads easily up.

21   Hidden Gully   350m   III/IV **   (1955)
An excellent route taking the narrow twisting gully well up right from
the lowest rocks above a large rock island at the entrance to the
subsidiary corrie on the west side of Stob Coire nam Beith. The gully
remains hidden until above the rock island. A 20m snow cone leads

to a cave; climb the icy left wall. Easy snow for 30m leads to another cave, avoided on the left by a short ice pitch. Snow with occasional ice and a gradual increase in angle lead in 90m to a saddle above a rock rib in the middle of the gully. Beyond this the gully steepens and narrows; 25m of snow leads to a 3m overhang above which a short chimney is climbed. A short distance above, a vertical rock rib divides the very narrow gully into two narrower exits. Take the left exit; a long, slanting open chimney with a vertical finish (35m). Above, finish by the right-bounding ridge of Summit Gully, which leads in 150m or so to the summit, or use the gully as a descent route, conditions allowing.

22   Alleyway   105m   III *   (1969)
This is the left-slanting gully starting right of Hidden Gully, to which it offers an alternative start. 30m of mixed rock, snow and ice followed by easy snow lead to a very narrow alley bridged by a large chockstone, obvious from below. From the top of the alley a 10m descent leads into Hidden Gully below its crux.

23   Bootneck Gully   240m   III   (1969)
Just up from Alleyway, this takes a chimneyline which has a steep rock wall on its right, with a possibly easier gangway start close under it. The route starts level with the base of a rib of rock descending to the right of the main face. Two pitches in the gully lead to a steep ice wall on the right. Climb this direct (crux) and continue to go up long easy snow slopes leading to the top, bearing right at a fork.

AN T-SRON
900m   (Map Ref 134 549)

This, the termination of the main Bidean ridge, is the ridge extending west then north from Stob Coire nam Beith to end in a steep hillside overlooking the Clachaig. The actual top only lies a short distance beyond the Bealach An t-Sron (134 547) and a few metres higher than it although the true and prominent nose of the hill is a few hundred metres further north. The only recommended descent is from this bealach into Coire nam Beith. The first two climbs are on the East Face, which presents a prominent 150m buttress directly across from Stob Coire nam Beith. Left of a long slabby section is a bay, above which two diverging gullies cleave the buttress.

Sack-o'-Coal Couloir   150m   III   (1969)
The left-hand line. Start up an easy snow ramp, heading for a
well-defined corner at the top. Enter this by a steep corner-crack and
continue up a slabby corner with chockstone finish.

Smashed Spectacles Gully   150m   II/III *   (1969)
The right-hand line gives a short steep pitch followed by an awkward
chimney. Easier climbing leads to the top.

The Chasm of An t-Sron   365m   III/IV   (1963)
This is the large gully, clearly visible from the road, which splits the
terminal north face of An t-Sron, starting some 300m up the hillside.
Most of the gully is easy. Scramble to the first big waterfall, turn this
on the right or left and re-enter above a second, 6m pitch. Continue
easily for 100m to a fork; the left fork is poor so take the right fork, a
45-65m icefall. Small ice pitches lead to a 30m icefall. At the top the
gully forks again, the left fork is the true one, but the right fork is better
and leads to a 30m icefall, above which an easy traverse left leads
back to the left fork. Easy ice scrambles lead to a short 5m pitch above
which the difficulties end. Seldom in true winter condition. Not recommended in summer; (Difficult 1932).

Outlying Peaks in Glen Coe and Appin

In addition to the climbs on the two main mountains in Glen Coe, Bidean nam Bian and Buachaille Etive Mor, which have been described in the preceding sections, there are other climbs on some of the other peaks of the glen and on a few neighbouring mountains in Appin. Although few of these climbs have the same quality as those in Glen Coe, they have other attractive features, not least a feeling of remoteness on mountains that are relatively unfrequented.

In addition, there are several low-lying crags in Glen Coe which give short and entertaining climbs very close to the road. Some of these climbs are also described in this section.

AONACH EAGACH
967m (Map Ref 141 583)

The Aonach Eagach forms the north wall of Glen Coe, stretching from the Devil's Staircase to the Pap of Glencoe. However, most mountaineers traversing the ridge are content to confine themselves to the section with the greatest interest, between Am Bodach and Sgorr nam Fiannaidh.

The Traverse   4km   Moderate ***   (1895)
A traverse of the ridge gives perhaps the finest and most difficult ridge scramble on the mainland. It is better done from east to west; not only is there 120m less ascent, but the views are finer. Start from a car park (173 567) about 300 metres west of the white cottage of Allt-na-reigh at a signpost. Either climb the broad south ridge of Am Bodach directly, following a fairly well-defined path for most of the way, or go to the right of the ridge along a branch path into the corrie east of Am Bodach from which easy slopes go up and left to the top.

The best and most interesting part of the ridge lies between Meall Dearg and Stob Coire Leith, where there is a narrow pinnacled section and an awkward slabby descent. The descent from Am Bodach also involves some down-climbing, where a step on the north side is made, then moving back south and down a short pitch.

Winter: II ***

In good conditions and good weather a traverse of the ridge provides a truly superb expedition in grand surroundings with magnificent views. Speed is of the essence if a party is to avoid benightment. It is difficult to pinpoint the amount of time necessary for a complete traverse. Five to eight hours seems fairly typical in good conditions for an average party. Where a competent party might quite happily solo, many would prefer to rope up and should certainly not feel embarrassed to do so. This is not a route for the winter hillwalker, a large number of whom have finished the route by helicopter.

Descent: There are no safe descent routes on the Glen Coe side of the ridge between the two peaks of Am Bodach and Stob Coire Leith. This point must be emphasised. If a party has run out of daylight, it is infinitely better to complete or reverse the traverse. The first safe descent route encountered on an east to west traverse is the long steep slope leading down to Loch Achtriochtan from Sgorr nam Fiannaidh. A descent due south from the peak is safe unless there is a risk of avalanche in soft snow conditions; do not go too far west into the rather rocky gully of a steep stream.

Another commonly used descent is down the path on the west side of the deep gorge of Clachaig Gully. The path is steep and suffering badly from erosion. Great care should be taken to avoid dislodging stones to the danger of climbers below. The best line is difficult to locate from above, especially in poor visibility.

Although the lure of a well-earned drink in the Clachaig Inn may be particularly tempting, the safest descent in bad conditions or after dark may well be to continue west then north from Sgorr nam Fiannaidh to the col before the Pap of Glencoe. From the col descend south-west to reach the old road midway between Bridge of Coe and Leacantuim farm.

Important : Would climbers descending from the west end of the Aonach Eagach ridge by the above route please avoid the fenced-off area above the Youth Hostel. This is private land which is used for livestock grazing. If climbers refuse to do so, then future access to this popular area could be put at serious risk.

The buttresses and gullies of the Aonach Eagach are of little climbing merit in summer. In winter, however, some of these routes provide first-class expeditions. Ideal conditions seem to be rare. Probably the best time is a heavy snowfall followed by a continuous freeze. The routes are described from east to west.

Chancellor Gully   525m   Severe   (1949)
This is the long slanting gully which scores the face, characterised by
the square-cut chimney which hangs above it at mid-height. The gully
goes up below the chimney, then bends up left. A long dry spell is
recommended.
The first five pitches are wet and vegetatious, and can be avoided by
the heathery buttress to the right. Further up the rock becomes clean
and sound, and there are several good long slab pitches on the
left-slanting section. Above the slabs the gully narrows again and leads
via a central fin to a chockstone pitch of classic line. Above it scree
leads to the top. (The square-cut chimney is Severe, but no further
details are available.)
Winter: III/IV **   (1960)
An excellent climb which is usually in condition during a period of
continuous freeze. The initial dog-leg is avoided by the ridge to its left.
From this point there are approximately eleven pitches of water-ice.
(The initial steep section is considerably harder.)

Old Man Gully   270m   III *   (1960)
This prominent gully gives a good climb to the summit of Am Bodach
in good hard snow conditions. The gully can be entered from the left
and some of the lower pitches can be by-passed. There are various
exits at the top which can be steep and corniced. Approach the gully
up a scree or snow slope from the main road directly below the col to
west of Am Bodach. Keep east of a small stream.

The Chancellor   180m   Difficult   (1920)
The Chancellor is an imposing buttress rising from the confluence of
Big Chock Gully and Old Man Gully and crowned by an isolated tower.
This forms the head and shoulders of a burly, strong featured, short-
bearded man, wearing a judical wig. The features are said to have
resembled an earlier Marquis of Salisbury. The route is open to
variation. The rock is poor and the most difficult section is in the middle.
A shattered arete connects the tower to the summit ridge.
Winter: III/IV *   (1965)
There are two starts, a shallow gully which runs up into the buttress
or the ridge to the right. The principal difficulty is route-finding on the
steep section at mid-height. This is solved by going well to the left and
climbing a grooved shelf, after which the crest is regained in two
pitches. The last pitch is the crux.

Big Chock Gully   210m   III   (1960)
The obvious gully left of The Chancellor, seldom in condition and
requiring a big build up of snow and ice. The main difficulties are in
surmounting the big chockstone pitch halfway up, climbed on ice on
the right wall.

Vice Chancellor Ridge   210m   III **   (1969)
Climb the exposed ridge left of Big Chock Gully to the first rocky tower.
Continue in two rope lengths to a more formidable tower, climbed by
a central line. Above, climb a rocky wall to a third, more exposed tower.
Traverse a narrow arete at its back to easier ground. In a further rope
length a steep step in the ridge is gained. This can be climbed direct,
slightly right of centre or take the easy gully on the right to easy ground
leading to the summit.

Twenty Minute Gully   180m   II   (1969)
This is the first narrow gully down from the crest of the ridge and below
the steep step to the west of Am Bodach. Start well up and left of Vice
Chancellor. The gully curves left leading to the summit ridge.

Chance   III   (1969)
The first gully left of Chancellor Gully, bounding the steep rocks of The
Chancellor on the left. It fades out about 210m above the road. The
gully contains four short ice pitches, the third of which follows a steep
V-groove capped by a chockstone.

Farm Gully   240m   II/III *   (1969)
Above the farm at the east end of Loch Achtriochtan is a wide gully.
Follow the right branch, awkward to start. Unless there is an unusually
heavy snowfall, the bottom few pitches are best avoided on the steep
snow slope to the left (tree belays). Several ice pitches remain. There
is a danger of stonefall during sunshine.

Blue Riband   600m   V ***   (1979)
One of the best water-ice routes in the Coe. Looking up from below
the pinnacled section of the ridge, three large icefalls can be seen
descending the buttress above. This route takes the central icefall.
Climb steep ice for two pitches (50m). A narrow ice runnel leads to a
steep icefall (35m). Climb this, then a further 75m of easier snow to
below a large icefall. (Possible escape at this point.) Climb the icefall
(35m). Follow the right branches of the gully over easy snow and small
ice pitches to a short steep ice wall (150m). Climb the ice wall, which
overhangs slightly (10m). 150m of easier climbing leads to the top.

Clachaig Gully   520m   Severe ***   (1938)
One of the great Scottish gully climbs; not to be underestimated. In
places the rock is compact and does not always lend itself to good
protection. The grade is for dry conditions. The climb starts just above
the Clachaig Inn on the south flank of Sgorr nam Fiannaidh. It receives
much sunlight, and is especially pleasant on a warm day in spring,
when the gully walls are covered in wild flowers. Beware of stone-fall
and avoid large parties.

To descend, follow the steep and eroded path down the west bank
with care.

   The route is obvious up to the Great Cave Pitch at 150m. This pitch
stopped all earlier attempts, from Collie's attempt in 1894 onwards.
Climb the right wall and slab to a small tree. From the tree traverse
down and round a rib, then left to the red wall opposite which leads to
the gully bed. The pitch above is the short but deceptive crux. Climb
the slabby shelf on the right flank then up a corner. Following a short
chockstone pitch, Jericho Wall is reached. This is on the right of a
waterfall, trending up and left to the top. Several good pitches then
follow including the Red Chimney, a distinctive 20m pitch on dark red
rock. A shallow cave rises 10m above. From the roof springs a 5m
chimney. Climb the right wall of the cave on the outside to a ledge near
the foot of the chimney. Finish up the chimney and the slab above.

   To descend, follow the steep and eroded path down the west bank
with care.

Winter: IV/V **   (1952)
Unfortunately, as with other climbs on the Glen Coe flank of the Aonach
Eagach, Clachaig Gully is seldom in good winter condition. The Great
Cave pitch will usually present the major difficulties along with Jericho
Wall and to a lesser extent the Red Chimney. Above this the gully may
well be snowed up and should not present any further difficulties.

Clachaig Gully West   Very Difficult   (1946)
The first gully to the left of Clachaig Gully. Vegetated and not recommended.

A'CHAILLEACH

901m   (Map Ref 189 580)

This hill is the extension of the Aonach Eagach ridge eastwards
beyond Am Bodach. The south side of the hill, which overlooks the
Glen Coe road above The Study, has several gullies, and a prominent
nose of rock high up is also a recognisable feature.

Red Funnel Gully   180m   II/III *   (1964)
This, the leftmost gully on the face, finishes near the prominent rock
nose. It is easily reached from the cairn opposite the Lairig Eilde about
one kilometre east of the Meeting of Three Waters. A fun route, ideally
suited for a short day or after a heavy snow fall. A series of short ice
pitches following the bed of the stream lead to a deeper section. A
steep 12m ice pitch (crux) is followed by a passage beneath a huge
chockstone and a final steep icy chimney-groove. The gully gives
many short pitches in summer (Very Difficult 1950).
    The quickest descent is by a long descending traverse to the east
but one may continue easily to the top of the mountain and descend
by the corrie between A'Chailleach and Am Bodach.

BUACHAILLE ETIVE BEAG
958m   (Map Ref 179 536)

Buachaille Etive Beag, which lies between Buachaille Etive Mor and
Beinn Fhada, is a long ridge consisting of two main summits, Stob
Dubh (958m) at the south-west end and Stob Coire Raineach (924m)
to the north-east. The north-eastern end of the ridge is the rocky peak
of Stob nan Cabar, which overlooks the Glen Coe road.

Red Campion Gully   300m   Very Difficult   (1950)
The south-eastern flank of the ridge between Stob nan Cabar and Stob
Coire Raineach is divided by four gullies, of which two are forked. They
are numbered 1 to 4 from left to right. Red Campion Gully is No.3; the
route follows the left-hand branch up a succession of short pitches.
The remaining gullies have been explored, but are disappointing

BEINN A'CHRULAISTE
857m   (Map Ref 246 567)

This hill rises on the north side of the A82 road two kilometres east of
Altnafeadh and the same distance north-west of Kingshouse Hotel.
There are two easy summer routes up the obvious rocky ribs on the
south side of the hill overlooking the road.

SGOR NA H-ULAIDH
994m   (Map Ref 111 518)

This fine but remote peak lies west of Bidean, hidden from the main road in Glen Coe by the projecting ridge of Aonach Dubh a'Ghlinne. About two kilometres west of Loch Achtriochtan the A82 goes over a bridge before it turns north (parking place before the bridge on the right). Follow the track along the Allt na Muidhe to the farm house of Gleann-leac-na-muidhe. The track continues for a further kilometre, ending near a junction of streams where the glen turns south and Sgor na h-Ulaidh comes into view.

The best descent from the summit is by the north-east ridge to gain the col just south-west of Stob an Fhurain from where steep slopes lead down to the head of the Allt na Muidhe. Alternatively, and probably more easily, continue over Stob an Fhuarain for about half a kilometre and descend by the west-facing slopes of its north ridge. It is also possible to descend by Vixen Gully but only if there is sufficient snow to bank out any pitches. The northerly slope of Corr na Beinne can also be descended, but it is very steep and has been the scene of several fatal accidents. The climbs are described from left to right.

Subsidiary Scoop   150m   II/III *   (1966)
This is a shallow gully immediately left of Red Gully and separated from it by a rocky rib. It usually gives one or two short steep ice pitches.

Red Gully   195m   III **   (1948)
The deep gully which leads directly to the summit. It usually gives three or four good ice pitches. The third will normally be the crux but can be turned on the right.

Brush Buttress   270m   III *   (1969)
The buttress right of Red Gully is divided into three tiers, the middle one being the hardest. Start from the lowest rocks. Start the main buttress in the central gully and move to the edge on the left. Gain a ledge above and belay (25m). Climb the chimney above to a belay on the left (20m). Continue up the chimney line and traverse right on a narrow ledge. Finish on the final buttress to the left of a steep edge, or up last section of the main gully.

Vixen Gully   150m   I   (1948)
The broad long gully in the middle of the face to the right of Red Gully gives a straightforward snow climb.

West Gully   300m   II   (1948)
This straightforward snow climb, sometimes a bit awkward at the top, follows the obvious gully on the extreme right-hand side of the corrie.

CREAG BHAN
710m   (Map Ref 102 531)

This outlying north-eastern spur of Meall Lighiche, one and a half kilometres north-west of Sgor na h-Ulaidh, has a steep rocky face overlooking the head of the Allt na Muidhe. The foot of this face is reached by the same route as that to Sgor na h-Ulaidh.

Humpback Gully   300m   II   (1965)
Viewed from Coire Dubh, it is the obvious gully in the north-east face leading to the right of the summit.

BEINN A'BHEITHIR
Sgorr Dhonuill   1001m   (Map Ref 040 556)

Central Buttress   90m   III/IV   (1988)
This climb is located on the front face of the northern spur of Sgorr Dhonuill, and is clearly seen from the Ballachulish Bridge. Climb the steep buttress in the centre of the crag.

The district of Appin is to the south-west of Glen Coe. At its centre, Glen Creran lies west of and parallel to Glen Etive and terminates below the south-west side of Sgor na h-Ulaidh several kilometres south-west of the Bidean nam Bian massif. It is best to approach the glen from the coast and Loch Creran to the south-west. From Glencoe village take the A828 around the coast for some 33 kilometres towards Oban. At the head of Loch Creran branch off and follow the minor road up into Glen Creran.
Glen Creran, and Glen Stockdale to the west, contain some limestone. Although there is little to interest the climber, it is one of the main centres for speleology in Scotland. Included within the caves of the area is the very fine Uamh nan Claig-Ionn *(cave of the skulls)* first descended in January 1977. For further information on the delights of the subterranean, *Scotland Underground* (1984) by Alan Jeffreys (Grampian Speleological Group) provides descriptions and surveys.

BEINN SGULAIRD
937m   (Map Ref 053 461)

Beinn Sgulaird rises on the eastern side of Glen Creran. High up under the summit of the mountain, and visible from the road, are the Sgulaird Slabs. The main slabs face south-west and are composed of solid clean granite some 180m high. In the centre are large overlaps. Above the Main Slab is the Upper Slab, while further to the right is the Bealach Crag. To its right, and at a lower level, are the Lower Bealach Slabs. The best and longest climbs are on the Main Slab.

MAIN SLAB

Safari   190m   Hard Severe   (1976)
Start at the lowest rocks on the left of the slab.
1. 45m Climb the slab direct, then trend left to belay.
2. 40m Follow a large slab corner, then move left to a small ledge.
3. 25m Climb left, then right above large blocks to belay on the right.
4. 45m Continue directly up the smooth slab above, move left, then up and through overlaps. Follow the slab above to a second overlap, break through and follow good cracks to a belay.
5. 35m Move up left into a corner, then up through an overlap to finish up the crest of the ridge.

Majuba   160m   Severe   (1976)
Start at the lowest rocks.
1. 45m Climb the slab direct.
2. 45m Continue directly up the slab right of the corner, then trend right to a small overlap. Break through this on the right, climb left, then directly to a belay.
3. 25m Climb the corner above direct to large overlaps, break through by a crack and grooves to a small stance.
4. 45m Continue directly via grooves and a small overlap to the terminal overlap which is taken direct to finish.

Tokalosh   165m   VS   (1976)
Start right of Majuba.
1. 45m Climb an easy rounded slab.
2. 45m Trend right to a bow-shaped corner on the central slab, climb to its top and step right onto a thin slab. Go up, then trend left to a shallow scoop and up to a belay.

3. 30m Climb steep grooves above a thin slab to large overlaps.
4. 45m Climb up to corner, large blocks, surmount the overhang to grooves and follow these directly to a rock nose, then climb a small corner slab. Belay under blocks at a grass ledge.

Assegai   160m   VS   (1976)
Start at the right side of the slab.
1. 45m   Climb an easy corner to a grass patch and surmount the overlap above to a belay.
2. 45m   Climb the grooves above.
3. 45m   Continue up a steep slab and grooves.
4. 25m   Finish up the corner groove above.

The following route is on slabs to the right of the main slabs.

Daktari   160m   E2   (1986)
Start 10m up and right of the lowest slab at a thread belay.
1. 40m 4c Climb straight up to the first overlap, turn it on the left, then up and slightly left to a belay.
2. 40m 5a Traverse 6m left to a short corner. Climb this to a good hold, move horizontally left and then slightly down until under an obvious nose of rock. Continue diagonally left and then slightly down to belay on a large flake.
3. 45m 5b Above the flake is an overlap with a thin diagonal crack below it. Make a hard move, then follow the crack to a good hold. Continue direct to belay on large boulders.
4. 35m 4c Move left along an easy ledge and take the centre of a blank white slab to finish.

UPPER SLABS
The following two routes climb the two obvious curving faults through overlaps in a series of steps.

39 Steps   90m   Severe   (1976)
The left fault.
1. 50m Follow small corners trending left to a belay.
2. 40m Follow cracks and grooves to the right, then climb up and through overlaps.

Tiptoe   90m   Severe   (1976)
Climb the obvious fault line right of 39 Steps in the centre of the slab. Break through overlaps on good holds.

BEALACH CRAG
This is the small but good steep slab below the Bealach Coire Allt Buidhe.

Creran Corner   65m   Severe   (1976)
1. 40m Climb directly up to the obvious large corner and follow it to a ledge.
2. 25m Climb a slab to the overlap, trend right to a second overlap, then take the slab above to a ledge. Climb the wall above to finish.

To the left and right of Creran Corner are a Severe and a Very Difficult (1978).

BEINN FHIONNLAIDH
959m   (Map Ref 095 498)

Beinn Fhionnlaidh lies at the head of Glen Creran, immediately to the south of Sgor na h-Ulaidh. Follow the minor road up Glen Creran for just over four kilometres to a parking place where the glen splits in two. The right fork leads past Elleric to the houses at Glenure where it may also be possible to park. From there the trackless Allt Bealach na h-Innsig is followed for some two and a half hours to reach the broken South Face of the mountain where it is split by a deep chasm, the Eas nan Clach Reamhar, that descends almost to the floor of the glen at (091 490).

Rapunzel   350m   IV ***   (1987)
The deep chasm gives an excellent climb with much character, a variety of interesting pitches and a general feeling of remoteness. Due to its relatively low altitude and south-facing aspect, a hard frost is required to bring the route into condition. It is reminiscent of the Dalness Chasm. Walk into the chasm and climb a short ice pitch to a steep corner. Climb thin ice on the right wall. Short ice steps and easy snow lead to a steep chimney which is climbed for 50m using thin icicles to pass two huge chockstones at its top. The gully splits and the right-hand branch is taken. Two long ice pitches followed by a short steep ice step lead to a general easing in the angle. Follow the gully up snow, with several short ice pitches, for 150m to the summit snow slopes.

The Witch   150   III/IV *   (1987)
About 150 metres right of Rapunzel, a shorter and less well-defined
gully system leads to a snow terrace at about half-height on the face.
A short ice pitch and easy snow lead to a longer ice pitch where the
gully narrows. Snow slopes and a short steep icefall lead to a split in
the gully. The right branch is followed on excellent ice to reach the
snow terrace.

MINOR CRAGS IN GLEN COE

ALLT DOIRE-BHEITH (Map Ref 179 562)
This is the hidden gorge on the lower slopes of Beinn Fhada above
the Meeting of Three Waters. The fastest approach is direct, parking
where the old road leaves the A82 a few hundred metres west of The
Study. The crags are numerous, the largest being a long slabby wall
split by an obvious crackline in the centre, with a further broken
diagonal crack system and line of roofs left of this. The crackline gives
a good well-protected pitch of about 20m (HVS 5a).

Smouldering   20m   E4 6a *   (1987)
Start to the right of the central crack, just left of a steep smooth slab.
Climb to good footholds and undercuts, pull right onto a slab with
difficulty and continue boldly to twin breaks. Step right at the break
and go up to a diagonal line of holds and a good nut crack. Pull slightly
right and up to finish.

Sweltering   20m   E3 5c *   (1987)
A direct line through the roof at its widest point to the left of the HVS
crack. Climb an easy stepped corner to a roof. Undercling this leftwards to good holds. Step right round the bulge and make a long reach
to the next break. Climb directly to the top. (A second rope is required
to establish a satisfactory belay on the boulders far back.)

Don't Talk to Strangers   20m   E4 5c   (1988)
A line just right of Smouldering. Follow Smouldering to the break. From
the break, climb straight up for 3m to place a Rock 4 in a horizontal.
Step left to a friable incut, mantelshelf and reach left again to a sidepull.
Climb direct to a good finger ledge (crux), and finish with a long reach
for good holds.

THE BENDY (Map Ref 175 565)
This is the steep wall overlooking the pool where the River Coe changes direction shortly before forming the Meeting of Three Waters. It is very sheltered, fast drying, and must be one of the most accessible crags in the Highlands, being only a minute (downhill) from the road. From Allt-na-reigh descend either the right bank of the stream or continue along the top and abseil in from one of the trees (fixed sling and belay ring on top of the tree above Roaring Silence). After prolonged wet spells, the bottom sections of the routes are often saturated by the spray from the waterfall, but the routes remain climbable under such conditions. On first appearance the crag is smooth and apparently holdless, split into two adjoining walls by a vegetated ramp. The right wall is just off the vertical, whilst the left gently overhangs.

The Roaring Silence   20m   E4 6a ** ⁕   (1987)
The best pitch on the crag, giving well-protected climbing up a series of thin incipient cracks running up the left edge of the crag. Start below the left end of a long ledge system at 6m. Climb past a good sidepull on the left to gain holds at the left end of the ledge. Step right and climb direct up the wall past a bulge to eventually reach a good small Friend placement in the diagonal crack on the left. Pull over second bulge rightwards to a good stopping place and finish up a short technical wall.

Quietly Burning   25m   E4 6a *   (1987)
A slightly eliminate line up the centre of the left-hand wall. Start as for In Seine and follow it to a ledge. Climb the thin crack directly above past a jammed nut until forced right on good holds to rejoin In Seine just below the small triangular niche. Pull up and left through the bulge to a hollow sounding spike. Launch directly up the headwall above (RP5) to good holds just below the top.

In Seine   25m   E3 5c   (1987)
Climbs an obvious natural line up the right-hand side of the left-hand wall. Strenuous and well protected, on good holds. Start at the base of the central vegetated ramp. Climb this for a few feet, then break out left and up a thin crack to gain the right side of the long ledge system. Step right and up the wall on good holds to a good triangular niche. Move diagonally right across the wall to good holds beneath an arching overlap. Pull over this slightly leftwards to finish past a good spike just below the top.

Virgin Waters   20m   E3 5c *   (1987)
The thin vertical crack up the left side of the right-hand wall. Start at a
broken uncleaned flake in the centre of the wall. Attain a standing
position on top of the flake, then go directly up on good holds to a tiny
spike runner. Move obliquely up and right (thin) to better holds which
lead to the top.

Cockleshell Journey   25m   E3 5c   (1987)
Follows the crescent-shaped crackline at the right side of the wall,
gained by a crucial traverse from the start of the previous route. From
the top of the flake traverse hard right to a ledge below the crack. Make
a long reach to place protection above, then follow the crack and pull
out left on good holds to a jugular finish.

GLEN COE GORGE (Map Ref 180 564)
This is the crag opposite the car park, just down from the waterfall.
Two short but worthwhile routes have been climbed, and can be easily
reached by a short scramble down from the A82 just after the cutting.

Chariots of Fire   15m   HVS 4c *   (1981)
The obvious right-hand crack.

Delusions of Grandeur   15m   E2 5b *   (1988)
Climb thin cracks just left of Chariots of Fire, exiting right at the top.

Gorge Crack   12m   HVS 4c   (1991)
The obvious crack in the wall on the road side of the river, opposite
Chariots of Fire. Start from large boulder in the river.

OTHER MINOR ROADSIDE CRAGS

Creag Drey is the small buttress situated above the old Glen Coe road,
and just below and left of The Study. There are about ten routes up to
E1.
    The Banana Crag, which is above the old quarry east of the Clachaig
Inn and is named for its curving rock strata, also has climbing up to
E1. Climbing is also possible in the old quarry, though one would have
to be pretty desperate.

Glen Etive

This section deals with the climbing in Glen Etive. For most climbers the name Glen Etive conjures up Beinn Trilleachan and the well-known slabs on the face of that mountain. There are also several other mountains overlooking the glen which have some interesting climbing: Ben Starav, Beinn Chaorach (a shoulder of the higher Stob Coir'an Albannaich), Sron na Creise, Beinn Mhic Chasgaig and Beinn Maol Chaluim. Although none of them can offer climbing comparable to that on the Trilleachan Slabs, they are all worthy of mention and are included here.

BEINN TRILLEACHAN
839m   (Map Ref 086 439)

THE TRILLEACHAN SLABS

These unique and beautifully situated sweeps of clean granite, better known as the Etive Slabs, lie at an altitude of about 300m on the east flank of Beinn Trilleachan at (097 446) above the head of Loch Etive. The slabs face east-south-east and catch the sun from early morning to early afternoon.

The climbing is sufficiently unusual to merit some comment. The rock is Starav Granite, set at an angle of about 40 degrees and coloured from pink to black depending on weathering and water streaks. As explained in the Geology section, the rock is smooth and good holds infrequent. However, visitors with experience of some of the granite slabs elsewhere in the world will be relieved to know that there is no glacial polish here, so friction alone is usually just sufficient to maintain position. This is fortunate, as the rarity of good cracks means frequent long runouts. The slabs are on several planes, separated by overlaps and walls which provide yet further entertainment and a marked contrast to the delicate slab climbing. After rain the open slabby areas dry relatively quickly, especially in the morning sun, although one should beware of seeps from grass ledges. There are more persistent weeps in the corners and below overlaps. Most routes include pitches with little protection, and perhaps some pure friction 'padding' moves. This makes for exciting but serious climbing, often requiring a high degree of commitment; it is not easy to reverse on the Slabs!

Shorts and lycra are not recommended except for the most 'gallous' of leaders, since the rock is particularly unforgiving on those unfortunate enough to take a slide; an 'Etive Kiss' is to be avoided at all costs. Modern rockboots and slippers have rendered the climbing a touch easier, although one does tend to become committed sooner on long runouts. Nevertheless, when 25m out from your last runner with composure wavering, spare a thought for those who have climbed this way before in not-so-sticky boots! The best technique is to keep the weight directly above the feet, searching for dimples and minute changes in angle, and to avoid long reaches. The 'gung-ho' approach is far more likely to lead to disaster!

It is neither necessary nor desirable to carry protection pegs. Although many of the routes were originally climbed with pegs for aid, runners and belays, the peg-damaged cracks now give nut placements. The *in situ* pegs which remain should be left in place, and although some are now very poor, they are nowhere necessary and should not be replaced. A good selection of nuts, Friends and micro wires is recommended.

There are two winter routes on the slabs, but due to their altitude and aspect a good freeze with low-lying snow is required. When this occurs the road is invariably very difficult to drive, if not impassable, unless recently ploughed. Frozen streams on the hillside can provide a little fun.

Helmets are sensible as stonefall is a regular occurrence. It is essential to take great care not to dislodge anything as leaders in the middle of a long runout are much more at risk on the slabs than they would be on a steeper crag.

Another hazard is *Culicoides impunctatum*, the dreaded biting midge. Carry insect repellent, and remember that the gentle breeze which keeps them at bay in the morning sun will go once the sun rounds the hillside; it is then that all hell breaks loose! Midges can make climbing here almost unendurable any time from June to September. Note also that many of the weeps dried by the sun in the early morning will reappear in the shade of the afternoon.

The approach to the slabs takes the single-track road which leaves the A82 just east of Buachaille Etive Mor. Follow this with some entertainment down picturesque Glen Etive to a car park where the road ends at a ruined pier and some ugly ruins at the head of Loch Etive. The pier formerly received steamers connecting with horse coaches to the Kingshouse Hotel, several thousand Victorians annually making the tour. During the summer months pleasure boats full of tourists sail up the loch, so remember that if you get caught short and find a spot hidden from climbers, you may be clearly visible to those with binoculars on the boats.

The slabs are clearly visible from the car park. From the ruin a muddy path, not suitable for trainers, branches off the lochside path and leads diagonally up in about 35 minutes, crossing a stream halfway. The path leads to the foot of the Great Slab where a large flat rock known as the Coffinstone provides a good viewpoint and gearing-up spot (but beware of stonefall). There are two belts of slabs, an upper and a lower, separated by a diagonal rake. The best climbing is on the lower slabs.

Above the Coffinstone the Great Slab is interrupted, first by one large curving overlap whose right end forms the Crevasse, then higher by a second major overlap lying just below the headwalls. Both main overlaps stop short of the left boundary of the Great Slab formed by the great corner of Agony, which runs the full height of the slab. Above and to the left, a narrow slab is taken by The Pinch, whilst the obvious corner on its left is climbed by Hammer. Left again, and set at a higher level, is the bulging Jaywalk slab whose left side is marked by the vegetated corner of Sickle.

To descend from the top of routes on the lower slabs, follow a heather rake which runs down diagonally right (north) above the steep headwalls.

Warning: The path has much loose rock, and since it runs above most of the routes, EXTREME CARE should be taken not to dislodge stones, either by clumsy footwork or by trailing equipment. In emergency there is a public phone box at Druimachoish, some two and a half kilometres from the car park. The routes are described from right to left on the main slabs, with the girdles at the end of the section, and from left to right on the upper slabs.

THE MAIN SLABS

The first five routes, together with the three girdles, start on the right-hand section of slab some 70 metres right of the Coffinstone and right of a large heathery slope. There are two narrow tongues of clean slab extending from the wall which forms a band across the slab beneath the larger upper slab. The brownish left-hand tongue is further identified by three short cracklines on its right side. Above the wall a number of thin cracklines and seams run up the slab. The first route takes the second crack from the right. The first crack has an old peg in it and is assumed to be the start of one of the girdles.

1   Seams Blanc   100m   E3 *   (1991)
Start at the base of the narrow right-hand tongue of slab. There is a
small sapling a short way up on the right.
1. 30m 5a   Climb the narrow tongue to an obvious short corner in the
wall. Climb the corner and pull out left to a small ledge.
2. 40m 5b   Gain the upper slab, follow a thin crack and continue to a
small ledge at an obvious red quartz band which cuts horizontally
across the slab. This is level with a heathery ledge on the right. Stand
on the quartz band and continue directly above for a few bold moves,
then move right and easily up to belay beneath heathery ledges.
3. 30m 4c   Climb the slab to the left of the ledges, then continue to
heather and belay in a corner.

2   Ba's   240m   HVS **   (1962)
A good route with poor protection on the hard sections. Start 70m right
of the Coffinstone at a tongue of clean brown slabs just right of a
heathery bay. Common start with The Grasshopper.
1. 35m 4c   Climb diagonally right to a small groove, then up to a
sloping ledge under a wall.
2. 40m 4c   Climb the wall on the right, then start up a thin crack in the
slab above, finally traversing left on a red band to ledges and a poor
flake.
3. 20m 5a   Traverse the ledges leftwards, then climb up left to a grassy
corner and ledge.
4. 20m 5a   Climb the corner at the left end of the ledge then the steep
corner to belay in the groove above.
5. 15m 5a   Traverse left and climb the wall to belay at the top of pitch
4 of Spartan Slab.
6. 45m 5a   Move left 6m across the slab, continue up the right-slanting
groove (do not take the first groove left of the belay) and traverse left
to belay on The Pause at the overlap.
7. 45m 5a   Trend up left to a fault which leads as for The Long Reach
to a sentry box, then climb a crack.
8. 20m 5a   As for The Pause, the corner.

3   Vein Rouge   95m   E1 **   (1991)
Start left of the three short cracklines at the base of the brownish
left-hand tongue of slab.
1. 35m 5a   A few moves gain first one pocket, then another. Continue
over some small steps, then move up right into an obvious scooped

depression in the wall. Climb the depression and continue to a grassy handrail.

2. 30m 5a Climb the crack above and continue to small ledges. A quartz band starts here and runs up the slab above. Move across and up right to belay at a crack.

3. 30m 5a Move back down left to the start of the quartz band and follow this to the top, then scramble to a belay in the corner.

4   Raspberry Ripple   95m   E2 *   (1991)
Starts as for Vein Rouge, then goes up just to its left. A very good second pitch.

1. 40m 5a Climb Vein Rouge to where it goes right into the scooped depression. Continue above, passing right of a heather ledge. Go up slightly left and climb to a small ledge at the foot of a crack.

2. 55m 5a The slab above is seamed with ripples. Follow the crackline which leads to the rightmost ripple, climb this to a small pocket midway up it (Friend 1). Continue up the ripple to holds and easier ground leading to a belay in the corner on rope stretch.

5   Frozen Ba's   IV *   (1979)
Follow the thickest ice smears, starting left of Ba's, crossing it, and finishing virtually straight up to gain the descent path.

The next routes lie just left of the large heathery slope some 15 metres from the Coffinstone.

6   The The   E3 †   (1990)
A route which takes the groove in the side wall below Spartan Slab, overlooking the Ba's slab. This, the first ascent description, may be difficult to follow.

1. 25m 5b Start right of Attila and climb the slab directly to a tree.

2. 20m 5a Follow Attila for 10m to a tree, then move horizontally right along obvious handholds to a ledge and poor belay (RP's).

3. 15m 4b Go diagonally right to belay on the third pitch of Spartan Slab.

4. 6a Move up and right, then follow an obvious groove to an old peg. Go up the obvious steep corner to easier ground. Belay on a tree in a corner.

5. 4c Pull over the overlap and follow the slab to the top of Spartan Slab.

7   Attila   200m   E3 *   (1965)
A direct line crossing Spartan Slab to climb up between it and The
Pause. Pitch 3 is very good. Start at tongue of slab 10m right of the
Coffinstone.
1. 40m 4c Climb the slab bearing right past two curious pockets, then
back left and up to heathery ledges. Spartan Slab Direct (1956) also
went this way before moving up left to join the normal line below the
Crevasse. Tree belay on right.
2. 40m 4c Continue directly to join Spartan after its hand traverse and
step up right to belay as for that route.
3. 40m 5c Climb the slab with a black streak to the overlap (peg and
wire nut relics) which is overcome by an entertaining move followed
by a bold section to a large quartz pocket. Continue up a crack and a
shallow groove to pull out left to an uncomfortable but good nut belay
at a small bulge.
4. 40m 4c Climb the crack above the belay, as for Ba's, then go straight
up to a tree-lined ledge.
5. 40m Either traverse right and escape up Spartan or take the corner
and short crack above to finish up a mossy slab.

8   The Long Reach   215m   E1 ***   (1963)
An excellent, sustained route with some boldish slab sections. Start
directly behind the Coffinstone.
1. 35m 5b Either climb the middle of the slab or bear left into the
groove, then up and back right to cross an overlap. Belay on the left
as for Spartan Slab.
2. 40m 5b Climb the twin grooves above onto the slab, step up to a
large pocket, then go horizontally left on a quartz band for 5m. Move
diagonally left then up to a small corner (The Pause) which is followed
to the overlap with a left traverse to belay on Swastika.
3. 15m 5a Surmount the overlap, then traverse right and climb the
slab for 8m to belay in the corner on Pause.
4. 40m 5b Traverse 3m left then climb the slab past a quartz pocket
to a small corner. Reach out left then go up to a small overlap.
5. 40m 5b Climb the overlap and a bulge in the slab, then move up
and traverse right beneath a large overlap to belay below and right of
an overhung groove.
6. 35m 5b Step up left, climb the overlap, then follow the groove to
ledge where a traverse left gains a sentry box and crack leading to
heathery ledges.
7. 10m 4c The small corner above.

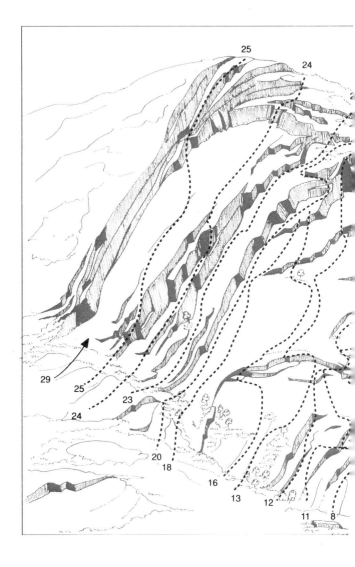

THE TRILLEACHAN SLABS

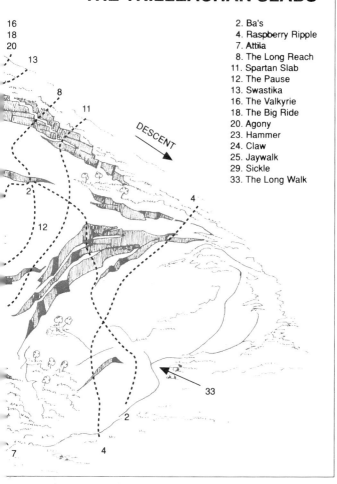

2. Ba's
4. Raspberry Ripple
7. Attila
8. The Long Reach
11. Spartan Slab
12. The Pause
13. Swastika
16. The Valkyrie
18. The Big Ride
20. Agony
23. Hammer
24. Claw
25. Jaywalk
29. Sickle
33. The Long Walk

DESCENT

9   The Band of Hope   210m   E3 **   (1971)
A fine direct line between The Pause and The Long Reach.
1. 35m 5b The Long Reach, pitch 1.
2. 40m 5c Step left onto a spike, climb to left end of the horizontal band of Long Reach and move up a short way. Go up and right for 6m to an invisible hold, then continue up left to the left end of the Crevasse.
3. 15m 4c Gain the slab above, move into a groove on the left and climb this over a bulge to the Long Reach belay ledge. (This follows the first part of The Pause, pitch 4.)
4. 40m 5a Continue straight up by bulges and small overlaps to belay below an overlap in a black corner.
5. 35m 5a Climb straight up to belay below the main overlap on Long Reach.
6. and 7. 45m 5b Finish up The Long Reach.

A succession of incredulous leaders have developed a number of equally improbable variations to pitch 2:
I. 40m 5c On departure from the Long Reach, gain the thin flange up on the right and follow this to the Pause, then traverse into the Crevasse.
II. 40m 5c On departure from the Long Reach, take the bald and very bold slab directly into the Crevasse, one of the hardest padding pitches on the Slabs, worth E4.
III. 40m 5c On departure from Long Reach, traverse horizontally right along a quartz seam almost into Spartan before moving back up left to the Crevasse.

10   The Long Wait   255m   E2 **   (1959)
Start behind the Coffinstone.
1. 35m 5b The Long Reach, pitch 1.
2. 40m 5a Climb twin grooves above to the large pocket on Long Reach, then continue slightly right up a line of weakness and a slab to the overlap. Traverse left below it then pull into the Crevasse.
3. 15m 4c Follow The Pause, pitch 3, to the Long Reach belay.
4. 25m 5b Descend diagonally left to an old peg just above the overlap, then back up left to the right end of grass ledge in a corner.
5. 25m 5b Climb the corner for 6m to a peg scar, then break out left and move up left to follow the slab on the left of a grass column. Step right to belay.
6. 30m 5a Follow a flange up right and continue to the top of another grass column (Long Walk belay).

7. 35m 5b Move up left to a diamond-shaped break in the overlap, cross this rightwards, then follow a shallow groove and flange left until a traverse left can be made to belay on the right end of grass ledge of Swastika.

8. 35m 5b Ascend the slab to a small niche, move up left and climb to a corner which is followed to a tree-lined ledge. Traverse right to the base of the Pause corner.

9. 15m 5a Finish up The Pause (the vertical corner on the left).

Variations to pitches 5-9 (5,6 and 7 are The Long Wait Direct, E3).

5. 25m 5b Climb the corner to the peg scar, then follow the corner up right and onto a grass ledge. Climb a flange and step left to belay on top of the grass column.

6. 30m 5b Follow the flange up right, then move up left to corner, step right and climb to the diamond-shaped break in the overlap by a ripple and two open quartz seams.

7. 35m 5c Cross the diamond-shaped overlap rightwards, then move up and left to runners before heading off up the slab on the right directly to the sanctuary of the tree-lined ledge.

8. 30m 5b Ascend the slab to a small niche and climb directly to grass ledges. See also Swastika for further variations on the right.

9. 25m (VS) The grassy right-angled corner at the left end of the tree-lined ledge.

11   Spartan Slab   190m   VS ***   (1954)

A good introductory route, offering pleasant interesting climbing: an excellent outing. Start 5m left of the Coffinstone.

1. 40m 4a Climb the groove for 30m, step right onto the lower slab and move up to a ledge.

2. 25m 4a From the right end of the ledge climb the slab and undercut flake to a ledge beneath the overhang.

3. 35m 4c Step left to the overhung recess where an entertaining move enables the overlap to be overcome. Move up a thin crack, then traverse right along a horizontal crack and continue to a belay near the edge.

4. 30m 4c From the right end of the ledge move up groove with a thin crack for 5m, step left to a steep slab and follow a thin crack for a short way until a step down right can be made. Climb the overlap and good cracks to a belay.

5. 35m 4b Continue up the right-trending crack to a ledge and tree.

6. 25m 3c Gain a tree-lined ledge via cracked blocks and take the fault on the left to easy ground.

12   The Pause   210m   HVS ***   (1960)
This superb route starts 10m left of the Coffinstone at a thin, peg-scarred groove running up the slab.
1. 25m 5a Climb the groove for 20m, move left to climb a bigger groove (peg runner) to a spike. Swing out left and belay by a tree.
2. 20m 4c Step right, follow the layback crack on the lip of the groove, then follow easy rock to belay on Swastika.
3. 40m 5b As for Swastika up the small block overlap, then traverse around its right side and up to the main overlap (peg runner). Continue delicately right into the Crevasse.
4. 40m 4c Gain the slab above, move into the groove on left and climb this over a bulge to a ledge at 15m (Long Reach belay). Traverse 3m right to a faint line of cracks and follow these to a small overlap; move right to a stance.
5. 40m 5a Continue up right to the right end of the higher overlap, then follow a thin crack to an easy groove which leads to a grass ledge beside an overlap.
6. 30m 5a Climb the overlaps on the left to the base of the terminal slab, then traverse left to an undercut edge near the right side of the slab, 5m right of The Long Reach sentry box. Climb the edge to a grass ledge.
7. 15m 5a The vertical corner on the left.

13   Swastika   200m   E2 ***   (1957)
Another superb route offering excellent climbing with fine situations. From the Coffinstone follow the path left for about 40m past a large silver birch tree to the foot of a clean slab. Start below the right-hand of two parallel cracks.
1. 35m 5a Follow the right-slanting crack to a heathery ledge.
2. 25m 4b Move right across the ledge to a slab below a small block overlap.
3. 10m 4c Climb the slab and move directly over a small overlap to beneath the main overlap.
4. 25m 5a Step up right and find a way to attain a standing position on the lip, then traverse left along the Moustache to a grass ledge. It is possible to protect the second by a Friend about 3m along the traverse.
5. 35m 4c Above is the first quartz band. Climb this to a grass ledge, tree belay.
6. 30m 5a Move up right to a ledge, draw breath, and climb the second quartz band.

7. 20m 5c Traverse 2m left beneath the upper overlap to climb a short corner and its ensuing groove, then go up and left to a tree below the final corner.

8. 20m 6a Climb the crack just left of the main crack for 10m, then move up and right to climb the corner to a ledge, finishing by a layback.

Variations to pitch 8.
I. 35m 5b The Long Wait, pitch 8.
II. 30m 5b From the right end of the ledge move up right to climb the blind crack right of the final slab pitch of The Long Wait.
III. 30m 5b From the right end of the ledge move up right passing the blind crack and climb the continuation of the quartz bands below.

14   Learning to Crawl   175m   E3 **   (1990)

Good open climbing taking the fine slab between The Long Wait and the quartz bands of Swastika. Apart from a few moves on pitch 2, the climbing is nowhere desperate, although the runouts are long and protection scarce.

1. 35m 5a Swastika, pitch 1.
2. 30m 5b Move up left towards a small grassy ledge, then traverse right onto the slab and climb directly to a huge leaning flange from whose top a grassy groove on the right can be gained. Move up to the main overlap and belay about 6m left of the Swastika belay.
3. 30m 5b Step left to a small sapling and stretch across the overlap (Friends 2-3 useful) to gain the slab above. Climb directly to a small ledge, then above to a hold, then bear up left to a good ledge and back up right to a small corner.
4. 40m 5a Move up left to a ledge, then climb to a small quartz pocket and follow the ripple up the middle of the slab to grassy cracks leading to the Swastika belay. This is just right of the upper quartz band; it is possible to stay on clean rock and finish up the last 5m of this.
5. 10m 5c Swastika, pitch 7.
6. 30m 5b Any of the variation finishes to Swastika.

15   Tous les Deux   190m   E2 **   (1970)

A direct line between Swastika and Valkyrie with a number of interesting overlaps. Start at the tree right of Swastika. Pitch 2 was originally part of Swastika Direct (1964).

1. 25m 5a Climb the slab, crossing Swastika, and corner to a grass ledge and belay as for Valkyrie.

2. 35m 5a Move up right to climb a line of weakness up the slab (old peg runner) to pass a small overlap and gain the main overlap which is followed rightwards to a belay.
3. 10m 5b Extend across the overlap and up to the Swastika belay.
4. 35m 5a Climb the quartz band for 5m then the slab and slender corner (Valkyrie) on its left to the ledge and tree of Swastika.
5. 10m 5a Climb the slab to the large overlap.
6. 30m 5b Surmount the large overlap from the left to reach a dubious flake which enables the slab above to be gained. Move up to the next overlap.
7. 25m 5c Awkwardly climb a steep corner to defeat the overlap, then follow the easier-angled corner above to a wall where a left traverse gains Agony, tree belay.
8. 20m 4c Follow Agony to easy ground (possible belay), then finish diagonally rightwards.

16   The Valkyrie 205m   E3 **   (1965)
A good, direct line, although some confusion has persisted over the line above the overlap, where unsuspecting leaders have taken various lines leading to even bolder ground. Start left of Swastika at the left-hand of two long parallel cracks. Pitches 1 and 3 were originally part of Swastika Direct (1964).
1. 25m 4c Climb the crack to a heather ledge and belay.
2. 30m 5a Move up and left to a small ledge, then climb straight up the slab to a cave below the overlap.
3. 15m 5b Traverse 3m left, climb the overlap and follow the lip back right to the Swastika belay at the foot of the quartz band.
4. 30m 5b From the middle of the ledge move up slightly left to a small quartz pocket, then follow a ripple diagonally up right some 5m left of the quartz band to gain a slender corner (long runout). Continue to the ledge and tree of Swastika.
5. 10m 4b Move up left to a flake belay beneath the overlap.
6. 20m 5b Surmount the overlap and continue up the slab slightly rightwards to a horizontal crack.
7. 30m 5b Continue up the slab and surmount the next overlap, step right, then move up a sloping corner and pull up left to join Agony.
8. and 9. 45m 5a Agony, pitches 4 and 5.

The Pea Brained Variation   E3 **   (1987)
Serious, bold and sustained, with some excellent blank padding.
4. 50m 5c From the left end of the Swastika belay ledge go up slightly left, then right, then back left to an obvious red pocket with an ancient

chipped spike (poor runner). Climb straight up for 5m to a small ledge (protection on right), then go diagonally up the blank slab to the left end of the overlap (junction with Fast Approaching and Big Ride). Regain Valkyrie by moving 10m right. It is also possible to cross this bald slab lower down, to join Fast Approaching midway up its third pitch.

17   Fast Approaching   170m   E3 **   (1981)
After a rather devious start, this route offers two good pitches. Not for timid seconds. Start as for Agony.
1. 25m 5c Climb the slab on the right to the base of the groove into which Big Ride traverses a little higher. Traverse right to the edge and step down to belay at the left end of the main overlaps.
2. 30m 5b Move up right, step over the overlap and move right to join and follow Valkyrie. A few metres below the Swastika belay ledge move back left to a small overlap then climb directly up to the Frustration abseil ledge. Traverse 5m left to a better belay.
3. 40m 5c Return to the Frustration ledge, then climb directly up to a small flange and follow the ensuing corners directly to the left end of the upper overlap (junction with The Big Ride). A superb pitch. If wet at top of the corner move left, then back right.
4. 30m 5b Surmount the overlap, move right and climb directly to the overlap above, passing a turfy crack, and belay in a corner.
5. and 6. 45m 5a Agony, pitches 4 and 5.

18   The Big Ride   145m   E3 **   (1964)
A fine direct line up the steep slab right of Agony with a substantial second pitch. Scramble to the tree just right of the corner.
1. 30m 5b Climb up right to a peg at 20m, then gain the groove on the right and follow it to ledges.
2. 30m 5c Ascend the obvious thin intermittent flange in the slab above to the haven of a ledge in the corner.
3. 40m 5b Traverse 5m right, then up to the left end of an overlap, climb crack and move up left to a ledge, old pegs. Continue above to the overlap and move up to belay in a corner.
4. and 5. 45m 5a Agony, pitches 4 and 5.

Variation:
3. 40m 5c An improvement on the original. Traverse 5m right and move up to a crack. Using a small pocket on the left gain a weakness and boldly follow this to the ledge and old pegs on the original line.

19   Frustration   HVS   (1960)
As the name implies, this was either an attempt on the The Big Ride
or the corners further right. It is now pointless. From the top of pitch 1
of The Big Ride traverse right to a decrepit peg. Those with a historical
bent (and suicidal tendencies) can abseil then climb up to the belay
of Swastika. Climb the quartz band then move left to rejoin The Big
Ride.

20   Agony   155m   E2 ***   (1957/71/78)
The great corner bounding the left side of the main slabs gives a
magnificent climb. Unfortunately, it is very slow to dry. Scramble to
base of corner.
1. 35m 5c Climb the corner for 15m (peg runner), then traverse right
on friction to a shallow recess. Now go straight up the slab past a small
overlap to a ledge. The corner has been climbed direct but it is dirty
and often wet.
2. 35m 5c Climb the corner to a ledge.
3. 40m 5c Climb the corner, usually wet, to grass at 25m. Now go
diagonally right up the slab to a small overlap and continue to a belay.
4. 25m 5a Move up the corner, traverse right, climb a short corner then
an overlap and move up to the terminal wall. Traverse left to tree.
5. 20m 4c Climb the wall behind the belay and continue to easy ground
(possible belay). Finish diagonally right.

21   The Pinch Direct   215m   E3 ***   (1968/78/84)
Another outstanding route, taking the corner and slab overlooking the
corner of Agony. The description is for the more direct line, as it is now
normally climbed; this does not belittle what was an impressive and
significant original ascent. Start as for Agony.
1. 35m 5c Move up the main corner for 3m, pull into the corner up left
and follow this to a very awkward hanging belay.
2. 25m 5c Continue up the corner, then exit left at the top to belay on
Hammer below the Scoop. With careful ropework and generous 50m
ropes it is just possible to run these two pitches together.
3. 20m 5b Move up right to a thin crack, then climb up right to the
obvious quartz pocket (passing the 'pinch'). Step right almost to the
edge and climb a crack to belay a short way below a small overlap.
4. 40m 5b Continue straight up the crack (the original line moved up
left to join Hammer) and over the small overlap to a finger slot 4m
below an overlap. Either go up, then left beneath overlap, or right, then
up and left above overlap; both finish at same belay on Hammer.

5. 40m 5a Move up the slab above to climb corners onto the upper slab and traverse left below the final wall to belay as for Claw.
6. 25m 5c Claw, pitch 7. Climb the steep chimney to a ledge, then walls and across to a recess and a tree.
7. 30m 5a Claw, pitch 8; the crack to the right of twin cracks.

22 Jackson E4/5 5c/6a †   (1989)
A bold eliminate taking the arete right of Pinch, with excursions back left to place protection. The crux section appears to be level with the Hammer Scoop. No further details are available.

23 Hammer 150m HVS ***   (1957)
Justifiably popular, this is a classic which frequently has queues. The route follows the large corner up to the left of the great corner of Agony. Start by following the path from the Coffinstone and scrambling up to the foot of the corner.
1. 15m 4a Climb the corner to a tree.
2. 35m 4b Follow the cracked slab right of the corner to a stance near the top of a heather cone.
3. 25m 5a Above is the celebrated Scoop, a concave steepening best climbed with a rush of blood to the head to gain the safety of the main corner. Continue to a fine belay halfway up the corner.
4. 40m 5a Climb the corner for 20m, ancient peg, tiptoe right for 3m, then follow cracks to a large overlap. Move right into a recess and pull over to the base of a corner.
5. 35m 4b Climb the corner, then undercut the overlap and move diagonally up right to gain the descent path. Take extra care not to dislodge rocks.

24 Claw 250m E1   (1957)
An uninspiring route to the left of Hammer. Start just left of boulders at the foot of some lower slabs, gained by descending leftwards from the Coffinstone.
1. 45m 4c Climb up and left to a diagonal heather rake.
2. 30m 4a Above a belt of slabs is a small rowan; gain this from the left. The Claw slab above gradually peters out onto the wall overlooking Hammer. Climb straight up to grass ledges.
3. 15m Move across the slab above a small tree into a groove and climb this for a metre or so.
4. 35m Follow the groove to its top, traverse right past a small spike to the arete, then continue to a ledge.

5. 35m Climb up, then right round an awkward edge and on to climb a short groove, then the flaw above to a slab and large block.
6. 35m 5a Climb two short overhangs, then the slab to a poor belay below the final wall.
7. 25m 5c Climb the steep chimney, move up to a ledge, then up walls and across to recess and a tree.
8. 30m 5a From the top of the recess climb a crack to the right of twin cracks to finish up slabs.

25 Jaywalk 190m E1 ** (1960)
A very good route on the upper slab left of Hammer, one on which to escape the crowds. Follow the path past Hammer and Claw to start beneath the right edge of the slab, 15m right of the vegetated left-retaining corner of Sickle.
1. 35m 5b Above is a two-tiered groove in the bulging slab. Climb this and follow its right-trending continuation onto the upper slab, step left, then up (or struggle directly) to gain a belay.
2. 45m 5a Move right and follow grooves to a belay.
3. 45m 5a Follow grooves to a grass patch, move left a metre or so and continue up slabs to a grass ledge.
4. 35m 5b From the thin grass ledge above climb a short wall using a spike then go up a crack and groove. Move right and layback into a grassy groove.
5. 30m Easier vegetated ground leads to the top. The first pitch is thought to have been previously climbed by **The Message** (1957), which then went left to join Sickle.

26 Aryan 175m E1 (1965)
A line between Claw and Jaywalk.
1. 35m 5b Jaywalk, pitch 1.
2. 45m 5a Traverse right to a crack on the edge and climb this to blocks, then step left and continue in the same line to step down right onto the upper of two grass ledges and a small sapling.
3. 45m 5a Climb grooves up and leftwards to reach and then climb the obvious wide crack in overlap, to gain a small sapling and belay.
4. 30m 5a Go up the groove on the right for 20m to an ancient peg, then traverse right under overlaps to reach good belay crack just above a tiny rowan.
5. 20m 5a Climb the overlap and slab to reach the final chimney of Claw. Either finish up this (5c, 5a) or by the wall and recess of Mistaken Identity (5a).

27   Mistaken Identity   195m   E2 *   (1981)
An attempt to find Aryan. Start from the top of Aryan, pitch 3.
4. 35m 5a Step left, then up to gain and follow small quartz seams up
right across the bald slab, long runout. This is between two large moss
streaks. Belay under the final walls.
5. 35m 5a Traverse right across the moss streak to reach the final
chimney of Claw, then climb the groove and wall on the right to a large
recess. Exit by a rightward dangle to reach easy ground.

28   Groundhog   200m   E3 **   (1972)
Another fine route, taking a line between Jaywalk and Sickle, starting
from the foot of the corner on the latter.
1. 35m 5c Move up right to climb cracks to a flake, go up right to an
obvious break in the big overlap and using the crack on the right gain
the upper slab. Continue up, then left to big holds, move up to a ledge
and climb a crack to a belay.
2. 45m 5a Continue up the crackline and grooves in the bulging slab,
never far right of grass ledges, until a short left traverse gains a belay
by a loose flake in a corner.
3. 45m 5a Climb the corner and move up right to a small circular
depression on the line of Jaywalk. Go straight up, then left to belay in
the flanking corner.
4. and 5. 75m 5b Gain the thin grass ledge of Jaywalk 15m above,
and finish up pitches 4 and 5 of that route.

29   Sickle   190m   VS   (1954)
This route, the pioneers' first excursion on the Slabs, provides a
scrappy and worthless experience by finding a way to the foot of the
sickle-shaped corner bounding the Slabs on their extreme left margin,
climbing the corner, then escaping out left somewhere. The corner is
reached either by climbing up, then left, just left of Claw, or by going
further along and climbing more directly. The most direct way, however, is to scramble up leftwards from the Coffinstone!

30   Mosquito   90m   Severe   (1972)
Start in a grassy corner on the extreme left edge of the Slabs where
they are bounded by a burn.
1. 45m Climb a steep crack to surmount an overlap, continue up a
prominent crack until a right traverse can be made, then move up
trending right on small footholds to a peg belay below a blank slab.
2. 45m Climb the blank slab, traverse right to a slab with twin cracks
and follow this, best by its left edge, to a grassy terrace and belay.

31   Buzzard Arete   200m   Very Difficult   (1970)
The main slabs are bounded on the left by a large gully. This route
follows the prominent ridge high up on the left-hand side of the gully.
From the base of the ridge a direct line leads to the top with many
short but interesting pitches on good clean granite.

THE GIRDLES

32   The Grasshopper   390m   E2 *   (1961/66/71)
A long sustained right-to-left low-level girdle beneath the first set of
overlaps. Start as for Ba's, 70m right of the Coffinstone at a tongue of
clean brown slabs just right of a heathery bay.
1. 35m 4c Climb the tongue and a groove to a belay.
2. 35m 4c Continue directly up to a poor flake belay on Ba's.
3. 20m 5a As for Ba's, traverse left to a grassy corner.
4. 25m 5a Descend 5m and climb a wall, then make a descending
traverse left to belay on Spartan Slab.
5. 30m 4c Spartan Slab, pitch 3 in reverse. Move left, hand-traverse
a horizontal crack and descend the overlap.
6. 20m 5b Traverse left under the overlap to belay on Swastika.
7. 30m 5a Traverse under the overlap to a small tree, descend 3m
and traverse under the lower overlap to the cave belay on Valkyrie.
8. 10m 5b Climb out of the cave on the right and go up to the belay
ledge of Swastika.
9. 35m 5b From the left end of the ledge step down and traverse
across to the abseil ledge of Frustration. This can also be done at a
lower level as described for Fast Approaching (p295). Continue across
to Agony.
10. 25m 5c Climb the wall with a peg for aid to enter, then follow the
corner of Pinch Direct to the belay on Hammer.
11. 25m 5a As for Hammer, climb the Scoop and corner to a belay.
12. 45m Climb the bay on the left, then a thin crack through mossy
slabs. Traverse slightly right and follow more thin cracks to reach the
upper wall.
13. 10m Move left to a large grassy bay.
14. 20m Move back slightly, climb an overhanging groove (peg for
aid) then traverse right to belay.
15. 25m Climb the wall on the left, then move up to climb an overhung
recess and the corner above to slabs. Finish up to the right.

33   The Long Walk   340m   E2 *   (1958)
A high-level, right-to-left girdle. Start at extreme right edge of Slabs.
1. and 2. 75m 4c Climb diagonally up and left to a stance beneath a
prominent corner in the first overlap.
3. 20m 5b Take the corner crack to the slab above.
4. and 5. 75m 5a Go diagonally left to belay on Pause at the edge of
the main upper overlap.
6. 25m 5a Traverse under the overlap across The Long Reach to a
grass ledge and the Long Wait belay.
7. 25m 5a Go left to a grass ledge on Swastika.
8. 20m 5c Swastika, pitch 7.
9. 45m 5a Go left along a zigzag line of overlap across Tous les Deux
and Valkyrie, then move up to a stance on Agony.
10. and 11. 55m 5a Agony, pitches 4 and 5.

Variation finish: 5b
From the belay at the end of pitch 7, traverse left beneath overlaps to
their end and a junction with The Big Ride, then follow this to finish up
Agony.

34   The Thin Red Line   460m   E3 A2 5c †   (1966)
A right-to-left mid-level girdle which finds a line between the two main
overlaps on the Great Slab. See article in SMCJ 1967, from which this
description has been gleaned.
    Start on extreme right of slabs and climb left along the obvious
horizontal red seam to overlaps, then go up to Spartan Slab (possibly
as for Ba's). Go left to a small overlap and up to a ledge. Another pitch
leads to a belay before a hard section which is then climbed (presum-
ably across the blank slab left of The Long Reach) to belay on The
Long Wait. Gain the quartz band on Swastika, then the belay at the
top of pitch 4 of Valkyrie, then by an 20m section to a flake belay
beneath the overlap. Gain Agony and climb the obvious overhanging
corner-crack (A2) to the upper slab. Cross Pinch to reach Hammer by
a hard, serious section, then abseil to the stance halfway up the corner.
Follow Grasshopper to Claw, then up to the upper slab, gain Jaywalk
and traverse to Sickle.

THE UPPER SLABS

The following four routes lie on the belt of slower-drying slabs above
and to the right of the main slabs. The lowest slab, just off the descent
path above the Ba's slab can be climbed fairly easily anywhere, and

leads to the rake from where the routes start. There are three prominent, right-facing corners at the left side of the slabs, running
diagonally from left to right. Descent is not easy but can be accom-
plished by abseiling off small trees down scrappy ground on the right.

35   Monsoon   150m   VS †   (1969)
Starts left of Dan and crosses that route to end up in scrappy ground
on the right. Start some 5m right of the centre corner at a crack. Climb
the crack and move left to a grass stance where the corner fades out.
Traverse obviously right to gain then climb a crack and go through a
small overlap to belay in a scoop. Continue up and right, following a
line of cracks and corners to a large scoop and belay. Climb the groove
above through a large bulge by a crack and finish up a wide crack in
the slab.

36   Dan   300m   E1   (1960)
Starts some 15m right of the rightmost of the three corners and goes
diagonally up left by a central line, crossing Monsoon to reach the
bottom left end of an obvious long left-to-right diagonal overlap near
the top of the slabs. Climb up right under the overlap to a loose
chockstone, move right, then climb by cracks and grooves to a nest
of roofs. Break through these leftwards and climb to more broken
rocks.

37   Cut the Grass   240m   HVS †   (1965)
Takes a line about 30m right of Dan all the way.

38   Winter Dan   IV **   (1980)
An obvious line of ice forms fairly regularly on these slabs, starting off
the descent path towards the right side, then going up and left to gain
an overlap. Above this a crack line leads up, bearing right to easier
ground at a tree in an obvious recess. The line probably equates more
to Monsoon.

THE RIGHT-HAND SLAB

Clearly visible from the approach path, and about 300 metres right of the main slabs beyond a small ravine, is a clean slab ending in steep scrappy ground. Descent by abseil to the right. There are two routes.

39 Curses 145m Severe   (1967)

Takes a left-to-right line. Start at the lowest tongue of slab.

1. 35m Climb to a vertical flake edge, then diagonally right along a groove and cross an overlap to belay in the groove above.

2. 25m Climb the groove, follow a band of red rock running right and go straight up to a poor belay.

3. 30m Follow a quartz band diagonally right for 15m, then go up just left of a black waterstreak to belay at a vertical flake (crux, little or no protection).

4. 30m Follow a grass ledge rightwards, then go up to a rock rib.

5. 25m Climb the rib for 12m, then traverse right to a tree.

40 Nausea 90m VS *   (1970)

Takes an obvious line straight up the middle of the slab on good clean rock. The following description is for a later route climbed in 1990 **(Comatose** 90m VS 4c), it is probable that this is the same as Nausea. Start just right of the lowest point of the slab.

1. 45m Climb past a small hole in the rock to reach an obvious right-slanting fault line. Follow this diagonally up right to a horizontal fault near the right edge of the slab (peg belay *in situ*).

2. 45m Climb back up left to a groove, which is followed to the top.

Finally, for those of an inquisitive nature, some three kilometres beyond the Slabs to the south-west there is a gully system whose right branch, The Chasm of Beinn Trilleachan (1973), is a remarkable rift which can provide an entertaining excursion.

SRON NA CREISE
900m   (Map Ref 240 520)

This is the fine hill at the head of Glen Etive opposite the Buachaille Etive Mor which is particularly well seen from Kingshouse Hotel. It lies to the west of the White Corries ski slopes and is best approached from Blackrock Cottage, less than one kilometre along the road to the chairlift car park. From the cottage bear west across the moor below the ridge of Creag Dubh to reach the Cam Ghleann beneath the east face of Sron na Creise. There are a number of easy-angled gullies and buttresses which give some pleasant winter climbing of a modest standard. The face holds a lot of snow and therefore can be fairly prone to avalanche.

The best descent is to follow the long ridge down north-eastwards from the top of Stob a'Ghlais Choire into the Cam Ghleann. Only one route has been recorded, but many others have been climbed. In the centre of the east face there is a broad V-shaped buttress, immediately left of what is known as Gully 5. The buttress top is a flat-topped tower; it was first climbed in summer 1903 by Dr and Mrs Inglis Clark.

Inglis Clark Ridge   140m   III ***   (1987)
An excellent mountaineering route up the well-defined ridge. Start at the right-hand end of the ridge, some 30m up Gully 5 from the foot of the buttress.
1. 35m Follow grooves, over an ice-bulge, and up a steep 5m ice pitch (crux), to reach a broad terrace.
2. 30m Easier climbing leads to the prominent rock tower.
3. 35m Climb the tower on its right to below a wall.
4. 40m Traverse 5m left along the wall and surmount blocks traversing back right. Finish up a right-angled chimney to gain easier rocks leading to the top of the tower.

BEINN MHIC CHASGAIG
862m   (Map Ref 203 502)

BIRD'S EYE BUTTRESS (Map Ref 203 502)
About seven kilometres down Glen Etive on the left, the west ridge of Beinn Mhic Chasgaig terminates in a west-facing, rounded granite buttress, well seen when looking back from further down the road near

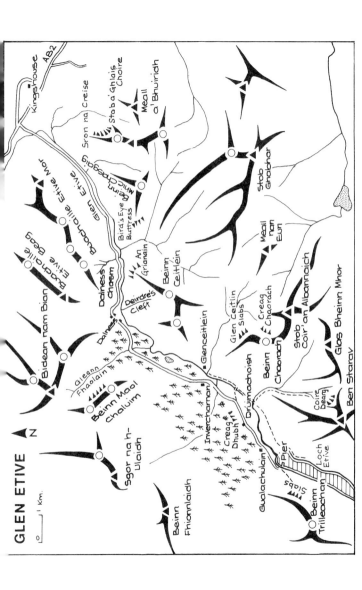

GLEN ETIVE

N

0   1 Km.

A82

Kingshouse

Sron na Creise

Stob a' Ghlais Choire

Meall a' Bhuiridh

Beinn Mhic Chasgaig

Bird's Eye Buttress

Buachaille Etive Mor

Glen Etive

Buachaille Etive Beag

Stob Ghabhar

Dalness Chasm

An Grianain

Meall nam Eun

Bidean nam Bian

Deirdre's Cleft

Dalness

Beinn Ceitlein

Glen Ceitlin Slabs

Creag Chaorach

Stob Coir' an Albannaich

Glas Bheinn Mhor

Glenceitlein

Gleann Fhaolain

Beinn Maol Chaluim

Invercharnan

Drumachoish

Beinn Chaorach

Coire Dearg

Ben Starav

Sgor na h-Ulaidh

Creag Dhubh

Gualachulain

Pier

Loch Etive

Slabs

Beinn Fhionnlaidh

Beinn Trilleachan

Dalness. Approach via the bridge (198 513) which has a 2m high corrugated iron gate, which is often locked, and follow the track to Alltchaorunn, then the footpath beyond leading up the east side of the Allt a'Chaorainn. The crag appears up on the left. The first route takes a steep narrow slab below and left of the main crag.

Secretion Slab   120m   Severe   (1966)
Start at the foot of the slab, surmount an overlap on the left, go straight up by large pockmarks, then trend left above a bulge (crux) to finish left of the final overlap.

Surprise Pea   80m   VS †   (1966)
Start at the foot of the main buttress, below two prominent corners.
1. 35m Climb the rib between the corners (crux), step left above an overhang and go diagonally left up a jam crack to a peg belay below a bulging slab.
2. 35m Climb the bulging slab and continue directly to a large overlap. Go diagonally left past a huge perched block and up to a sloping ledge.
3. 10m Finish up the rib above, wet.

Fish Finger   75m   VS †   (1966)
Start 10m up right from the lowest rocks.
1. 10m Climb a wall to a grass ledge and peg belay (crux).
2. 35m Move round a bulge to a sloping ledge and follow a prominent corner on the nose of the buttress to slabs above. Belay below the final wall.
3. 30m Climb bulging slabs rightwards past a good spike to the top.

BEINN CEITLEIN

832m   (Map Ref 178 492)

This is the next hill down Glen Etive from Beinn Mhic Chasgaig. Opposite Dalness Chasm the termination of the east ridge of the hill forms an interesting afforested, tower-like crag known as An Grianan (formerly called A'Cioch). This faces north-east, and is at a height of 300m, at (193 205). Approach as for Bird's Eye Buttress, then just beyond the farm at Alltchaorunn cross the Allt a'Chaorainn by a footbridge and so gain the crag.

Weevil's Way   90m   Hard Severe   (1960)
Start on slabs at the left end of the crag. Climb rightwards to a tree belay in a corner just right of a yellow overhang. Continue up the right

wall to a large flake, then straight up to below an overhang. Traverse right to a groove with small ash trees and climb this to a tree belay. Traverse right along a grassy terrace for 12m, then climb to the top by grooves and ribs.

Bo Weevil   40m   VS †   (1960's)
Climb the steep wall on the left of the crag.

Further down Glen Etive, just east of Dalness House, an obvious cleft can be seen rising up Beinn Ceitlein, starting from a ramp. Access is via the footbridge (172 512) over the river behind Dalness House.

Deirdre's Cleft   245m   II/III *   (1970's)
There are no particular difficulties in the lower section. Higher, either climb a steep chimney direct or break out right up a scoop to exit just right of the main gully line.

BEINN MAOL CHALUIM
847m   (Map Ref 143 518)

This hill, which is on the north-west side of Glen Etive three kilometres west of Dalness, faces the south side of the Bidean nam Bian massif across Gleann Fhaolain. The north-east face presents a long wall of high though broken crags. Due to their nature the crags allow endless route variation at about Grade II, although harder pitches can be found. Approach from Inbhirfhaolain (one kilometre south-west of Dalness) via Gleann Fhaolain. One route has been recorded **(Lone Ranger,** 220m II 1987) which takes a line right of the centre of the wedge-shaped buttress which is separated by a shelf from the sprawling buttress with a steep base.

BEINN CHAORACH
840m   (Map Ref 157 464)

This steep rocky hill on the south-east side of Glen Etive six kilometres south of Dalness is the north-west shoulder of Stob Coir'an Alban-naich. There are two climbing areas, both reached from Glen Ceitlein. Leave the Glen Etive road about two kilometres south of the deer farm at Invercharnan (136 469) and follow the private track (not readily seen from the road) which drops east to cross the River Etive. On the other side a track carries on north-east towards the foot of Glen Ceitlein.

GLEN CEITLIN SLABS (Map Ref 164 464)

These west-facing slabs are located at an altitude of 500m on the north-east side of the hill overlooking Glen Ceitlein. Follow the glen for about 600 metres and turn up the hillside just beyond a low crag. The slabs form the east wall of a prominent gully. Follow the west bank of the gully to their base.

The rock is rough granite at a comfortable angle, extending upwards for 300m but narrowing rapidly above the gully base. Prominent features are an area of reddish quartz-banded grooves at half-height on the left and a large square slab high on the right. Routes are described from left to right, with the first route lying on the right before the main slabs are reached. On the approach to these slabs in winter an impressive icefall is seen on the right, some 400 metres before the slabs are reached. The ice forms down the largest of the watercourses.

The Fall Line   220m   III **   (1991)
Climb the impressive icefall direct, finishing up a deep narrow chimney just below the top.

The Whore's Apron   310m   Very Difficult   (1989)
The main mass of slab is bounded on the left initially by steep ground, and higher up by an obvious corner. This route takes a fairly direct line up the area of clean slab close to the left edge of the slabs. Avoid any possible escapes up disintegrating rock and heather on the left. The main interest lies in the route-finding.
Winter: III **   (1991)
Copious amounts of ice form on these slabs in a good winter, the best down the line of The Whore's Apron. Climb this icefall direct.

Limburger Slabs   305m   Very Difficult   (1986)
Scramble up 15m from the gully bed to a prominent bollard at the lowest point of the slabs.
1. and 2. 80m Move up right and follow an indistinct crack to a steepening. Move right to a recess above a heather patch.
3. and 4. 60m Leave the recess on the right and traverse right and up to reach prominent twin quartz grooves. Climb either groove to easy slabs above.
5. and 6. 60m Move up and right easily to a niche below the left-bounding groove of a large square slab.
7. and 8. 90m Follow this groove to a higher slab and climb this by a thin crack to easy ground. From 150m up it is possible to make a less than satisfactory finish on the extreme left of the slabs.

Gruyere   150m   Very Difficult   (1986)
About 30m above the lowest rocks there is a second easy access to
the gully bed from the west bank. Above this point a prominent corner
stretches up the crag, defining the large square slab on the right in its
upper reaches. Gain the corner system by a ramp and steep chimney-
crack (awkward to enter) and follow it in four pitches to easy ground.

CREAG CHAORACH (Map Ref 161 454)

This compact granite crag faces south-east across the head of Coire
Glas towards Stob Coir'an Albannaich. It is clearly seen in profile from
the summit of Buachaille Etive Mor. Follow Glen Ceitlein till it forks,
then scramble up the gorge into Coire Glas between Beinn Chaorach
and Stob Coir'an Albannaich. A striking pinnacle is passed on the way.
The scramble up the gorge is recommended as an expedition in itself.
    The crag is divided into two portions by a well-defined central area
of cracks and deep V-grooves. On the left is an expanse of steep slabs
and on the right more slab, on whose right at three-quarters height is
a prominent black overlap. Routes are described from left to right.

Patey's Old Man   20m   Unclassifiable   (1967)
This is the striking pinnacle passed on the approach. It protrudes from
the left wall of the gorge. Lasso the top and climb the rope. Treat it
gently!

The Glutton   120m   VS   (1990)
Start just right of a large cracked block some way left of Prey.
1. 20m 4c Climb to a scoop, turn an overhang on the left, then continue
up and right to belay.
2. 40m 4b Traverse left to an edge overlooking a corner, then climb
the edge to a ledge. From the right end of the ledge follow a slabby
rib to grass ledges.
3. and 4. 60m Two easy pitches lead to the top.

Prey   120m   HVS *   (1990)
Probably the best route on these slabs. Left of Eezay Edge is a large
square slab with a bird-like overlap top left.
1. 20m 4c Follow a diagonal crack in the slab to belay short of the
overlap.
2. 40m 5a Surmount the overlap at its right-hand end, traverse left a
few metres, then climb a short wall to gain the slab above. Climb
rightwards up the slab to below a short wall.
3. and 4. 60m Two easy pitches lead to the top.

The two original routes on this crag lie somewhere on the central section, where the rock can be climbed virtually anywhere.

To the right of the central raised area there are three narrow buttresses, the leftmost of which has a striking pink slab capped by a line of overhangs. **Eezay Edge** (105m Severe 1967) follows its left edge. **Central Rib** (120m Difficult 1967) takes the line of least resistance to finish up the rib bounding the pink slab on the right. Another line, which may approximate to Eezay Edge, takes an easy introductory pitch to a ledge and thread belay, then goes left and up to a fine traverse right to pull over a red wall. The climbing was good and just short of VS.

The following routes lie to the right of the raised area in the centre of the crag.

Deadline   140m   Severe   (1972)
Start at a large boulder 15m left of the small curving overlap above the lowest rocks, 6m left of Xenolith. Climb fairly directly up, always on the left of a natural watercourse, to the left end of the prominent black overlap at three-quarters height.

Xenolith   145m   VS *   (1972)
At the right end of the crag and at three-quarters height is a prominent black overlap. This route climbs the slabby rib leading directly to the right end of the overlap. Above the lowest rocks is a small curving overlap. Start 8m to its left.
1. 30m Climb slabs to a steep rib, move up, then left to a small stance at pink rocks.
2. 35m Climb a steep slab past a large block and follow a system of quartz veins to enter an obvious rectangular recess. Step left and move up to a flake belay.
3. 45m Climb a groove, then the thin crack at the right end of the large overlap and continue by slabs to a peg belay just below a grass ledge.
4. 35m Finish by a choice of routes up short walls, better to the left.

Xenolith Right-hand Start   60m   VS   (1990)
To the right of the normal start is a slab bounded on the left by a corner and topped with an overlap.
1. 40m 4b Climb the slab to belay below an overlap.
2. 20m 4c Gain the rib on the left, then trend left to join Xenolith at the rectangular recess.

CREAG DHUBH (Map Ref 127 470)

This is the small south-east facing granite crag which sits at 250m on the little hill behind Druimachoish, near the foot of Glen Etive. It is clearly visible from the road and is approached through the trees. Three Severes were climbed on this crag by W. Skidmore and the Greenock MC; **Crab, Scalp and Jungle** - no descriptions available. Routes are described from left to right.

Turnaround   25m   E1   5b   (1986)
Climb the obvious thin crack at the left end of the crag, with three steep sections.

Graceland   35m   HVS   5a   (1987)
Just left of Conscience Corner climb a left-trending corner to a steep wall. Pass a flake on the wall to a ledge. Climb the top wall using two sloping ramps.

Conscience Corner   35m   VS   4c   (1987)
Climb the small corner just left of Ivy Corner direct. Maintain line by following grooves and cracks to top.

Ivy Corner   35m   HVS   5a   (1987)
Climb an ivy-filled corner direct to a small overhanging nose. Pass the nose on the left and continue by easier ground to the top.

Gestation   35m   HVS   5a   (1986)
Climb a steep wall and crack 4m left of Tattieman towards a tree. Move right before the tree and climb a rib, then step back left onto a wall with a left-trending crack leading to a corner. Move out right of the corner to easier ground.

Tattieman   35m   HVS   5a   (1986)
At the foot of the highest section of crag climb a steep wall past a loose block on the right to an oak tree. Pass the tree on its left to gain a left-trending crack leading to the final wall.

Druim nan Gillean   30m   E2   5c   (1987)
The sharp arete at the right-hand side of the crag. Climb a steep crack, then follow the arete to a flake. Wedge gently up this to finish up a blunt arete.
On the right of the arete is a large block. The shallow corner above its left side is VS 4c, but escapable, and the corner above its right side is Severe.

BEN STARAV
1078m   (Map Ref 125 427)

The vast bulk of Ben Starav rises from the head of Loch Etive opposite the Etive Slabs. From its summit a ridge runs out east to Glas Bheinn Mhor (997m) forming four small corries, all clearly visible from the road. Stob Coire Dheirg is at the head of Coire Dearg, the second corrie east of the main summit. The crag faces north-east, and since its foot is at some 900m, it readily comes into good condition for winter climbing.

Approach from the road in Glen Etive at (136 467). Follow a private track which drops east to cross the river and leads to the cottage of Coileitir. Continue south-west along a path to the Allt Mheuran, then south-east to cross a bridge 200 metres upstream and follow the path below the east side of the long north ridge of Ben Starav. This path follows the west bank of the Allt nam Meirleach towards the corrie high above. Routes are described from left to right.

On the left is the main east ridge of Stob Coire Dheirg. A broken buttress sits on this, bounded by a short gully on its right flank.

Parting Shot   70m   II   (1986)
Climb the broken buttress by a shallow icy scoop just right of centre to reach the ridge.

On the right, beneath the summit, are three buttresses separated by deep gullies.

Flexi Rib   120m   II   (1986)
The left-hand buttress, starting at its lowest point. Climb a snow gully between rock ribs to a small col. Move left to the edge and follow it to a snow arete. The tower above is climbed direct (crux) although it can easily be outflanked on the left.

Hidden Ridge   200m   III/IV **   (1986)
The central buttress, which becomes a narrow pinnacled ridge in its upper part, gives a route of quality and variety. Start on the right side of the buttress just above its foot at an open gully. Climb the gully, which becomes a groove then a ramp, for about 60m to a block belay. Ascend a short steep groove (crux) and interesting mixed ground above to the top of the buttress. A narrow ridge with two pinnacles lies

ahead. The second one can be outflanked, but for maximum enjoyment it should be taken direct. Easy ground leads to the summit of the mountain.

Shadow Groove   100m   III   (1986)
The broad right-hand buttress. Just to the right of the lowest point is a snow bay with a steep ice groove above. Climb the groove (sustained) and easy ground above to the top of the buttress.

STARAV SLABS (Map Ref 120 446)
Some 200m up the hillside level with the head of Loch Etive is an area of slab clearly seen from the road end. Approach from Coileitir. The Greenock MC note that they found three pleasant 140m climbs (all Very Difficult). MacInnes is also reported to have climbed there.

Garbh Bheinn of Ardgour

The districts of Ardgour and Sunart lie between Loch Sunart and Glen Tarbert in the south and Loch Eil in the north, with Loch Linnhe being its eastern limit. The mountain of most interest to climbers is the aptly named Garbh Bheinn (the rough hill, 885m), which lies two kilometres north of Glen Tarbert and some four and a half kilometres north-west of Inversanda on the west side of Loch Linnhe.

The rock is a beautifully striped gneiss, wonderfully rough even when wet. The area is quiet, a ferry being the way of easiest access from the 'mainland', while the climate is definitely different from Glen Coe. It is often possible to climb on Garbh Bheinn while watching rain squalls hit Glen Coe. Conversely, 'West Coast' weather can lie on the Ardgour hills for days, with mist and drizzle. Spring is easily the best time to visit Ardgour; the weather is better than in mid to late summer, and stalking takes place between September and February (enquire at Inversanda House, 940 595).

To approach, take the drive-on Corran Ferry (022 635), which runs during the hours of daylight only, from about 8 a.m. to 8 p.m. in summer; an early start is advised. The bus service along the A82 goes past the ferry. Should the return ferry be missed, the penalty is a tedious drive north along the A861 single-track road to the A830 Mallaig road at the head of Loch Eil. There are hotels on either side of the Corran Narrows, and camping sites are easily found along the shore of Loch Linnhe, thus avoiding confrontations with landowners.

There are two approaches to the climbs on Garbh Bheinn; Coire an Iubhair (scenic), or Coire a'Chothruim (fast but brutal, unnamed on the 1:50000 map). For the former, from the Corran Ferry follow the Strontian road (A861) to about one kilometre west of Inversanda at an old bridge (928 596). Follow the path up Coire an Iubhair to the junction with the Garbh Choire Mor, then the less distinct path through the narrow entrance to the upper corrie. The Great Ridge lies ahead, bounded on the right by Great Gully. Allow about 2 hours.

For the Coire a'Chothruim route, useful especially for the South Wall and Garbh Choire Buttress climbs, follow the A861 westwards for about three kilometres past the old bridge to the mouth of the corrie. Follow the east side of the burn up an indistinct path (avoiding the incredibly deep bracken jungle), before heading up right to the bealach south of the summit. The walking is rough and steep, but leads to the bealach in just over an hour from the road. From the bealach continue

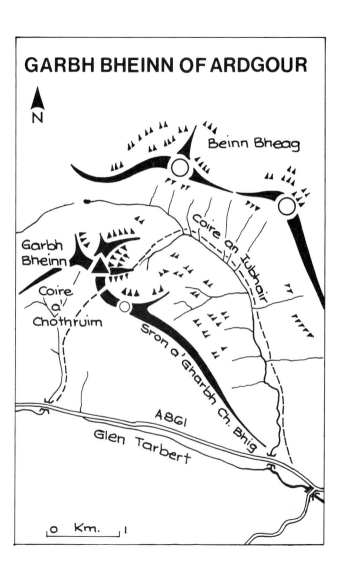

GARBH BHEINN OF ARDGOUR

N

Beinn Bheag

Coire an Iubhair

Garbh
Bheinn

Coire
a'
Chothruim

Sron a' Gharbh Ch. Bhig

A861

Glen Tarbert

0   Km.   1

up the ridge towards the summit until the sloping shelf under the South Wall is seen. Descend this to the foot of the lower tier. For the Garbh Choire Buttress, from the bealach descend slightly then contour towards the buttress.

LEAC BEAG BUTTRESS

The buttress low in the south-east corner of the Garbh Choire Mor. There are two sections, divided by a vegetated groove, while deep gullies define the buttress on both flanks. The routes are described from left to right.

1   Sinister   120m   Very Difficult   (1954)
Climbs the left-hand section of the buttress, starting at the lowest rocks. Indifferent climbing leads to scrambling above half-height.

2   Dexter   145m   Severe *   (1954)
A pleasant route with good situations, starting at the lowest rocks of the right-hand section of the buttress below a prominent arete.
1. 30m Climb the arete for 15m, then a 10m wall to an overhang. Climb this directly to a stance near the edge.
2. 35m Follow the edge until holds lead left to overhanging rocks. Move right below these to a recess near the right edge and follow the obvious groove up left on good holds to a belay.
3. 35m Move right and follow the arete directly to a grassy rake.
4. 45m Scramble to the top.

3   Left Edge Variation   55m   Severe   (1954)
An indifferent variation, starting about 10m left of Dexter, below and right of a vertical nose. A wall, the nose, scrambling, and then a right traverse below overhanging rocks leads to a junction with Dexter at its extreme right edge.

4   Drongo   120m   VS *   (1973)
A very obvious line, well seen from the South Wall. Start 45m up the gully on the right flank of the buttress below a huge sloping corner on the left wall of the gully.
1. 40m 4c Enter the corner and climb its right wall until almost level with a large recess on the left, then step right into a groove on the edge (crux) and so to a belay.
2. 35m Climb up and left across a steep wall to join the arete of Dexter, which leads to a belay.
3. 45m Scramble to finish.

GARBH CHOIRE BUTTRESS

This compact buttress, high in the south-west corner of the Garbh Choire Mor and about 250 metres right of Leac Beag Buttress, provides excellent climbing. It is easily approached by a downward traverse from the Bealach. The routes are described from left to right.

5 Percussion 55m VS **   (1974)
Near the left end a corner crack rises behind a large block.
1. 25m Climb the corner to a slab. Follow this rightwards below an overhang to a flake belay below a groove with an overhanging crest.
2. 30m Climb the groove and overhang to finish.

6 Swingle 70m Severe **   (1978)
Start 8m right of Percussion, at a wall just left of an edge.
1. 25m Climb the wall and move right to climb a crack to a grass ledge with a loose block.
2. 25m Follow a broken arete up right to a smooth corner. Climb the left wall, cross an overlap and climb a cracked slab to a comfortable stance at the foot of a groove capped by a roof.
3. 20m Climb the left wall of the corner, step left into a groove and swing left below the roof to step back right and finish by the corner above.

7 Sugarplum 85m E1 **   (1987)
Climbs the central depression of the buttress between Swingle and Cantata, including the overhanging headwall above. Start about 8m right of Swingle and scramble up to a slab beneath the furthest left of the three grooves that run up through the depression.
1. 35m 5b Climb the groove past two steep difficult bulges to a stance below the overhanging corner that cuts through the headwall.
2. 20m 5a/b Make a rising traverse across the left wall on sharp incut holds, then move back right to the overhanging corner which leads to an awkward finish. Continue easily to a belay.
3. 30m Broken rocks and an easy slab lead to the top.

8 Cantata 75m VS **   (1976)
Climbs the buttress just right of centre. Scramble to the point where a downward-jutting nose abuts on a slab and begin at a loose flake.
1. 20m Move up and slightly right, then go left and climb a corner to a stance.
2. 25m 4c Climb the corner above to a ledge, then a short wall and slab to a belay at the right edge of a steep wall with twin grooves.

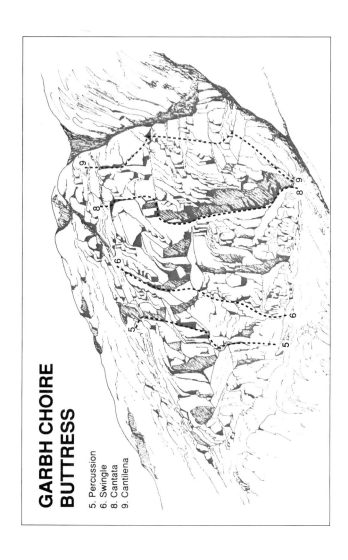

GARBH CHOIRE BUTTRESS

5. Percussion
6. Swingle
8. Cantata
9. Cantilena

3. 30m Go right under the wall for a few metres until a good flake leads back left to the foot of a slab. Bear left up the slab to finish over an overhang.

9 Cantilena 100m Severe *   (1974)
At the right end of the crag is a flying buttress. Start up a corner to its left.
1. 40m Move onto and climb a rib to a slab, go up and left, climb an overlap by a rib and then a second slab and wall to a belay.
2. 35m Climb to a block overhang, pass this on the left, move right and climb a wall on good holds to a ledge.
3. 25m Scramble to finish.

GARBH CHOIRE SLABS

These obvious and pleasant slabs are just down and left of the bealach, facing the South Wall. They can be climbed virtually any-where at about Very Difficult or Severe standard, and though slow to dry the rock is so good as to be climbable in almost any condition. They were probably first climbed by a party from Moray M.C. in 1948, but the only properly recorded routes are:

10 Rampage 105m Very Difficult *   (1971)
Start at the lowest rocks at the left-hand side and follow a system of cracks and grooves to a belt of overhangs, which is climbed to the left.

11 Lodestone 105m Severe *   (1973)
Start 6m right of Rampage. Climb a crack to a detached block. Gain the main slab and climb this directly. Move right at its top and finish up short walls.

BEALACH BUTTRESS
BEALACH GULLY BUTTRESS

These are just below and right of the bealach at the head of Garbh Choire Mor. Bealach Buttress is defined on its right by a deep-cut gully on whose right lies Bealach Gully Buttress.

12 Bealach Buttress 105m Very Difficult   (1952)
Start at the lowest rocks and take the line of least resistance to the left-hand of two narrow aretes. This leads to the top. Much variation is possible.

The two following climbs are on Bealach Gully Buttress.

13 Sapphire 60m E1   (1972)
Start at a chimney on the right wall of the deep-cut gully about 10m
up from its entrance.
1. 20m 5b Climb the chimney to a ledge on the right (peg runner),
traverse 6m right (crux, peg runner on loose block) and climb an
overhanging corner to a ledge and peg belay.
2. 40m Climb the groove above to its conclusion, then continue up
the wall to a good flake belay.

14 Garnet 55m HVS **   (1971)
Start from the gully at some slabs forming the toe of the buttress. The
route takes the prominent line of corners up the buttress nose.
1. 45m 5a Climb slabs and a short corner to step right and follow the
main corner line to a belay.
2. 10m Finish more easily.

THE SOUTH WALL OF GREAT RIDGE
The two tiers of this superb crag, separated by a terrace, form the
upper part of the south flank of the Great Ridge. The routes on the
upper tier finish at the summit of Garbh Bheinn. The best approach is
from the bealach, taking the path towards the summit but turning down
right before it to gain the left end of the Wall. Easy slabs continue down
giving access to the lower tier, while the terrace leads across to the
final rocks of the Great Ridge. Routes are described from left to right,
taking the lowest routes first. An alternative approach is to climb one
of the following three routes from Garbh Choire.

15 Jock 65m Very Difficult   (1971)
Below the broad grassy rake under the lower tier of the South Wall is
a somewhat broken face, in the middle of which is a large area of
continuous sound rock, about 60m high. This and the following route
may be common in part. Follow the edge of a prominent corner up the
line of a steep crack for 25m to the base of an overhang. Traverse
delicately right across a slab and belay below a short wall. Climb the
wall, trending left to a large ledge. At the back of the ledge is a wall
split at its left end by prominent crack. Climb it to easier rock and the
grassy rake.

16   The Final Judgement   70m   Very Difficult   (1986)
Below and to the right of Bealach Gully Buttress an easy-angled gully
leads up and left towards the bottom tier of the South Wall. Left of the
gully is a small buttress. Climb a series of grooves and ribs near the
right edge of the buttress to easy ground below the lower tier of the
South Wall.

17   South-East Chimney   210m   Very Difficult   (1936)
The easy-angled gully-ramp, starting in the Garbh Choire, some
distance up and left from the initial slabs of the Great Ridge, which
leads to below the South Wall. Traverse right on a grass ledge and
enter the chimney proper, climbing it to where it steepens to form an
arch. Continue either by the right wall to the crest of the Great Ridge
or by the chimney. As the ramp is often wet and is prone to stonefall
(a large rockfall occurred above it in 1988) it may be better to miss it
out, beginning with the traverse from the foot of the South Wall.

18   Plod   210m   I   (1966)
Climb the initial chimmney of South-East Chimney to the terrace and
continue below the South Wall to the top.

19   Anathema Gully   180m   Severe   (1954)
An unpleasant slabby gully on the flank of the Great Ridge to the left
of South-East Chimney. The final chimney, finishing about 15m below
the summit, is easily seen from some distance up Garbh Choire Mor.
The exit is the crux.

THE LOWER TIER
Near the left end of the lower tier is a large open right-facing corner.
Scimitar starts near there at the point where a shattered ledge curves
up to the right. The lower tier ends on the left below roofs as a short
arete, taken by Brack.

20   Dirk   25m   Very Difficult   (1952)
Climb the prominent chimney near the left end of the tier. Loose.

21   Brack   40m   E3 5c *   (1986)
Climb the short arete to a break, pull left over the roof (crux) and take
the next bulge to the wall above, which leads to the next roof. Move
right and pull over the roof at a break, then continue up passing left
through two bulges to the terrace. Steep, with a short difficult section.

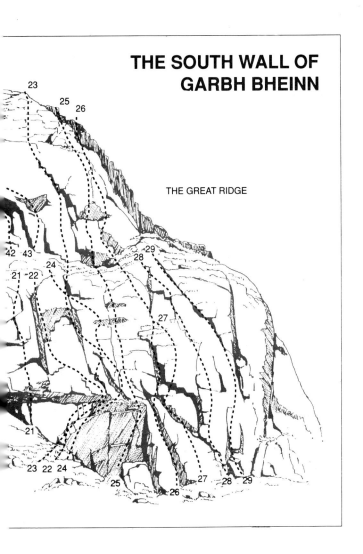

THE SOUTH WALL OF GARBH BHEINN

THE GREAT RIDGE

22   Gralloch 45m   E2 5b *   (1981)
Start as for Scimitar at the shattered ledge. After a few moves continue
up and left via thin cracks and ramps to the main right-facing corner.
Climb this more easily to the terrace.

23   Scimitar 105m   VS **   (1952)
This route climbs both tiers. Start at the shattered ledge about 30m
left of the huge boulder leaning against the face.
1. 30m 4c Follow the ledge up right to a horizontal section. From its
left end climb a steep crack to an overhang. Traverse right in a brilliant
position to an edge with good holds, move up and left to a ledge and
belay at the foot of a corner.
2. 25m 4a Climb easier rocks and an open chimney to the terrace.
3. and 4. 50m Continue directly by a smooth vertical groove and move
right to a flake. Climb a left-facing corner or the slabs on its left to
easier slabs and the ridge crest. A VS variation to pitch 3 climbs the
first corner and overhang to the right of the original line, rejoining the
route at the flake (1983).

24   Razor Slash 75m   Severe *   (1956)
Start at the huge boulder.
1. 25m Climb the boulder and a corner to a platform beyond the right
end of a shattered horizontal ledge.
2. 20m Traverse 10m left along the ledge to a left-sloping layback slab
ledge. Climb this, move delicately over the nose at its top (crux) and
go right then left to a belay.
3. 30m Go up and left by a diagonal fracture, crossing the chimney
of Scimitar, to the terrace.

25   The Golden Lance 95m   E2 **   (1984)
This climbs both tiers, taking the obvious thin crackline left of Butterknife on the lower tier. Belay on top of the huge boulder at the start of
Razor Slash.
1. 20m 5c Climb a thin crack in the steep wall above (crux), pull up
left then move up and right to belay on the traverse ledge of Razor
Slash.
2. 40m 5c Step right and climb a thin crack past an area of loose rock
to pull over a short leaning wall. Continue in the same line to the
terrace.
3. 40m 5b Above is a short corner leading to a small roof. Climb the
corner and pull over right to easier ground. Move up and left into the
middle of the wall, then climb up to a short leaning wall. Pull over this
and continue to easier ground.

26 Butterknife 105m   VS ***   (1956)
Climbs both tiers, starting up the corner near the right end of the lower
tier. Start at a shallow chimney bounding the right side of the large
pillar immediately right of the huge boulder. This classic line, on the
best rock in the world, is low in the grade.
1. 25m Bridge up the chimney and corner (slow to dry), moving left
to belay below the prominent corner crack. If the initial corner is wet,
take easier rocks on the left.
2. 25m 4a Climb the corner on superb rock to belay at its top.
3. 25m Continue more easily to the terrace, reaching a point below
an overhang at the far right end of the upper tier.
4. 30m Climb the overhang and trend right to gain the final rocks of
the ridge.

27 Bodkin 85m   HVS *   (1979)
The wall and steep edge starting immediately right of Butterknife.
1. 25m 5a Climb to a steepening at 15m. Step left (crux) and continue
up left to belay on an edge below bulges.
2. 25m 4b Move right and up to an overhang, then left to and up the
edge overlooking the corner of Butterknife.
3. 35m Follow Butterknife to the terrace.

28 Mournblade 80m   VS **   (1976)
The main feature is a corner some 12m right of and parallel to the
corner of Butterknife. Start 6m right of the initial chimney of Butterknife
at a rough flake.
1. 35m 4b Climb up, then right to the corner. Enter it, step right into a
groove and so to a ledge below a bulge. Climb this using a downward-
pointing spike to a ledge and belay.
2. 45m Climb the wall above on the left. Continue to the terrace.

29 Targe 105m   VS   (1971)
Start 30m right of Butterknife, below a bottomless corner.
1. 25m Climb the wall to the corner, move left into a corner crack (crux)
and continue up this past a large flake to a ledge.
2. 30m Continue directly, passing a small pinnacle on the left, to a
broad ledge.
3. 50m Climb the final section directly up two walls broken by large
cracks.
    This route probably coincides for much of its length with **Right-hand
Route** (100m Severe)

THE UPPER TIER
Near the left end of the upper tier is a deeply incised, right-facing chimney, formed by a large flake, taken by Sgian Dubh. A steep smooth wall then leads right to a steep corner climbed by Chela; the right edge of this is The Pincer. Further right again are two large roofs, under which traverse The Clasp and The Foil. Routes are described from left to right. The first two routes begin to the left of Sgian Dubh.

30 Bayonet 35m Severe   (1978)
Climb the crack to the left of the flake of Sgian Dubh.

31 The Peeler 45m HVS *   (1961)
Start on the outer face of the large flake of Sgian Dubh, near the left end of the tier.
1. 10m Climb the crest of the flake to a platform and belay.
2. 35m 5b Take a groove on the right and pull up left over a small roof. Go up a short steep crack (strenuous) which falls back into a groove, and continue to the top. A sustained pitch.

32 Sgian Dubh 60m Very Difficult **   (1956)
An interesting and varied climb. Near the left end of the upper tier is a chimney formed by a large flake.
1. 10m Climb the chimney, crack at back, to a platform.
2. 25m Traverse left and go up cracked ledges to a stance.
3. 25m Move left and over an overhang and follow a groove to the right, then up a nose and steep rock to finish near the summit.

The following three routes start from the platform at the top of pitch 1 of Sgian Dubh.

33 Sala 30m HVS 5a   (1982)
Move up Sgian Dubh, then climb the flange in the wall above (just left of the obvious crack of Menghini) to where a diagonal crack comes in from the right. Continue to a ledge, move right and climb to the top.
Direct Start: E2 5c   (1990)
Start just left of Menghini. Climb up to the right end of the diagonal crack. Follow this left to join Sala.

34 Menghini 30m E1 5a   (1982)
The obvious crack just left of The Peeler.

ILLUSTRATIONS
Opposite: Above the Crevasse on Pause, Trilleachan Slabs

(Climber, Philip McAra)

Next Page: The long corner of Hammer, Trilleachan Slabs

(Climber, Davy Gardner)

35 Cesta Kurva 30m E1 5b   (1990)
Climb Menghini over first overhang, gain good holds above the second
overhang, then step 2m left before climbing straight up the wall above.

36 Kelpie 45m E6 ***   (1986)
Starting midway between the groove of Chela and an obvious black
streak running down the wall to the left, this route climbs the left-
slanting crack in the leaning wall between The Peeler and Tru-Cut.
1. 25m 6b Climb the initial bulge as for Tru-Cut, then move across left
to follow a flake line leading to the halfway ledge (bold). Struggle up
the crack above to a belay perched on the edge of the leaning wall.
2. 20m 5b Continue up the crack leftwards until a groove can be
followed to easier ground which leads to the top.

37 Tru-Cut 50m E3 5c *   (1982)
Start as for Kelpie. Gain the groove above the initial overlap from the
left and follow this to pull out left to a junction with the crack of Kelpie
at the halfway ledge. Continue up until a hard move right enables a
ramp-groove to be reached. Follow this over the initial bulge to reach
a belay or continue to the top.

38 Chela 45m E3 **   (1981)
The left-facing groove left of the lower of the two roofs.
1. 25m 6a Follow the groove direct to a nut belay.
2. 20m 5b Continue more easily in the same line to the top.

39 The Pincer 50m E2 5b **   (1978)
Climb the arete right of Chela with interest, passing a bulge on the left
to reach a small overhang. Pull round its left side and enter a steep
corner. Continue up this and its left arete to the top.

40 White Hope 55m E4 ***   (1984)
A dazzling and intricate line up the white wall right of The Pincer; barely
adequate protection. Wear sunglasses.
1. 45m 6a Start in the centre of the wall below a thin vertical quartz
seam. Climb this to a right-slanting flake at 12m. From its right end,
hard moves gain jugs below a small isolated roof. Take the thin crack
out left above the roof into the centre of the wall. Continue up and right
to blocks below the short leaning headwall and go up this to a ledge.
2. 10m Continue easily to the top.

ILLUSTRATIONS
Previous page: Excalibur, South Wall (Climber, Ken Crocket)
Opposite: Scimitar, South Wall (Climber, Ken Crocket)

41 The Clasp 60m HVS ** (1960)
This route follows a left-trending line below the left-hand and lower of the two roofs, starting below the right end of the roof.
1. 10m 4b Climb the wall, moving up and left to a belay.
2. and 3. 50m 5a Continue up under the roof for 6m, then traverse 10m left to a shallow groove (crux). Climb a chimney above and trend left to the top.

42 The Foil 80m E2 * (1978)
The steep wall between the two roofs, with spaced protection. Start at a short wall below the right end of the upper right-hand roof.
1. 40m 5c Climb up to the roof, move left directly below the roof and follow it left to where it fades (hard), exiting left onto steep slabs.
2. 40m Climb the cracks above to the top.

43 Excalibur 75m VS *** (1972)
This route gains then traverses the lip of the right-hand, upper roof, with some fine situations. Start below the right end of the right-hand roof, just right of The Foil, at a groove left of a yellow wall and rib on right.
1. 20m 4c Climb the groove, moving right onto the rib (superb spike). Go up steeply to easier rock and belay at the right end of a large ledge.
2. 20m 4b Traverse hard left above the lip of the roof (several small wires) to a steep corner. Climb this to a chockstone and pull out left onto the flake edge. Step left to a ledge and belay.
3. 35m Go 3m left and climb walls above to the top.

44 Chib 60m VS * (1983)
This route may be the same as **Brogue**, H. MacInnes, M.C. MacInnes (1968). Start at the next corner right from Excalibur.
1. 40m 4b Climb the corner, go straight up, trend slightly right to large flake and go straight up to a grass ledge.
2. 20m 4b Continue directly to the top.

To the right of Chib is the smooth vertical groove on the wall taken by the upper part of Scimitar. The corner and small roof further right are taken by the Scimitar variation. Finally, the continuation of Butterknife takes the overhang at the far right-hand end of the upper tier.

45 Girdle Traverse of the South Wall VS * (1975)
A left-to-right traverse of the upper tier. Keeping fairly high, most of the climbing is of a pleasant Severe nature, except for one excellent pitch across The Clasp.

46   The Great Ridge   300m   Difficult *   (1897)
The fine ridge dropping from the summit of Garbh Bheinn into Garbh
Choire, between South-East Chimney and Great Gully. The ridge
swells in its lower stretches to form slabby rock, crossed by two grassy
rakes. Gain the lower rake by vegetated slabs next to Great Gully, or
move well left below the lowest rocks and gain the left end of the same
rake by the slabby gully start of the South-East Chimney. From either
start, the rake leads right to the beginning of the Ridge. Continue
directly up the crest on good holds with a superb view to the summit.
Winter: III   (1908)
Follow the summer line; rarely in true winter condition.

47   Crescent Route   130m   III/IV *   (1988)
A natural winter line up the area of cliff left of the Great Ridge Direct
Start.
1. 15m Begin up the Direct Start, moving up and left to the ramp.
2. 40m Move left and climb an ice column (crux) to a big corner line.
Continue first right then left by icy grooves to belay.
3. 40m Continue in this line, which curves round left, to belay under
a steep wall at the top of a snowfield.
4. 35m Move left and breach the final rockband by twin grooves to
belay on the lower rake.

48   Great Ridge Direct Start   105m   Very Difficult **   (1952)
In combination with the upper part of the Great Ridge, this makes an
excellent expedition with some sustained initial climbing. Start at the
lowest rocks, just right of a twisting crack with a slab on its right. This
is well right of a steep wet crack. Climb the slab to gain a prominent
right-running slabby ramp with an overhung left wall; two pitches lead
to a broad grass ledge at 65m. Move left round an edge and climb to
a second grass ledge, and an obvious flake chimney (12m). Climb the
awkward chimney then easy rocks to the lower rake. Move right to
continue up the original route.
Winter: IV   (1987)
Follow the summer line except for the first pitch, which is avoided by
coming in from the right. At the broad ledge traverse left at a lower
level then go diagonally back right.

49   Great Gully   270m   Very Difficult   (1946)
The shadowy gully right of the Great Ridge. Avoid the initial 90m on
the right then traverse in where the gully deepens. After a pitch the

gully widens and is divided by a 30m rib. Climb 10m up the rib and traverse right to a chimney which leads to a saddle. Return to the left fork where easier climbing leads to the Great Cave (escape left to the ridge below the cave if necessary). Start 20m out from the cave on the right wall. Pull over an overhang by a flake, move right past a bulge and climb parallel to the gully to finish by a short wall just left of the gully bed. A short pitch and scrambling leads to the main fork of the gully. Climb the buttress between the forks, starting to the right. A third of the way up, traverse left round a nose and continue to the top.

Rib Variation: Very Difficult   (1952)
Where the 30m rib divides the gully take the left fork. Following a mossy chockstone, climb a pitch right of a waterfall, then a chimney to finish.

Left Fork Direct Finish: 45m   VS   (1953)
The direct line up the left fork for the final 45m of the gully, finishing directly up the 30m vertical chimney high above the Great Cave.
Winter: IV ***   (1969)
First climbed during an exceptionally icy winter, this gave a superb route, including the initial 90m and the Left Fork Finish.

PINNACLE RIDGE
To the right of Great Gully there is a broad and very broken buttress called Winter Buttress. It was climbed in 1897 (Moderate). To its right is a more prominent ridge which appears from below to have two pinnacles on its crest.

50   Pinnacle Ridge   Easy   (1898)
The pinnacles which look quite steep and impressive from below are steepenings on an easy scrambling ridge. On the south-east sides of the pinnacles steep faces provide climbing.

LOWER PINNACLE

51   Shiver   40m   HVS 4c   (1987)
Start in a gully about 10m left of a prominent chimney on the left side of the buttress, below a left-facing corner formed by a large flake. A steep pitch with large but suspect holds. Climb the flake (loose) and pull onto the steep wall above on good holds. Gain the crack line above from the left and follow it to the top.

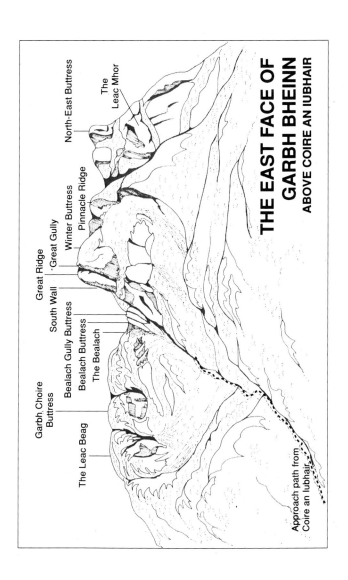

THE EAST FACE OF GARBH BHEINN
ABOVE COIRE AN IUBHAIR

Garbh. Choire Buttress

The Leac Beag

Bealach Gully Buttress

South Wall

Great Ridge

Great Gully

Winter Buttress

Bealach Buttress

The Bealach

Pinnacle Ridge

North-East Buttress

The Leac Mhor

Approach path from Coire an Iubhair

52   Tottie's Route   50m   VS   (1972)
Some dubious rock, but otherwise interesting climbing. Start at a
prominent chimney on the left side of the buttress.
1. 35m Climb the left wall for 10m, enter the chimney and follow it to
the point where it opens into a corner. After a few metres in the corner
gain the left edge which leads to a belay.
2. 15m Climb the corner and its left edge to the top.

53   Blockhead   60m   E1 *   (1957)
Serious and strenuous. A dark crack takes the centre of the front face.
Start at a 5m pillar just right of the crack.
1. 35m 5b Climb the pillar, moving left below its top into a shallow
groove which leads to small flakes. Move left and up to a shallow
corner with a cracked right wall. Move up and break out right below a
small overhang. Pull left round a loose block to a recess and climb a
slab on the right to a belay.
2. 25m 4a Follow the arete on the right to a huge block belay.

54   Wild Spot   60m   E1   (1985)
Start just right of Blockhead below a white wall split by a smooth
groove.
1. 35m 5b Scramble up to a crack which leads to a roof. Go over this
(small spike runner high on right) to the easier groove above. Make a
rising traverse left to the arete on the left. Follow this in an excellent
position to the stance of Blockhead.
2. 25m 4a Finish up Blockhead.

55   Bear's Picnic   90m   VS   (1972)
Start 15m right of Blockhead, left of whitish slabs.
1. 40m Climb the edge to a grass ledge and chockstone belay.
2. 40m Continue up the groove and move onto the right rib to reach
a ledge and chockstone belay.
3. 10m Move down and left a few moves then climb a short chimney
to the top.

UPPER PINNACLE

56   Interrupted Slabs   90m   VS †   (1956)
This climb lies high up in the gully on the left side of this indifferent
face, not far below the summit ridge. There are two white slabs,
separated by a large roof. Climb a corner to the roof and traverse right

below it (two aid points) to turn the roof on the right. Move up then left to the edge of the slab and continue across a terrace to belay in a chimney. The chimney and then slabs lead to the summit ridge.

57   Iubhair Grooves   135m   VS †   (1956)
Start just above the lowest corner of the face. The crux is the overhanging chimney taken by the first pitch. Above is a cave, corners and chimneys.

58   Outside Edge Route   120m   VS †   (1956)
Start below a small chimney-gully at the right-hand end of the face. The crux is the first pitch up the slimy overhanging crack on the left of the gully. Corners and slabs lead to scrambling.

NORTH-EAST BUTTRESS
This is the huge 360m buttress to the right of Pinnacle Ridge, divided into four tiers by three grassy terraces. The tiers of most interest to climbers are the second and third ones, the latter being known as the Leac Mhor or Great Slab. The rocks require several days to dry. Routes are described from left to right, beginning with two lines which begin up the first tier.

59   Route I   330m   Difficult   (1936)
A rambling route which starts at the bottom left of the first tier. Climb 75m by slabs and walls to the first terrace. Walk up to the main face near its left end and climb 10m on difficult slabs to the left end of a right-slanting ledge. Traverse the ledge and climb 80m, trending right by a series of corners to the second terrace. At the right end of the Leac Mhor slabs lead in 60m to the third terrace. Climb the buttress above by any line.
Winter: III   (1986)
Follow the summer line.

60   Route II   330m   Very Difficult **   (1939)
A good route with a plethora of variations on the third tier, The Leac Mhor, which lead to a choice of finishes up the final tier. Take the first tier as for Route I to near the left end of the second tier. Climb 10m up difficult slabs to the left end of the ledge of Route I. Continue directly to a stance below an overhanging band of rocks. Traverse right below these until the overhang can be passed and the second terrace gained (75m).

Original Route:
The Leac Mhor is girdled near its top by a long line of overhangs. Start to the left at a long narrow chimney and climb this to a stance just above a huge semi-detached block at 35m. Follow grooves which lead right across the slabs, curving upwards to a stance below a short overhang (45m). Go right up the slabs above to the third terrace (the corner above the short overhang is wet and Severe).

Turret Variation: Very Difficult **   (1952)
From the top of the short overhang, traverse easily left to a grassy niche below the Turret. Step left round an exposed nose and climb the Turret on splendid holds to the third terrace.

Variation A: VS   (1954)
From the top of the short overhang, climb rightwards round the foot of the overhanging belt for about 6m. Embark on the overhang by a long step up onto a sloping hold using a small sidepull, then pull up. Continue to a belay at 20m and finish up a fine steep arete.

Variation B: Very Difficult   (1953)
From the top of the short overhang, traverse briefly right and look for a big flake belay on the left wall. Descend a little from the belay, traverse left a little to turn an overhang and go up steep broken rock.

Direct Finish: Severe   (1954)
Follow the original route on the Leac Mhor past the semi-detached block to the recess above (40m). Climb the grey slab on the right of the recess, trending left to its crest. Step left into a groove which is climbed for 15m to a narrow rock ledge and rock finger belay. Move left and follow the left flank of the overhanging rocks above to a steep corner, which is climbed to the third terrace.

Variation C: Severe   (1954)
Follow the Direct Finish to a position on the grey slab where a rightward traverse can be made to the crack which splits the rock directly above the recess. Follow the crack up to the foot of the overhanging band of rocks. Traverse hard left to rejoin the Direct Finish at the finger belay.

Variation D: Severe   (1954)
Follow the Direct Finish to the grey slab. Go up the grey slab between the groove of the Direct Finish and the crack of Variation C to the overhanging band of rocks. Traverse hard left to rejoin the Direct Finish at the rock finger belay.

61   March Buttress   180m   VS †   (1956)
Takes a line well to the right of Route I. Begin on the first grass rake about 10m right of the right-bounding chimney of the slab.

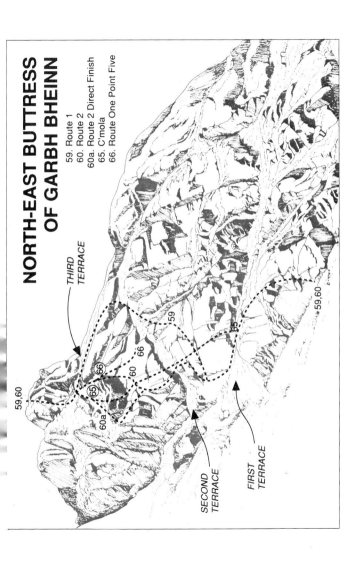

NORTH-EAST BUTTRESS OF GARBH BHEINN

59. Route 1
60. Route 2
60a. Route 2 Direct Finish
65. C'mola
66. Route One Point Five

THIRD TERRACE

SECOND TERRACE

FIRST TERRACE

59,60

1. 35m Climb a crack past loose blocks and a turf ledge. Where it peters out move round a corner to the right and then up to a shaky spike high on the right.

2. 25m Go up the groove on the left, step right onto a slab and climb up to a wide grass bay.

3. and 4 . Step left onto a nose and move up easily to a small spike right of a slab rib on the edge of the bounding chimney. Climb the slab rib, step left into a scoop and go up to a small belay on the right wall.

5. and 6. Climb scoops for 45m and a final 15m wall.

7. Finish by any good line on the fourth tier.

SECOND TIER

62   Near Enough   95m   Severe   (1975)
At the far right end of the tier is a prominent corner. Start 7m right of this at a crack line. Hard for the grade.

1. 40m Take the crack to a small recess, belay on the right.

2. 40m Continue up the crack trending slightly left and aiming for a shallow scoop. This is just right of the top of the corner. Climb the scoop to a belay.

3. 15m Traverse left and up to easier ground.

63   Mayday   75m   Very Difficult   (1966)
Start left of the lowest rocks at the north end of the second tier. Climb a shallow corner and an arete, then slabs to a grassy platform. Continue by two short vertical walls and a shallow right-slanting groove over more slabs to the top.

THIRD TIER

64   Hauchmagundie   145m   E2   (1988)
Start about 10m right of Routes I and II and 5m left of C'mola, below an obvious triangular niche 15m up a slab.

1. 20m 5a Climb the slab and a crack to the niche, then continue up a thin crack to a grassy ledge and belay.

2. 25m 5c Immediately above the belay, climb a very thin right-slanting crack until it fades. Traverse 2m right until a mantelshelf can be made onto a small lip. Climb directly up to an obvious right-slanting crack (crux), then hand-traverse the crack to join C'mola.

3. 25m 5b Step up and right to a ledge and gain a right-slanting crack. Climb the crack and when it fades climb the slab slightly leftwards to

another right-slanting crack. Hand-traverse on improving holds to easier ground. Pull up to a grass rake.
4. 40m 4c Cross the rake to a recess and climb an obvious thin crack left of Route One Point Five. Belay below overlap.
5. 35m 5a Step left and pull over an overlap, then follow a thin crack up a slab trending slightly left to an obvious corner. Climb the corner on good holds to the top.

65   C'Mola   150m   VS *   (1970)
An enjoyable route, though slow to dry, which takes a left-trending line across the second and third tiers, climbing directly the overhanging wall near the top of the Leac Mhor. Start on the first terrace, about 15m right of Routes I and II, just left of a shallow, grassy groove.
1. 25m Climb the groove and gain the traverse ledge of Route I.
2. 40m Go up a left trending crack to the second terrace.
3. 25m Move 12m right to a thin crack. Climb this, crossing Route II after 25m, to belay at the ledge beyond.
4. 25m Climb directly to and climb a short right-trending groove. At its top step left over an overlap to a slab. Move a short way up the steep dirty groove above and cross its left wall and round the edge to a gully; belay up and right.
5. 35m Climb easy slabs rightwards to the third terrace.

66   Route One Point Five   75m   Severe   (1966)
Start from the terrace below the Leac Mhor, well right of the chimney of Route II and below the right end of the overhanging band of rock at the top of the tier. There is a recess with a cracked slab above. Gain the slab and follow cracks and grooves, crossing the original finish of Route II to reach the upper terrace.

67   Girdle Traverse   115m   Severe   (1966)
1. 20m On the left of the third tier there is a smooth streaky wall. Traverse under it to a grass ledge below a greasy corner. Go up, then right across a slab below an overhung wall to belay below a steep corner.
2. 25m Go down and right along a ledge, then up and right across the main slab to the large block on Route II.
3. and 4. 70m Climb the original Route II for two pitches to a belay in the corner forming the right flank of the central overhanging section. Tension right into the grooves of Route One Point Five. Continue rightwards to easy slabs.

THE NORTH FACE

This face overlooks the Bealach Feith'n Amean between Garbh Bheinn and Beinn Bheag. There are some fine masses of steep rock on which many ill-defined routes may be found.

North Face   150m   Difficult   (1939)
A fence runs from the bealach up to the foot of the rocks. Start at the toe of the buttress, some 100 metres left of the fence. Climb directly to a long, steep slab lying to the right. Cross the slab on good small holds and climb its exposed right edge. Continue directly on moderate rock to the top.
Winter: III   (1986)
Start at the lowest point of the buttress. Keep left of obvious rightward trending slab ramps. Follow grooves and walls heading towards a shallow central depression. Follow this to the top. Good sustained climbing.

Unnamed Gully   (1939)
The narrow curving gully between the North Face and the North-East Buttress has been descended. In parts it is a tight chimney.

Numerous small masses of rock can be found elsewhere. A small buttress on the north wall of Coire an Iubhair, for example, yields a two-pitch Severe. Other routes can be found in the Garbh Choire, though the biggest and best may well have been found by now.

BEINN NA SEILG

342m   (Map Ref 456 642)

Far to the west of Garbh Bheinn, this shapely peak lies about three kilometres west of Kilchoan in the Ardnamurchan peninsula, and might be regarded as the westernmost hill on the Scottish mainland. The rock is gabbro, as rough as that on Skye. The north top has a fine steep cliff on its west flank which gives pleasant climbing, total solitude and a superb outlook. Approach from Ormsaigmore to the Lochan Ghleann Locha, then go round the western slope. Viewed from the west the cliff is divided into two masses by an area of easy scrambling, the Central Break. To the right, Hebrides Wall stretches to the South-West Buttress. The cliff narrows at its centre to Gabbro Slab, which provides easy access to or from the summit. To the left lies Cuillin Buttress. Routes are described from right to left.

South-West Buttress   Moderate   (1949)
The right-hand boundary of Hebrides Wall. The best line remains close above the wall.

Faradh Dubh   55m   Very Difficult   (1949)
Start below a prominent crack on the right side of the wall.
1. 20m From the small ledge near the bottom of the crack move steeply up left to a small belay.
2. 20m Climb straight up to two bulges, turn the left-hand one, then up to the right. Thread belay.
3. 15m Traverse left until the overhang can be climbed, up to right, then easy rocks to the crest of the buttress.

Trident Climb   35m   Very Difficult   (1949)
Start at three prongs of rock between Faradh Dubh and Gabbro Slab.
1. 10m Climb the prongs. From a shaky spike above make a long step right. Gain a roomy ledge by a mantelshelf and belay on the left.
2. 15m Traverse right to a small crack. Follow it for several metres, then turn a small overhang on the left. Block belay.
3. 10m A choice of routes leads to easy ground.

Gabbro Slab   15m   Moderate   (1949)
Start from highest ground at the foot of Hebrides Wall. Climb the slab above, keeping left.

Geologist's Groove   30m   Difficult   (1949)
Start halfway between Gabbro Slab and the Central Break.
1. 10m Climb a heather-filled crack until it overhangs, go left then back to a wide bay and belay.
2. 20m Continue up a crack to easier rocks.

Sunset Wall   45m   Very Difficult   (1949)
Start on a grass terrace below Cuillin Buttress, halfway between the Central Break and a large rock step.
1. 20m Climb inclined ledges to a grass platform.
2. 15m Traverse left, then up steep rocks to a pulpit.
3. 10m Climb the slab on the right, belay up and left.

List of First Ascents

The following abbreviations are used:

BEM	(Buachaille Etive Mor)	LVMB	(Lost Valley Minor Buttress)
[DF]	(Direct Finish)	NFAD	(North Face Aonach Dubh)
[DS]	(Direct Start)	NFGA	(North Face Gearr Aonach
EFAD	(East Face Aonach Dubh)	p	(pitch)
EFNB	(East Face North Buttress)	pa	(peg aid)
FFA	(First Free Ascent)	SCnB	(Stob Coire nam Beith)
[FWA]	(First Winter Ascent)	SCnL	(Stob Coire nan Lochan)
GGB	(Great Gully Buttress)	Var	(Variation)
GSWC	(Glencoe School of Winter	[W]	(First Ascent in Winter)
Climbing)		WFAD	(West Face Aonach Dubh)
LVB	(Lost Valley Buttress)	WFBF	(West Face Beinn Fhada).

1868 Summer	Ossian's Ladder N.Marquis
1894 March	Collie's Climb N.Collie, G.A.Solly, J.Collier
1894 March	Collie's Pinnacle (Short Side) N.Collie
1894 March	East Wall Climb N.Collie, G.A.Solly, J.Collier
1894 March [W]	Central Gully (Bidean) N.Collie, G.A.Solly, J.Collier
1894 Summer	Great Gully (BEM) N.Collie
1895 July	West Route (North Buttress BEM) W.Brown, Rose, W.Tough
1895 Aug	Aonach Eagach Ridge A.R.Wilson, A.W.Russell, A.Fraser
1895 Dec	The Chasm North Wall J.H.Bell, J.W.McGregor, J.Napier, R.G.Napier
1896 July	Curved Ridge G.B.Gibbs
1896 Aug	Naismith's Route, Crowberry Ridge W.W.Naismith, W.Douglas
1897 April	Winter Buttress G.Hastings, W.P.Haskett-Smith
1897 April	The Great Ridge J.H.Bell, W.Brown
1898 April	Easy Route W.W.Naismith, J.Maclay, Boyd
1898 April 9	D Gully G.T.Glover, Collinson
1898 April 10	Crowberry Gully H.Raeburn, E.W.Green 1st ascent in 'mixed' conditions
1898 April 10	The Chasm to Crowberry Traverse G.T.Glover, Collinson
1898 April 11 [W]	Curved Ridge/Easy Gully G.T.Glover, R.G.Napier
1898 April	E4F5 Route J.Maclay, W.Inglis Clark, J.Gall Inglis
1898 July	Flake Route H.Raeburn J.H.Bell, R.G.Napier. An historic and epic ascent
1898 July	Pinnacle Ridge J.H.Bell, J.S.Napier, W.W.Naismith

1900 May	Direct Route, Crowberry Ridge G.D.Abraham, A.P.Abraham. The hardest climb in the area
1900 Oct	Lady's Gully Mr & Mrs G.D.Abraham
1900 Oct	Amphitheatre Scoop Mr & Mrs G.D.Abraham
1900 Oct	Arch Gully Indirect Mr & Mrs G.D.Abraham
1900 Oct	No 3 Gully (upper part) Mr & Mrs G.D.Abraham
1900 Oct	Winifred's Pinnacle Mr & Mrs G.D.Abraham
1903 Oct 13	D Gully Buttress W.C.Newbigging et al
1905 April	East Ribs Newbigging, Morrison, Burns
1906 April [W]	North-West Gully (SCnB) G.T.Glover, Wordsell
1907 April	Greig's Ledge Variation, Direct Route F.Greig, C.R.Baird
1907 April [W]	Ordinary Route (SCnL Central Butt) H.Raeburn, Dr & Mrs Inglis Clark
1908 Jan [W]	The Great Ridge W.Ling, H.Raeburn
1908 June	Shadbolt's Chimney A.C.McLaren, L.G.Shadbolt
1909 April [FWA]	Crowberry Gully H.Raeburn, W.A.Brigg, H.S.Tucker - the party was avalanched!
1910 Sept	Crowberry Gully H.Raeburn, F.Greig, S.M.Cumming, D.H.Menzies 1st summer ascent
1912 July	Crack Climb J.H.Hirst, R.E.Workman
1920 April	The Chasm R.F.Stobart, Mr & Mrs Odell. Partial winter ascent
1920 April	The South Chimney N.E.Odell, R.F.Stobart, Mrs Odell
1920 Sept 15	Crypt Route & Collie's Pinnacle (N.Chimney) R.Morley, M.Wood, J.Wilding, A.S.Pigott
1920 Sept	Shelf Route J.Wilding, A.S.Piggott
1920 Sept	South Gully A.S.Piggott, J.Wilding
1920 Sept	The Chancellor M.Wood, A.S.Piggott, J.Wilding
1929 Summer	North Face Route J.H.B.Bell, A.Harrison
1930 June	Ordinary Route J.H.B.Bell, A.Harrison
1930 Aug	North Route (Diamond Buttress) J.H.B.Bell, LStC.Bartholomew, A.Harrison
1930 Sept	Lagangarbh Chimney P.M.Barclay, A.R.Ramsay
1931 May	Centre Route (SCnB) A.Harrison, A.J.Don
1931 May	No 4 Buttress A.Harrison, J.Don (FWA not known)
1931 June	No 1 Buttress A.Harrison, N.Allan, AJ.Don
1931 Aug	Direct Route (Diamond Buttress) J.H.B.Bell, C.M.Allan
1931 Aug	The Direct Route, The Chasm I.G.Jack, J.G.Robinson
1931 Sept	No 2 Buttress LStC.Bartholomew, A.Harrison
1931 Sept	North Face (SCnL) J.H.B.Bell, C.M.Allan
1931 Sept	North West Gully (SCnB) I.Campbell, A.Horne
1931 Sept	Ordinary Route (SCnL Summit Buttress) J.H.B.Bell, C.M.Allan
1931 Sept	SC Gully J.H.B.Bell, CM Allan
1931 Oct	West Face Collie's Pinnacle FAs unknown

1931 Nov	Central Chimney (Central Buttress BEM) C.M.Allan, J.H.B.Bell
1931 Nov	Direct Route (Diamond Buttress) C.M.Allan, J.H.B.Bell
1932 April	The Chasm of An t-Sron J.H.B.Bell, J.McNab FWA unknown
1932 May	Bell's Pinnacle J.H.B.Bell, C.M.Allan
1932 May	The Pinnacle Face J.H.B.Bell, C.M.Allan
1933 Dec [W]	Arch Gully Direct C.M.Allan, J.H.B.Bell
1934 March	No 3 Gully J.W.Crofton, Evans
1934 March [W]	SC Gully P.D.Baird, E.J.A.Leslie, H.A.Fynes-Clinton
1934 March [W]	Sron Na Lairig P.D.Baird, Coulson, Allberry, Kendall, T.M.Wedderburn
1934 May	Crest Route G.G.MacPhee, G.F.Todd
1934 May	The Chimney of Creag a'Bhancair G.G.MacPhee, G.F.Todd
1934 June	Route 1 G.C.Williams, G.F.Todd, G.G.MacPhee, I.G.Jack
1934 June	The South Wall of The Chasm C.M.Allen, J.H.B.Bell, Miss V.Roy
1934 July	Spillikin Route C.M.Allen, J.H.B.Bell, Miss M.B.Stewart
1934 Sept	Original Route (EFAD) C.M.Allan, J.H.B.Bell
1934 Sept	The Central Chimney (Cuneiform Buttress BEM) E.A.M.Wedderburn, J.H.B.Bell
1934 Nov	Ledge Route E.Derzaj, E.A.M.Wedderburn (E.Derzaj led Slav Route on Ben Nevis)
1935 June	C Buttress J.D.B.Wilson, G.A.Collie
1935 June	Pleasant Terrace A.A.B.Martin, A.M.Spence, G.A.R.Spence
1935 Sept	West Chimney A.A.B.Martin, J.Bell
1935 Nov	Central Ridge J.H.B.Bell, C.M.Allan
1935 Nov	Original Route (F Buttress WFAD) J.H.B.Bell, C.M.Allan
1936 March	Deep-Cut Chimney J.A.Brown, T.D.MacKinnon. FWA made in the month of April (1939)
1936 May	Crest Route, Lagangarbh Buttress J.H.B.Bell, J.R.Wood
1936 June	Shackle Route S.H.Cross, Miss A.M.Nelson
1936 Aug	Agag's Groove J.F.Hamilton, A.Anderson, A.C.D.Small
1936 Aug	South-East Chimney A.R.Macdonald, A.R.Wilson
1936 Sept	North Face Route (including last 45m) D.Scott, J.C.Henderson
1936 Oct	Route I J.K.W.Dunn, A.M.MacAlpine, W.H.Murray
1937 March [W]	Shelf Route W.M.MacKenzie, W.H.Murray
1937 May	High Level Traverse Naismith's-Haven A.C.D.Small, J.F.Hamilton
1937 May	Slanting Ledge W.H.MacKenzie, J.K.W.Dunn, J.Ewart

1937 June	Raven's Gully J.B.Nimlin, B.Braithwaite, G.McArtney. Hardest pre-1940 route.
1937 July	West Face Route (Church Door Buttress) W.H.Murray, J.K.W.Dunn, W.G.Marskell
1937 Aug	South Tower, Lady's Gully I.G.Jack, C.R.Steven
1937 Sept	High Level Traverse Haven-Agags A.C.D.Small, J.R.Wood
1937 Summer	Route 1, Route 2 J.G.Robinson, G.F.Todd
1938 April 3 [FWA]	Direct Route, Crowberry Ridge A.C.D.Small and party. Impressive partial WA
1938 May	Clachaig Gully W.H.Murray, A.M.MacAlpine, J.K.W.Dunn, W.G.Marskell
1938 Sept	D Buttress W.A.Gilmour, J.D.B.Wilson
1939 April 7 [FWA]	Deep-Cut Chimney W.M.Mackenzie, W.H.Murray (alts). Short axes, hard route.
1939 July 30	North Face B.K.Barber, J.Lomas
1939 July 30	Unnamed Gully B.K.Barber, J.Lomas (in descent)
1939 July	Left Wall (SCnB) R.L.Plackett, R.Bumstead
1939 July	Route II B.K.Barber, J.Lomas
1939 Sept 5	Satan's Slit, Red Slab H.I.Ogilvy, Miss E.Speakman. Bold ventures.
1940 Jan 10	January Jigsaw H.I.Ogilvy, Miss E.Speakman
1940 May 1	Overhanging Crack B.Nelstrop, J.E.Byrom
1940 May 13	Pluto E.R.Zenthon, B.V.Fox
1940 May 1	Overhanging Crack (Rannoch Wall) B.Nelstrop, J.E.Byron
1940 June 10	Girdle Traverse, Rannoch Wall H.I.Ogilvy, F.R.Frere
1940 June 11/12	North East Zig Zag P.L.M.McGeoch, H.W.Grant, Miss Drummond
1940 June 11/12	Slanting Groove H.W.Grant, P.L.M.McGeoch, Miss Drummond
1940 Sept 15	Belial J.H.B.Bell, J.R.Wood
1940	Original Route (B Buttress WFAD) M.Slesser et al (1940s)
1941 Sept 11	Direct Route (SCnL S. Buttress) R.L.Plackett, Miss C.M.Curtis, A.Bumstead, G.C.Curtis
1941 Summer	Bottleneck Chimney R.G.Donaldson, G.R.B.McCarter
1941 Summer	Hangman's Crack R.G.Donaldson, G.R.B.McCarter. Continuation to Bottleneck Chimney
1942 March 18 [W]	Flake Route G.R.Scott, F.W.Cope. Combined tactics used
1942 July	Lost Valley Upper Gorge J.B.Nimlin, R.Gowers
1942 Summer	North East Crack Variation R.G.Donaldson, P.E.Burt
1942 Summer	Original Route (LVB) R.G.Donaldson, J.E.Spence
1943 Sept 16	Crowberry Gully Left Fork B.N.Simmonds, A.C.Marriot
1945 Feb [W]	Centre Route (SCnB) J.G.Parish, D.H.Haworth, D.McIntyre

1945 Sept	Echo Crag Route J.B.Nimlin, Mrs Nimlin, D.Easson, J.Stevenson
1946 April 22	Hole And Corner Gully L.Greenwood, S.Fry
1946 April 22	North-East Nose J.Neill, A.H.Henson
1946 April	The Upper Bow J.Neill, A.H.Henson
1946 June	Crow's Nest Crack J.Cunningham, J.C.P.McGonigle. Originally graded Severe in rubbers
1946 June	Great Gully (Garbh Bheinn) W.H.Murray, D.Scott
1946 June	Shattered Crack J.C.P.McGonigle
1946 Aug	The Gangway J.Poole, F.R.Brooke
1946 Oct	Autumn Slab J.Cunningham, W.Smith. Now the first pitch to Whortleberry Wall
1946 Oct	Clachaig Gully West J.F.Hamilton, D.Paterson
1946 Oct	Curving Groove J.Cunningham, W.Smith
1946 Oct	Direct Route GGB S.Smith, I.Dingwall
1946 Oct	Fracture Route K.Copland, W.Smith. Previously top roped by another party
1946 Oct	Grooved Arete J.Cunningham, W.Smith
1946 Oct	Juniper Groove K.Copland, C.Lyon
1946 Oct	Waterslide Wall W.H.Murray, R.V.Waterhouse, H.Cameron
1946 Nov	Lady's Gully, Right Fork W.M.MacKenzie, J.K.W.Dunn
1946 Nov	The Pyramid W.H.Murray, R.Smith. First recorded ascent, route already nail-marked
1946 Nov	The Sphinx W.H.Murray, R.Smith. Climbed the same day as The Pyramid
1946 Dec [W]	Twisting Gully W.H.Murray, D.Scott, J.Cortland-Simpson
1947 April 20	Original Route (Staircase Buttress BEM) D.H.Haworth
1947 May	Archer Ridge W.H.Murray, D.B.McIntyre
1947 May	Barn Wall Route D.B.McIntyre, T.J.Ransley, W.H.Murray
1947 May	Basin Traverse W.H.Murray, T.J.Ransley, D.B.McIntyre
1947 May	East Face (Lagangarbh Buttress BEM) D.H.Haworth, I.McPhail
1947 May	East Route (Creag na Tulaich BEM) D.H.Haworth, G.G.Williams
1947 May	Lower Bow D.B.McIntyre, T.J Ransley, W.H.Murray
1947 May	Quiver Rib D.B.McIntyre, W.H.Murray
1947 May	Rowan Tree Wall W.H.Murray, D.B.McIntyre
1947 May	The Bowstring D.B.McIntyre, W.H.Murray
1947 June	Gallows Route J.Cunningham, I.Dingwall 2nd Ascent D Whillans
1947 June	Great Flake Route J.Cunningham, I.Dingwall
1947 June	Sunset Groove J.Cunningham, I.Dingwall
1947 June	Sunset Rib I.Dingwall, J.Cunningham

1947 July	East Face (SCnL North Buttress) D.H.Haworth, IapE.Hughes
1947 Aug	Arrowhead Grooves D.H.Haworth, I.McPhail
1947 Aug	Basin Chimney D.Scott, J.Currie Henderson
1947 Aug	Weeping Wall Route D.Scott, J.C.Henderson
1947 Summer	Sassenach Groove D.H.Haworth, IapE.Hughes
1948 Feb	West Gully J.G.Parish, D.H.Haworth, J.S.Berkeley
1948 March	Vixen Gully D.H.Haworth and party
1948 May	Raven's Gully, Direct Finish J.Cunningham, W.Smith, T.Paul
1948 June 12	June Crack W.Smith, J.Cunningham
1948 June	Direct Route (WFAD) A.S.Parker, H.G.Nicol
1948 June	Guerdon Grooves J.Cunningham, W.Smith
1948 July	Domino Chimney W.Smith, J.Cunningham, T.Paul
1948 Oct 31	Left Edge T.J.Ransley, A.Johnson
1948 Dec 20	Lefthand Route (SCnL SW Face) J.Purser, D.G & M.J.Turnbull
1948 Dec 20	Righthand Route (SCnL SW Face) H.W.Turnbull, G.Pratt
1949 Jan [W]	Boomerang Gully J.Black, R.G.Donaldson, W.H.Murray
1949 March [FWA]	Crowberry Gully, Left Fork C.M.G.Smith, R.J.Taunton, I.C.Robertson
1949 April 17	Six routes on Beinn na Seilg, Ardnamurchan R.E.Chapman, G.H.Francis
1949 May	South West Rib W.W.Clarkson, N.S.Tennent
1949 July	Chancellor Gully J.F.Hamilton, T.D.MacKinnon
1949 July	Shattered Crack Variation W.Smith
1949 Aug	Chimney and Face Route D.Scott, J.C.Henderson
1949 Sept	The Direct Route (WFBF) A.Hill, N.S.Tennent
1950 Feb 23 [W]	Central Couloir J.G.Brown, J.G.Parish
1950 Feb 26 [W]	Red Gully D.Scott, J.C.Henderson, R.Anderson
1950 Feb [W]	Right Chimney H.MacInnes
1950 June 19	Red Campion Gully J.G.Parish, T.G.Brown, R.Fox
1950 Aug 24	Blaeberry Rib J.R.Lees, J.G.Parish
1950 Aug 28	Red Funnel Gully J.G.Parish, T.G.Brown
1950 Summer	Gallows Variation D.D.Stewart, J.R.Marshall
1951 Jan 28 [W]	Dorsal Arete J.Black, T.Shepherd, J.Allingham, J.Bradbury
1951 March 30 [W]	No 6 Gully D.H.Munro, P.D.Smith
1951 April	Lament J.Cullen, C.Vigano
1951 May	Wall and Crack Route G.Batty, K.Miller
1951 June 2	Dalness Chasm, Left Fork J.Cunningham, H.MacInnes, S.Jagger, C.White
1951 Aug	Rose Innominate A.E.Maskey, P.G.White
1951 Sept	Deep-Gash Gully J.Cunningham, W.Rowney, W.Smith
1951 Sept	Engineer's Crack H.MacInnes, C.Vigano, R.Hope

1951 Summer	Drain Pipe Corner W.Smith, C.Vigano
1951 Summer	Right Hand Route W.Smith, C.Vigano
1951 Oct	Waterslide Gully D.D.Stewart, C.M.G.Smith
1952 Jan 3 [FWA]	Clachaig Gully R.Hope, H.MacInnes
1952 Feb 24	Original Route (Lagangarbh Buttress BEM) J.R.Lees, J.G.Parish
1952 Feb 28	Rehabilitation Route J.G.Parish, J.R.Lees
1952 March 9	North East Zig Zag Variation J.Mason, G.K.Armstrong, E.Furness
1952 April 12	Bealach Buttress D.D.Stewart, D.N.Mill
1952 April 12	Great Ridge [DS] D.D.Stewart, D.N.Mill
1952 April 13	Dirk D.D.Stewart, D.N.Mill
1952 April 13	Route II Turret Variation D.D.Stewart, D.N.Mill
1952 April 13	Scimitar D.D.Stewart, D.N.Mill
1952 May 6	May Crack R.Hope, W.Smith
1952 May 18	Shattered Wall W.Smith, H.MacInnes
1952 May	Alcoholics Arete J.Cullen, C.Vigano
1952 June 8	Bollard Slab, Nameless Wall W.Smith, W.Rowney
1952 July 15	Crypt Route (The Gallery Var) I.G.Norris, P.R.C.Barker, AN Other
1952 July	Peasant's Passage W.Rowney, H.MacInnes
1952 July	Wappenshaw Wall W.Smith, H.MacInnes
1952 Aug 16	Grochan Grooves J.Cullen, C.Vigano
1952 Sept 7	Ledgeway W.Smith, R.Hope
1952 Sept 21	Bludger's Route P.Walsh, H.MacInnes, T.Lawrie
1952 Summer	Bunny's Route H.MacInnes, Mrs T.Lawrie, Miss A.Williamson
1952 Summer	East Chimney Variation
1952 Summer	Great Gully Rib Var. (Garbh Bheinn) W.Scrimgeour, AN Other; G.S.Johnstone, T.J.Ransley
1952 Oct 5	Curving Crack L.S.Lovat
1952 Nov	November Wall W.Smith, H.MacInnes, H.Currie
1952 Dec 26 [W]	No 4 Gully J.Brown, D.Whillans
1953 Feb 8 [FWA]	Agag's Groove H.MacInnes, K.MacPhail, C.Bonington, J.Hammond, G.McIntosh
1953 Feb 13 [FWA]	Crowberry Ridge Direct Route H.MacInnes, C.Bonington 1 pa
1953 Feb 14 [FWA]	Raven's Gully H.MacInnes, C.Bonington
1953 March 1	Rose Late, Rear Exit L.S.Lovat, J.M.Johnstone
1953 June 6	The Long Crack L.S.Lovat, J.M.Johnstone
1953 June 7	Arrow Wall L.S.Lovat, J.M.Johnstone
1953 June 18	Pinnacle Buttress NE Face D.H.Haworth, Miss J.Tester
1953 July 2	Route II Variation D.H.Haworth, Miss J.Tester
1953 July 3	Great Gully Left Fork Finish D.H.Haworth, Miss J.Tester
1953 Summer	Nameless Groove J.R.Marshall, A.H.Hendry

1954 May 15	Bent Crack, Bent Crack Rib C.E.Wood, C.Ford
1954 May 15	The Wabe J.M.Brockway, J.S.Orr, D.J.Parlane
1954 May 16	Mome Rath Route J.S.Stewart, Mrs M.A.Stewart, Miss C.B.Stewart. A family outing
1954 May 17	Outgrabe Route (Upper Section) J.M.Brockway, J.S.Orr
1954 May 23	Anathema Gully L.S.Lovat
1954 May 23	Route II Direct Finish L.S.Lovat, D.C.Hutcheson; D.Scott, Miss E.Stark
1954 May 30	Scabbard Chimney L.S.Lovat, I.D.McNicol, A.Way
1954 May	Adam's Wall J.Cullen, C.Vigano
1954 May	Archer Ridge Direct L.S.Lovat, I.D.McNicol, A.Way
1954 May	Kinloss Corner D.D.Stewart, A.W.Hay
1954 May	Terrace Arete P.Walsh, J.Cullen
1954 May	Winifred's Pinnacle North-West Arete L.S.Lovat, C.G.M.Slesser
1954 June 13	Sickle E.D.G.Langmuir, M.J.O'Hara, J.A.Mallinson. The first route on the Slabs
1954 June 14	Spartan Slab E.D.G.Langmuir, M.J.O'Hara, J.A.Mallinson 3 pa
1954 June	Route II Variation C C.E.Wood, J.M.Johnstone, A.S.Dick
1954 June	Route II Variation D.D.Goldie, J.Dunn
1954 July 4	Dexter L.S.Lovat, C.Ford
1954 July 4	Left Edge Variation C.E.Wood, W.Harrison
1954 July	Hawker's Crack P.Walsh, C.Vigano
1954 July	Pedlar's Groove P.Walsh, C.Vigano
1954 Aug 15	Route II Variation G.Shields, T.Low, W.Nelson
1954 Sept	Lady's Gully, Left Fork D.Goldie, R.Goldie, J.Dunn
1954 Sept	East Chimney Variation L.S.Lovat, C.E.Wood
1954 Summer	Brevity Crack P.Walsh, C.Vigano
1954 Summer	Sinister C.E.Wood, W.Harrison
1955 Feb 6 [W]	North Route (Diamond Buttress) J.Clarkson, F.King
1955 Feb 13 [W]	Shadbolt's Chimney D.Goldie, R.Goldie
1955 Feb 13 [W]	Hidden Gully L.S.Lovat, W.J.R.Greaves. Originally called Red Caves Gully
1955 Feb 20 [FWA]	East Chimney Variation
1955 March 13 [FWA]	North Route Direct (Diamond Buttress) L.S.Lovat, W.Harrison
1955 April	Overhanging Groove D.Stevens, I.Provan
1955 May 15	Gully A L.S.Lovat, W.J.R.Greaves, A.G.Daley, G.A.Warmbath
1955 May 23	Pedestal Arete J.R.Marshall, L.S.Lovat
1955 May	The Long Chimney D.Stevens, Miss D.M.Lawrie
1955 June 5	North West Gully (NFGA) T.Low, A.Ferguson, R.Simpson
1955 June 18	G String W.Smith, W.Rowney

1955 June 5	Wappenshaw Wall [DS] W.Smith, G.MacIntosh
1955 July	Wappenshaw Wall, Variation J.R.Marshall, A.H.Hendry
1955 Aug 3	August Crack W.Smith, J.Cunningham
1955 Aug 3	Trident Crack W.Smith, J.Cunningham
1955 Aug 4	Guillotine W.Smith, T.Paul 1 pa
1955 Aug 2	Boomerang, Little Boomerang J.Cunningham, M.Noon
1955 Aug 4	Garrotte J.Cunningham, M.Noon
1955 Aug 21	Dalness Chasm, Central Branch J.R.Marshall, A.H.Hendry, D.Boston, L.S.Lovat, T.Weir
1955 Aug	Mainbrace Crack P.Walsh, W.Smith
1955 Aug	Pendulum P.Walsh, J.Cunningham 1 pa Lasso for flake. FFA Spence & Porteous
1955 Aug	White Wall Crack W.Smith, G.MacIntosh. 2 pa FFA B.W.Robertson 1963
1955 Sept 11	West Chimney (Church Door Buttress) L.S.Lovat, A.S.Dick
1955 Sept 17	Waterfall Wall D.Goldie, R.Goldie
1955 Sept 18	Chimney Route (LVMB) L.S.Lovat, W.J.R.Greaves, G.K.Armstrong
1955 Sept 18	Left Wall Route L.S.Lovat
1955 Summer	Dalness Chasm, Right Fork D.Whillans and party
1955 Dec 4	Fingal's Chimney J.Brown, L.S.Lovat
1956 Jan 29 [W]	North Face (SCnL) L.S.Lovat, K.Bryan
1956 Feb 12 [W]	Scabbard Chimney L.S.Lovat, J.R.Marshall, A.H.Hendry. Combined tactics & aid
1956 March 29	March Buttress Mr & Mrs G.J.Sutton
1956 March 30	Iubhair Grooves Mr & Mrs G.J.Sutton
1956 April 1	Interrupted Slabs, Outside Edge Route Mr & Mrs G.J.Sutton
1956 April 1	Razor Slash J.R.Marshall, L.S.Lovat, A.H.Hendry
1956 April 1	Sgian Dubh J.R.Marshall, L.S.Lovat
1956 May	Clevedon Way D.H.Briggs, A.J.J.Moulam, Miss D.Shortall
1956 June 9	Left Edge J.R.Marshall, I.D.Haig
1956 June 9	Pang J.R.Marshall, G.J.Ritchie, A.H.Hendry
1956 June 17	Ledgeway [DS] J.R.Marshall
1956 June	Bloody Crack P.Walsh, J.Crawford. Considered by Walsh to be as hard as any Coe route.
1956 June	Doom Arete P.Walsh, C.Vigano
1956 June	Girdle Traverse P.Walsh, C.Vigano
1956 June	Revelation P.Walsh, C.Vigano
1956 July	Nightmare Traverse P.Walsh, M.Noon
1956 Aug 5	Abomination J.R.Marshall, A.H.Hendry
1956 Aug 26	The Vent L.S.Lovat, R.Reid
1956 Sept 9	Gibbet E.Taylor, W.Smith
1956 Sept 9	Hangover J.R.Marshall, A.H.Hendry

1956 Sept 15	Butterknife J.R.Marshall, A.H.Hendry, G.J.Ritchie, I.D.Haig
1956 Sept 15	The Gut J.Cunningham, W.Smith
1956 Sept 16	Whortleberry Wall J.Cunningham, W.Smith
1956 Summer	Corridor Wall J.A.White, D.Hill
1956 Nov 18	Centre Rib L.S.Lovat
1956 Dec 24 [W]	Boomerang Arete J.Clarkson, R.Keltie
1957 Feb 24 [W]	Deep-Gash Gully J.Cunningham, M.Noon
1957 Feb 24 [FWA]	Lady's Gully, Left Fork J.R.Marshall, I.D.Haig, G.J.Ritchie
1957 Feb 24 [FWA]	Lady's Gully, Right Fork L.S.Lovat, W.J.R.Greaves
1957 March	Blockhead R.Smith, V.Burton
1957 Winter [FWA]	North East Zig Zag J.R.Marshall, A.H.Hendry, G.J.Ritchie
1957 April 6	Agony J.Cunningham, M.Noon, W.Smith. Aid. FFA June 1978 B Duff W Todd
1957 April 7	Hammer M.Noon, J.Cunningham 1 tension FFA unknown but certainly before the mid 70s
1957 April	Spider J.R.Marshall, R.Marshall, A.H.Hendry
1957 May 5	Crest Route K.Bryan, M.Thom
1957 May 25	Claw M.Noon, A.Charles, T.Lawrie
1957 May	Preamble J.R.Marshall, L.S.Lovat, G.J.Ritchie
1957 May	The Walk J.R.Marshall, R.Marshall
1957 June 25	Swastika M.Noon, E.Taylor
1957 June 30	Ledgeway, Final Variation L.S.Lovat, C.G.M.Slesser
1957 June 30	Facade L.S.Lovat
1957 June	Bogtrotter E.Taylor, W.Smith. Originally an aid route, FFA K.Johnstone, W.Todd 1977
1957 July	Bludger's Revelation Link J.R.Marshall, J.Griffin, G.Adams, R.Marshall
1957 Sept	Herbal Mixture J.R.Marshall, R.Marshall, G.J.Ritchie
1957 Sept	Pegleg J.R.Marshall, G.J.Ritchie
1957 Dec 15 [FWA]	Ordinary Route (Cuneiform B) J.R.Marshall, D.N.Mill, G.J.Ritchie
1957 Dec 15 [FWA]	The Long Chimney R.Smith, D.Leaver
1958 Jan 4 [W]	No 2 Buttress R.D.Stewart, R.R.Shaw
1958 Jan 5 [W]	No 1 Buttress R.D.Stewart, R.R.Shaw
1958 Jan 5 [W]	Pinnacle Buttress Groove L.S.Lovat, N.G.Harthill
1958 Jan 12 [W]	Central Gully (SCnB) J.Clarkson, J.Waddell
1958 Jan 12 [W]	Crack Climb L.S.Lovat, N.G.Harthill. Several earlier winter ascents discredited
1958 Jan 12 [W]	Spectre K.Bryan, J.Simpson
1958 Jan 12 [W]	The Pyramid, The Sphinx J.R.Marshall, I.Douglas. Both in a day as for summer
1958 Jan [W]	North Face Route J.R.Marshall, J.Stenhouse
1958 Jan [W]	Twisting Gully Right Fork J.R.Marshall, I.D.Haig. Part climbed 1952 Lees & Parish

1958 May	The Long Walk J.Cunningham, M.Noon 3 pa
1958 June	July Crack R.Smith, A.Fraser
1958 June	Shibboleth R.Smith, A.Fraser
1958 Aug 9	Carnivore J.Cunningham, M.Noon. Some aid, FFA E Cleasby and party 1978
1958 Aug	Bluebell Grooves J.Cunningham, F.Finlayson. FFA W Todd D.Cuthbertson 1978
1958 Sept 13	Rainmaker, Persuasion R.Marshall, J.Moriarty
1958 Sept	Dingle D.Haston, J.Stenhouse
1958 Sept	Original Route (E Buttress WFAD) J.R.Marshall, G.J.Ritchie
1958 Summer	Trapeze J.R.Marshall, D.Leaver
1958 Oct	Left End L.S.Lovat, N.G.Harthill
1959 Jan [W]	Chimney Route (LVMB) J.R.Marshall, J.Moriarty
1959 Jan [W]	Ciotach Route H.MacInnes & party
1959 Jan [W]	Direct Route (Diamond Buttress) J.McLean, M.Noon
1959 Feb [W]	Right Edge (LVMB) J.R.Marshall, J.Stenhouse, D.Haston
1959 March 22 [W]	The Gash I.Clough, M.Hadley, M.Large
1959 March	Meander J.R.Marshall, D.Haston
1959 March	The Prowl D.Haston, J.R.Marshall
1959 Winter [W]	Left Edge Route (LVMB) J.R.Marshall, G Tiso
1959 April 19	Swansong D.Haston, J.Stenhouse
1959 April	Pontoon J.R.Marshall, R.Marshall, J.Moriarty
1959 April	Stook R.Smith, D.Haston
1959 April	The Mappie J.Moriarty, J.R.Marshall
1959 May	North Ridge South Wall D.Haston, J.R.Marshall, J.Moriarty
1959 May	The Kneepad D.Haston, J.Moriarty, J.R.Marshall Aid
1959 May	Yo-Yo R.Smith, D.Hughes
1959 June 11	Isis I.Clough, M.Large, M.Hadley
1959 June 21	Hee-Haw J.Moriarty, D.Haston
1959 June	Stickleback J.R.Marshall, R.Marshall, R.Anderson
1959 June	Lecher's Route D.Haston, J.R.Marshall
1959 June	Shibboleth True Finish R.Smith, J.McLean 2nd ascent J.Cunningham or J.McLean
1959 Aug	Cayman Grooves J.McLean, J.Cunningham
1959 Aug	Pirhana J.McLean, J.Cunningham
1959 Sept 15	The Black Crack M.H.Crawford, J.R.Mills
1959 Sept	Apparition J.R.Marshall, J.McLean
1959 Sept	The Long Wait J.Cunningham, R.Smith
1960 Feb [W]	Big Choc Gully H.MacInnes
1960 Feb [W]	Crypt Route (The Tunnel Route) H.MacInnes & party
1960 Feb [W]	Rev Ted's Gully H.MacInnes, Rev. Ted
1960 Winter [FWA]	Chancellor Gully H.MacInnes
1960 Winter [W]	Old Man Gully H.MacInnes

1960 Winter [W]	Avalanche Gully (Upper Left Fork) H.MacInnes & party (1960s)
1960 April	Frustration D.Haston, A.Wightman 1 tension and abseil
1960 April	The Clasp J.R.Marshall
1960 May	Dan J.Moriarty, R.Smith 1 tension
1960 May	Marshall's Wall R.Smith, G.J.Ritchie. An outstanding route for the time
1960 May	Mimsy I.McFadzean, H.Noble
1960 May	Screw R.B.Evans, I.F.Howell
1960 May	White Spiral R.B.Evans, I.F.Howell
1960 May	Yo-Yo continued J.Moriarty, R.Smith
1960 July 2	Weevil's Way J.Stenhouse, R.Marshall
1960 July 3	Central Grooves K.Bryan, R.Robb 1 pa (Recorded a second time as East Face!)
1960 July	The Pause J.R.Marshall, G.J.Ritchie, G.Tiso, R.Marshall 4 pa 1 tension
1960 Sept 9	Buttress Route R.Birbeck, M.R.Wilson
1960 Sept	Jaywalk J.R.Marshall, J.Moriarty, J.Stenhouse 4 pa
1960 Summer	Bo Weevil D.Haston, J.Moriarty, G.B.Wakefield (1960s)
1961 April	The Grasshopper J.Stenhouse, J.R.Marshall, G.Tiso Pitches 1-7 1 tension
1961 May	The Kneepad Direct D.Haston, J.Moriarty. Aid
1961 June	The Peeler J.Moriarty, R.Smith
1961 Aug	The Big Top R.Smith, J.Gardner
1961 Oct 2	Turnspit D.Haston, R.Smith
1962 March 11 [W]	Twisting Grooves W.Sproul, T.Carruthers (alts)
1962 April 23	Consolation G.Grandison, I.Clough
1962 April	Girdle Traverse NFAD R.N.Campbell, D.Haston, N.MacNiven, R.Smith
1962 May	Superstition D.Todd, W.Gordon
1962 June	Carnivore [DF] D.Whillans, D.Walker 1 pa
1962 June	Plumbline J.Stenhouse, J.R.Marshall
1962 Aug	Ba's J.McLean, W.Smith 2 pa
1962 Sept 2	Buckshee Groove, Rough Slab R.T.Richardson, P.McKenzie, W.Skidmore
1962 Sept 24	Hiccup B.W.Robertson, J.Houston
1963 Jan 2 [W]	The Chasm of An-t-Sron H.M.Brown, J.Matyssek, R.K.Graham, M.Smith
1963 June	The Long Reach J.McLean, W.Smith 1 pa
1963 Summer	Yam A.Fulton, J.Cullen
1963 Oct	Kuf D.Haston, R.N.Campbell
1964 Jan [W]	Pterodactyl H.MacInnes, D.Crabbe. Aid, FFA via icicle probably T.Denholm & partner
1964 Feb 14	The Lid B.W.Robertson
1964 March 7	Marmalade A.McKeith, J.Brumfitt

1964 March 7	Oz B.W.Robertson, G.Anderson
1964 March 7	The Shake B.W.Robertson, G.Anderson
1964 March 8	Iron Cross J.Brumfitt, A.McKeith, B.W.Robertson
1964 March 28	Toast J.Brumfitt, M.Strong
1964 Winter [W]	Red Funnel Gully R.Baillie, H.MacInnes
1964 Winter [W]	Gully A Right Fork H.MacInnes, D.Crabbe
1964 May 23	Via Dolorosa B.W.Robertson, A.McKeith
1964 May	Raven's Edge D.Bathgate, J.Brumfitt
1964 June	Goldfinger E.Cairns, J.Knight
1964 July 25	Cornflake A.McKeith, Miss M.A.Thompson
1964 July	The North Wall N.Tennent, Miss M.McLeod
1964 Aug 1	Paladin J.Renny, F.Harper
1964 Aug	The Big Ride D.Haston, R.N.Campbell. 2 tensions 2 pa FFA R.Carrington, I.Nicolson 1970s
1964 Oct 11	Swastika Direct B.W.Robertson, R.K.Holt, F.Harper, A.McKeith
1965 Jan	Shiver (EFAD) J.Knight, M.Harcus
1965 Feb	C-D Scoop D.Bathgate, J.Brumfitt
1965 Feb	The Screen D.Bathgate, J.Brumfitt
1965 April	Rock Climb A.McKeith, J.Knight
1965 April	Slaver D.Haston, J.Heron
1965 May 5	Kak R.Burnett, A.McKeith
1965 June 13	Harry J.Knight, A.McKeith
1965 June	Cut the Grass D.Haston, T.Shearer, J.Heron
1965 June	Trapeze [DF] J.Falkener, C.Higgins
1965 June	The Widow J.R.Houston, C.Mitchell
1965 July	Pocks R.N.Campbell, J.R.Marshall
1965 Sept 4	Tom D.Gray, Miss M.A.Thompson, A.McKeith
1965 Oct 17	Slimcrack I.Clough, C.G.M.Slesser
1965 Oct 24	Tober I.Clough, D.G.Roberts
1965 Oct	Aryan D.Haston, G.Tiso 1 tension 1 pa
1965 Oct	Attila D.Haston, J.Brumfitt 2 pa
1965 Oct	Dick D.Haston, M.Sclater
1965 Oct	Greez D.Haston, M.Sclater
1965 Oct	Smersh D.Haston, M.Sclater
1965 Oct	The Valkyrie B.W.Robertson, F.Harper. Pea-Brained Var Everett, Gaffney, Kaiser 1987
1965 Nov 6	Novity I.Clough, D.G.Roberts
1965 Nov [W]	Humpback Gully J.Renny, I.MacEacheran
1965 Nov [FWA]	Barn Wall Route J.Renny, I.MacEacheran, A.McKeith
1965 Dec 25	Christmas Couloir I.Clough, D.G.Roberts
1965 Dec [W]	The Chancellor W.Skidmore, R.T.Richardson
1965 Dec [FWA]	Drain Pipe Corner D.Haston, A.McKeith
1966 Jan 13 [W]	Broken Gully Mr & Mrs I.Clough
1966 Feb 18 [FWA]	Amphitheatre Scoop I.Clough, G.Lowe, J.Hardie. From Middle Ledge
1966 Feb [W]	Hourglass Gully I.Clough & party

1966 March 31 [W]	Subsidiary Scoop I.Clough, N.Clough
1966 March [W]	Rescue Team Gully H.MacInnes & party
1966 April 17 [W]	Pearly Gates I.Clough & party
1966 April 30	High
1966 May 7	Leg Stump J.Renny, A.McKeith
1966 May 7	Off Stump A.McKeith
1966 May 23	Mayday C.Blenkinsop, B.T.Hill, A.S.Macdonald
1966 May 28	Tilt (Original Route) I.Clough, J.Hardie 1 pa, FFA R.Anderson on FWA 1991
1966 May 29	Appauling A.McKeith, P.Brian
1966 May 29	Rock Climb [DS] P.Brian, A.McKeith
1966 May	Sideshow J.R.Marshall, R.Marshall
1966 May	The Grasshopper II J.R.Marshall, D.Bathgate. Pitches 8-15 aid
1966 June 6	Outgrabe Route (Lower Section) I.Clough & party
1966 June 11	Intruder, The Jester, Juggler I.Clough, G.Arkless
1966 June 12	Angor I.Clough, G.Arkless FFA & [DF] K.Johnstone, A.Ramsay 5/9/80
1966 June	The Whip J.R.Marshall, J.McLean 1 pa
1966 July 3	Hesitation J.Cunningham 1 pa. FFA K.V.Crocket, I.Fulton Summer 1972
1966 July	Yak H.Small, J.Graham, R.Marshall
1966 July 31	Tight Rope J.Cunningham, J.McLean. Superceded by Bannockburn
1966 Aug 21	Triangle T.Low, G.Skelton
1966 Aug 22	The Mummy I.Clough, C.Kynaston, J.G.Garster
1966 Aug 23	Stumblebum J.Cunningham, W.Smith
1966 Aug 26	Nirvana Wall I.Clough, C.Kynaston, J.G.Garster
1966 Aug 26	Nobad, So So A.McKeith
1966 Aug 27	Jabberwock I.Clough, C.Kynaston
1966 Aug 28	Plutocrat J.R.Marshall, M.Galbraith
1966 Aug 28	Whimsy I.Clough, Mrs N.Clough
1966 Aug 29	Yen C.Kynaston, J.G.Garster
1966 Aug 30	Delusion I.Clough, C.Kynaston
1966 Aug	19th Nervous Breakdown H.Small, K.Haggerty
1966 Aug	Girdle Traverse Leac Mhor I.G.Rowe, P.M.MacDonald
1966 Aug	Jabberwock I.Clough, C.Kynaston
1966 Aug	Route One Point Five I.G.Rowe, P.F.MacDonald
1966 Sept 3	Dinnaeken, Seek Tochil, Uhuh A.McKeith
1966 Sept 11	Bag, Shasmakelmanov A.McKeith, R.MacDonald
1966 Sept 11	The Dial A.McKeith
1966 Sept 26	Sgub W.Sproul, M.Galbraith
1966 Sept	Tober Variation Start H.Small, K.Haggerty
1966 Summer	The Thin Red Line B.W.Robertson, P.Nunn. Aid
1966 Summer	Awrite, Awrong A.McKeith
1966 Oct 2	Secretion Slab A.McKeith
1966 Oct 29	Surprise Pea, Fish Finger A.McKeith, A.W.Ewing

1966 Dec 10	Plod B.T.Hill, D.Stone, M.Durham
1967 Jan 25 [W]	Broken Gully Left Fork I.Clough & party
1967 Jan 26 [W]	Pinnacle Buttress NE Face I.Clough, J.R.Woods
1967 March 29 [FWA]	Bunny's Route I.Clough, C.G.Kynaston
1967 April 23	Curses A.Kirk, C.Kilpatrick
1967 April	Central Rib J.R.Marshall, R.N.Campbell
1967 May 13	Eezay Edge J.Brumfitt, B.Sproul
1967 May	Patey's Old Man I.Rowe, B.Sproul
1967 June 11	Agoraphobia M.Galbraith, A.McKeith
1967 June 12	Flake Groove I.Clough, G.Brown, J.G.Donnison, R.A.Logan
1967 June 18	The Duel I.G.Rowe, B.Sproul. Consolation for being beaten to Unicorn
1967 June 18	Unicorn J.R.Marshall, R.N.Campbell
1967 June 19	Flip-Out D.Bathgate, A.W.Ewing. Climbed free (K.Johnstone unseconded 2/7/77)
1967 June 23	Way In C.Higgins, B.Sproul
1967 June 24	Girdle Traverse E Buttress M.Galbraith, A.McKeith
1967 June 25	Tilt (Var Start) Mr & Mrs Clough
1967 July 1	Freak-Out D.Bathgate, A.McKeith. Aid. FFA 1979 D.Mullin, J.Melrose
1967 July 9	Rabbit's Hole J.R.Marshall, R.Marshall, R.N.Campbell
1967 July	Blind Pew J.Ferguson, C.Higgins
1967 Aug 8	Direct Route (SCnB The Sphinx) Mr & Mrs I.Clough, J.Simpson
1967 Aug 18	Slithy I.Clough, P.McLeod, R.Morgan
1967 Aug	Girdle Traverse (NE Nose AD) J.Porteous, K.Spence
1967 Aug 23	Sundown Slab I.Clough and party
1967 Aug	The Late Late Show K.Spence, J.Porteous
1967 Aug	The Tumbler K.Spence, J.Porteous
1967 Sept 21	Annie's Route D.A.Knowles, D.R.Knowles, J.Loxham
1967 Sept	Girdle Traverse EFNB J.R.Jackson, K.Robson
1968 Jan [W]	John Gray's Buttress H.MacInnes
1968 March [W]	Jim's Gully J.McArtney & party
1968 Winter (or 1969) [W]	Ingrid's Folly/Peregrine Gully GSWC party
1968 April 18	The Pinch J.R.Jackson, R.Carrington
1968 May	Fall-Out J.Ferguson, C.Higgins
1968 May	Snowbas C.Higgins, J.McLean
1968 June 14	Crack-line J.Hardie, W.Thomson
1968 June 15	Inquisition J.Hardie, W Thomson
1968 June 17	The Crook, Mitre J.Hardie, W.Thomson. Back again after a day's rest
1968 Aug 17	Ambush D.N.Thomson, R.Turner
1968 Aug 17	How-Do R.Bannatyne, J.Magee
1968 Aug 17	Kingpin J.Hardie, W.Thomson. Aid. FFA complete 1978 D.Cuthbertson, D.Mullin

1968 Aug	Lecher's Direct K.Spence, J.Porteous
1968 Sept 1	Meson I.Fulton, N.Muir
1968 Sept 1	Yamay I.Nicolson, K.Spence
1968 Summer	The Cheek H.MacInnes, M.C.MacInnes
1969 Jan 14 [FWA]	Pleasant Terrace I.Clough, J.McArtney et al
1969 Jan [FWA]	Original Route (F Buttress WFAD) H.MacInnes et al
1969 Jan [W]	Twenty Minute Gully H.MacInnes and party
1969 Jan [W]	Gully A Central Branch D.Haston, J.Stenhouse 1 pa
1969 Feb 3 [W]	McArtney Gully H.MacInnes, GSWC party
1969 Feb 8 [W]	Chance G.Anderson, A.J.Trees
1969 Feb 8 [W]	The Graduate D.A.Knowles, J.Loxham, D.Wilson, A.Wilson
1969 Feb 8 [W]	West Chimney, The Gangway A.Fyffe, H.MacInnes.
1969 Feb 9 [W]	Sabre Tooth, Trilobite I.Clough, H.MacInnes
1969 Feb 12 [W]	The Corridors I.Clough, M.A.Hudson, C.Hutchinson, C.Williamson, D.Davies
1969 Feb 13 [W]	Lost Leeper Gully H.MacInnes, A.Gilbert, P.Debbage, D.Layne-Joynt, D.Allwright
1969 Feb 14 [W]	Lady's Choice Mrs N.Clough, A.Fyffe
1969 Feb 16 [W]	Mome Rath Face Route A.Fyffe, J.McArtney
1969 Feb 16 [FWA]	The Wabe H.MacInnes, J.Hardie, I.Clough
1969 Feb 18 [W]	Sack-o'-Coal Couloir J.McArtney & party
1969 Feb 18 [W]	Smashed Spectacles Gully I.Clough, F.Jones, R.Fox, C.Wood
1969 Feb 18 [W]	Vice Chancellor Ridge H.MacInnes & GSWC party
1969 Feb 18 [W]	No 5 Gully (WFAD) A.Fyffe, C.MacInnes, N.Clough
1969 Feb 20 [FWA]	Great Gully (Garbh Bheinn) C.J.S.Bonington, T.W.Patey, D.Whillans
1969 Feb 21 [W]	Farewell Gully/Grand Finale J.McArtney, D.Selby, C.Wood
1969 Feb 26 [FWA]	C Buttress J.McArtney, A.Smith, A.Thompson, A.Taylor, K.Withall
1969 Feb 26 [W]	Chaos Chimney A.Fyffe, E.Viveash, B.Jenkins, P.Hardman, J.Snodgrass
1969 Feb 27 [FWA]	Amphitheatre, North Ridge I.Clough, J.Choat, A.Taylor, K.Withall, R.Viveash
1969 Feb 27 [W]	D Buttress F. Tier D.Power, P.Hardman, J.Friend, A.Thompson, A.Fyffe
1969 Feb [W]	North Ridge J.Choat, I.Clough, A.Taylor, K.Withall, R.Viveash
1969 Feb [W]	Righthand Gully (Stob Coire a'Chearcaill) J.Grieve
1969 Feb [W]	999 H.MacInnes, Miss G.Marshall, J.Friend
1969 Feb [W]	Broken Lip Gully I.Clough, F.Jones & party
1969 Feb [W]	Frostbite Groove H.MacInnes & GSWC party
1969 Feb [W]	Frostbite Wall H.MacInnes, A.Gilbert, P.Debbage, D.Layne-Joynt, D.Allwright

1969 Feb [W]	Lost Leeper Gully H.MacInnes, A.Gilbert, P.Debbage, D.Layne-Joynt, D.Allwright
1969 Feb [W]	Main Buttress H.MacInnes, D.Layne-Joynt
1969 Feb [W]	The Cleg H.MacInnes, D.Layne-Joynt
1969 Feb [W]	The Midge H.MacInnes & party
1969 Feb [W]	Twine Climb J.McArtney & party
1969 Feb [FWA]	D Buttress J.Choat, I.Clough, J.Friend, P.Mallinson, D.Power
1969 March 2 [W]	Central Scoop I.Clough, N.Clough
1969 March 5 [W]	Adagio H.MacInnes, R.Birch, D.Chen, P.Judge, R.O'Shea
1969 March 5 [W]	Tyrannosaur I.Clough, D.Morrish, E.S.Taylor. Aid on pitch 2
1969 March 23 [W]	Alleyway K.V.Crocket, D.Jenkins, C.Forrest, J.McEwan
1969 March 26 [W]	The Smear I.Clough, I.F.Duckworth, F.M.Wells, R.E.B.York
1969 March 26 [W]	The Slot (WFAD) I.Clough, R.York
1969 March [W]	Bootneck Gully H.MacInnes, I.Duckworth, P.Wells, R.Ward, J.Parsons
1969 March [W]	Brush Buttress H.MacInnes and party
1969 March [W]	Langsam H.MacInnes, M.C.MacInnes & party
1969 March [W]	The Ramp H.MacInnes
1969 March [FWA]	Fingal's Chimney W.Tauber, D.Gardner
1969 Winter [W]	Farm Gully. Probably H.MacInnes and party
1969 Winter [W]	Dislocation C.J.S.Bonington, F.Mitchell
1969 Winter [W]	Innuendo H.MacInnes, R.Birch, P.Judge, R.O'Shea
1969 Winter [W]	Quintet H.MacInnes, D.Chen, R.Birch, P.Judge, R.O'Shea
1969 Winter [W]	Middle Ledge K.Spence et al
1969 Winter [W]	The Wasp A.Fyffe, C.MacInnes, A.Laing, J.McCatten, R.Sherman
1969 June 1	Line Up C.Higgins, I.Nicolson
1969 June 7	Plink D.Gardner, R.J.Gorman
1969 June	Apocalypse C.Higgins, I.Nicolson. 1 pa 2nd ascent and FFA W Todd and N.Donelly 1976
1969 July	Monsoon A.Fyffe, W.March
1969 Aug 31	Bosco G.Anderson, J.Porteous
1969 Aug	Backing Out G.Adams, C.Higgins
1969 Aug	Lift Off I.Fulton, C.Higgins
1969 Sept 14	Eve's Arete J.Buchanan, J.Forbes, F.Jack, G.Skelton
1969 Sept 16/17	Girdle Terrace Face (EFAD) K.V.Crocket, D.C.Forrest, D.M.Jenkins
1969 Sept 17	Tartan Slab J.Buchanan, J.Forbes, G.Skelton
1969 Summer	Impresario D.A.Knowles, S.Whimster
1970 Jan [W]	Cyclops H.MacInnes et al
1970 Feb [FWA]	Gully A Left Branch H.MacInnes GSWC party

1970 Feb [FWA]	Raven's Gully [DF] Y.Chouinard, D.Tompkins
1970 Winter [W]	Midnight Special K.Spence, I.Clough et al
1970 Winter [W]	Deirdre's Cleft H.MacInnes, C.Williamson
1970 Winter [W]	GSWC Memorial Route D.Knowles & D Knowles (1970s)
1970 May 16	Buzzard Arete G.N.Hunter, D.F.Lang, S.Littleford
1970 May 23	Mainbrace Crack [DF] 1 pa/tension S.Belk, I.Fulton
1970 May	Tous les Deux R.Carrington, J.McLean 1 pa & combined tactics
1970 June 7	C'Mola S.J.Crymble, K.Schwartz
1970 June	Blister R.MacDonald, J.Porteous
1970 June	Raven's Edge [DF] J.Porteous, M.MacDonald
1970 July 8	Pilliwinks K.V.Crocket, I.Fulton
1970 Aug 25	Rannoch Traverse B.Dunn, D.MacArthur
1970 Aug	Waterslide Corner D.Jenkins, I.Fulton
1970 Summer	Paleolith P.Brian, R.N.Campbell, A.W.Ewing
1970 Summer	The Knowles-Spence Route D.Knowles, K.Spence (early 70s)
1970 Summer	Nausea A.Fyffe, I.Nicolson, D.Knowles
1971 Jan 31 [FWA]	The Pinnacle Face K.V.Crocket, C.Stead
1971 Feb [FWA]	Bowstring A.Fyffe & party
1971 Feb [FWA]	Basin Traverse A.Fyffe & party
1971 Feb [W]	Ordinary Route (SCnL Summit Buttress) K.Spence & party
1971 Feb [W]	The Hash H.MacInnes AN Other. Formerly known as Caradhras Cleft
1971 Winter [W]	North-West Face Route (NFAD) K.Spence et al
1971 Winter [W]	Evening Citizen K.Spence, H.MacInnes, A.Thompson (poss 1970)
1971 May 1	Sinus K.V.Crocket, C.Stead
1971 May 2	Steptoe, The Verger K.V.Crocket, C.Stead
1971 June 5	Targe R.G.Ross, R.Watters
1971 June 6	Jock A.M.James, Miss C.L.Purdey
1971 June 26	The Cough S.Belk, D.M.Jenkins
1971 June	Rampage M.H.Moar, J.D.Roberts-James
1971 June	Slake J.Crawford, W.Skidmore
1971 Aug 14	The Band of Hope J.Newsome, C.Stead, I.Anderson, K.V.Crocket
1971 Aug 22	Garnet K.V.Crocket, C.Stead
1972 Jan 8 [FWA]	Direct Route (SCnL South Buttress) D.Knowles, J.Loxham or D.Wilson. Hard.
1972 Jan 30 [W]	Moonshadow K.V.Crocket, C.Stead
1972 Feb [FWA]	Route 1 (Rannoch Wall) H.MacInnes & partner
1972 March [W]	Alpen S.Belk, I.Fulton, K.V.Crocket, C.Stead
1972 Winter [W]	Cleftweave B.Clarke, A.Strachan
1972 April 15	Mosquito R.G.Ross, L.D.Wilson
1972 May 20	Bear's Picnic, Tottie's Route B.Dunn, C.Higgins

1972 June 10	Excalibur K.V.Crocket, C.Stead
1972 July 2	Xenolith K.V.Crocket, Miss K.Simpson
1972 July 8	Deadline K.V.Crocket, C.Stead
1972 July 22	Footpad, Sidewalk K.V.Crocket, C.D.Grant
1972 July	Bumblebee P.Brian, R.N.Campbell
1972 Aug 12	Neolith, Limbo K.V.Crocket, C.Stead
1972 Aug 13	Flamingo, Whispering Grooves K.V.Crocket, C.Stead
1972 Aug 15	Sapphire K.V.Crocket, C.Stead
1972 Sept 2	Scansor P.Braithwaite, G.Cohen
1972 Sept 23	Groundhog D.Dinwoodie, G.Strange. Aid FFA M.Hamilton, P.Greenwell
1972 Summer	Littlekin K.V.Crocket, J.Armour
1973 Winter [W]	Midnight Cowboy D.Knowles, D.Knowles, W.Thomson
1973 May 26	Mutchkin J.Armour, C.Stead
1973 June	The Chasm of Beinn Trilleachan I.Rowe, G.Tiso. Rumours of earlier ascents
1973 July 7	Drongo, Lodestone K.V.Crocket, I.Fulton
1973 Sept 16	Satyr P.Nunn, J.Morgan, J.Street
1973 Oct 14	Stitch B.Clark, J.Mackenzie
1974 April	Percussion J.Cant, P.Gribbon
1974 May 5	Snowstormer J.Burns, D.Rubens
1974 June 16	Cantilena K.V.Crocket, I.Fulton
1974 Aug 17	Saturday Rock B.Dunn, C.Higgins
1975 May	Girdle Traverse South Wall R.Archbold, G.Strange
1975 May	Reptile C.Heap, G.Skelton
1975 June	Near Enough W.Anderson, G.Grassom
1976 April 23	The Fly Man N.Colton, W.Todd
1976 June 4	Le Monde N.Colton, W.Todd 2nd ascent K.Johnstone
1976 July 24	Cantata K.V.Crocket, I.Fulton
1976 July 31	Mournblade K.V.Crocket, C.D.Grant, J.A.P.Hutchinson
1976 Aug 29-Sept 5	Safari and others on the Creran Slabs GN Hunter N Quinn In the early 70s
1976 Aug	The Clearances E.Grindley, C.Grindley, J.Main
1976 Sept 19	Nirvana C.Hill, D.N.Williams
1976 Oct 30	Venison Dagger A.Paul, G.Reilly, J.Reilly
1977 June 3	Gambado W.Todd, D.Cuthbertson, R.Anderson (Pitch 3)
1977 June 3	Solitude D.Cuthbertson, R.Anderson, W.Todd
1977 June 4/5	Crocodile D.Cuthbertson, M.Hamilton (W.Todd, R.Anderson pitches 1 & 2)
1977 June 18	Bannockburn D.Cuthbertson, W.Todd
1977 June 18/19	Massacre A.Grigg, K.Johnstone
1977 June 22	Eldorado K.Johnstone, M.Worsley. FFA M.Hamilton, D.Mullin 1980 May
1977 June 23	Serenade K.Johnstone, M.Worsley
1977 June 25	Gazebo C.Hill, D.N.Williams
1977 July 9	Quietude D.Cuthbertson, W.Todd

1977 July 9	The Fly D.Cuthbertson, W.Todd
1977 July	Lady Jane D.Cuthbertson, D.Jamieson
1977 Aug 12	Easy Going D.Cuthbertson, M.Hamilton
1977 Summer	Demoniser J.Leinster, T.Plommer (or 1978)
1977 Dec [W]	The Corridors [DS] I.Fulton, J.Hutchinson
1978 Winter [W]	Findlay's Rise I.Nicolson et al
1978 April	Spacewalk K.Johnstone, P.Ogden. FFA D.Cuthbertson, M.Hamilton 1978
1978 May 21	Blast-Off B.Duff, K.McCluskey
1978 May 21	Triceptor P.Greenwell, K.Johnstone
1978 May 27	Blockbuster, Layla P.Greenwell, K.Johnstone
1978 May 27	Sir Chancealot B.Duff, K.McCluskey
1978 May 27	Sticky Fingers K.Johnstone, P.Greenwell
1978 May 27	The Challenge D.Cuthbertson, R.Anderson, D.Mullin
1978 May 28	Walk With Destiny D.Cuthbertson, D.Mullin
1978 May 29	Daredevil, Exellerator B.Duff, K.Johnstone
1978 May 29	The Foil P.Moores, M.Tighe
1978 May 29	Trichord B.Duff, K.Johnstone
1978 May	Bayonet Mr & Mrs A.Fyffe
1978 May	Double Exposure K.V.Crocket, C.J.Gilmore
1978 May	Marathon Man A.Crocket, K.V.Crocket
1978 June 1	Routes right & left of Creran Corner S.Kennedy, C.Moody
1978 June 11	Storm Trooper K.McCluskey, C.McLean
1978 June	Grogblossom M.Hamilton, D.Jamieson 2nd ascent D.Cuthbertson, D.Mullin 1978
1978 June	Swingle A.Matthews, C.Stead
1978 July 20	Gutrot G.A.Christie, P.Ogden
1978 July	De Vreemde Stap M.Hind, H.van Ryswick
1978 Aug	The Pincer D.Dinwoodie, R.A.Smith
1978 Sept 2	Guinness K.Johnstone, M.Worsley
1978 Summer	Triple C Special B.Duff, C.Patterson, AN Other
1979 Jan 30 [W]	The Flute D.Cuthbertson
1979 Jan [W]	Venom R.Anderson, D.Brown, M.Duff, A.McAllister
1979 Jan [W]	White Snake R.Anderson, D.Brown, M.Duff, A.McAllister
1979 Jan [W]	Amphitheatre Scoop Direct R.Bruce, R.Anderson, A.McAllister. Climbed before?
1979 Feb 18 [W]	Blue Riband J. 'Spider' MacKenzie, G.Rooney
1979 Feb 18 [W]	Heart of Glass D.W.Cuthbertson, K.Johnstone, W.Todd
1979 Feb [W]	Elliot's Downfall D.Cuthbertson. One rest point used to place protection
1979 Feb [W]	Venom Viper Start R.Anderson, D.Brown
1979 Feb [FWA]	Dalness Chasm Right Fork H.MacInnes, C.Williamson
1979 March 17 [W]	Cuneiform Corner, Misty High A.Paul, D.Sanderson
1979 March [FWA]	Direct Route, GGB M.Hamilton, K.Spence

1979 Winter [W]	Frozen Ba's M.Hamilton, K.Spence, A.Taylor
1979 May	Freakout FFA D.Mullin, J.Melrose. An on-sight ascent in one day with no yo-yoing
1979 June 10	Bodkin K.V.Crocket, S.N.Smith
1979 Summer	The Zig-Zag Roof D.Gunn & Party
1980 Jan 20 [FWA]	Tilt M.Hamilton, K.Spence, A.Taylor. A significant step forward
1980 Jan 26 [FWA]	Dan R.Anderson, M.Hamilton, K.Spence
1980 Jan [FWA]	Outgrabe Route/Mome Rath Direct R.Anderson, R.Milne
1980 Feb 7 [FWA]	Rainmaker D.Cuthbertson, M.Duff
1980 May 17	Perambulator K.V.Crocket, S.N.Smith. Old abseil sling found below crux pitch
1980 May 17	Sentinelle Rouge D.Cuthbertson, K.Johnstone
1980 May 18	Sundance K.V.Crocket, S.N.Smith
1980 May 19	En Garde G.Rooney, I.Dalley
1980 May 23	Performance M.Fowler, P.O'Sullivan
1980 May 24	The Slot K.V.Crocket, S.N.Smith
1980 May 28	The Risk Business. p1,2 P.Whillance, R.Parker. p3,4 P.Whillance, P.Botterill 1980
1980 June 6	Spacewalk FFA M.Hamilton, D.Cuthbertson
1980 July 31	Carnivore [DS] P.Whillance, D.Jamieson
1980 Dec 20 [FWA]	Consolation R.Anderson, K.Spence
1981 Feb 12 [W]	Central Buttress (SCnL) K.Spence, M.Hamilton (alts)
1981 Feb 19 [W]	Financial Times R.Anderson, A.Taylor (alts)
1981 May	Chela M.Hamilton, A.Murray
1981 June 26	Chariots of Fire R.Anderson, M.Lawrence
1981 June 26	Outlandos A.Kay, N.Morrison
1981 June 26	Revengeance D.Cuthbertson, R.Anderson, M.Lawrence (p1, p2 on June 27)
1981 June	Gralloch M.Diggins, A.Fyffe
1981 July	Fast Approaching R.Anderson, A.Russell
1981 July	Mistaken Identity R.Anderson, A.Taylor
1981 Summer	Prophet of Purism D.Cuthbertson, R.Williamson. A very bold lead
1981 Summer	Short But Sweet D.Cuthbertson, R.Williamson
1981 Summer	Yamay [DS] M.Hamilton, A.Murray
1981 Dec 6 [W]	Bop Till You Drop M.Garthwaite, A.Foster
1981 Dec 28 [W]	Darwin's Dihedral D.Cuthbertson, M.Lawrence
1982 Jan 2 [W]	The Bubble S.Kennedy, C.MacLeod, M.Slater
1982 Jan 9 [FWA]	Dalness Chasm, Left Fork A.Nisbet, G.Allen. Barrier pitch omitted
1982 Jan 10 [FWA]	Dalness Chasm, Central Branch D.Cuthbertson, E.McArthur
1982 Feb 18 [W]	Closer C.Dale, A.Kassyk, D.Talbot
1982 Feb [W]	North Face Route (NFAD) K.Spence, R.Anderson
1982 Feb [W]	Yankee Go Home G.Reid, T.Swain

1982 March 20 [W]	East Face Route (SCnL) M.Hamilton, R.Anderson
1982 June 13	Tru-Cut M.Hamilton, R.Anderson
1982 June 20	Menghini A.Taylor, R.Anderson
1982 June 20	Sala A.Taylor, R.Anderson
1983 Jan/Feb [W]	Minute Man M.Hamilton, R.Anderson (alts)
1983 Feb 18 [W]	Cuneiform Continuation P.Moores, C.Butler
1983 Feb [W]	Winter Route K.Spence, J.McKenzie (alts)
1983 Feb [FWA]	Central Grooves K.Spence, J.McKenzie (alts). A route with a complicated history
1983 Feb [FWA]	Rowan Tree Wall P.Moores & party
1983 Winter [W]	Mr Softee M.Fowler, A.Saunders
1983 May 11	The Wellie Boys T.McAuley, A.Paul
1983 June 23	Plonk T.McAulay, D.Sanderson
1983 July 16	Chib T.McAuley, D.Sanderson
1983 July 27	The Lost Ark P.Whillance, R.Parker. Whillance strikes again
1983 Summer	Fawlty Tower P.Whillance, T.Furnis
1984 Jan 21 [W]	Divergence A.Nisbet, C.Murray, S.Taylor
1984 Jan 21 [W]	Special K R.Anderson, A.Russel
1984 Jan 21 [FWA]	Direct Route by the Chimney Route (Central Buttress BEM T.McAulay, D.Sanderson
1984 Jan 21 [FWA]	Raven's Edge, Ordinary Route S.Allen, B.Sprunt
1984 Jan 24 [W]	Two Shakes M.Duff, A.Greig
1984 Jan 26 [FWA]	June Crack D.Hawthorn
1984 Jan 28 [W]	Paul Rodger's Wake P.Moores, H.McNicoll
1984 Jan 28 [FWA]	Guerdon Grooves D.Cuthbertson, A.Paul
1984 Jan 30 [FWA]	Jabberwock A.Paul, D.Cuthbertson
1984 Jan 31 [FWA]	Snowstormer D.Cuthbertson, A.Paul, C.McLean
1984 Jan [FWA]	Kinloss Corner A.Paul, D.Sanderson
1984 Jan [FWA]	Whimsy R.Clothier, D.Hawthorn
1984 Feb 3 [W]	Southern Death Cult J.Tinker, K.Howett
1984 Winter [FWA]	The Walk C.Dale, D.Kay
1984 May 5	White Hope P.Whillance, R.Anderson, M.Hamilton
1984 May 6	Bloodline M.Hamilton, P.Whillance, R.Anderson
1984 May 21	The Twarf M.McLeod, C.Moody
1984 May	Romantic Reality D.Cuthbertson, K.Howett
1984 June 9	Has Been T.McAulay, D.Sanderson
1984 June 30	The Golden Lance R.Anderson, A.Russell
1984 June	Gone With The Wind D.Cuthbertson, P.Moores
1984 June	Too Cold For Comfort D.Cuthbertson, P.Moores
1984 July 21	Temple of Doom M.Hamilton, G.Livingston, R.Anderson. Previously attempted by others
1984 Aug 26	Twilight K.Johnstone, A.Leary
1984 Dec 9 [FWA]	Crypt Route (The Through Route) T.McAulay, D.Sanderson, D.Hawthorn
1985 Jan 2 [FWA]	Great Flake Route T.McAulay, D.Sanderson
1985 Jan 3 [W]	The Corridors, Alt Start M.Duff, S.Picknett

1985 Jan 24 [FWA]	May Crack C.Jamieson, E.Todd
1985 Jan 24 [FWA]	Unicorn C.Maclean, A.Nisbet. A testpiece climbed when plastered in hoar frost
1985 Feb 1 [W]	Spectre, Alt Start M.Duff, M.Garret, R.Nowack
1985 May 4	Symposium A.Tibbs, D.Hainsworth, A.Winton
1985 July 28	Wild Spot M.Fowler, S.Richardson
1985 Nov 24 [FWA]	Crest Route R.Anderson, M.Hamilton (alts). Var by A.Nisbet, M.Duff
1985 Dec 28 [W]	Ephemeron Gully K.V.Crocket, A.Walker, P.Craig
1985 Dec 31 [W]	People's Friend A.Nisbet, M.Duff
1986 Jan 2 [W]	Ordinary Route Var (Summit Buttress) M.Duff, N.Kekus, A.Nisbet
1986 Jan 25 [W]	Hidden Ridge G.E.Little, D.Saddler
1986 Feb 7 [W]	Silent Running M.Duff, R.Nowack
1986 Feb 9 [W]	Diamond Route D.Rubens, G.Cohen
1986 Feb 9 [FWA]	Waterslide Gully T.McAulay, C.Murray
1986 Feb 15 [FWA]	Route I S.Richardson, N.Kekus
1986 Feb 17 [W]	King Cobra M.Duff, R.Nowack
1986 Feb 20 [W]	Veil/Waterslide Corner T.Brindle, A.Moore
1986 Feb [W]	Exellerator W.Todd. Icefall left of Lady Jane
1986 Feb [W]	Newsholme's Groove G.Hornby, C.Schaschke
1986 April 3 [W]	Flexi Rib, Shadow Groove, Parting Shot G.E.Little
1986 April 5 [FWA]	North Face (Garbh Bheinn) W.Hood, R.Turner
1986 June 13	Daktari P.Hyde, G.Szuca
1986 June 21	Brack, Kelpie M.Hamilton, R.Anderson
1986 June 21	The Final Judgement K.V.Crocket, L.S.Lovat
1986 June 30	Limburger Slabs, Gruyere R.N.Campbell, J.R.Marshall
1986 June	Gravity and Grace W.Todd, I.Rea
1986 June	Uncertain Emotions D.Cuthbertson
1986 July	Fated Path G.Livingstone
1986 July	Waltzing Ostriches D.Cuthbertson, A.Moist
1986 Aug 14	Turnaround, Tattieman, Gestation W.Hood, R.Turner, B.Williamson
1987 Jan 11 [W]	Rapunzel, The Witch S.Richardson, R.Clothier (alts)
1987 Jan 11 [FWA]	Great Ridge [DS] A.Matthewson, J.MacLaurin
1987 Feb 14 [W]	Neanderthal R.Anderson, G.Nicol (alts). The first fine modern winter routes here
1987 Feb 23 [W]	Dubiety F.Yeoman, J.Mathie. An obvious line missed (?) by others
1987 March 14 [W]	Inglis Clark Ridge R.A.Napier, S.Downie
1987 March 14 [W]	Lone Ranger G.E.Little
1987 May 9	Graceland, Conscience Corner, Ivy Corner W.Hood, B.Williamson
1987 May 24	Showcase A.Tibbs, S.Steer
1987 May 24	Celtic Dawn G.Livingston, A.Ross, D.Dinwoodie
1987 May	Baptism of Fire M.Edwards, R.Edwards

1987 May	The Chant of Jimmy Blacksmith M.McGowan, B.Campbell
1987 June 16	Druim nan Gillian N.Horn, C.Moody
1987 June 16	Para Andy A.Cunningham, A.Nisbet
1987 June 16	The Primordial Soup Kitchen A.Nisbet, A.Cunningham
1987 June 20	Admission G.Livingstone
1987 June 20	Shiver (Garbh Bheinn) S.Richardson, G.Muhlemann
1987 June 20	Sugarplum G.Muhlemann, S.Richardson
1987 June 20	Twilight Zone G.Livingston, A.Ross
1987 June	The Railway Children D.Cuthbertson
1987 Aug	Salome K.Howett, G.Latter
1987 Sept	Creag Dhont Woll M.McGowan, C.Bell. Prize for the worst route name
1988 Jan 8 [FWA]	Para Andy A.Cunningham, A.Nisbet, A.Newton
1988 Jan 10 [W]	Minor Issue R.Anderson, G.Taylor (alts)
1988 Jan 16 [W]	Barracuda R.Anderson, R.Milne
1988 Jan 21 [W]	Central Buttress (Sgur Dhonail) A.Clark, P.Yardley
1988 Jan 23 [FWA]	Fall-Out G.Taylor, R.Anderson
1988 Jan 27 [W]	Moonlighting R.Anderson, G.Taylor (alts), N.West
1988 Jan 30 [W]	Flying Scotsman H.Henderson, R.G.Ross
1988 Jan 31 [W]	Savage G.Taylor, R.Anderson (alts)
1988 Jan [FWA]	Red Slab C.Gilchrist, M.McGowan
1988 Feb 1 [W]	Ziggy M.Duff
1988 Feb 7 [FWA]	Chimney & Face Route R.Anderson, R.Milne, J.Naismith
1988 Feb 7 [W]	White Rhino A.Cave, M.Duff
1988 Feb 10 [W]	Trumpeting Elephants M.Duff, I.McLeod, A.Owen
1988 Feb 14 [W]	Against All Odds M.Fowler, C.Watts
1988 Feb 14 [W]	Crescent Route A.Matthewson, M.Potter
1988 Feb 14 [W]	Intruder R.Anderson, G.Nicoll. Attempted by others
1988 May 14	Game of Dice G.E.Little, R.Reid, G.Ettle
1988 May 14	Pandava's Progress G.E.Little, R.Reid, I.Marriot, W.Wright, G.Ettle
1988 May 8	Delusions of Grandeur A.Tibbs, G.Jones
1988 June 11	Hauchmagundie R.Carchrie, G.A.McEwan
1988 June 17	Eyes of Mica A.Nelson, K.Howett
1988 June 17	Fringe Benefits K.Howett, A.Nelson
1989 Feb 19 [W]	Minor Adjustment R.Anderson, C.Greaves
1989 Feb 25 [FWA]	The Long Crack R.Anderson, C.Greaves, A.Williams
1989 March 11 [W]	Dream Topping S.Richardson
1989 March 16 [W]	Double Entendre A.Nelson, G.Szuca
1989 March [W]	Directosaur G.Ettle, R.Anderson (alts), R.Milne
1989 May 14	The Whore's Apron S.Kennedy, C.Grindley
1989 May 27	Eugallt A.Tibbs, D.Saddler
1989 July 2	Batura Wall A.Tibbs, H.Shannon
1989 July 9	Sentry Slabs Direct S.Steer, I.Roberts, C.Scollick
1989 Summer	Jackson C.Murray, G.Harrison

1990 May 12	Comatose I.Barron, S.Kennedy
1990 May 12	Satori, Shibumi K.V.Crocket, G.Jefferies
1990 May 12	The Burning A.Tibbs, S.Cameron
1990 May 13	Mad Mackerel I.Roberts, V.Ross
1990 May 13	Smiley's Indecision S.Steer, C.Scobie
1990 May 19	Farewell Arete K.V.Crocket, A.Walker. Walker emigrates to NZ!
1990 June 10	Impulse R.Everett, T.Prentice
1990 June 10	The Glutton W.Hood, I.Taylor, A.Caren, J.Ferry
1990 June 10	Xenolith Righthand, Prey W.Hood, I.Taylor
1990 June 13	Baldrick G.Ettle, S.Cameron
1990 June 13	The The G.Lawrie, G.Szuca. Second worst route name
1990 June 16	Sunstroke, Sunnyside Up, Sunset Strip R & C.Anderson
1990 July 22	Augley Crack I.Taylor, B.Williamson, W.Hood
1990 Aug 18	Learning to Crawl R & C.Anderson
1990 Summer	Tribeswoman P.Laughlan
1991 Feb 2 [W]	Orient Express R & C.Anderson, R.Milne
1991 Feb 9 [FWA]	Yen R & C.Anderson
1991 Feb 10 [W]	The Whore's Apron S.Kennedy, D.Ritchie
1991 Feb 14 [W]	The Fall Line S.Kennedy, A.Paul
1991 Feb 17 [W]	Inclination R.Anderson, C.Anderson, R.Milne
1991 March 2 [W]	Dalmation Couloir, Huandoy Revisited G.E.Little, A.Baker
1991 March 23 [FWA]	Isis R & C.Anderson, R.Milne
1991 April 14	Wounded Knee, Two-Step Arete K.V.Crocket, B.Dullea
1991 June 1	Seams Blanc, Vein Rouge, Rasberry Ripple R & C.Anderson
1991 July 6	Cross-Over Wall, Eastern Promise, The Straight Climb, Turkish Delight R & C.Anderson
1991 July 7	Anniversary Arete R & C.Anderson
1991 July 29	Up with the Sun G.Farquhar, G.Latter
1991 Aug 18	Wall Climb R & C.Anderson
1991 Aug 31	Paleface, The Snake T.McAuley, C.Higgins
1991 Sept 1	Raptor T.McAuley, D.Gardner, C.Higgins
1991 Sept 8	Gorge Crack R & C.Anderson. By hook or by crook...

Graded List Of Rock Climbs

Although the following list has been compiled after consultation with several of the most active climbers of the area, it comes with all the normal disclaimers and health warnings. In particular, the positions of routes marked with the dagger symbol in the text could be wildly inaccurate. Perhaps unusually, its accuracy may diminish towards its lower end. For this reason, no attempt has been made to continue the list below HVS.

E7	
Romantic Reality	6a,6b,5b

E6	
Revengeance	6b,5c
Up With the Sun	6b,6b
Prophet of Purism	6a,5c,5a,5b
Gone With the Wind	6b,6a
The Tribeswoman	6b
Fated Path	6b
The Railway Children	6b
Admission	6b
Kelpie	6b,5b
Waltzing Ostriches	6a
Twilight Zone	6b
Uncertain Emotions	6b

E5	
Fringe Benefits	6b
Creag Dhon't Wall	6b
The Chant of Jimmy Blacksmith	6a
Celtic Dawn	6a
Spacewalk	5c,6b
Eldorado	5c,6b,6a,5a
Salome	6a
Triceptor	5c/6a,5c,5b
The Risk Business	6a,5c,6a
Le Monde	5c,5b
Baptism of Fire	6a,5c

E4	
Grogblossom	4b,6a,4c
The Lost Ark	6a,5b
Carnivore Direct Start	6a
Quietly Burning	6a
Dont Talk To Strangers	5c

Eyes Of Mica	6a
Bannockburn	5c,5b,5c
Bluebell Grooves	5b,6a
Freak-Out	5c,6a
White Hope	6a
The Roaring Silence	6a
Smouldering	6a

E3	
Chela	6a,5b
Virgin Waters	5c
True Cut	5c
Massacre	5b,6a,5b
Sentinel Rouge	5c,6a
Stormtrooper	6a
King-Pin	6a,5c,5b,5b
Playmate of the Month	6a
Carnivore Original Finish	6a,5c,4c
Temple of Doom	6a,5c
The Clearances	5c,5c,4c
Bloodline	5c,5c,5c
Cockleshell Journey	5c
Mr Bates	5c/6a
Sweltering	5c
In Seine	5c
Too Cold for Comfort	5c
Brack	5c
Fawlty Tower	5c,5a
Sticky Fingers	5c
The Challenge	6a
Crocodile	5c,5b,5c
Dizzy Lizzy	5b/c
Meat Beater	5c
Apocalypse	4b,5c,5c,5b,4b
Solitude	5b
The Fly	5b

E2

Hamburg	-,5b,5c,5a
Performance	4c,5b,-,5b
Twilight	5c
NFAD Girdle	5b/c
Short But Sweet	5b
Flip-Out	5b
Gravity and Grace	5c
Walk With Destiny	5b,5b/c,5a
Bogtrotter	5c
Gambado	5c
Yamay Variation	5c
Symposium	5c,-
The Golden Lance	5c,5c,5b
The Foil	5c,-
Hauchmagundie	5a,5c,5b,4c,5a
Sir Chancealot	5b,5c
The Pincer	5b
Pendulum	5c
Shibboleth True Finish	5b,5c
Carnivore, via Villains Finish	5b,4b,5a,5c,-
Marshall's Wall	5b,5b,4c
Lady Jane	5b
Yamay	5b
Easy Going	5b
The Fly Man	5b
Lechers Superstition	-,5c,5b,5b,4c
Scansor	5b,5b,4c,5a
Shibboleth	4b,5c,5a,5b,5a,4b
Nightmare Traverse	5b/c
Druim nan Gillean	5c
Sala Direct	5c
Outlandos	5b,-
Cross-Over Wall	5b,5b
Gralloch	5b
Delusions of Grandeur	5b
A Game of Dice	5b,4c
Daktari	4c,5a,5b,4c
Big Al's Arete	5b

E1

The Cough	5b,-,-
The Whip	4c,5b,4c
Blast Off	5b
Gallows Route	5c
Stumblebum	

Hee-Haw	5b,4b,4c,4c,-
Pontoon	5a,5a,-
Sunset Strip	5c
Happy Valley	5b
Girdle Traverse of Slime Wall	5b
Satyr	5a
Yo-Yo	5b,5a,5a
Cayman Groove	5b,4c
Doom Arete	4c,5a/b,4b
Bloody Crack	5a/b
Yam	5b
Eastern Promise	5a,5b
Apparition	4c,5b,5a,4b
Engineers Crack	5b,-
19th Nervous Breakdown	5b,-,-
White Wall Crack	5b,4c
Sideshow	5b
Big Top	4c,5a,5a,5b
Trapeze	-,5b,4c,5a
Unicorn	5a,5a,5a,5a
Gutrot	5b
Girdle Traverse of NE Nose	5b
Raven's Direct Finish	5a
Dalness Chasm Right-hand Branch	5a
Anniversary Arete	5b,4b
Wild Spot	5b,4a
Yak	5a,-,-
Daredevil	5b
Sugarplum	5b,5a/b
Sunnyside Up	5a
The Kneepad Direct Start	5a
Cresta Kurva	5b
Blockhead	5b,4a
Smiley's Indecision	5a,-
The Burning	5a,-
The Zig-Zag Roof	5b
Mad Mackerel	5a,5a
Turnaround	5b
Sapphire	5b,-
Menghini	5a

HVS

Blind Pew
Gazebo
Mainbrace Crack Direct
Girdle Traverse of E Buttress

The Peeler	5b	Exellerator	5a
Waterslide Corner	-,5a,5a,-	Blockbuster	4c,4c/5a
En Garde	5a	Persuasion	5a
The Duel		Snowstormer	5a
Pilliwinks	5a,5a,4c	Spider	5a
Pegleg	4a,5a,4a	Dick	
The Late Late Show		Impressario	-,5a,-
Rose Inominate		Girdle Traverse GGB	4a,4c,4c/5a,5a,-
Guillotine	5b	Hesitation	4c,5a
Layla	5b	Lift-Off	5a,4b/c,-
De Vreemde Stap	5b,4c	Turkish Delight	5a
The Clasp	4b,5a	Dwindle Wall	5a
Plink	4c,5a,4c/5a	Augley Crack	-,5a
Line-Up	4c,5a,5a	July Crack	4a,5a
Crack-line	5a	Trapeze Direct Finish	4c
The Crook	5a,4b	Stickleback	5a,-,-
Guinness	5a,4c	Bludger's Revelation	-,5a,4c,4c,4a
The Tumbler		Raven's Edge Direct Finish	5a
Raptor		Raven's Gully	5a
Wappenshaw Wall Variation	5a	Dingle	-,5a
Trichord	5a,4c,4c	Prey	4c,5a,-,-
Hee-Haw Direct Finish	5a	Triple C Special	5a
Brevity Crack	5a	The Primordial Soup Kitchen	5a
Mainbrace Crack	5a	Guerdon Grooves	4c,4c,4b,-
Girdle Traverse E Face of		Graceland	5a
North Buttress		Ivy Corner	5a
Gibbet	5a	Annie's Route	5a
Via Dolorosa	5a,5a,4b	Tattieman	5a
Kuf	5a	Quietude	4a,5a
Angor	5a,5a,4c	Gestation	5a
Has Been		Showcase	5a,4a
Perambulator	5a	Garnet	5a
The Kneepad	5a	Bodkin	5a,4b,-
Whortleberry Wall	4c,4c,4c,4b	Sala	5a
Sunstroke	5a	Eugallt	4c/5a
Impulse	4c	Shiver	4c
Boomerang	5b,4b	Chariots of Fire	4c
Peasant's Passage	4c,4c,4b	Gorge Crack	4c

Due to the uniqueness of The Etive Slabs, it is difficult to compare the routes with those of the rest of the guide. Therefore they have been compiled into their own graded list:

Jackson	E5	6a	The Long Wait Direct	E3	5c
Band of Hope Direct	E4	5c	Valkyrie, The Pea Brained		
The Thin Red Line	E3	5c	Variation	E3	5c

The Big Ride	E3	5c
Pinch Direct	E3	5c
The The	E3	6a
The Band of Hope	E3	5c
Valkyrie	E3	5c
Learning To Crawl	E3	5b
Attila	E3	5c
Groundhog	E3	5c
Seams Blanc	E3	5b
Fast Approaching	E3	5c
The Grasshopper	E2	5c
The Long Walk	E2	5c
Tous Les Deux	E2	5c
Swastika	E2	5c
Agony	E2	5c
Rasberry Ripple	E2	5a
The Long Wait	E2	5b
Mistaken Identity	E2	5a

Aryan	E1	5b
The Long Reach	E1	5b
Vein Rouge	E1	5a
Jaywalk	E1	5b
Claw	E1	5c
Dan		E1
Ba's		HVS 5a
The Pause		HVS 5b
Hammer		HVS 5a
Cut the Grass		HVS
Spartan Slab		VS 4c
Nausea		VS 4c
Monsoon		VS
Sickle		VS
Mosquito		Severe
Curses		Severe
Buzzard Arete		Very Difficult

A Proposed Extension to the Scottish Winter Grading System

Since the introduction of the numerical system for the grading of Scottish winter climbs more than two decades ago, several developments have taken place in equipment, technique and attitude. These developments have placed such a strain on the grading system that the leading activists have agreed that it must be extended to take these changes into account. In particular, the new modern mixed routes must be graded so as to indicate their high levels of technical difficulty, while taking into consideration the frequently greater seriousness of the older-style ice routes. The elements of this extended system can be summarised as follows:

(i) Nearly all grades up to and including grade IV will remain unaltered.

(ii) Climbs of grade V and above will have two grades, an overall grade in roman numerals, and a technical grade in arabic numerals. Some hard, technical mixed grade IV routes have also been given a technical grade.

(iii) The overall grade will take into account all factors affecting the difficulty of reaching the top of the climb, including its technical difficulty, seriousness (frequency of protection and reliability of belays) and sustainedness (length of hard sections of climbing and number of hard pitches).

(iv) The technical grade will reflect the actual difficulty of the hardest section(s) of climbing, without reference to seriousness. It is not intended to be used as a technical pitch-by-pitch grading.

(v) The technical grade will normally vary not more than two below or two above the overall grade. Thus V,5 can be taken as an average grade V route of the old system. A higher technical grade than the overall grade would indicate greater technical difficulty, offset by better protection (as frequently found on mixed routes); a lower technical grade would indicate easier but more serious climbing. Thus the system has some parallels with the E-grade system for summer rock climbs.

(vi) The previous artificial ceiling of grade V (and reluctant VI) has been removed, so as to reflect more realistically the differences between the old classic grade V's and the current state-of-the-art routes.

The following list includes Glen Coe winter routes from hard grade IV. Routes formerly given the split grade of IV/V, or considered as hard for Grade IV, on account of their technical content, are now given Grade V. It is not the size that counts but the way that you climb it! In this list, a technical grade of 5 would indicate relatively straightforward, steep ice climbing; a technical grade of 6 would generally indicate more technical mixed climbing; technical grades of 7 and 8 would indicate much more intricate and harder snowed-up rock moves. A high overall grade linked with a lower technical grade indicates steep, serious ice routes such as Mr Softee. A low overall grade with a high technical grade indicates a short but technically hard and safe route, such as Yen.

Some degree of variability will undoubtedly occur, but the grading has to be take account of what are thought to be average conditions. These proposals should be a great improvement over the ridiculous cramming of the grades that had developed. By way of illustration, how could Point 5 (Ben Nevis; grade V), which has been soloed in 45 minutes, have the same grade as Savage (which took 6 hours or more but is three times shorter). Under the new system Point 5 is V,5 and Savage is VII,8 (Savage involves HVS 5a snowed-up rock).Obviously there will be errors, especially when one considers that a great number of routes have had few ascents. In some cases where the precise grade is unsure, a split grade has been used. Do you remember when the E-grade system was introduced? We do - have fun!

It should also be noted that, while this list has been compiled after consultation with many of the leading figures in Scottish winter climbing, despite broad overall agreement it is possible that the use of this system in practice may lead to a revision of the boundaries between the overall grades. It is hoped that publication of this list will not only be useful to the higher grade winter climber, but that it will also lead to lively debate and exchange of information so that it can be progressively refined and improved.

Guerdon Grooves	IX,8	Dalness Chasm Central	VI,5
Unicorn	VIII,8	North Face Route	VI
Inclination	VIII,8	Kinloss Corner	VI,6
Red Slab	VIII,7	June Crack	VI,7
Against All Odds	VIII,8	Direct Route (GGB)	VI,6/7
Fall-Out	VIII,7	May Crack	VI,7
Central Grooves	VIII,7	Snowstormer	VI,5/6
Central Buttress	VIII,7	Jabberwock	VI,5
Neanderthal	VIII,7	Rainmaker	VI,5
Agag's Groove	VIII,7	Exellerator	VI,5
		Midnight Cowboy	VI,5
Tilt	VII,7	Consolation	VI,7
People's Friend	VII,7	Southern Death Cult	VI
Savage	VII,8	Chimney Route (SCnL)	VI,7
Isis	VII,8	Direct Route (SCnL)	VI,7
Intruder	VII,7	East Face Route (SCnL)	VI,7
Para Andy	VII,7	Diamond Route	VI,7
Winter Route (Diamond Butt)	VII,7	Blue Riband	VI,5
Fingal's Chimney	VII,7		
Crowberry Ridge Direct	VII,7	Moonlighting	V,7
Mr Softee	VII,6	Barracuda	V,7
Elliot's Downfall	VII,5	Ordinary Route Direct(SCnL)	V,6/7
Darwin's Dihedral	VII,6/7	Pterodactyl	V,5/6
		Raven's Gully	V,6
The Long Crack	VI,7/8	Scabbard Chimney	V,6
Directosaur	VI,7	The Chasm	V,5
Tyrannosaur	VI,7	The Veil	V,5
Raven's Edge	VI,7	Misty High	V,5
Chimney & Face Route	VI,7	Outgrabe Route	V,5
Raven's Gully Direct	VI	Newsholme's Groove	V,5
Dalness Chasm Left	VI,5	Mome Rath Face Route	V,5

The Wabe	V,5	Ordinary Route (Cuneiform)	V,6
White Rhino	V	The Long Chimney	V,6
Venom	V,5/6	Minor Adjustment	V,6
Venom, Viper Start	V,5	Minor Issue	V,6
Midnight Special	V,5	Frostbite Groove	V,5
Amphitheatre Scoop Direct	V,5	Frostbite Wall	V,5
Clachaig Gully	V,5	The Walk	V
The Flute	V,5	Shadbolt's Chimney	V
Yen	V,7	Evening Citizen	V
Route 1 (Rannoch Wall)	V,6	Crest Route	V,6
Shelf Route	V,6	Direct Route (Diamond Butt)	V,6
Ordinary Route (SCnL)	V,6	West Chimney Route	V,6
Innuendo	V,6	The Screen	V,5
Double Entendre	V,6		

ADDENDUM

The miserable winter of 1991/2 has allowed little winter climbing, but the following route has just made it into the guide (with one day to spare!):

EAST FACE OF AONACH DUBH, FAR EAST BUTTRESS

Eastern Slant 120m III/IV *
This may correspond in part to the summer line of Left Edge. Start at the base of the obvious groove just left of the cleanest and highest section of cliff. This is just right of Orient Express.
1. 40m Climb the groove or the rocks to its left to the belay of Orient Express.
2. 40m Traverse left beneath the icefall of Orient Express. Go around the edge, then pull up and left across a slab to a short corner. Pull out left and belay.
3. 40m Continue the left bias, up and across a fault-line, then climb a groove to finish up a short chimney.
R.Anderson, C.Anderson and R.Milne; 16 February 1992

And it came to pass that, just as the General Editor was on his way out of the house to deliver the last disc to the Publication Manager (when the rest of the book was already in page-proofs), the phone rang. So this route can be said to have made it into the guide at absolutely the last minute:

LOST VALLEY BUTTRESS

Primordial Soup Kitchen V
An ascent by the summer line, taking the left side of the monolithic pinnacle. In the revised grading sytem this climb is VII,7.
B.Davison, A.Nisbet; 19 February 1992.

Index of Routes

GARBH BHEINN OF ARDGOUR

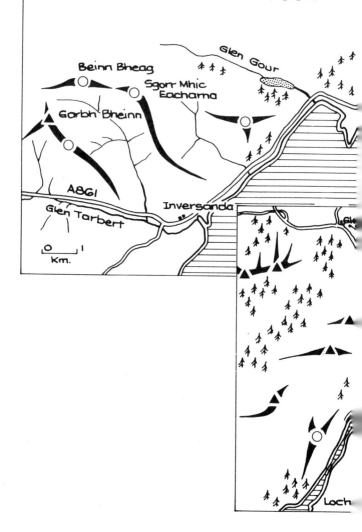

Glen Gour

Beinn Bheag

Sgorr Mhic
Eacharna

Garbh Bheinn

A861

Glen Tarbert

Inversanda

0   1
Km.

Loch